The Authoritarians

PRAISE FOR *THE AUTHORITARIANS*

"Jonathan Emord is a warrior out to save our rights. In *The Authoritarians*, he has done just that. Now if our leaders will read it and follow through . . . we just might make it."

—**George Noory,** Host of *Coast to Coast AM*

"The passionate and knowledgeable writing found in these pages is the perfect—and necessary—antidote to the sniveling, condescending, and yes, dangerous machinations of this nation's far-gone Left, whose legions of autocratic Democrats, Antifa and BLM rioters, delusional media members, and misguided educators seek to replace our great Republic with their own perverted version of Marxist reality. These authoritarians seek to enslave us all through the false narrative of, among other things, inherent white privilege and racism. This threat to our individual liberty, as the recent election shows, is not some distant pipe dream of the progressive movement's new revolutionaries. It is real and it is here. Jonathan Emord explains in great detail how and why this has occurred and, most importantly, how to reverse this tragic course of history before it's too late."

—**Wayne M. Barrett,** Publisher, *USA Today Magazine*

"*The Authoritarians,* from title to breathtakingly well-researched last page, offers an astonishing and eye-opening look at the many issues Americans must confront in order to stay free. Jonathan Emord does an admirable job of weaving together historical truths with modern day news to show readers the sad, raw reality—that yes, communism could indeed come to America. Like Paul Revere atop his horse—like John the Baptist crying from the wilderness—*The Authoritarians* is America's twelfth hour call to arms. This is a great book to put in the schools to teach America's emerging leaders the horrors of unfree states. They'll be frightened enough to grab hold of the Constitution tight and keep our country on a path of limited government for decades to come."

—**Cheryl Chumley,** Online Opinion Editor, *The Washington Times* and author of *Socialists Don't Sleep*

"*The Authoritarians* answers the question: How did we stray so far from the high ideals of the Founding Fathers and Framers of the Constitution? What if teetering on the edge of becoming a socialist nation was not an accident, but the deliberate effort of a progressivist agenda begun well over 100 years ago? The history not taught but revealed by Jonathan Emord's meticulous research provides a critical road map to recovery for a nation founded on the principles of defense of life, liberty and property. How do we stop progressives who would abolish rights endowed by our Creator and replace them with privileges from authoritarian collectivists? Read this book. Before it's too late."

—**Robert Scott Bell,** *The Robert Scott Bell Show*

"[*The Authoritarians*] ought to be must-reading for anyone who loves freedom . . . [Jonathan Emord] is, in our opinion, an intellectual warrior for the rights and freedoms of people in America and around the world."

—**Congressmen Dan Burton and John T. Doolittle,**
as written in the Foreword

THE
AUTHORITARIANS

Their Assault on Individual Liberty,
the Constitution, and Free Enterprise
from the 19th Century to the Present

JONATHAN W. EMORD

NEW YORK
LONDON • NASHVILLE • MELBOURNE • VANCOUVER

THE AUTHORITARIANS

Their Assault on Individual Liberty, the Constitution, and Free Enterprise from the 19th Century to the Present

Published in New York, New York, by Morgan James Publishing. Morgan James is a trademark of Morgan James, LLC. www.MorganJamesPublishing.com

Morgan James
BOGO™

A **FREE** ebook edition is available for you or a friend with the purchase of this print book.

CLEARLY SIGN YOUR NAME ABOVE

Instructions to claim your free ebook edition:
1. Visit MorganJamesBOGO.com
2. Sign your name CLEARLY in the space above
3. Complete the form and submit a photo of this entire page
4. You or your friend can download the ebook to your preferred device

ISBN 9781631953927 paperback
ISBN 9781631953934 eBook
ISBN 9781631953941 jacketed hardcover
Library of Congress Control Number:
2020950450

Cover and Interior Design by:
Chris Treccani
www.3dogcreative.net

Morgan James is a proud partner of Habitat for Humanity Peninsula and Greater Williamsburg. Partners in building since 2006.

Get involved today! Visit
MorganJamesPublishing.com/giving-back

For all who cherish liberty.

TABLE OF CONTENTS

ACKNOWLEDGMENTS

I have benefited greatly in the writing of this book from the able assistance of a select group of highly talented people. I am grateful to Morgan James Publishing Company for its expert editing, publication, marketing and promotion of this book. I am thankful to Cortney Donelson of vocem, LLC, whose expert proofreading enriched the text in so many ways. I also thank Constance Wood for her excellent copy editing.

I thank my external editors Norman Singleton, President of the Campaign for Liberty; Dr. Charles B. Simone, medical scientist, scientific advisor, and insightful and indispensable friend; and USA TODAY Magazine's own brilliant Editor Wayne M. Barrett for his thoughtful guidance and cautionary notes. Wayne is an intellectual, a very fine journalist, and a great defender of liberty.

I am grateful to my law partner, the masterful litigator, analytical thinker and strategist Peter Arhangelsky for his tempered wisdom, calm resolve, and perspicacity. I am grateful to my talented associates Bethany Kennedy, Bryan Schatz, Eric Awerbuch and Joshua Furman for tirelessly tracking down sources.

I am particularly indebted to my client Donna Kasseinova for her willingness to help readers understand the horrors of collectivism by reliving in Chapter 9 the harsh conditions her family experienced under the former Soviet Union.

It has been my pleasure over the years to work with two great statesmen and defenders of liberty whose personal integrity and fidelity to the American cause, keen wit, love of country, and stalwart, and unwavering advancement of our founding principles have inspired generations to never surrender to tyranny. I speak of Congressmen John T. Doolittle and Dan Burton. I thank them for their patriotism (love of country over self), generous Foreword to this book, wise advice over many years of our friendship, and constant advance of the principles of liberty.

In addition, two fine radio talk show hosts have always been supportive and have found issues related to the struggle for individual liberty worth broadcasting to millions: George Noory of Coast to Coast AM and Robert Scott Bell of the Robert Scott Bell show. How very grateful I am to them for getting the superior claim of liberty out to those deluded by the false allure of socialism.

There are certain people who in the darkest days of our nation's recent and explosive travails have inspired me to double, triple, and quadruple my resolve to oppose the machinations which aim daggers at the heart of the Constitution from the authoritarian radicals and reactionaries. Those great and courageous Americans include Florida Governor Ron DeSantis; Texas Governor Greg Abbott; and, most notably, that brilliant rising star from the free state of South Dakota who shines brightly in defense of life, individual liberty, private property, and free enterprise, the Honorable Governor Kristi Noem.

There are those in my early career whose examples of legal scholarship and analysis, draftsmanship, and defense of constitutional principles caused me in my teens and 20's to choose a career in the law and dedicate my life to the fight against government bureaucracy and tyranny. I thank the late U.S. Congressman from Illinois Philip M. Crane; the late President Ronald W. Reagan; the former FCC Chairman Mark S. Fowler; the former FCC Chief of Staff Jerry Fritz; Wiley Rein Partner Richard J. Bodorff; University of Illinois Political Science Professor Stephen P. Cohen; the late Professor and Ulysses S. Grant Scholar John Y. Simon; the late Professor and Abraham Lincoln Scholar at the University of Illinois Robert Johansson; the late Notre Dame Constitutional Law Professor Charles E. Rice; DePaul University Constitutional Law Professor Jeffrey M. Shaman; and University of Illinois Professor and American Colonial History Scholar John H. Pruett. I owe them all very much and am deeply grateful for their wisdom and guidance over the years.

I am grateful to Chris Treccani of 3dogcreative for the cover and interior design of this book.

Finally, I would be remiss if I did not at least try to convey the depth of my gratitude to my beautiful wife Sheryl and my wonderful children Justice and Angelica for their months of support and patience as I have labored on this book atop a heavy schedule of litigation, pleading practice, business management, lectures, and articles.

I would also be remiss were I not to thank those too numerous to list who have read my other four books and have provided me with useful information, recommendations, and support since the 1991 publication of my first book, *Freedom Technology and the First Amendment*. Thank you all!

FOREWORD

Jonathan Emord is a distinguished attorney who leads the top-rated firm, Emord & Associates, based in Washington, DC, Virginia, and Arizona. Since 1985, Jonathan has specialized in constitutional law, federal administrative law, and complex civil litigation.

We have known him for years and have been consistently impressed with his integrity, his knowledge of the law and of history, his meticulous preparation, his fearless advocacy on behalf of his clients, and, most importantly, his devotion to America and to its principles enshrined in its founding documents—the Declaration of Independence and the United States Constitution. He loves America and the values on which our country is based. He fights in court and before administrative agencies to protect those values and principles against those who would take them away. His career is a powerful example of how best to put principles of liberty into action in ways that make freedom continuously ascendant.

What impressed us and will impress those reading the book is the research that Jonathan put into it.

As America in the twenty-first century is being pushed by "progressives" toward socialism and communism, it is essential that Americans (and readers around the world) realize that those who are pushing us toward socialism and communism are using the term "progressivism" to mask their ultimate goal. Through the research he has done in writing this book, Jonathan Emord has shown the reader that Hegel, Karl Marx, and others had as their ultimate goal complete control by the state. Individual freedoms guaranteed by the Constitution and the Bill of Rights would be eliminated and replaced by a "benevolent state."

Jonathan's book ought to be must-reading for anyone who loves freedom. The last election shows a lack of knowledge by many who voted for "progressivism" and who are causing a socialist agenda to be implemented by one political party in control of Congress and the White House.

We as conservative former congressmen believe that this book should be presented to school boards across the United States as a text that all students should use. It is a bedrock of American principle, history, law, economics, and exceptionalism. It defines at root what it means to be American to all who read its pages. It is an instant classic.

The war between freedom and radical progressivism is raging, and Jonathan Emord is, in our opinion, an intellectual warrior for the rights and freedoms of people in America and around the world. He is making an enormous difference and is deeply respected by the courts, intellectuals in law, and by leaders, like us, who value his insights.

Jonathan provides a concise and accurate history of the United States, greatly at variance with the far-left authoritarian orientation of the *New York Times'* 1619 Project, designed to falsely taint with racist motivations the founders and the founding documents and the American republic created by them. In this book, the reader will discover how slaveholders in the South came to adopt a foreign philosophical justification for slavery. That justification caused them to reject the principles of the Declaration of Independence and to embrace authoritarianism advocated by the Eighteenth- and Nineteenth-Century German philosopher Georg Wilhelm Friedrich Hegel (1770–1831). Following the Civil War, the book then traces the birth and growth of authoritarianism, also based on Hegel's underlying philosophy, and carries it forward to the twentieth and twenty-first centuries, where it has now become the driving intellectual force of the Democrat Party.

For many Americans, there seems to be an insufficient understanding of the origin and true meaning of far-left authoritarianism and its adverse impact on the values enshrined in America's founding documents. Jonathan describes and documents the rise of the administrative state brought about through progressivism and demonstrates how it has in essence replaced the limited government established in the Constitution.

The Authoritarians is essential reading for anyone interested in learning *how* our government has moved so much in the direction of socialism and away from the limited government established by our United States Constitution through the creation of independent administrative agencies within the federal government wielding the combined powers of the legislative, executive and judicial branches of government in its dealings with the citizenry. The principal actors included both Democrat and Republican Presidents such as Grover Cleveland, Theodore Roosevelt, Woodrow Wilson, Franklin Delano Roosevelt, and Herbert Hoover. The book will cause the reader to reevaluate the records of these men as well as many other historical figures. Jonathan relies on a wealth of historical evidence to sound the alarm that the present stark divide between the authoritarians and the constitutionalists closely parallels that irreconcilable fissure between the abolitionists in the capitalist North and the advocates of slavery in the plantation South. He says we need a Lincoln, but do not have one in Biden. He thinks we have one in that great Governor of the free state of South Dakota, Kristi Noem.

He offers a way forward to launch a return to the principles contained in the founding documents. The book is unique in its perspective and will be of immense value to illuminating the understanding of any reader who loves America and wishes to turn away from authoritarianism and maintain the values of its founding.

President Ronald Reagan said, "Freedom is never more than one generation away from extinction. We didn't pass it on to our children in the bloodstream. It must be fought for, protected, and handed on for them to do the same, or one day we will spend our sunset years telling our children what it once was like in the United States when men were free."

President Abraham Lincoln said, "If destruction be our lot, we must ourselves be its author and finisher. As a nation of free men, we must live through all time or die by suicide."

Jonathan Emord captures what Presidents Lincoln and Reagan said in this great analysis of our country's movement away from its founding values and toward authoritarianism. Every freedom-loving American should read *The Authoritarians*. It is a monumental work of immediate, critical importance.

Dan Burton, Republican Member of Congress
from Indiana (1983–2013)

John T. Doolittle, Republican Member of Congress
from California (1991–2009)

INTRODUCTION

Who are authoritarians? They are people who believe in submission to a governing will imposed at the expense of individual rights to life, liberty, and property. They are paternalists. Some demand pure democracy or majority rule at the expense of minority rights. Some demand rule by elites, called experts, who operate through bureaucracy to regulate enterprise. Some demand government take-over of private property and elimination of private worship and political dissent. Beginning in May of 2020, thousands of far-left authoritarian radicals committed crimes against life and property across the United States, including vandalism, robbery, arson, assault, and murder. Those authoritarian radicals received vocal support from the mainstream media, liberal politicians, and Big Tech companies, among others who either endorsed or condoned their actions and did not condemn them. On January 6, 2021 as Congress began to consider certification of Joe Biden and Kamala Harris in the 2021 Electoral College, hundreds of authoritarian reactionaries including anarchists, nihilists, QAnon zealots, and others with no respect for the rule of law breached Capitol security and occupied the Capitol buildings, destroying property and entering the private confines of the Senate and House chambers. Those authoritarian reactionaries were universally condemned by the mainstream media, by virtually all politicians, and by Big Tech companies. The authoritarian reactionaries were part of a well-orchestrated, armed vanguard that planned in advance to overwhelm capitol defenses simultaneously from different points of vulnerability. Their assault on the Citadel of Democracy was a pre-planned domestic terrorist attack. Vehicles filled with weapons caches were found on capitol streets. After the riot subsided pipe bombs were found strategically placed around the Capitol and at Democratic and Republican offices.

Whether they call themselves progressives, socialists, or communists, anarchists, nihilists, or anti-capitalists, they share an opposition to the fundamental tenets of constitutional government: They do not believe all are created equal and endowed by God with unalienable rights to life, liberty, and property; they do not believe that the very purpose of government is to secure rights; and they do not believe governments derive their just powers from the consent of the governed.

Since the mid-1800s, authoritarians have justified the taking of life, liberty, and property as necessary to achieve a so-called "common good." That common good is invariably a reflection of their own moral outrage and interests in furtherance of personal quests for political power and control. It is born of a belief that those in power know better than the typical person what is in that person's self-interest.

To gain popular support for the confiscation of private wealth through taxation and political control, they stoke the public into class warfare. They endeavor to make employees turn on employers, and low and middle-income earners on the wealthy. As a prelude to confiscation, they villainize private wealth and call for "soaking the rich," whereby they can pillage through confiscatory taxation and then parcel out the spoils, enriching themselves and favored constituencies in the process, in a feeding frenzy of legalized looting and self-dealing. Calls for class warfare invariably lead to acts of violence, such as looting, arson, anarchy, terrorism, and treason.

As they draw ever more wealth out of the economy, they destroy the engine of economic growth, the ability of entrepreneurs to provide employment and opportunity, innovate, and uplift the standard of living. And while they condemn wealth, they themselves obtain unimaginable riches, living lavishly and turning their political offices into vehicles for private gain through influence peddling.

By deceiving the public with a false allure (e.g., the promise of things of great value for nothing: free health care, free education, or a free guaranteed minimum income), far-left authoritarians have succeeded in obtaining popular support for breaking down legal barriers that defend individual liberty and property, indeed all constitutional barriers that stand in the way of total government control. Because authoritarians have ordinarily operated in the shadows (in academia, executive branch advisory roles, and the bureaucracy), their threat to liberty and property has been until recently invisible to most Americans. But in recent years, after decades of eroding constitutional barriers, they have now become bold, public, vocal, insistent, and violent. They no longer shy away from the moniker "socialist." They embrace it. They no longer leave it to the bureaucracy to undermine free enterprise. They lead the battle against private wealth. They no longer feign respect for the rule of law. They violate it with impunity and a sense of moral superiority based not on persuasion but on brute force.

Authoritarians have succeeded repeatedly in overcoming obstacles to unlimited government. They have overcome every defense of individual liberty except one: the commitment of an American majority against mob action that destroys or steals property, causes physical injury, or compels allegiance to causes Americans oppose. That powerful counterforce, fueled by generations who have a deep and abiding commitment to liberty, forms a uniquely American strength against authoritarianism and the greatest prospect for restoration of constitutional government.

Today we are witnessing a national uprising even greater than the war protests of the 1960s and the series of anarchistic attacks that caused such horror and damage during the economic contraction known as the Panic of 1907. Egged on by sympathizers within the Democratic Party who either welcome a coup d'état in America or who remain silent in the face of one, the Marxists rioting in the streets have powerful allies. They have become a political and paramilitary force with which to be reckoned. What started as an isolated urban phenomenon of orchestrated chaos has reached suburbia and even otherwise banal settings, such as restaurants. Those who love liberty can no longer perceive the threat as distant. It is omnipresent, and it imperils American lives, liberty, and property, the rule of law and the constitutional Republic itself.

AUTHORITARIAN EFFORTS TO DESTROY THE REPUBLIC, RELIGION, AND FREE ENTERPRISE

Under the cover of protests arising from isolated instances of police brutality involving black victims, Marxists, anti-capitalists, and anarchists have engaged in violent insurrection, turning cities into places of mayhem and conflagration as they seek to trigger a Marxist revolution. Destruction of civil society, installation of prosecutors who will not defend the people from crime, elimination of cash bail, and the neutering and defunding of police are not coincidental or isolated events. They are planned steps to bring about a violent overthrow of American governments. The revolutionaries aim to install Marxist regimes, which they will control, bringing an end to the greatest bastion in defense of individual liberty the world has ever known, the constitutional republic of the United States.

It is false that racism is non-existent in America, but it is also false that racism is common in our society or in policing; rather, racism is the exception, not the rule, and ordinarily when it arises, it comes under siege from every part of our society. Despite those facts, isolated instances of racism have given rise to a popular lie (lies being the currency of Marxist revolutionaries): that every police officer is racist; that, indeed, all American governments and businesses are inherently, irredeemably, systemically racist; and that every person who lacks dark pigment is inherently racist. If those falsehoods are accepted, then logic dictates an end to government and business, a redistribution or destruction of private property, and a rearrangement of society based on skin color. It is a perfect Bolshevik recipe for government overthrow.

Under this perverse theory, all institutions must be destroyed because they are, every one of them, guilty of a wrong by their simple existence. In their place, the Marxists demand a new regime that owns and distributes all property and polices all speech, indeed all human behavior. The BLM organization and Antifa build their support for a Marxist takeover by fueling popular sentiment against racism; channeling that sentiment into race-based hatred, character assassination, and scapegoating; and directing popular animus against obstacles in the way of their total control: the police, property owners, and government.

Since the 1917 Bolshevik revolution in Russia, scapegoating to provoke violence (pitting an alleged "Oppressed" against their alleged "Oppressors"); the felling of symbols of all prior governmental regimes, history, and institutions, such as the church; the looting and destruction of private property; the occupation of cities to the exclusion of law enforcement; the assault and murder of police; and the assault and murder of innocents— have all been hallmarks of communist revolution. Each instance, whether to create or to perpetuate a communist state, has been accompanied by gruesome violence, torture, gulag or concentration camps, forced slave labor, and forced migrations that sacrifice millions to starvation and death. These movements depend on hate, directed against class, race, and private wealth. They mean to tear everything down and replace it with a totalitarian government that they rule. They mean to enslave us all.

The Bolshevik Red Terror in Russia killed approximately two million people between 1917 and 1922. Joseph Stalin's Reign of Terror killed about 23.2 million between 1930 and 1938 in the former Soviet Union. Mao Zedong's Great Leap Forward (1959 to 1961) and Cultural Revolution (1966 to 1976) killed a combined sixty million people in China. Pol Pot's Khmer Rouge killed approximately two million people between 1975 and 1979 in Cambodia. North Korea's communist dictatorship has killed an estimated 3.2 million people. Rudolph J. Rummel estimates communist governments worldwide have killed approximately 148 million between 1900 and 1999.[1] The Victims of Communism Foundation conservatively estimates at least 100 million have been killed by communist regimes worldwide. *The Black Book of Communism* puts that figure at between eighty-five million and 100 million, explaining, "the Communist record offers the most colossal case of political carnage in history."[2] By comparison, in all of World War II, 291,557 Americans died in battle between 1941 and 1945. Quite obviously, the most extensive destruction of human life on the planet has come not from natural disasters or wars but from communism and socialism.

In the United States, the Marxist riots have arisen in the middle of a coronavirus pandemic, which has left streets and businesses largely void of pedestrian traffic, and largely undefended. The rioters are well organized and well-funded by sympathetic industry and individuals, the funds of which finance weapons from bricks to improvised explosive devices strategically hidden in street caches for later retrieval by the rioters. The rioting is aimed not only at provoking the police and destroying property but also at intimidating citizens into inaction and bending weak political leaders into anemic defenses, no defense at all, or complicity with Marxist demands. These are precisely the kind of methods used in communist coups world-wide. The tactics are the same as those used to install communist regimes in Russia, China, Laos, Cambodia, Vietnam, Albania, Cuba, Angola, Ecuador, El Salvador, Ethiopia, Nicaragua, and Venezuela, to name a few.

The rioting, vandalism, looting, arson, assaults, rapes, and murders have been unleashed by diverse groups variously describing themselves as Marxists, socialists, anti-capitalists, and anarchists, all sharing a profound hatred of the United States, its Constitution, its history, and its free-market economy and all sharing a zealous commitment to authoritarianism. Austin, Oakland, Aurora, Omaha, Minneapolis, St. Paul, New York, Los Angeles, San Francisco, Oakland, Albuquerque, Cleveland, Raleigh, Louisville, Nashville, Salt Lake City, Atlanta, Dallas/Fort Worth, Washington, D.C., Baltimore, Manassas, Williamsburg, Richmond, Charlotte, Bakersfield, Boston, Chicago, Columbus, Des Moines, Denver, Detroit, Kenosha, Madison, Green Bay, Houston, Memphis, Kansas City, Phoenix, Portland, Olympia, Sacramento, San Jose, Seattle, New York City, Rochester, Cincinnati, and Dayton are among the cities that have suffered violent attacks, a major uptick in homicides, assaults, and rapes, and billions of dollars in property damage.

Over 200 people have been killed by rioters as of this writing (including infants, youth, and police). Thousands have been injured. Billions of dollars have been lost from vandalism, arson, and looting. Most of the killed and injured have been minorities. Over 1,000 police and 200 federal government agents have been injured. Over 6,500 people have been arrested. Most admit affiliation with the Black Lives Matter organization, Antifa, or similar Marxist, socialist, anti-capitalist, or anarchist groups. The FBI has initiated over 500 domestic terror investigations. Attorney General William Barr announced Operation Legend in July 2020, a federal law enforcement initiative to combat rioters and criminal syndicalists named after four-year-old Legend Talifero who was shot and killed while sleeping in his bed during rioting in Kansas City on June 29, 2020. Operation Legend has made a total of over 2,000 federal criminal arrests in Kansas City, Chicago, Albuquerque, Cleveland, Detroit, Milwaukee, St. Louis, Memphis, Indianapolis, Washington, D.C., Baltimore, and Philadelphia. Of those, 150 have been charged with murder. The arrests have also netted over 500 guns and seven kilos of fentanyl.

Ordered reductions in police patrols in urban areas across the United States and the imposition of new laws that free criminals, eliminate cash bail, prevent police from using the force necessary to stem riots and make arrests, eliminate qualified immunity for police, eliminate plainclothes (undercover) police, and eliminate police special weapons and tactics (SWAT) units have dramatically increased the carnage and misery suffered by residents who dwell in major American cities. Morale among law enforcement officers is at an all-time low. Many police have filed for early retirement, are taking extended leaves of absence, and are calling in sick in atypically high numbers. Police recruitment efforts have been severely hampered by the vilification of law enforcement and by the lack of support for police by political leaders.

Dedicated to the dismantlement of law enforcement and the transformation of the United States into a socialist country, socialist billionaire George Soros, via his Justice & Public Safety PAC, among others, has paid over $2 billion in campaign contributions to replace law and order county, state's, and district attorneys in San Francisco, California; Contra Costa County, California; Fairfax County, Virginia; Arlington County, Virginia; Delaware County, Pennsylvania; Suffolk County, Massachusetts; St. Louis, Missouri; Cook County, Illinois; Maricopa County, Arizona; and Multnomah County, Oregon with socialists. These new socialist anti-law enforcement officials have refused to prosecute those accused of misdemeanors, certain felonies, and attacks on police, have given early release to depopulate jails, have expanded the scope of investigations and prosecutions against the police, and have fired assistant district attorneys with distinguished careers enforcing the law. In short, Soros-backed county, states, and district attorneys are destroying the rule of law in America and breaking down all barriers to the violent overthrow of the government. They are dismantling the essential governmental defenses against a Marxist revolution. They are laying a foundation for the end of the republican form of government and rights to private property and liberty.

Since the 1840s, Karl Marx and Friedrich Engels' vision of a workers' revolt against the bourgeoisie capitalist has led to violent installations of totalitarian regimes, which then turn their murderous rampages against the very people who supported, or, at least, did not oppose the revolutions. While proclaimed the natural evolution of capitalism, the proletarian revolt is never actually serendipitous but is always provoked by Marxist organizers, as they are doing in the United States presently.

In rapid succession, newly installed communist leaders once in power use force to suppress revolution and kill the opposition, demanding absolute allegiance to the state and absolute control over all aspects of life. Those regimes engender hatred for the propertied classes, confiscate private property, incarcerate or murder the former property owners, and indoctrinate the masses in the new order, insisting that all reveal publicly their support and suffer arrest and punishment for any dissent, which is said to be treason. In this way, the entire population is converted into slavery.

The common Marxist method is to force dissenters to suffer public humiliation, torture, and even death. In Marxist regimes, the common exemplars of freedom are condemned, including those of conscience (such as the media, schools, and churches). Many formerly free institutions of communication, learning, and worship are required to serve as organs of the state, to ensure one uniform propaganda message. All media, art, and literature are controlled by the state. Institutions that teach youth rewrite history to condemn the non-Marxist past and to glorify, unceasingly, the Marxist state and its leaders. The people are denied the right to practice their religions and are threatened with arrest, incarceration, or death for professing allegiance to God rather than the state. Violent Marxist condemnation of religion reminds Christians and Jews of the persecution of Jews in Pharaoh's Egypt and reminds Christians also of the persecution of the disciples of Christ by secular Roman authorities in the first century following Christ's crucifixion (and of the exile, murder, and crucifixion of Christ's apostles by Roman imperial decree). "The abolition of religion as the illusory happiness of the people is required for their real happiness," wrote the atheist Marx.

Thus, for example, Cuba's Fidel Castro struggled mightily to destroy the Catholic faith of his people, incarcerating and killing many, albeit so strong was the church among the nation's people that the faithful remain.

All Americans are witnessing Marxists' repressive tactics in the streets of our cities and suburbs. Most media, Big Tech, and major universities have created an environment hospitable to Marxist ideology and "cancel culture," an environment that invites personal attacks on all who celebrate American history, culture, and law, demanding instead that there be no debate and that only one view be tolerated (indeed, celebrated), that of condemnation of American history, government, business, and culture. That anti-Americanism is often taught as the only viewpoint acceptable even in grade schools, both public and private. That anti-Americanism underlay Joe Biden's executive order to abolish the 1776 Commission as a true historical retort to the critical race theory of the *New York Times'* 1619 Project.

For example, variously in reliance on the *New York Times'* 1619 Project (under the direction of Times' reporter Nikole Hannah-Jones), many American youth are being taught that the United States did not arise out of the great promise of the 1776 Declaration of Independence (that all men are created equal and endowed by their Creator with certain unalienable rights) but out of a society of white supremacists, a slave-owning aristocracy of whites in the 1619 Jamestown colony, which white supremacy is said to infect every white person ever since, every institution of government, and every business in America.

The project neglects to tell the truth about the Jamestown colony. Its leaders first tried a form of what today we call Marxism (common ownership and equal distribution of the harvest), resulting in widespread starvation and death. That error was corrected thereafter by the introduction of what today we call capitalism, allowing the settlers to obtain their own land and retain their own harvests, resulting in self-sustaining abundance. They thus rejected Marxism and adopted free enterprise, transforming the colony from near extinction to prosperity. The 1619 Project also maintains a false narrative regarding the color of slaves in the Jamestown colony. As explained in Chapter 11, four months before twenty black slaves arrived in Jamestown, one hundred white slaves arrived and toiled under the same conditions as the later black arrivals. Moreover, from 1619 until at least the American Revolution, white and black slaves existed not only in Jamestown but also throughout the colonies, laboring in bondage side by side.

In short, the true quest for freedom that defines America's unending struggle from its founding in the American Revolution through the Civil War and on through the Civil Rights era to the present, in defending and expanding the blessings of liberty to embracing all regardless of race and gender, has been erased in our schools and replaced with a false narrative that defines America as hopelessly racist, replete with unending white patriarchal dominance, racial and cultural insensitivities, and "white privilege." This false propaganda is designed to prepare America's youth for dismantlement of American government and capitalism in favor of collectivism, i.e., socialism. Those who propound the false teachings are indoctrinating American youth to hate their own country so that its foundational principles in defense of liberty and free enterprise may be destroyed and its Constitution overturned.

The BLM organization and Antifa promote this essential thesis, denouncing "white privilege," describing it as an inextricable characteristic of all white people in America, baked into their DNA, and of all American institutions. In BLM organization and Antifa circles, there is no such thing as black racism, only white racism (hence, while BLM and Antifa are married to the label, "black lives matter," they condemn the fundamental truth that "all lives matter"). Non-whites who favor individual liberty and free enterprise (the overwhelming majority) are labeled as not truly "black." Under this illogic, you must be a Marxist to be black, and there is no such thing as a black capitalist.

When one comes to the realization that the BLM organization and Antifa are fundamentally Marxist, it then comes as no surprise that Black Lives Matter activist Shaun King, a self-avowed Marxist, complements BLM calls for the toppling of statues to famous Americans, including George Washington, with calls for the destruction of all Christian statues and symbols. Marx, of course, was an atheist and believed religion the "opiate of the masses," i.e., a harmful delusion.

King calls Christian symbols, especially those of Christ, "tools of oppression" and "racist propaganda." As with all enemies identified by the BLM organization, the Christian subjects of Shaun King's vitriol are all labeled racist, a particularly ill-fitting charge when levied against Jesus Christ, the savior of the entire world, who repeatedly professed himself to be "no respecter of persons" (meaning that he did not discriminate among people), received and ministered to all victims of discriminatory mistreatment throughout his mortal ministry, and preached a doctrine of love and inclusion of all, defining every person without exception to be in the image of God. Indeed, in no small measure, one of the reasons given by the Pharisees for Christ's crucifixion was that he did not discriminate among people but broke bread with the faithful and sinners alike, violating the Pharisees' segregationist table customs, which demanded that those deemed holy among the Jews and, thus, "clean," not dine or fraternize with any who were deemed unholy or "unclean," which included famously the Samaritans and common sinners, and indeed all outside the Pharisees' tight-knit religious circle.

True Christians are thus not racists because they adhere to Christ's example of non-discrimination. Rather, Christians view racism as sinful and contrary to Christ's teachings. Shaun King thus reveals the insincerity of the BLM mantra by condemning true Christians and their art in sacred remembrance of Christ.

While condemning Christianity as "white supremacy," King aligns himself with bigots throughout history who have persecuted the faithful. Shifting focus away from Christ's doctrine of inclusion to a supposed white tone of Christ in statues and stained glass windows, Shaun King proclaims the statues and windows exemplars of white hatred for blacks, demands that they all be destroyed, and encourages an assault on churches and Christianity all over America, writing: "I think the statues of the white European they claim is Jesus should . . . come down. They are a form of white supremacy. Always have been."[3] It does not matter to him that those of all races and ethnicities venerate these images and statues and look to them as reminders of the deep, powerful, and abiding doctrines of Christ which transcend all peoples and reject superficial distinctions (such as pigment). As the logic follows, if the statues venerated by Christians are forms of white supremacy and must come down, then those who venerate them are irredeemably racist and must be condemned. King thus pits his pedestrian demagoguery of hate and violence based on race, which only begets bigotry and intolerance, against the teachings of love, non-violence, and inclusion that have led to the greatest erosion of racial barriers and expansion of civil liberties in the history of the world, from Jesus Christ, the prince of peace, to Martin Luther King, Jr., the father of non-violent civil rights protest.

Heeding Shaun King's call, BLM and Antifa rioters have torched American churches and toppled religious statues in cities nationwide. The beautiful 250-year-old San Gabriel Mission Church outside of Los Angeles, founded by Saint Junípero Serra in the eighteenth century, was set ablaze and gutted. The iconic exterior of the eighty-three-year-old Our Lady of Mt. Lebanon, Maronite Catholic Church in Los Angeles, was defaced. The Baba Sale Synagogue of Moroccan Jewish Refugees in Los Angeles was vandalized. The Congregation Beth Israel of Los Angeles was defaced with profane graffiti. Orthodox Jewish synagogues in Los Angeles were looted, defaced, and vandalized, including Beit Medrash Kehilat Yaakov; the Synagogue of Rabbi Gershan Best; the Congregation of Tiferes Tzvi; and Young Israel of Hancock Park. Jewish religious schools in the city were also vandalized. Statues of St. Junípero Serra throughout California have been destroyed by BLM supporters. In Ocala, Florida, a man drove a van through the front doors of the Queen of Peace Catholic Church, coming to a stop in the lobby, while parishioners prayed inside the chapel. Exiting the vehicle, he poured gasoline in the lobby and lit the gas on fire. Statues of Our Lady (Mary, the virgin mother of Jesus) were torched and vandalized in Boston and New York. The Cathedral Basilica of the Immaculate Conception in Denver was defaced by BLM rioters in the church and rectory. They left behind the spray-painted words "God is dead" and "there is no God." The iconic doors to the rectory were permanently damaged and the cathedral windows were smashed. The exterior of the 142-year-old St. Patrick's Cathedral in New York was defaced with "BLM" graffiti and profanity. The basement of St. John's Episcopal Church in Lafayette Square, a block away from the White House, was set ablaze in its basement and adjacent building. Since its construction in 1816, every sitting president has attended that church at least once, beginning with James Madison. In Minneapolis, BLM rioters burned part of the interior of the Catholic Basilica of St. Mary, one of the oldest Catholic churches in the United States. BLM rioters firebombed the one-hundred-year-old Lewis Street Church of Christ in Little Rock, Arkansas, and the resulting blaze destroyed the roof of the church. BLM rioters assaulted Catholics praying for peace and unity in front of the St. Louis statue in St. Louis, Missouri, beating, among others, an elderly man who walked with a cane. Father Stephen Schumacher bravely stood in front of the statue and defended it, explaining to the rioters, that St. Louis (King Louis IX) aided the poor and needy. BLM rioters smashed the windows of the 116-year-old Beth Ahabah Reform Jewish Congregation in Richmond, Virginia. BLM rioters defaced the 175-year-old St. Paul's Episcopal Church in Richmond and smashed the rectory windows of The Cathedral of the Assumption, the third oldest Catholic cathedral in the United States. They also broke the windows of the West Broad Church of Christ in Richmond, which serves an African-American congregation. The St. Jude Chapel in Richmond had its windows smashed.

Those who have instigated, participated in, or supported the violence, vandalism, and arson include the Black Lives Matter and Antifa organizations and their affiliates. The title "Black Lives Matter" is a deceptively innocuous one that engenders sympathy from almost all people, many of whom choose to protest peacefully, but gives cover to those who have looted and destroyed even black-owned businesses, assaulted and murdered black policemen and black Americans, including even infants, and destroyed public property, including monuments to the Great Emancipator Abraham Lincoln; to the abolitionist Hans Christian Heg; to the President who refused dictatorship, George Washington; to the author of the Declaration of Independence, Thomas Jefferson; and to the first major black proponent of black freedom and equality and women's suffrage in America, Frederick Douglass. The BLM organization has conspicuously refused to show any sympathy for black victims of the rioting it instigates or the mayhem, assaults, and murders its police defunding and elimination of cash bail policies predictably cause. Indeed, it is precisely because the BLM organization and Antifa seek the Marxist overthrow of the United States that to them, black lives ultimately do not matter; rather, black lives have become acceptable casualties of a Marxist revolutionary struggle to topple American governments.

Antifa, short for Anti-fascist, is another deceptive title, suggesting opposition to fascism. Attaching the epithet "fascist" to capitalists is an old Leninist saw, ironic because fascism, or state socialism, is nascent communism (the very thing Antifa supports) and is the antithesis of capitalism. Ironic today, as well, because many Antifa members dress in fascist attire, cloak themselves in paramilitary wear, and don black helmets with face shields, indicative of the paramilitary troops who imposed fascism in the 1930s. Like the fascists of the pre-World War II era, Antifa is entirely intolerant of any view but their own Marxism. While self-proclaimed Anti-fascist, they are virtually indistinguishable from fascists.

Antifa and BLM members toss bricks, bottles, Molotov cocktails, improvised explosive devices, bags and bottles filled with frozen water, human feces or urine; they wield brass knuckles, knives, bats, and boards with nails protruding from them; they attack police; set fire to police vehicles; loot, vandalize, and burn businesses and government buildings; and they attack all who voice opinions contrary to their own. In "A Brief History of Antifa: Part I," the Gatestone Institute's Soeren Kern explains, "Antifa is . . .[a] highly networked, well-funded" organization that "has a global presence." Its "stated long-term objective, both in America and abroad, is to establish a communist world order." It intends to achieve communist overthrow by employing "extreme violence and destruction of public and private property to goad the police into a reaction, which then 'proves' Antifa's claim that the government is 'fascist.'"[4]

Others, opportunists, have joined in the riots, including radical Islamists, white supremacists, anarchists, arsonists, and thieves (with no apparent ideological agenda). Attorney General William Barr has explained that BLM, Antifa, and anarchist rioters carefully plan the "hijacking" of peaceful protests. They blend into the protests and use protestors as shields to cover their criminal actions.

Founders and leaders of BLM and Antifa have publicly and repeatedly declared themselves to be Marxists. BLM Co-Founder, Patrisse Cullors, was interviewed in 2015 by Jared Ball. In that interview, she, in reference to herself, to her fellow BLM co-founders Alicia Garza and Opal Tometi, and to BLM organizers in general, said: "We are trained Marxists." She explained that she, Garza, and Tometi formed the organization in 2013, following the shooting of seventeen-year-old Trayvon Martin by neighborhood watch coordinator George Zimmerman in Sanford, Florida.[5] Cullors is an understudy of Eric Mann, a leader of the Weather Underground. In 1969, the FBI classified the Weather Underground as a domestic terror organization. In that same year, Mann was sentenced to two years in prison for conspiracy to commit murder in association with the firing of two bullets into the Cambridge, Massachusetts police headquarters on November 8, 1969. In that same year, he was sentenced to eighteen months in prison for assault, battery, disturbing the peace, damaging public property, defacing a building, and disturbing a public assembly.

Consistent with Marxism, BLM and Antifa leaders applaud violence used to exclude and condemn those who do not follow their dictates in lockstep. Theirs is a doctrine of hate that demands complete obedience. They hate free speech, except their own. They hate free enterprise and wish to confiscate private property for their own use. They hate the police and want to abolish them. They hate American history and want to "cancel" it. They find no hypocrisy in condemning anti-black racism while advocating anti-white racism. They favor restructuring society into governing and subservient classes defined by race. They hate all governments in the United States, which they describe as "systemically" racist; they want to replace those governments with Marxist states that preside over a socialist economy. They want to replace the free market with government ownership, operation, and control of all private property and means of production. They want to redistribute income from those who earn it to those who do not. They want a guaranteed minimum income. They want reparations for all black Americans based on the assumption that whites alive today are responsible for acts of enslavement by whites over one hundred and fifty-five years ago. They ignore the fact that whites were also enslaved in the colonies, and that manumitted blacks were also slaveowners. They demand the elimination of all prisons and cash bail. They want to destroy the Constitution along with what remains of limited government, the separation of powers, and the system of checks and balances. They mean to rule America through a dictatorship.

BLM and Antifa inflame popular passion by making the unsubstantiated claim that white police routinely shoot and kill black people. In 2019, scholars published a study in the *Proceedings of the National Academy of Sciences* reviewing data from 2015 to discern the extent to which white police were more likely to shoot minority civilians than non-white police. The sponsors of the study concluded: "We find no evidence of anti-Black or anti-Hispanic disparities across shootings, and white officers are not more likely to shoot minority civilians than non-white officers." In short, while there are isolated instances of police brutality, and even individual instances of racism in policing, there is no foundation to the BLM charge that white officers are more likely to shoot minority civilians than non-white officers or that racism is common in policing. Police shootings, regardless of the race of the officer, occur in up to 95% of the cases in instances where the party shot by the police was attacking police or other civilians. Among those engaged in the attacks against the police or other civilians, 90% were armed.[6] These statistics thus support the conclusion that BLM claims of black shootings are exaggerated. The greater BLM claim, that all whites are racists is fictive and itself a discriminatory claim that demeans the overwhelming number of whites who do not judge others based on skin tone. In this way, BLM departs from the legacy of civil rights activists in America of the Jim Crow Era at least through the time of the passage of the Civil Rights Act of 1964.

Moreover, BLM and Antifa leaders reject the ideology of civil rights movement leaders. The civil rights leaders were believers, mainly Christians and Jews, who staunchly opposed violence and embraced non-violent protest as the means to overcome racial inequality in America. As Dr. Martin Luther King, Jr. put it in his April 16, 1963 letter from Birmingham jail, those who seek change through violence have chosen a corrupt means that taints the very ends they seek: Injustice does not beget justice. Or, as Dr. King more eloquently put it: " . . . the means we use must be as pure as the ends we seek. I have tried to make clear that it is wrong to use immoral means to attain moral ends." And again, in his August 28, 1963, "I Have a Dream" speech at the Lincoln Memorial: "In the process of gaining our rightful place we must not be guilty of wrongful deeds." He consistently preached nonviolence.

The civil rights leaders did not destroy historic monuments; they spoke in front of them. They did not shout down those who opposed their cause, they debated them in a civil manner. They did not riot in the streets, they peacefully protested. They did not murder, rape, loot, vandalize, and commit arson; they set an example of dignity, self-restraint, and just purpose. They suffered much physical abuse, incarceration, and vilification for their convictions but they never sought to destroy the people and the institutions that vexed them; rather, they sought to persuade an American white majority to see the hypocrisy inherent in actions and laws that treated the races differently, and they succeeded magnificently. Rather than murder, pillage, rape, and destroy the civilization surrounding them, they understood that such destruction would magnify the horror and oppression they sought to eliminate. They proved the righteousness of their cause by powerful examples of civility, nonviolent insistence on reform, and peaceable assembly. They spoke, in the words of Abraham Lincoln, to the "better angels of our nature," presuming all people, regardless of race, fundamentally just, even if momentarily misled into bigotry. They thus sought to expose the injustices of bigotry itself, of the injustice imposed on a just people, not adopting a new form of bigotry to combat the old. They had faith in mankind, in free choice, and in the power of persuasion. They believed in the superiority of their message and understood that it would only take lasting root if those receiving it were persuaded. They knew well, as the Antifa and BLM Marxists do not, that forcing an ideology on a people was impossible.

They did not attack those who did not speak in favor of their cause or destroy institutions run by political opponents; they instead made paramount to every person of fair mind the inevitable necessity in a nation born of freedom to grant freedom to those still disenfranchised. They did not expect society at large to bear the immediate costs and burdens of their demands. They bore those costs and burdens themselves in a Christ-like manner, thereby revealing to the majority that the minority that suffered was possessed of human dignity and a completely understandable desire for justice. It was thus that Dr. King persuaded white Americans to sympathize with his cause, to understand that discrimination was beneath the greatness of America, beneath the promise of the Declaration of Independence, and could not be tolerated. Dr. King won the argument: the minds of the majority changed and then the law changed.

Dr. King's quest was not to overthrow the Constitution and the government, which held out the promise of freedom; it was to extend that promise to all, regardless of race. Dr. King believed in the Declaration of Independence, understanding that the generation alive during its promulgation did not extend its promise of liberty to all but also understanding that the Declaration's promise was true and could only be fulfilled when the blessings of liberty reached all. He sought equal justice under the Constitution and protection for the unalienable rights to life, liberty, and the pursuit of happiness of all people. As Dr. King put it: "We have waited for more than 340 years for our constitutional and God given rights." He did not condemn unalienable rights because they had originally been legally recognized in another race. Rather, he explained the hypocrisy of limiting those rights to some of God's children, when because they are God-given, and in accord with Christ's doctrine, they necessarily applied to all. He revered the Declaration and the Constitution, stating in his "I Have a Dream" speech: "When the architects of our republic wrote the magnificent words of the Constitution and Declaration of Independence, they were signing a promissory note to which every American was to fall heir. This note was a promise that all men, yes, black men as well as white men, would be guaranteed the unalienable rights of life, liberty, and the pursuit of happiness."

Dr. King and the non-violent civil rights activists who joined him were thus adherents of the Lockean philosophy that underlies the Constitution, not the Hegelian and Marxist philosophy used to justify state enslavement of all America, i.e., to justify socialism and communism. Martin Luther King, Jr. and other non-violent civil rights leaders, Coretta Scott King, Martin Luther King III, Alveda King, John Lewis, Reverend James E. Orange, Rosa Parks, Dolores Huerta, Dorothy Height, Diane Nash, Daisy Bates, Julian Bond, James Farmer, and Ralph Abernathy, among others, each believed fervently in the promise of the Declaration of Independence and favored fulfillment of that promise through the creation of a color-blind society in which people would be judged, as Dr. King famously said, not based on the color of their skin but on the content of their characters.

It was in appreciation for that great legacy of peaceful civil rights struggle to extend the promise of the Declaration of Independence to all Americans that I accepted an invitation from the late Reverend James E. Orange, a protégé of Dr. Martin Luther King, Jr., to speak at the 21st Annual Martin Luther King Jr. March and Rally Celebration on January 16, 2000, in Atlanta. There, in front of the King Center and the Ebenezer Baptist Church, I spoke for a few minutes to an audience filling several city blocks. I was honored on a more solemn occasion, on February 8, 2006, when my wife Sheryl and I were invited to attend the funeral service for, and burial of, Coretta Scott King, driving to and from the event in the number one bus of the King family itself. On those occasions, the non-violent teachings of Dr. King filled my mind and were honored as people of all races, united in love of God, of country, and of the Declaration and the Constitution, reflected on the achievements of the great non-violent leaders of the civil rights movement. Their views and deeds in support of the promise of the Declaration of Independence, the Constitution, and freedom for all stand in stark contrast to the Marxist BLM organization and Antifa activists who are not advocates of liberty. To them, race is an excuse for Marxism, which is enslavement.

The Marxist BLM and Antifa rioters together with those who support their cause of violent overthrow, including leading figures in the Democratic party, condemn the Declaration, the Constitution, and all American institutions and, thus, oppose the philosophy of freedom that drove the Civil Rights movement. The Marxists receive either express or tacit support from mayors like Bill De Blasio of New York; Jenny Durkan of Seattle, Eric Garcetti of Los Angeles, and Ted Wheeler of Portland, among others; members of city councils in Minneapolis, Seattle, Los Angeles, and Portland, among others; governors like Andrew Cuomo of New York, Gavin Newsom of California, Kate Brown of Oregon, Gretchen Whitmer of Michigan, and Jay Inslee of Washington; members of Congress like avowed socialists Alex- andria Ocasio-Cortez, Ilhan Omar, Ayanna Pressley, and Rashida Tlaib; and United States Senators like Kamala Harris (now Vice President),

Charles Schumer, Edward Markey, Elizabeth Warren, Kirsten Gillibrand, Amy Klobuchar, Richard Blumenthal, Ron Wyden, Jeff Merkley, and Bernie Sanders (another avowed socialist). BLM and Antifa's violent actions are trivialized or left unopposed by House Speaker Nancy Pelosi (who said that if socialist Bernie Sanders were the Democratic nominee she would support him and indicated that the toppling of statues across the nation was a trivial matter ("People will do what they do")); the House Judiciary Committee Chairman Jerry Nadler; House Financial Services Committee Chairman Maxine Waters; Senate Majority Leader Charles Schumer; and several other United States Senators and Congressmen, including Senator Cory Booker and Congressman Eric Swalwell. Collectively these politicians by overt statements in support of the revolutionaries, expressions of sympathy for them, or silence in the face of violence and destruction have advanced the Marxist movement to overthrow United States governments.

Violence, the defenestration of the police, and the toppling of governments are actions rejected by most Americans. Those criminal acts are favored by a tiny fraction of the population. The failure of the government to interdict those actions and arrest the perpetrators has led isolated instances to become chronic national phenomena, threatening the safety, liberty, and property of every American.

As one would expect, most Americans regardless of race oppose defunding the police, violent overthrow of United States governments, destruction of property (including statues, private businesses, and homes), and assaults, rapes, and murders of citizens. A Gallup poll from June and July 2020 revealed that 81% of black Americans want the same amount of, or more, policing in their neighborhoods (with 61% wanting the same amount and 20% wanting more). In those parts of urban America where low-income earners of varying races and ethnicities reside, they are now suffering from an extraordinary rise in murders, assaults and rapes, a rise that corresponds directly with the decrease in policing mandated by those cities' governments whose leaders pander to the BLM organization and Antifa. Urban populations, particularly in the areas hardest hit by crime, overwhelmingly support the police and understand that lives depend on a reliable police presence.

The violence has become the very end sought by the rioters with the originally claimed basis for protest, an end to police abuse of blacks, no longer a primary justification for the violence that has ensued. At first befuddled, Americans are increasingly realizing that the racial injustice said to justify protest does not justify the destruction of monuments, federal buildings, churches, and private property together with assaults against the police and innocent citizens. Those acts of violence and destruction have nothing at all to do with justice, create new injustices, and destroy the basic foundations of our society. Violent crime is the very soul of injustice. It is a repeat of, not a reversal of, the wrongs perpetrated against those who have suffered from instances of police brutality motivated by racism. The BLM organization and Antifa do not want reform, they want overthrow--from the toppling of monuments to the looting and burning of private property to the ultimate toppling of governments federal, state, and local.

That lesson is taught well by several examples of political patronizing that have backfired on those who either fundamentally misunderstood or naively sympathized with the rioters. The saga of Portland Mayor and Police Chief Ted Wheeler is illustrative. After weeks of professing sympathy for what he misperceived to be the aims of BLM and Antifa rioters (those who nightly endeavored to burn and gut the Mark O. Hatfield United States Courthouse), Wheeler flattered himself with the notion that he would be warmly greeted by the rioters. He was convinced the rioters wanted what he wanted: eliminating the federal presence in Portland, defunding the police, ending cash bail, and replacing capitalism with socialism. The rioters, however, weren't wielding rocks, golf balls, ball bearings, bricks, bottles of urine, bottles of bleach, baseball bats, sledgehammers, Molotov cocktails, boards embedded with nails, brass knuckles, lasers, commercial fireworks, and improvised explosive devices because they wanted "reform." No, people destroy buildings where law and order are dispensed, attack police, and try to injure or kill agents defending those buildings because they want an end to law and order. Wheeler presumed himself an alter ego of the mob and one of their favorites, and he presumed they, like he, wanted an end to the federal presence in Portland, not an end to all government, including his own.

With five armed guards surrounding him (a right to self-defense he wants to deny all other citizens), Wheeler ultimately placed himself in a prime spot adjacent to the fence surrounding the federal courthouse. From there he in- tended to give an anti-federal speech to what he presumed to be a supportive crowd, believing it would boost his standing among them. Poking his head above the crowd, he tried to be heard. The rioters took notice, quickly discerned who he was, and made clear that they did not want to listen. They pressed forward and drowned out Wheeler's every word with loud shouts of condemnation and demands that he resign. Initially unperturbed, Wheeler pressed on, thinking if the crowd could just see who he was, they would lis- ten to his message. Nonplused, the crowd pitched water bottles at him and other projectiles, aiming for his head. They swore at Wheeler, screamed at him to shut up, drowned out his feeble voice with their multiple and loud taunts and jeers, pressing him and his bodyguards against the fence.

With the rioting intensifying, federal agents then fired tear gas, and Wheeler came within the gas cloud. He choked as his armed entourage then whisked him away to the confines of the nearby County Justice Center. The rioters followed on his heels, demanding that Wheeler get out of the area and out of elective office. When he retreated within the Center, they at- tacked the Center, pitching projectiles at it and condemning Wheeler. In the Center, Wheeler gave up his quest for mob stardom, leaving in a fast-moving car. Although most would understand from these circumstances that the mob despised Wheeler, the Portland government and police, and the agents of the Federal Bureau of Investigation and the Department of Homeland Security (in short, all existing authority), Wheeler, even after his public humiliation, operated on the delusion that the rioters were still "his people." In fact, shortly thereafter he again railed against President Trump and praised the protestors. Whatever favor he thought his remarks would curry with the rioters, he soon discovered that neither BLM leaders nor Antifa cared one iota for his left-wing politics. They assembled *en masse* in front of his condominium demanding his ouster and hurled incendiary devices to burn his condo to the ground. Wheeler did not understand that it is the BLM and Antifa goal to overthrow the existing government and install *their own*

Marxist regime, not his. Were it not for the Portland police and fire department, whom Wheeler regularly fails to support, he would have been forcibly evicted and, likely, brutalized, if not killed.

AMERICANS SHARE MUCH IN COMMON CONTRARY TO THE CLAIMS OF BLM AND ANTIFA

Americans of all skin tones and backgrounds share much more in common than the shrill army of revolutionaries and their media supporters would have us believe. As famed neurosurgeon and Housing and Urban Development Director Dr. Ben Carson is fond of saying, our brains lack pigment and are visually indistinguishable one from another. While there are certain people of every race who harbor a sophomoric hatred for those not of the same race, that kind of base prejudice is in America generally condemned, is the exception, not the rule, and when acted upon is against federal and state law.

There is among Americans a strong desire to ensure that neither the police nor the courts engage in acts that deprive any citizen of equal justice under law and a strong desire to ensure that neither government policy nor private acts discriminate based on race or gender or deprive individuals of equal opportunity. What binds the citizens of this country together is a united commitment to individual liberty and the impartial administration of justice. That consensus present for at least the last half-century has distinguished the United States as the most racially diverse, non-discriminatory, and opportunity-rich country in the world. Ironically, it is the goal of the BLM organization and Antifa to make us believe that this consensus does not exist, not to end the vestiges of discrimination but to achieve a Marx- ist overthrow of the United States, based, in part, on a revival of bigotry (against whites, against Christians, and against those who have political be- liefs different from their own). They raise the banner of black lives in their quest to destroy the very legal and commercial institutions that have done the most to eliminate prejudice, provide equal justice, and supply opportunity in America. Their Marxist state is full of prejudice; it is the very definition of a slave state in which a select minority of political leaders control all aspects of American life, dictating acceptable views, denying religious liberty, directing where and for whom Americans work, and taking from Americans all private property, removing it from those who have earned it and providing it to those who have not. Indeed, their hero, Karl Marx, was unabashedly anti-Semitic and racist.

Nearly every American detests racial discrimination and almost everyone agrees with the factual proposition that black life matters, but BLM and Antifa leaders who assert claims of racial injustice do not proclaim black lives matter as a stand-alone fact but as a response to the very existence of non-black life, which they do not say matters. They condemn those who proclaim that all lives matter, asserting that this proposition, another self-evident truth, is reflective of the concept of equal justice under law which they reject, perpetuates white supremacy, and fails to admit the falsehood to which they subscribe: that whites are biologically racist. It has become fashionable in certain BLM circles to demand that whites kneel in front of blacks as an expression of guilt over "white privilege," indicative of subservience to a new master race.[7] That kneeling to dictatorial authority is a microcosm of the Marxist state, wherein we would all be forced to kneel to a communist regime.

What the BLM organization refers to as "racism" is in their world a one-way street, a condemnation of all possessed of pale pigments, even the overwhelming majority who have engaged in no overt acts of discrimination. By BLM definition blacks cannot be racist, even those (including their leaders) who condemn white people as irredeemably racist. To BLM leaders, racism imbues everything touched by lightly pigmented hands, in perpetuity. So, all business, all government, and all institutions in the United States, whether controlled by blacks or not, are infected with "systemic racism," irredeemably so, and must be destroyed. The "destroy everything" mentality belies their professed concern for black life because they sweep within their destruction all elements of black capitalist success: black-owned businesses, black victims of their violence (e.g., retired St. Louis Police Captain David Dorn), and black voices that differ from their Marxist monologue.

BLM and Antifa do not seek racial equality, equal justice under law, or that all be judged based on the content of their character rather than the color of their skin. They do not want a color-blind society; they want a color-conscious society in which slavery returns in the form of Marxist masters enslaving the rest of us. After all, the communism they seek is the communism history records as depriving freedom universally, what we may term "systemic slavery."

They advocate defunding the police not to achieve racial justice, as they publicly claim (indeed, most urban police forces are run by professionals whose officers overwhelmingly do not engage in unlawful conduct, are not racist, and are substantially non-white), but to remove that primary defense to their planned violent overthrow of governments and their confiscation of all private property.

The BLM organization and Antifa can point to no Marxist success story. Every nation that has succumbed to the false dogma of socialism, to centralized government planning, has experienced a profound loss of human wealth and worth inextricably intertwined with each individual's freedom, has experienced a deadening of the soul and a loss of hope, and has experienced a near-universal reduction in productive enterprise and rapid rise in mass poverty. The poorest nations on earth are ordinarily those, like Venezuela and North Korea, which adopt socialism and communism. Communist China yields a novel exception, not because its annihilation of political and religious liberty is any less horrific, but because of its embrace of capitalism. Thus, while the Chinese people are not free to speak and worship as they wish, they market goods and services profitably, albeit for only so long as the state neither takes offense nor wishes to control the industry directly. The Peoples Republic of China continues to imprison disfavored minorities in labor camps and torture the Muslim Uighurs; Christians; the Falun Gong; Taoists, and the Tibetan Buddhists, among others. The persecuted minorities are forced to renounce their faiths, pledge allegiance to Xi Jinping, undergo re-education, and be enslaved in forced labor. Those resistant are variously tortured into submission or executed.

THE DEMOCRATIC PARTY IS DOMINATED BY AUTHORITARIANS

Despite popular will against the aims of the BLM organization and Antifa, political leaders at the local, state, and national level, particularly in urban jurisdictions, have pandered to those groups, professing considerable support for them and meekly cowing to their demands: defunding police, eliminating cash bail, and releasing back onto the streets those arrested for all manner of serious crimes. The moves in Minneapolis, New York, Portland, and Seattle, among others, to neuter power to arrest criminal acts have logically led to more violence, reaching more cities nationwide, bleeding into the suburbs. Almost one-half of the 258 police departments in the United States have experienced budget cuts favored by politicians who pander to the Marxists and anarchists in the BLM organization and Antifa. If the trend of defunding police, ending cash bail, and releasing criminals continues, there will invariably be far more instances of violent crime across the United States in urban and suburban areas alike. The spread of destruction from the center of the cities to the suburbs is progressing apace. Civilization is very much at stake. In the absence of police protection, self-defense will become the order of the day with all fending for themselves because legal protection will be unreliable or unavailable. For the many who love America, who have been willing to fight and die for liberty overseas, the planned Marxist revolution is unacceptable and will face their stiff opposition.

Never in American history until now have communists and socialists assumed positions of such great political power at every level of American government, enjoyed near-constant national media coverage and promotion of their views, amassed enormous war chests from corporate donations, and received sympathetic mass media and political support for statements condemning their own country, its Constitution, its free-market system, and its defense of rights to life, liberty, and property. Never in American history until now have those same political leaders and media minimized the significance of, condoned, or turned a blind eye to acts of violence against citizens, property, police, and governments. But we did not get here overnight. The movement has been a long, continuous struggle against republican forms of government, beginning in the antebellum South.

The genesis of the movement lies in the political philosophy of Georg Wilhelm Friedrich Hegel, whose influence extends through nearly 200 years of American history. Slaveowners invoked Hegel to justify the institution of slavery as perfect socialism. Communists and socialists were loud in their complaints preceding and during World War I. They were vocal again during the Great Depression. Dozens assumed power in the administration of Franklin Delano Roosevelt. They were again loud in their denunciations of

America preceding and during World War II. They were vocal again during the Vietnam War and ever since the 1960s on all major college campuses. But never have they had so many adherents, so much sympathy for their cause from those in power, so many representatives in government, and so much money as they do now. Never have they so successfully dominated a political party as they do the Democratic Party today. Never have they received such assurances of support for the implementation of their agenda as they have from Joe Biden.

Indeed, for the first time in history, the Democratic Party openly avows support for socialist policies, adopting almost all aspects of Senator Bernie Sanders and Congresswoman Alexandria Ocasio-Cortez's agendas for America, as revealed in Joe Biden's Build Back Better plan and in the Biden-Sanders Unity Task Force Report. Biden's catalog of heavy taxation, redistributionist policy, heavy regulation, planned elimination of fossil fuels, redirection of funding away from law enforcement and to social services, elimination of Customs and Border Patrol enforcement of border protection, grant of amnesty and welfare for those illegally in the United States, and Medicare for all promises to destroy the essential institutions in defense of freedom and free enterprise that radical Marxists have long endeavored to eliminate. According to economists Timothy Fitzgerald, Kevin Hassett, Cody Kallen, and Casey Mulligan in a recent Hoover Institution Study, the Biden plan will cause almost five million Americans to lose their jobs.[8] Some estimates of job loss due to his planned transition away from fossil fuels are far higher, upwards of seven million. Fitzgerald, Hassett, Kallen, and Mulligan conclude that "Biden's full agenda reduces full-time equivalent employment per person by about 3 percent, capital stock per person by about 15 percent, real GDP per capita by more than 8 percent, and real consumption per household of about 7 percent." They anticipate a drop in median household income of $6,500 by 2030.[9]

Biden intends to "reimagine policing" by using federal mandates to re-direct certain local spending away from policing and toward social services, precisely at a time when more policing is needed to combat massive crime increases. He offers no plan to stop what will be even more murders, rapes, assaults, and burglaries as policing is drawn down further, even as jurisdictions in Minneapolis, New York, and Seattle experience multiple hundred percent increases in those crimes from their defunding actions. He intends to raise individual and corporate taxes in the current recession, a recipe that will all but ensure a greater economic downturn, perhaps even a depression, by increasing unemployment and reducing job opportunity. He intends to defund municipalities unless they agree to federal control of urban planning and zoning (what was the former Obama Administration's "Affirmatively Favoring Fair Housing" (AFFH) initiative) and dictate everything from park services and locations to school curricula and education, essentially replacing much of what constitutes local government. He intends to end immigration law enforcement, abolish immigration detention centers, and end all deportations (including those of MS-13, criminal sex traffickers, murderers, rapists, and repeat offenders). He intends to end the prosecution of all illegal border crossings and expand asylum for all new illegal immigrants. He intends to cancel all asylum cooperation agreements in the West- ern Hemisphere. He intends to provide all new illegal immigrants federal welfare, taxpayer-funded legal counsel, taxpayer subsidies, work permits, government-financed health care, federal student aid, and free community college. He intends to end the requirement that illegal aliens demonstrate self-sufficiency as a condition of citizenship and to grant amnesty to all who seek it. He intends to expand substantially low skill immigration into the United States. He intends to increase refugee admissions into the United States by 700%. He intends to end border wall construction. He intends to end all travel bans, including travel bans from jihadist regions. He voices no concern for any resulting massive increase in illegal immigration, loss of citizens' jobs, an explosion in the cost of welfare, and a predictable rise in violent and non-violent crime and terrorism.

He intends to expend $2 to $4 trillion on "green" initiatives, such as the nationwide building of windmills and the installation of solar energy panels. He intends the federal government to finance the installation of 500 million solar panels and erect 60,000 wind turbines throughout the West over millions of acres, turbines responsible for decimating bat, bald eagle, raptor, night-migrating songbird, and grassland bird populations. He intends to impose federal mandates and regulations to eliminate oil, clean coal, natural gas, and fracking in the United States, a source of over ten million jobs and of American energy independence. He intends to prohibit the emission of all building greenhouse gasses by 2030, putting an end to central air conditioning and heating. He intends to prohibit the emission of all greenhouse gasses from businesses by 2050, shuttering all petroleum, oil, and natural gas production in the United States. He intends to expand Medicare to include a public option to cover all health care deemed medically reasonable and necessary by the federal government at a likely cost of trillions annually and to rationing of medical care. He intends to limit the sale and transfer of weapons to the police and to law enforcement agencies. He intends to limit private ownership of firearms, further constricting individual's Second Amendment rights. He does not calculate the extent to which these actions will increase the loss of life due to violent crime. He intends to abolish the death penalty and solitary confinement. He intends to provide free federal housing to former inmates. He intends to appoint "social justice" prosecutors who will expand the release of those accused of violent crime, such as the dozens on the state level whose campaigns were heavily financed by George Soros. He intends to promote the closure of jails, prisons, and detention centers, and to redirect that funding to community-based welfare programs. He does not explain how the nation will cope with the corresponding rise in violent crimes that predictably will follow these reforms. He intends to have the United States rejoin the Paris Climate Accord (estimated to cost businesses in the United States tens of trillions of dollars and to result in the closure of many domestic companies in the manufacturing and energy sec- tors, to cause higher unemployment, and to inflate the cost of all goods and services). He intends to ban for-profit charter schools, end school choice, and ban funding for charter schools in poor neighborhoods. He shows noconcern for the many poor families whose children have prospered in the private and charter schools he plans to ban and defund.

Biden's new open border policy combined with amnesty, welfare, paid education, paid healthcare, subsidies, and paid legal services for all illegal immigrants will result in wave after wave of illegal immigrants entering the United States from all over the world with no effective evaluation to weed out those who lack employable skills, have histories of violent crime, are members of gangs, or are engaged in criminal sex or drug trafficking and with no regard to the effect that the new immigrants will have on the employment prospects of workers who are citizens. That, combined with his proposed support for sanctuary cities and states, and redirection of funding away from policing, elimination of jails and prisons, and reduction in the incarceration of serious offenders will predictably increase murder, rape, assault, home invasion, and robbery in the United States.

Not including the trillions for reparations, his plans will cost taxpayers about ten trillion dollars per year, doubling current federal spending and threatening the financial solvency of the nation as it labors under the weight of federal spending associated with the pandemic. His promised destruction of school choice and charter schools will lock children in urban areas in substandard public schools, robbing them of opportunities to break out and achieve academic excellence. His promise of significant tax increases and industry choking regulations while the nation endeavors to recover from a pandemic-induced recession will create enormous unemployment and prevent economic recovery—forcing the nation into a downward, ruinous spiral. It is hard to imagine a more complete plan to destroy the United States in a single presidential term than that of Joe Biden, and, sadly, perhaps that is the point.

Taken together, Biden's planned interventions into the economy define a new socialist order. They betray the Constitution and Bill of Rights by replacing a republican form of government with a bureaucratic oligarchy administering a socialist economy. It is precisely the government our Constitution forbids.

The dramatic weakening of the United States caused by this radical agenda will create new opportunities for enemies of the United States, likely leading to more aggression by those nations to eliminate American influence in the world and advance the causes of communist and theocratic dictators. China will accelerate its move to replace the United States as the world's predominant military and economic superpower and replace the dollar with the renminbi as the world reserve currency. China, Russia, North Korea, and Iran can be counted upon to promote more violence, economic hardship, internecine conflict, and destabilization of the United States and allied governments.

The authoritarians who occupy the streets and dominate the Democratic Party differ from their predecessors in that their Marxist agenda no longer hides in the shadows, on the fringe, in the bureaucracy, or in academia as was common before 2020. They overtly control most of the media and agencies of the government, run the Democratic Party, and fill seats in Congress, and some of like mind riot in the streets, destroy property, kill police, and kill innocents, even children, all with enormous financial backing from major corporations and well-healed individuals. For example, the BLM Global Network Foundation and aligned organizations have received over $1.4 billion in donations from entities and individuals, including the following: Bank of America ($1 billion); George Soros's Open Society Foundation ($33 million); Amazon ($10 million); Door Dash, Inc., Deckers, Gatorade, Glossier, Airbnb, Nabisco, and Dropbox ($500,000 each); Microsoft ($250,000), Square Enix ($250,000), and Pokemon ($100,000). A billion dollars is more than enough money to foment a violent revolution. Due to their unprecedented prominence, wealth, power, and proclivity for violent overthrow, the authoritarians pose the greatest threat to the survival of constitutional government and individual liberty and private property our nation has ever faced.

AMERICANS MUST RISE TO RESTORE CONSTITUTIONAL GOVERNMENT

There is, of course, an alternative to the violence and oppression of Marxism. That alternative first arose following the 1776 publication of the Declaration of Independence and the publication that same year of Adam Smith's *Wealth of Nations*. That alternative protects the individual's right to choose his or her own beliefs and his or her own pursuits of industry and improvement, free of government coercion, restriction, and control. That alternative is historically proven to work; it created in America the most prosperous and productive nation ever to exist, a nation that raised the standard of living, produced more innovation and innovative thought, and alleviated the poverty of more people than any other nation that has ever existed. The flourishing of capitalism in America is responsible for the elimination of more human suffering, the arrest of more disease and discomfort, the extension of life and the quality of life, and the creation of more inventions, which have lessened the burdens of life, than any other economic system.

Americans must awake to and oppose the real agendas of the Marxist BLM organization and Antifa, or they will witness the demise of our republic and the precious freedoms we hold dear. The great blessings of that republic and the freedoms protected by it will be lost. What we see unfolding across the United States hauntingly echoes the threat another Marxist gave America in 1956: "We will take America without firing a shot," said Nikita Khrushchev, First Secretary of the Communist Party of the Soviet Union. "We do not have to invade the U.S.," he said. "We will destroy you from within . . ."

The counter to the current Marxist revolution in America depends on a resounding rejection of its adherents by Americans united in their patriotism across all pigments, faiths, creeds, and party affiliations, a rejection in the streets, at the ballot box, in the state legislatures and governorships, and in the courts. The days of emerging authoritarian rule and liberal tolerance for Marxist policies and for mass violence are upon us. Economic depression, significant increases in crime across the country, and the destruction and erosion of all private property and liberty will be ushered in through waves of redistributionist and individual rights disabling laws and regulations unless we stop them now. Those who cherish freedom are on the front lines. They must not let socialism take root in America.

If the American people turn back socialism, we may yet save the republic. If we do not, we will be reduced to a degree of burden, suffering, poverty, and social unrest unlike anything Americans have experienced, not even in the Great Depression. And in that lies the threat not only of a Marxist take-over of all things private but also of a clear invitation to our enemies around the world, to China, to Russia, to North Korea, and to Iran to seize the day and hasten our destruction so that the last, best hope for freedom on earth is reduced to a slave satellite of totalitarian regimes.

For those who live in cities controlled by mayors who, and city councils that, defund the police, it is past time to move to locations where the police are respected, thereby removing the tax base of support for policies that turn those cities into killing fields. That mass exodus is happening, with large numbers of people leaving New York, California, Oregon, and Washington to the interior and southern states, likely effecting one of the greatest demographic redistributions of the population in American history.

Consistent with the example first set by President George Washington in July of 1794 to quell the whiskey rebellion in western Pennsylvania, the President must be implored persistently to invoke the Insurrection Act of 1807 and dispatch the armed forces of the United States to quell riots in the cities where local authorities either cannot or will not. Attendant to the Article II duty of the President to ensure that the laws are faithfully executed is the fundamental obligation to protect American lives, liberties, and properties against assault when local leaders fail to or refuse to do so. That duty is made manifest in Article IV, section 4 of the Constitution (the Guarantee Clause), which guarantees each state a republican form of government. President George Washington set the example of leadership in this as in so many other instances throughout his heroic life. After three years of insurrection at the hands of armed men who refused to pay the federal tax due on whiskey, culminating in 500 of their number threatening the life of federal Tax Inspector General John Neville, President Washington federalized 12,950 militia from Virginia, Maryland, New Jersey, and Pennsylvania to form an army under his command to put down the rebellion. While President Washington and that army were enroute to engage the insurrectionists, the mob's leaders reconsidered and the insurrectionists returned home. Likewise, today, in the face of overwhelming force, those intent on fomenting revolution through cowardly acts of violence and destruction against innocent people, against public and private property, and against the police should be forced either to relent or be crushed, thus restoring law and order.

In addition to deploying all force necessary to quell riots, local, state, and national governments must coordinate efforts to uncover the planning underway for acts of subversion and must bring terrorism, criminal RICO, seditious conspiracy, Smith Act, and, in cases of violence intended to topple the government, treason charges against the offenders, prosecuting each to the full extent of the law and imposing just punishments. Those who mean to maim, rape, kill, overthrow the government, and destroy public and private property need to be prosecuted and incarcerated. If guilty of murder or treason, their lives should not be spared.

In the chapters that follow we will explore the authoritarians' ugly history in the United States: their power grabs, deprivations of liberty and life, discrimination, eugenics, destruction of the rule of law, corruption, disenfranchisement of disfavored classes, perversion of education, and selective ruin of private enterprise. We will contrast authoritarianism based on expert divination of a "collective" will with the classical liberal model of the founding era based on individual liberty, free enterprise, and individual sovereignty. We will discover why only the latter is compatible with human nature, human dignity, self-fulfillment, innovation, equal justice under law, and equal opportunity.

The historical record confirms that authoritarianism is parasitic, enslaving, and oppressive. It demands that the individual abandon liberty to serve the dictates of the state. It reduces all that which is excellent to a pervasive condition of mediocrity. It destroys the human spirit, stifles innovation, and degrades the quality and value of human life. By contrast, classical liberalism protects individual independence and fosters a rise to excellence through freely chosen beliefs and service to others, which redounds to greater prosperity for all. It respects the individual, elevates the human spirit, inspires innovation, and raises the quality and value of human life. The oppression that comes when government enslaves its people ensures a perpetually low standard of living, mass poverty, hopelessness, and universal abasement. That is the legacy of socialism, of liberties lost, and of state control of life. The freedom that comes when government protects the people's rights to life, liberty, and property against the rapacious acts of the state, and protects their freedom to engage in their own chosen pursuits of industry and improvement, ensures a rise in the standard of living, prosperity, and happiness. That is the legacy of limited government under our Constitution.

As an attorney who has practiced before agencies of the federal government since 1985, I have long observed the persistent presence in the bureaucracy of those who favor government control over individual liberty. In case after case, some of which I document here, authoritarians in the bureaucracy have destroyed private enterprise and deprived individuals of liberty, and even life, in pursuit of an ever-elusive ideological agenda driven by the unelected heads of the agencies. As the cases demonstrate, in the minds of those who lead the bureaucracy the ends justify the means and the law, indeed fundamental fairness, is no barrier to the achievement of political ends. In short, for most agency heads, the rule of law is no rule at all because nothing is permitted to stand in the way of their preferred political outcomes. In this way, our federal bureaucracy has for years embodied authoritarianism antithetical to the core values evinced by and the restrictions on power contained in the Constitution.

The seeds of authoritarianism were planted in America before the Civil War, gained deep roots between the 1880s and the 1930s, and came to fruition in the administrative state from the 1930s to the present. In case after case, authoritarianism has exacted an enormous toll on American freedom, property, and life, dragging the nation down and limiting its true potential. The Progressives of today are the authoritarian offspring of the Progressives of the mid-nineteenth and early twentieth centuries. Those Progressive forebears are themselves the offspring of authoritarian monarchs and administrators who ruled in England and Europe from the thirteenth to the nineteenth Centuries. Then, as now, the Progressives are defined by a common insistence on centralized power beyond constitutional limits to achieve desired social and economic ends, circumventing the democratic process and violating the rights of the people. Then, as now, the Progressives' core beliefs mirror those of Friedrich Hegel, the nineteenth-century German Historical School philosopher who rejected classical liberalism. The Progressives of our time fully embrace the concept of collectivism, and worship state power, efficiency, and direction of all things economic and social, trusting unquestioningly in the will of bureaucratic "experts."

The Progressives of today have much in common with the enemies of liberty that the founding fathers defeated; the Progressives wield power in a manner akin to absolute monarchs and the infamous English Courts of High Commission and of Star Chamber in the fifteenth to seventeenth centuries.

They harbor disdain for constitutional limits on power, constitutional separation of powers, and legal protections for individual liberty, preferring imposition of administrative rule unencumbered by constitutional limits. They employ combined legislative, executive, and judicial powers, making the prosecutor also the judge and legislator, rendering justice for individuals impossible. They elevate a collective right of the state to pursue a "public interest" defined by agency experts over individual freedom of choice and the right to be protected against arbitrary deprivations of life, liberty, and property.

For one hundred years, the federal courts have been largely tolerant of these federal agency abuses, rarely disallowing them since the late 1930s, permitting the abuses to pass by largely unmolested, establishing broad judicial deference for authoritarianism. In this way, an agency that has served as both prosecutor and judge, an inherent conflict of interest, is rarely made to account for that conflict or its actions.

Although by its very nature beyond constitutional limits (a source of independent governance nowhere authorized by the Constitution), the administrative state came to be by usurpation, not by amendment to the Constitution under Article V as the supreme law requires. The disdain with which Progressives of the late nineteenth century held the Constitution led them to usurp the power to create the first major federal agency, the Interstate Commerce Commission, and forego the Article V amendment process. Had they proceeded in a manner that respected the sovereignty of the people, they would never have created the administrative state without first securing a constitutional amendment authorizing it. Instead, Progressives, like President Woodrow Wilson, argued that the courts need not interpret   the Constitution to mean what it says but could view it from a higher level of abstraction and presume it "living." It could therefore be said to mean the opposite of what its authors intended, permitting the establishment of an all-powerful administrative state nowhere authorized by the document and, indeed, forbidden by its power limiting provisions. In this way, the separation of powers doctrine, the non-delegation doctrine, and the independence of the judiciary could be emasculated. Indeed, the powers of the legislative, executive, and judicial branches could be drained from their constitutional repositories and poured into single agencies, circumventing the Constitution's design and requirements.

The product of relentless Progressive advocacy in its favor and tepid efforts on the part of the federal courts to defend the Constitution, the administrative state is today all-powerful, deeply political, destructive of liberty and property, and committed to an anti-competitive agenda that channels market activity into politically preferred pursuits and grants anticompetitive protection for certain industry players over others. Its unelected heads rule with few limits on their power. They, and not the Congress of the United States into which the law-making power is exclusively vested by the Constitution, make, enforce, and judge the violation of nearly all federal laws today. That extra-constitutional system, sometimes referred to as the "fourth branch" of government, has transformed our polity from a limited federal republic into a centralized bureaucratic oligarchy, one which Marxist and socialist leaders of the Democratic Party wish to empower further to make America a socialist state.

As I have come to learn profoundly from thirty-five years of practice before federal agencies and courts, Congress may pass laws but the agencies, not the federal courts, define the meaning of those laws through regulation. And the agencies do just as they please, often effectively rewriting their enabling statutes (sometimes to mean the opposite of the plain and intended meaning of the law). The agencies pursue their own legal agendas without the consent of the governed and with little care for what Congress wants, what the Courts require, or what the American people can tolerate. The all-powerful federal bureaucracy acts in ways the public would abhor were it fully exposed, but the public has little awareness of, and no legal say in, the matter.

While the republic created by the Constitution could be controlled through the ballot box, the federal bureaucracy cannot be. The Constitution's founders condemned legislation without representation, yet today federal bureaucrats promulgate and enforce thousands of regulations each year adopted without a single elected representative having any role to play in that lawmaking and with no serious judicial check on the bureaucrats who enforce the regulations. The principal author of the Declaration of Independence foresaw the dangers of collectivism before Hegel introduced the concept. Jefferson condemned a society where "every man shall be bound to dedicate the whole of his industry to the common interest," explaining, "were we directed from Washington when to sew, and when to reap, we should soon want bread."[10]

Freedom is thus besieged on many levels. We face a revolution in the streets led by Marxists intent on transforming the United States into a communist country. We face elected representatives who either favor that Marxist take-over or intend to stand by while it takes place. We see for the first time a dominant political party, the Democratic Party, openly embrace a socialist agenda. We face an internal, governmental threat that has already replaced the republic defined by the Constitution with a bureaucratic oligarchy created by acts of usurpation by Progressives since the end of the Civil War. There will be no domestic tranquility and no adequate defense of individual liberty unless we arrest the Marxist revolution in the streets, remove the Marxists and Marxist sympathizers from elected office, and end the administrative state.

There is a far better way than this massive embrace of collectivism with its threat of imminent oppression. It defines a world in which the government does not interfere with the exercise of freedom of choice except when that exercise violates the equal rights of others. It requires that government be instituted for the very purpose of protecting the rights of the governed, who, if so protected, are sovereign. It requires that government exist only by the consent of those sovereigns. It presumes people innocent of wrongdoing unless the actions they take are proven beyond a reasonable doubt to violate the rights of others in an independent court dependent upon rules of procedure that guard against bias. It does not allow any law to be created except by those the people elect, and it does not allow any who create the law to judge law violation or to enforce the law, thus guarding against an all-powerful tyrant through a genuine separation of powers. Individual liberty arising in such a system is maximized by limiting government.

The intrinsic value of freedom for all humanity vastly exceeds the value of control for a select few. By nature, we are inquisitive, seek betterment, and obtain satisfaction from the delivery of goods and services we freely provide and others freely choose to obtain. In this way, capitalism, which depends on free exchange, near perfectly complements individual liberty while socialism does the opposite by depriving the productive of the fruits of their labor for purposes chosen by political masters who confiscate those fruits and redirect them as they please. Thus, in the socialist state, only the leaders, those who control the dispensation of wealth earned by others, enjoy a meaningful degree of freedom. They live a parasitic existence, sucking the life's blood out of their host, a host that increasingly delivers less value as it receives little or none in return for labor. Because socialism is parasitic and draws ever more wealth out of the private sector to fuel government expansion and control, it invariably implodes. Its private sector host can only endure so much exsanguination.

Satisfaction in life is dependent on proof from the fruits of our labors that those labors, freely chosen, have improved the lives of others who express their satisfaction whenever they make a purchase. In this way, freedom begets human dignity, self-fulfillment, and progress.

No amount of theoretical communitarian ideology offered to salve the conscience can substitute for the real self-confidence, self-worth, self-fulfillment, and happiness derived from the exercise of free choice. We are happiest when we are free to select that part of education and experience to mold into our unique contribution, our innovation, leading ultimately to our individual success and prosperity. No political planner can better determine how best to serve our own interests than we can ourselves. In a free society, unencumbered by government, success and prosperity are direct reflections of others' appreciation for our pursuits of industry and improvement, upon which they and we depend for advancement. In this way, freedom invariably raises the standard of living and enables progress while ensuring the greatest degree of self-satisfaction.

Against this, the false promise of socialism and of Marxism provides a depraved alternative that depends on removing individual freedom of choice and sovereignty and vesting all power and control in the state. That unnatural separation of people from their freedom and possessions is slavery and destroys the soul, robbing us of our dignity, individuality, wealth, and self-determination. The collective will is, in fact, a fiction, an excuse, a ruse to take away individual liberty. Few of us freely choose to be in precise agreement with anyone else on matters as complex as those affecting the economy, society, and politics. The collective will is, in reality, nothing more than the political desires of those with the authority to direct the enforcement of government power. To serve what is in fact the dictatorial will of those few in control, our individual will is suppressed and our freedom is deprived, because we must do as directed by political leaders, by a new class of slaveowners. It is, then, no wonder that Hegel and all authoritarians since have viewed direct enslavement of individuals, or by arresting and constricting their choices and markets, to be preferable to the classical liberal model where individual freedom reigns.

How did the many grave threats to liberty we now face arise in America? How did those who favor communist and socialist doctrines of absolute state power and against individual liberty gain such tremendous political clout? How were constitutional barriers to the exercise of administrative state power defeated? What effect has the administrative state had on freedom, innovation, and enterprise? Will the rule of law be restored such that the rule of the mob, so freshly in our experience, will be arrested? What is life like under socialism and communism; what is the perspective of those who have experienced that life? What can we do to block the advance of socialism and communism, reign in the administrative state, and restore constitutional governance to America? Answers to those questions follow.

CHAPTER 1

THE BIRTH AND GROWTH OF AUTHORITARIANISM IN AMERICA

A uthoritarianism in America has its roots in the antebellum South. Confronted with northern cries for abolition of slavery along with a loss of majority control of Congress, southern leaders rejected the classical liberal model of the Founding generation (individual rights, limited government, and free enterprise) and embraced an authoritarian collectivist model, socialism, derived from the German Historical School of the 1820s. In 1821, the German philosopher Georg Wilhelm Friedrich Hegel, a darling of modern-day Progressives, socialists, and Marxist communists (indeed, Karl Marx was for the most part his doting student), heralded slavery as a form of societal progress, by which an "inferior" people (Africans) could be lifted to a higher level of social progression by association with a "superior" people (Europeans).[11] Endeavoring to fend off abolitionist attacks on the evils of slavery rooted in the promise of the Declaration of Independence (that all men are created equal), southern leaders latched on to Hegel's view[12] and condemned the Declaration and its principal author, fellow southerner Thomas Jefferson.

Hegel's defense of an all-powerful state that would dictate the collective will and impose it on the people was celebrated by social, economic, and

1

political reformers in the antebellum South. Later, after the South was vanquished by the Civil War, Progressives continued to demand a Hegelian socialist state.

Today's authoritarians who advance Hegel's philosophy include leading members of the Democratic Party and almost every chairman of every committee in the House of Representatives. Joe Biden is a captive of this way of thinking. Those who dominate the Democratic Party routinely define collectivist objectives, then command adherence to those objectives at the expense of individual rights to life, liberty, and property, and condemn any form of dissent. Consistent with Marxism, dissenters are the victims of character assassination and doxing. Once the Marxists overthrow the government, then dissent becomes a crime against the state (seditious libel) and dissenters are variously arrested, tortured, or killed for that crime.

The Hegelian construct devalues the individual, except as he or she is useful to the state. It calls for the creation of an unelected, independent government of so-called experts, unrestricted by a separation of powers and need to account to the electorate, entrusted with authority to define the universe of lawful pursuits of industry and improvement. While the classical model at the Founding gave legal protection to each person's freedom to decide for him or herself all pursuits of industry and improvement, save those which resulted in a violation of the equal rights of others, the Hegelian model gives that power to a highly paternalistic state and denies the public any freedom to deviate from the state's sanctioned path. In this way, control over basic life-affecting decisions is removed from the individual and given to the state, and all thereby become *de facto* slaves of the state.

In short, the Hegelian model was adopted as a primary defense for slavery in the antebellum South. It was then adopted as the justification for the authoritarian administrative state by Progressives in the late nineteenth and early twentieth centuries. And it has again been adopted in our time as the basis for massive redistributive tax programs, wholesale elimination of private property and industry, government regulatory control over all industry, reparations for populations based on race, destruction of the rule of law, cancel culture, and mob violence. It aims fundamentally at transferring control over all attributes of ownership and life-affecting decisions from the individual to the state. The authoritarians mean to constrict individual liberty to such an extent that no private action of any significance can occur without state sanction, thus placing the state in the role of the plantation slave master.

While in days past servitude was the legacy of those enslaved by plantation owners in America, increasingly today, servitude has become the universal fate of all Americans. To halt and reverse that trend requires that we oppose the authoritarians' quest for control at the ballot box, in court, and in legislative and executive decision-making; end the administrative state; and revivify constitutional barriers to the exercise of government power.

THE BIRTH OF AUTHORITARIANISM IN THE ANTEBELLUM SOUTH

Before the Civil War, southerners were forced to confront a dilemma created by the Lockean teachings enshrined in the preamble to the Declaration of Independence, a preamble their forebears taught them to revere:

> We hold these truths to be self-evident, that all men are created equal, that they are endowed by their Creator with certain unalienable rights, that among these are life, liberty, and the pursuit of happiness. That, to secure these rights, governments are instituted among men, deriving their just powers from the consent of the governed. That, whenever any form of government becomes destructive of these ends, it is the right of the people to alter or to abolish it, and to institute new government, laying its foundation on such principles, and organizing its powers in such form, as to them shall seem most likely to effect their safety and happiness.

In the antebellum South, southerners had strong familial affections for the struggle for Independence in which their fathers, uncles, and grandfathers fought to harvest from British usurpations the Declaration's self-evident truth that "all men are created equal" and "endowed by their Creator with certain unalienable rights," including among them "life, liberty, and the pursuit of happiness." Having been taught in very personal terms how freedom wrenched from the British should remain a protected inheritance for all generations to come, they struggled to explain how the promise of the Declaration could be squared with the reality of human bondage.

Northern abolitionists, like William Lloyd Garrison, salted southern wounds by condemning slaveholders as unchristian and hypocritical in not allowing the blessings of liberty to reach all peoples, regardless of race and gender. As sectional strife mounted between the societies of North and South, southerners were forced to defend slavery as moral. Indeed, they were forced to provide an explanation for why southern slavery was not only consistent with Christianity but also superior to free labor in the industrialized North.

In their quest to defend what South Carolina Senator John C. Calhoun called the "peculiar institution" (a term he meant to depict slavery in a positive light), southern slaveholders found themselves unable to reconcile black bondage with the Declaration's promise, the inherent logic of which begs universality: that all men are created equal. Thus stymied, they turned to Hegel's argument in defense of slavery, which is born of a paternalistic prejudice: that slaves benefit by association with an allegedly more sophisticated race, the race of those who enslave them.

Acting on the command of Lincoln's 1863 Emancipation Proclamation, that all slaves in the states then in rebellion "shall be then, thenceforward, and forever free," the Union Army ended the institution of southern slavery, but it was not able to terminate the Hegelian doctrine, which justified enslavement. Forced out of the plantation, that doctrine simply relocated itself in the salons of "Progressive" intellectuals, who cleaved to the Hegelian idea that no one is born endowed by their creator with unalienable rights, that all rights are effectively privileges permitted by the state, and that the state is the absolute master of all, controlling all life, liberty, and property. Upon that basis, Progressives justified enforced segregation via Jim Crow laws and eugenics, among other forms of identity politics that persist to this day.

As C. Bradley Thompson explains in *America's Revolutionary Mind*, "Proslavery thinkers came to realize that the greatest intellectual obstacle to promoting slavery in the United States was the Declaration of Independence and its psychic hold on the minds of ordinary Americans, including patriotic

Southerners."[13] Among southern leaders who rejected the Declaration's promise were South Carolina's Governors James H. Hammond and George McDuffie, who stated (the former quoting the latter): "I repudiate, as ridiculously absurd, that much lauded but nowhere accredited dogma of Mr. Jefferson that 'all men are born equal.'" Adopting Hegel's rejection of the Lockean concept of unalienable rights expressed in the Declaration, slavery's advocates held to be false that man was born with rights; rather, rights were not inherited, they were acquired from the state based on earned privileges, they said. South Carolina Congressman William Porcher Miles was a famous advocate of this Hegelian view, which he held in common with Hammond and McDuffie. Historian Eric H. Walther summarizes:

> [Miles held to be false doctrine] the idea that liberty was a birthright at all. He maintained that liberty was an "Acquired Privilege," not an unalienable right. Asserting that individuals and societies must prove themselves worthy of liberty, he maintained that not every person or society could do so. Those who believed otherwise subscribed to the "monstrous and dangerous fallacy of Thomas Jefferson," which proclaimed that all men were created equal. "Men are born neither Free nor Equal," Miles insisted . . . Miles categorically rejected any faith in natural equality, thereby fitting African slavery comfortably within American republicanism.[14]

Moreover, advocates of slavery believed fundamentally that this bifurcated system wherein liberty was acquired by a "superior" white race but never by an "inferior" black one undergirded a state of plantation socialism said to be far superior to northern capitalism. Southern sociologist George Fitzhugh explained that slaves lived in a socialist plantation system that was paternalistically compassionate and enabled southern whites to achieve a standard of living substantially greater than could be achieved by northerners dependent on hired labor. Slaves were cared for from cradle to grave, he emphasized; the plantation system gave them food, shelter, health care, and opportunities to learn skills, all without need for payment. In this way slaveholders fulfilled the role of caretakers, fitting neatly within Hegelian doctrine, which teaches the state to be the paternalistic caretaker of all people without need for recognition or defense of individual rights. As Thompson writes:

> Anticipating Marx's famous slogan—'From each according to his ability, to each according to his needs'—[George] Fitzhugh claimed that the plantation system holds 'all property in common' and divides 'the profits, not according to each man's input and labor, but according to each man's wants.' Plantation socialism, he continued, provides 'for each slave, in old age and in infancy, in sickness and in health, not according to his labor, but according to his wants.' The kind of 'free society' built into the principles of the Declaration, he wrote, is an unmitigated 'failure' and must be replaced by 'domestic slavery,' which he called 'the oldest, the best, and the most common form of socialism.' In fact, a 'southern farm,' he continued, 'is the beau ideal of communism.'[15]

Southern leaders celebrated the slave plantation as a socialist ideal. They explained that capitalism produced an underclass of labor that was destitute and depraved with living conditions beneath that of plantation slaves. In substance, they argued that slavery benefited the slave in ways that capital did not benefit northern labor. Thompson cites *The Political Economy of Slavery* (1857) by Edmund Ruffin as illustrative of this southern dogma. Ruffin was a Virginia slave owner and "Fire-eater" who claimed falsely that he fired the first cannon shot of the Civil War against the United States garrison at Fort Sumter; he committed suicide rather than be taken captive by the Union Army at the war's end.[16] Ruffin believed socialist doctrine "right" and reasoned: "Our system of domestic slavery offers in use, and to the greatest profit for all parties in the association, the realization of all that is sound and valuable in the socialists' theories and doctrines . . . Thus, in the institution of domestic slavery, and in that only, are most completely realized the dreams and sanguine hopes of the socialist school . . ."[17] Ruffin applauded the authoritarian nature of socialism and its reliance on an all-powerful governor to dictate the course of labor. He said that the institution of domestic slavery best achieved the socialist ideal. Indeed, if capital were replaced by one all-powerful ruler in the northern states, Ruffin expected the North would soon resemble the South by raising northern labor to a presumed higher living standard defined by "domestic slavery." He wrote: "Supply the one supreme head and governing power . . . [with] the association of labor . . . and the scheme and its operation will become as perfect as can be expected of any human institution. But in supplying this single ruling power, the association is thereby converted to the condition of domestic slavery."[18]

As Thompson explains, like their modern Marxist comrades, authoritarians in the South "challenge[d] the Declaration's understanding of truth, nature, and reason, as well as its four substantive truth claims about equality, rights, consent, and revolution, and they also turned against the political, social, and economic institutions of a free society."[19] To justify slavery, they of necessity moved away from defense of individual liberty and cleaved to an alleged superior social progress derived from forced labor, wherein natural rights theory could stand as no impediment to the betterment of the white race achieved on the backs of the black.

Reverend James Warley Miles of South Carolina, who Thompson identifies as "the South's leading Hegelian," wrote that man should not be viewed as an individual but, rather, as part of "the organic body of humanity" who could only reach his full potential through "the organism of the state."[20] At the South's stage of historical development, Miles explained, "the slave plantation . . . represented a new kind of state superior to all others."[21] Consistent with Hegel's view, Miles argued that blacks benefited from slavery in ways they could not if they were free. "[T]he inferiority of the black to the white race is an actual fact," he wrote, "the former race is benefitted by its subjection to the latter."[22] In particular, like Hegel, he concluded that the black race was naturally savage and a product of inferior social development and progress. By associating with whites of European descent, blacks acquired refinement, beyond what they achieved in social progress over millennia in their native Africa. Miles wrote: "Left to himself, he is a savage . . . placed as a permanent peasant in the Southern States, he reaches his highest development, and he fulfills an important mission in the world."[23] Slavery's antebellum apologists form a chorus on this point, uniting in their defense of slavery as the best means to achieve progress for the white race and to elevate the black race from savagery. Quoting Ruffin: "When the Caucasian mind thus commands and directs the bodily powers of the ignorant Negro, it is the best possible form of slavery, and the condition which conduces most to the benefit of both the white and the black race—and especially is best for the happiness and improvement of the latter. Indeed, it is the only condition in which the Negro race has received much enlightenment, or civilization, or real Christianity, in the thousands of years during which African barbarism has been known to exist."[24]

Another Hegelian, William Harper of South Carolina, believed that "without slavery . . . there could be no accumulation of property, no providence for the future, no taste for comforts or elegancies, which are the characteristics and essentials of civilization."[25] In other words, the standard of living white southerners enjoyed from the bondsmen's involuntary toil could not be maintained without slavery. For Harper, white southerners' progress demanded black bondage. Not only that, but because Harper perceived blacks as inferior, he presumed bondsmen incapable of presently appreciating or truly benefiting from freedom, professing that at some future date following greater association with the white race black slaves might then be ready to be free. He wrote: "[I]f in the adorable providence of God, at a time and in a manner which we can neither foresee nor conjecture, [slaves] are to be rendered capable of freedom and to enjoy it, they would be prepared for it in the best and most effectual, because in the most natural and gradual manner."[26] This idea, that blacks were an inferior race incapable of appreciating freedom and fit for menial labor into the indefinite future, was pervasive among southern slavery apologists. As antebellum William & Mary Law Professor Nathaniel Beverley Tucker taught, white Anglo-Saxons had been created by God as "a master race of unquestionable superiority," while black Africans had hardly "the lineaments of humanity" and had an "intellect scarcely superior to brutes." Tucker shared Harper and slave owners' general view that forced labor of black bondsmen was not an evil

THE BIRTH AND GROWTH OF AUTHORITARIANISM IN AMERICA | 9

but an unquestionable good because the black race, Tucker believed, was mentally incapable of making good use of freedom and "unable to live honestly without labor."[27]

Hegelian thought so prominent as a justification for slavery leads naturally to the communist teachings of Karl Marx, who, indeed, was a dedicated student of Hegel. Marx studied Hegel at the University of Berlin in 1836 where Marx joined youth groups dedicated to rejecting the then current German system of governance in favor of a more Hegelian, collectivist model. Marx disagreed with certain Hegelian precepts, most notably Hegel's belief in God, as Marx subscribed to atheism. Marx's belief that religion was fictive and an opiate of the masses led him, in part, to define the communist ideal as atheistic and to regard religion as a source of power and influence competitive with, and destructive to, the communist state's control over the people. This thinking also fueled Marx's abhorrence for the nuclear family and preference for plural marriage.

Marx held profoundly racist and anti-Semitic views. Walter Williams explains: "Marx's son-in-law, Paul Lafargue, was viewed as having Negro blood in his veins. Marx denigrated him as 'Negillo' and 'The Gorilla.'" Marx had similar hatred for Jews. He referred to his fellow socialist labor organizer Ferdinand Lasalle as a "greasy Jew," "the little kike," "water polack Jew" and "Jewish n---er."[28] In his 1844 essay, "The Jewish Question," Marx asks, "What is the worldly cult of the Jew?" He answers, "Haggling. What is his worldly God? Money."[29] The BLM organization and Marx are thus strange bedfellows, and were the organization's true agenda anti-racist, its leaders would not have identified Marx as the group's source of inspiration.

Although Marxian communism had not reached American shores in the antebellum period before the formation of socialist justifications for slavery, its foundational principles mirror those that southern leaders raised in slavery's defense. As C. Bradley Thompson observes: "Many proslavery writers in the American South were, in effect, pre-Marxian socialists. Their critique of capitalism was virtually indistinguishable from Marx's, and they saw the plantation system as the only practical way in which to successfully implement the socialist ideal."[30]

Calhoun's so-called "peculiar institution" thus begat a peculiar philosophy that presumed the state "an organism" and the people essential cells that must support that organism. That philosophy operated on the assumption that the epoch of southern slavery was part of the unfolding historical dialectic described by Hegel. Under this view, it would be a mistake to abandon slavery because to do so would cause a regression in white progress, economically and socially. Supplanting individualism and free choice with collectivism and government control was the answer: Slavery would be legally protected and blacks would remain legally classed as chattel under the supervision (slavery apologists said "care") of white gentry.

Southern leaders thus abandoned the promise of the Declaration in favor of the pro-slavery views articulated by Hegel. As Ronald J. Pestritto explains, consistent with slaveowners' preferences, Hegel contended, "that the slave trade was truly liberating for Africans. Slavery may have meant defeat and subjugation on one level, but to Hegel it marked historical progress because it brought the African race into contact with more advanced civilizations." Hegel insisted that "enslavement by the race of the West literally freed [the African race] from their historical backwardness."[31]

Reverend James Warley Miles taught the antebellum graduating class of the College of Charleston the Hegelian view that "man can only develop all of his capacities in the organism of the state." He described the slave plantation as a model of Hegelian government, elevating whites to a standard of living higher than any other civilization and enabling slaves to improve their primitive station through association with a "superior" race. This mirrored Edmund Ruffin's view. So long as "the drudgery and brutalizing effects of continued toil" were restricted to "the inferior races," white southerners could enjoy "leisure and other means to improve mind, taste, and manners," which was essential to maintenance of the "mental and moral qualities" of the "superior" white race.[32]

Slavery's apologists condemned the industrial North for what they perceived to be labor's inferior quality of life due, they claimed, to a conflict between capital and labor. As with Marx, so too with slavery's apologists, the classes of capital and labor were artificially presumed to be constantly at odds and falsely presumed to be static without revolution. As with Marx, the only way to move from, in Hegel's terms, the historical conflict phase (thesis versus antithesis) to an ultimate resolution phase (synthesis) was through an inevitable proletarian uprising in which capital would be deposed and replaced by a proletariat-led government that would confiscate all property and wealth and redistribute it from each according to his ability, to each according to his need. As Marx put it in *Critique of the Gotha Program*: "In a higher phase of communist society, after the enslaving subordination of the individual to the division of labor, and therewith also the antithesis between mental and physical labor, has vanished; after labor has become not only a means of life but life's prime want; after the productive forces have also increased with the all-around development of the individual, and all the springs of co-operative wealth flow more abundantly—only then can the narrow horizon of bourgeois right be crossed in its entirety and society inscribe on its banners: *From each according to his ability, to each according to his needs!*"[33]

Slavery's apologists presumed that essential outcome would be achieved in what they viewed as the ideal socialist state: plantation slavery. On the plantation, society was ordered to ensure that the betters (slaveowners) were kept in their elevated status by laws that caused the inferiors (slaves) to do the most arduous, time-consuming manual labor. The inferiors' work was said to be equal to their intellectual station; menial for whites, it was deemed just right for blacks, who were said to be primitives incapable of appreciating freedom or exploiting it for just ends. Slavery's apologists argued that black slaves lacked the intellect and aptitude necessary to be free. As such, they were best served by performing menial labor under the supervision of their betters, whose example they could learn from and perhaps one day emulate and understand fully, at which point they might deserve freedom. Just as in Marx's communism, so too on the plantation, the laborers would not be allowed to choose their pursuits, own property, or retain the wealth they generated. Rather, the state would paternalistically choose their rightful occupations, and the fruits of their labor would all go to the state (or, in the case of the South's proxy for the state, the plantation), which would paternalistically "care" for the laborers. The state then, or the plantation, governed by the betters, would own a monopoly over all property and over all pursuits. While freedom would be non-existent, life's essentials would be taken care of from cradle to grave.

As with Marxism, so too with plantation slavery, the system invariably fails because dictating labor's pursuits with no escape to alternative employment, robbing labor of its earnings, and denying labor the prospect of property ownership, retention of wealth, and self-fulfillment causes labor to lose every incentive to work efficiently and productively. State or plantation coercion must then be applied to force each laborer to produce to a set quota, which oppresses and leads to labor's neglect, sloth, gross inefficiencies, and inferior quality production. In this way, the presumed injustice of capital touted by the Marxists is magnified in institutions of slavery, not reduced, when that monopoly on force called the state becomes the sole master, yielding a grand hypocrisy because the universe of several competing capitalists from which labor may choose to seek employment is reduced by force of law to one totalitarian master with absolute control over the entire economy and the police.

Run by dictators whose selfish demands define all lawful pursuits of industry and improvement, the Marxist "utopia" is in fact a workers' hell indistinguishable from slavery under an all-controlling master. In this world of inescapable oppression, labor groans under the weight of a state master and can never break the bonds of servitude or rise above a level of mediocrity. In short, the Marxist offers a pipe dream, a false promise, that the destruction of free enterprise will yield freedom for the proletariat when in fact it leads to the enslavement of the proletariat by the state. In that way, the slave plantation is indeed a perfect microcosm of the communist state; both are prescriptions for perpetual misery. The socialist state, whereby the state regulates all industry (as opposed to the communist state, whereby the state owns all industry), imposes misery on the people in comparable measure.

Senator James Henry Hammond of South Carolina coined a term used by southerners from the antebellum period through the end of the Civil War to express the essential thesis undergirding their commitment to slavery, the "mudsill theory." Consistent with Hegelian historicism, the mudsill theory held that in every era in history there had been a lower class to undergird all other classes else the other classes could not progress. In the construction trade, a "mudsill" is the lowest threshold supporting a building foundation; it rests next to the dirt and without it the building cannot stand. As Hammond put it:

> In all social systems there must be a class to do the menial duties, to perform the drudgery of life. That is, a class requiring but a low order of intellect and but little skill. Its requisites are vigor, docility, fidelity. Such a class you must have, or you would not have that other class which leads to progress, civilization, and refinement. It constitutes the very mud-sill of society and of political government; and you might as well attempt to build a house in the air, as to build either the one or the other, except on this mud-sill. Fortunately for the South, she found a race adapted to that purpose . . . A race inferior to her own, but eminently qualified in temper, in vigor, in docility, in capacity to stand the climate, to answer all her purposes. We use them for our purpose, and call them slaves.[34]

In *The American Political Tradition and the Men Who Made It*, Richard Hofstadter referred to the mudsill theory as "the Marxism of a Masterclass" and to Senator John C. Calhoun, who argued slavery was a "positive good," as "the Marxist of the Masterclass."[35] Senator Calhoun gave national prominence to the defense of slavery based on the mudsill theory. He argued that plantation slavery was a superior social and economic order to capitalism in the North. He did so early in the budding contest between North and South in his February 6, 1837 address to the United States Senate, stating:

> [T]here never has yet existed a wealthy and civilized society in which one portion of the community did not, in point of fact, live on the labor of the other. Broad and general as is this assertion, it is fully borne out by history. . . . Compare [the slave's] condition with the tenants of the poor houses

in the more civilized portions of Europe—look at the sick, and the old and infirm slave, on one hand, in the midst of his family and friends, under the kind superintending care of his master and mistress, and compare it with the forlorn and wretched condition of the pauper in the poor house. . . . There is and always has been in an advanced stage of wealth and civilization, a conflict between labor and capital. The condition of society in the South exempts us from the disorders and dangers resulting from this conflict; and which explains why it is that the political condition of the slaveholding States has been so much more stable and quiet than that of the North . . .[36]

Before the word Marxism entered the American vernacular, Abraham Lincoln exposed its analytical shortcomings when he attacked the "mudsill theory" as one of slavery's justificatory rationales. In his September 30, 1859 address before the Wisconsin State Agricultural Society in Milwaukee, Lincoln rebutted the "mudsill theory." He revealed the assumption that labor in the North was not free and that the condition of a free laborer was worse than that of a bondsman to be false. Lincoln said:

By some it is assumed that labor is available only in connection with capital—that nobody labors, unless somebody else, owning capital, somehow, by the use of that capital, induces him to do it. . . . [T]hey proceed to consider whether it is best that capital shall hire laborers, and thus induce them to work by their own consent; or buy them, and drive them to it without their consent. . . . [T]hey naturally conclude that all laborers are necessarily either hired laborers, or slaves. They further assume that whoever is once a hired laborer, is fatally fixed in that condition for life; and thence again that his condition is as bad as, or worse than, that of a slave. This is the "mud-sill" theory. But another class of reasoners hold the opinion that there is no such relation between capital and labor, as assumed; . . . [T]here is no such thing as a freeman being fatally fixed for life, in the condition of a hired laborer, that both these assumptions are false, and all inferences from them groundless. . . . The prudent, penniless beginner in the world, labors for wages for a while, saves a surplus with which to buy tools or land, for himself; then labors on his own account another while, and at length hires another new beginner to help him. This, say its advocates, is free labor—the just and generous, and prosperous system, which opens the way for all—gives hope to all, and energy, and progress, and improvement of condition to all. If any continue through life in the condition of the hired laborer, it is not the fault of the system, but because of either a dependent nature that prefers it, or improvidence, folly, or singular misfortune.[37]

The authoritarianism inherent in the institution of slavery did not die as a casualty of the Civil War but, rather, re-emerged among Progressives, who adopted Hegelian doctrine yet again to justify creation of another authoritarian model, the extra-constitutional administrative state. As C. Bradley Thompson explains: "The Union army destroyed the Confederacy, slavery, and plantation socialism, but many of the core ideas held by proslavery intellectuals in the 1840s and 1850s were given a second life (albeit in new forms) by progressive intellectuals in the decades after 1865."[38]

PROGRESSIVE REJECTION OF THE CONSTITUTION IN FAVOR OF AUTHORITARIANISM (1865 to the 1930s)

In the first few decades after the Civil War, dramatic economic and social changes in America led to a degree of unease so profound that it brought radical elements to the forefront. Until that time, most Americans favored the classical liberal model of government embraced by the Declaration and embodied in the Constitution: substantial protection for individual rights against the state, which, consistent with the Declaration of Independence, were understood to be derived from God; a limited federal republic replete with multiple barriers against the exercise of arbitrary power; a *laissez-faire* economy; private property; and private education.

After 1877, however, and continuing through World War I, leading reform elements and a supermajority of political leaders believed individual rights no impediment to pursuit of what they defined as the "common good" or "public interest." Those reformers increasingly believed their subjective wishes for restructuring society had to be implemented posthaste without resort to constitutional amendment or even the passage of legislation. They favored a controlled economy with pursuits limited by extra-constitutional agencies. They supported public instead of private education to enable the malleable minds of youth to be molded in ways supportive of law made and enforced outside of the Constitutional system and supportive of the Progressive ideal of citizenship. They wanted each generation to exhibit unquestioning adherence to the dictates of the state.

The source of modern argument in favor of government intervention to alter private choice largely springs from Progressive thinking in America that arose in the late nineteenth and early twentieth centuries. More ominously, the roots of authoritarian governance in the United States at the expense of individual freedom and private property has its principal origins in the "progressive" reforms of this age.

The transformation of America from rural agrarian to urban industrial between 1865 and 1917 resulted not only in new forms and concentrations of wealth, greater material abundance and prosperity, a large middle class, and more economic opportunity but also in factory labor sometimes under onerous and unsafe conditions, urban slums, urban sanitation problems, pollution, and vice. Although in 1890 only 35% of Americans lived in cities, by 1920, 51% did.[39] During that same period the United States experienced two depressions that shook confidence in free markets, one in the 1870s and another in the 1890s.[40] In their aftermath, from 1897 to 1904, business mergers proceeded apace. Some 1,800 firms merged into 157 with the new enterprises controlling over 40% of each respective industry's market (and with one-third dominating 70% of their respective markets).[41] While industry efforts at monopolization occurred with some regularity, Gabriel Kolko and Murray N. Rothbard have convincingly explained that those private efforts were, contrary to popular belief, universal failures.[42] Far from leading to industry dominance sufficient to control prices, competition reigned throughout the period from 1877 to 1917 except in those instances where government ordered cartelization and only then did monopoly arise.

From 1865 to 1891, substantial growth in manufacturing and interstate commerce combined with falling retail prices to create a new and fulsome middle class with access to a wide array of consumer goods. That transformation dramatically increased the standard of living in America, catapulting the nation from a largely subsistence economy of farmers and domestic manufacturers to a far more prosperous one with greater potential for upward mobility and hundreds of medium to large sized concerns engaged in mass manufacturing. Rothbard records:

> Gross National Product per capita in constant 1929 prices rose by 80% in the 20 years from 1871 to 1891 . . . [T]he average daily wage in all industry rose by 13% from 1865 to 1891, while the cost of living fell on the average of 31% in the same period. The average daily real wages (corrected for price changes) increased by 64%. Then, when we consider that average hours worked dropped from 11 to 10 hours a day in this period, we should add 10% to the average real wage.[43]

Immigration levels peaked between 1890 and 1914 with more immigrants coming to the United States from the Austro-Hungarian Empire, Italy, Russia, Greece, Romania, Turkey, and Southern and Eastern Europe than ever before.[44] Fifteen million immigrants, representing about 14% of the American population, became a part of the American family in those years. The profound economic, demographic, and social changes that influx of new Americans created were regarded with alarm by many in academia, the clergy, the philanthropic community, the intelligentsia, and the burgeoning middle class. Influential Americans expressed disillusionment with capitalism, with classical liberalism, and with the apparent inability of republican government to compel the social, economic, and political changes they desired, giving rise to a widespread discontent that fueled drives for extra-constitutional government.[45]

The prolonged depression of the 1890s shook middle-class faith in free markets, and even economic recovery did not assuage that loss of confidence. A movement arose from diverse sectors in favor of interventionist government in pursuit of disparate utopian ideals. Self-described socialists, like Upton Sinclair, endeavored to hasten the movement toward socialism through yellow journalism. Sinclair's *The Jungle*, a work of fiction, falsely described the Chicago meatpacking plants as ones that not only ground filthy beef but also ground workers into sausages. The popular book appalled readers and inspired passage of the Meat Inspection Act (a law favored decades before by the meat packers themselves because "governmentally-coerced upgrading of quality" not only ensured access to European markets but also greater industry cartelization).[46] Sinclair hoped his book would lead government to require a better standard of living for packinghouse workers but, instead, it led to a law that principally benefited the leading meatpacking firms. Sinclair lamented, "I aimed at the public's heart, and by accident I hit it in the stomach."[47]

As historian Steven J. Diner records: "The dissenters who believed that an informed polity could use government to solve the problems caused by industrialism and economic concentration now moved to the center of American political debate."[48] Richard Hofstadter, a communist in 1938 and 1939 and thereafter a socialist (writing, "I hate capitalism and everything that goes with it"[49]) observed: "Progressivism . . . affected in a striking way all the major and minor political parties and the whole tone of American political life"[50] and the consistent demand was "for more government intervention." The Progressives insisted on "a new form of government, one that was disinterested, nonpartisan, scientific, and endowed with discretionary powers to investigate and regulate." Despite internecine battles and varying demands for government action, the Progressives "agreed that the best means to their several ends was the administrative state."[51]

Many leading industrialists in the 1860s, particularly those who dominated the railroad industry, came to regard government intervention as a solution to the risks and pitfalls of rigorous competition. Indeed, rather than the exclusive product of lobbying by political idealists, socialists, disgruntled farm groups, labor groups, and small business groups, the expansion of government over the private sector during this period largely came about because industrialists aligned themselves with Progressive politicians to achieve a "government-sponsored and enforced cartelization" of industry, a cartelization that had eluded industry leaders in the market where robust competition was the norm.[52]

In *The Progressive Era*, Murray N. Rothbard documents how early in the effort to build the transcontinental railroads, industry leaders wed themselves to government, calling for regulation that would guarantee set rates of return at profitable levels, would cull the small rail competitors, and would eliminate the highly competitive practice of granting rebates. At the start of railroad development, the Central Pacific, Southern Pacific, Union Pacific, and Northern Pacific railroads successfully lobbied Congress for a heavy dose of government support in the form of massive federal land grants, loans, and subsidies. Rothbard describes the typical method used:

> Of nearly 200 million acres of valuable land in the original federal grants, almost half were handed over to the four large transcontinental railroads: Central Pacific, Southern Pacific, Union Pacific, and Northern Pacific. The typical *modus operandi* of these railroads was as follows: (1) a small group of inside promoters and managers would form the railroad, putting up virtually no money of their own; (2) they would use their political influence to get land grants and outright loans (for the Union and Central Pacific) from the federal government; (3) they would get aid from various state and local governments; (4) they would issue a huge amount of bonds to sell to the eager public; and (5) they would form a privately-held construction company, issuing themselves bonds and shares, and would then mulct themselves as managers of the railroad (or rather, mulct railroad shareholders and bondholders) by charging the road highly inflated construction costs.[53]

That pattern repeated itself in the oil, iron, steel, copper, automobile, agricultural machinery, electrical manufacturing, chemicals, meatpacking, and sugar industries. In each, dominant market players aimed to achieve monopolies and fixed, above market rates of return, but small market competitors and new market entrants with technological innovations frustrated those goals, that is, until government entered presumptively on behalf of beleaguered consumers, but, in reality, at the behest of industry to impose state-enforced cartelization.[54] As Gabriel Kolko explains:

> The dominant fact of American political life at the beginning of the [twentieth] century was that big business led the struggle for the federal regulation of the economy. . . . Important business elements could always be found in the forefront of agitation for such regulation, and the fact that well-intentioned reformers often worked with them— indeed, were often indispensable to them—does not change the reality that federal economic regulation was generally designed by the regulated interest to meet its own end, and not those of the public or the commonweal.[55]

In other words, incapable of arresting competition to achieve monopoly on their own, leaders of American industry professed sympathy with the cause of Progressive reformers. Those leaders then lobbied for the creation of new, extra-constitutional agencies that were said to be in aid of reform but were, in fact, industry-dominated and intent on cartelizing industries. The new regulators created barriers to market entry, set above market fixed rates, and banned competitive rebating, thereby ensuring above market rates of return not possible before government imposed cartelization.

The typical Progressive Era reformer was motivated by a desire to defend his or her own social standing, to obtain legal protection for enforcement of his or her own social mores and religious preferences against diverse populations, and to eliminate those deemed "undesirable." Historian Michael McGerr seized upon Theodore Roosevelt's apt description of a "fierce discontent" in the land, a "movement of agitation throughout the country . . . to punish the authors of evil," a movement led by Progressive reformers.[56] Prohibitionists, suffragists, union organizers and protestors, voting test advocates, evangelists, trust busters, redistributionists, segregationists, eugenicists, and socialists, all clamored for reforms. The Progressives were impatient with the pace of reform and, oftentimes, with each other, but they were united in their desire for use of authoritarian government to compel societal reformation. In *The Age of Reform*, Richard Hofstadter, himself a proponent of Progressive reforms during this period, recalled, "[t]he ferment of the Progressive era was urban, middle-class, and nationwide."[57] The mix of diverse cultures, religions, ethnicities, and nationalities combined with the rise of cities, industry, and urban dwellings to stoke public support for Progressive leaders' demands that government intervene to control, change and direct society to achieve outcomes those leaders preferred.

On June 6, 1900, armed with brickbats and Schlitz-Malt bottles, Christian Prohibitionist Carrie A. Nation raced feverishly from her home in a buggy to each of four saloons in Kiowa, Kansas. There she hurled her weapons with fury, smashing liquor bottles and marring bar woodwork. She railed against the evils of drink and the commercial liquor houses (which she called "murder mills"[58]). In Wichita, Kansas, she expanded her moral crusade, accosting the painting of a naked woman displayed in a bar, declaring it the bane of feminine virtue and insisting that every nude painting rendered all women toys "with no will power of [their] own" and "parasite[s] of" man.[59] In a tip of the hat to today's cancel culture, Nation demanded that all nude paintings of women be destroyed.

Other Protestant reformers, including Jane Addams, insisted that immigrants conform to Protestant theology, social norms and hygienic practices. Protestant reformers created some 400 settlements across urban America by 1900 to house, feed, and "socially adjust" immigrants.[60]

Miners and laborers joined unions (like Samuel Gompers' American Federation of Labor, John Mitchell's United Mine Workers, and Socialist Eugene Debs' American Railway Union) and struck over 1,098 times in 1898 alone; then 1,839 times in 1900; and then fully 3,012 times in 1901, demanding better working environments, reduced hours, and increased pay.[61]

Voting reform movements gave women the right to vote in the Progressive Era, but "[s]tricter voter registration laws," writes historian Steven J. Diner, "made it more difficult for Americans, especially from working-class and immigrant backgrounds, to vote, while Southern progressivism disenfranchised African-American voters completely" as a part of the rise of Progressive-endorsed Jim Crow laws.[62]

Although occasionally at odds with one another, Progressives were united in their dissatisfaction with the slow pace of republican government and their opposition to laws protective of individual rights against the use of authoritarian power to pursue what Progressives deemed the "common good" or "public interest." They were insistent on expert and efficient government solutions through extra-constitutional agencies. Progressives aimed to have their preferences imposed on society by force of administrative law. In that way, their demands for urgent change would not have to wait for the evolution of democratic processes under the Constitution.

Although before the Progressive Era, science was in its comparative infancy and did not ordinarily feud with religion, science became increasingly viewed as hostile to religion and, indeed, to be its own sort of secular religion, especially for the Progressive intelligentsia. The conflict between science and religion in no small measure arose because of the popularization of Darwinian theories of evolution (so-called social Darwinism) derived from Charles Darwin's 1859 publication, *On the Origin of Species*, which theories were pitted against Creationism, famously so in the Scopes Trial (1925). In that trial, atheist and agnostic Progressives, like famed defense attorney Clarence Darrow, battled against Progressive Christian reformers, like William Jennings Bryan.

Dayton city attorneys Herbert E. and Sue K. Hicks, who brought the case against school teacher John T. Scopes, and the newly minted American Civil Liberties Union, that originally defended Scopes, sought to narrow the debate to the question of whether local school boards could control public school curricula or whether teachers were protected by the freedom of speech against laws that would forbid the teaching of specific topics. Progressive leaders intervened, however, exploding the issues to embrace the validity of Creationism itself (and, implicitly, whether rights were God-given or state created) in what became known as the "trial of the century." Clarence Darrow, defendant Scopes' preferred attorney (against the wishes of the ACLU), and William Jennings Bryan, the volunteer "attorney" for the prosecution (who had no law degree) and gained national notoriety as a three-time unsuccessful presidential candidate, sought to make the Scopes Trial a contest between Darwinian evolution and Creationism. The Progressive contest that played out over radio nationwide was a clash of extremes, but it need not have been. As Professor Edward J. Larson explained, "[m]iddle ground did exist between modernism and fundamentalism but gained little attention in the public debate surrounding the Scopes trial."[63]

The Scopes trial carried with it an underlying theme of Progressivism, indicative of the extent to which Hegel's thinking had become mainstream. No longer would it be taken for granted that rights came from God because, as in the case of Clarence Darrow, a majority of intellectual elites in America had come to the view that in the advent of Darwinism, religion was bunk, and that rights, therefore, could only come from the state, there being no God. Indeed, that was the preferred teaching of the German historical schools. The German model of the administrative state and its Hegelian underpinnings swept the field of academy and inspired a reconsideration of the origins of government and rights, resulting in a rejection of individual rights and constitutional governance in favor of more efficient authoritarian measures through the new extra-constitutional administrative state.

Progressive reform leaders largely viewed science as capable of providing both an explanation for, and, in the hands of "experts," an answer to every social ill. Man, not God, would provide all the answers. Everything, even government, politics, and history, were to be appreciated in "scientific" terms, thus yielding new courses of study, such as "social science," "sociology," "psychology," "economics," and "political science." Science had become the new theology. Progressive leaders increasingly believed every human endeavor could be the subject of scientific study, evaluation, and expert adjustment. The law could be evolutionary, redefined by psychology in a case-by-case approach. There would no longer be strict adherence to the rule of law and legal formalism, as the Realists, like Jerome Frank of Yale Law School, now taught. The market could be understood as a form of capitalist exploitation of labor as economists and sociologists, like the socialist Scott Nearing of the Wharton School, taught. Experimental psychology could be used to discover human motivations in employment interviews, in trials and in the creation of civil and criminal laws, as Harvard psychologist Hugo

Munsterberg taught in *On the Witness Stand* (1908). Even human evolution (as eugenicists like George Hunter taught in his popular *Civic Biology* (1914)) could be used to justify state actions to compel those deemed hereditarily "defective" and "undesirable" to be sterilized.

Consistent with the emerging doctrine of social Darwinism, economists, psychologists, sociologists, eugenicists, and law professors endorsed the idea that government ought to use extra-constitutional powers to redirect society, to channel industry to serve the "public interest," to eliminate from humanity all "defectives" and "undesirables" (to achieve a utopian society of intelligent and healthy Anglo-Saxons), and to employ government as a moral force in place of religion, individual free agency, and laissez-faire.

There was perhaps no greater prophet of social Darwinism in the Progressive era than Herbert Spencer whose *Social Statics* (1850) and *The Man Versus the State* (1884) were among many works he wrote that translated a generalized interpretation of Darwin's theories into a socio-economic doctrine of progress. Spencer coined the term "survival of the fittest," writing in his *Principles of Biology* (1864) that "[t]his survival of the fittest, which I have here sought to express in mechanical terms, is that which Mr. Darwin has called 'natural selection,' or the preservation of favored races in the struggle of life."[64] Wielding enormous influence in the latter part of the nineteenth century, Spencer swayed the thinking of academics in economics, political science, sociology, education, and history into believing that progress depended on "betters" (i.e., the fittest) being able to advance unencumbered by "inferiors." This, then, invited the view that the "common good" was superior to claims of individual right, particularly when legal recognition of that individual right might encumber progress. We see in this a throwback to the Hegelian doctrinal justifications for slavery in the antebellum South.

Academics who championed reform possessed a near universal dislike for classical liberalism, for the Constitution, for individual rights, for the Courts, for the free market, and for the rule of law, believing each a relic of a bygone era, incapable of addressing the rapidly evolving problems of the industrial age, which they thought demanded constant legal oversight by and intervention from "experts" in government. They demanded the creation of fully empowered entities outside of constitutional government. They could not tolerate delays arising from adherence to the separation of powers and the system of checks and balances under the Constitution. They found intolerable normal delays attendant to the operation of republican government; delays from judicial procedural and substantive rules created to protect individual rights; and delays attendant to legislative debate and representative democracy.

They had considerable difficulty tolerating views contrary to their own and views contrary to "expert" opinion, which they lauded profusely and marshaled in support of reforms. They demanded rule by "experts" unencumbered by constitutional restraints. As the Progressive Lester Frank Ward wrote in *Dynamic Sociology* (1883), progress depended not on the invention of free people everywhere but on governmental direction imposed on the market and society by "an educated class trained for leadership."[65] Progressives presumed experts capable of identifying a remedy for nearly every social and economic ill, if freed from constitutional constraints. They argued that a "visible hand of a powerful administrative state, guided by expert social scientists"[66] was preferable to, and needed to replace, the invisible hand of the market, guided by the free choice of individuals.

They meant to remake the United States into that society and economy dictated by bureaucrats who would daily "correct" private choices whenever they veered from the utopian ideal. In short, they demanded authoritarian governance in place of both individualism and the republican government created by the Constitution. While the founding generation feared concentrations of government power and unbridled official discretion, demanding a Constitution dedicated to rendering the people sovereign and protecting the rights of the governed, the Progressives embraced concentrations of government power in a virtually unbridled bureaucracy of experts, demanding that the Constitution be side-stepped to enable agency action against private rights that encumbered establishment of utopia. They believed the ends urgent and the means justified, even at the expense of the Constitution.

Largely taboo in the Gilded Age, calls for socialism and a government-planned society and economy became commonplace in the Progressive Era, as many disillusioned by the status quo cleaved to state power, favoring either regulatory control of the market or government ownership of private enterprise. McGerr writes:

> In the 1880s and 1890s, impassioned discussions of socialism spilled across the pages of magazines and rang through lecture halls and the rooms of [Jane Addams' immigrant settlement] Hull-House. For middle-class Americans repelled by individualism, socialism offered an appealing insistence that society's needs were more important than those of selfish individuals . . . Socialism also provided an intriguing example of the willingness to use the power of the state to regulate society. Numerous middle-class reformers and even politicians acknowledged their interest in socialism. . . . A few middle-class reformers declared themselves socialists outright.[67]

Indicative of the extent to which the public had been swayed to favor unconstitutional government, overtly socialist candidates won several local elections for the first time in American history, principally in the northeastern United States. The Socialist Party was formally established in the United States in 1901. By 1911, there were eighteen socialist mayors, governing in America's cities. Seats in the New York and Rhode Island legislatures were held by socialists. Socialists held 1,150 offices in thirty-six states. Eugene Debs ran for president on the Socialist Party ticket in 1908 and again in 1912 and was a popular stump speaker.[68] Progressives studied socialist teachings and methods, selectively picking those that impressed them and inculcating socialist ideas into reform party platforms. "The characteristic Progressive thinker carried on a tolerant and mutually profitable dialogue with the Socialists of the period," writes Hofstadter, ". . . interested to learn what he could from Socialist criticism."[69]

Creation of unconstitutional government, of commissions given combined legislative and executive or legislative, executive, and judicial powers independent of the elected branches of government, occurred in many states, as governors and mayors implemented Progressive Party platforms. Before the federal government in earnest endorsed the notion of government untethered from the Constitution, the states led the way, heavily opting for commission control of industry prices and sales practices between the 1860s and 1914. "Administrative and regulatory agencies, which barely existed before the Progressive Era," observes Diner, "now virtually constituted a new branch of government."[70] State legislatures abandoned their constitutionally mandated exclusive role of making the laws, deferring to the newly minted commissions to create regulatory laws, enforce them, and adjudicate their application.

PROGRESSIVE AND SOCIALIST EMBRACE OF FORCED STERILIZATION

While many Progressives were Protestants, with a considerable number supporting charity for those less fortunate, many (perhaps nearly all) did not allow Christianity to stand in the way of actions to limit opportunities for those not of their "own kind," i.e., not of their religion, race or ethnicity (including Blacks, Asians, Irish, French Canadians, Italians of the Messogiorno, other non-Anglo-Saxons, Jews, and Catholics). They sought extra-constitutional means to limit the "undesirables" and the "unfit" from advancing beyond unskilled labor, from exercising political power, and from procreating.

As Richard Hofstadter remembered of the Progressives during this period: "Everyone remote and alien was distrusted and hated."[71] Once again, as with their embrace of authoritarianism in general, Progressives and Socialists aimed, like their intellectual forebears in the antebellum South, to deny equal justice under law to those deemed "inferiors." Many Progressives and Socialists in academia viewed those outside of their race and class not only as undesirable but also as suspect, as "hereditary inferiors," as threats to their race, undeserving of equality with whites, and, concerning some, undeserving of life itself. Many Progressive and Socialist leaders demanded that government do their bidding by rearranging the economy and society in ways calculated to ensure the dominance of a "master" Anglo-Saxon race.

Progressives and Socialists thus put their prejudices into administrative law and brutally enforced them against various minorities they despised, creating that very tyranny of the majority that the Founding Fathers feared if constitutional limits on power were ignored: wherein a majority political faction could rule with impunity against a dissenting minority, taking away that minority's rights.[72]

As economic historian Thomas C. Leonard explains in *Illiberal Reformers*:

> The roster of progressives who advocated exclusion of hereditary inferiors reads like a Who's Who of American economic reform. It includes the founders of American economics: Edward Bemis, John R. Commons, Richard T. Ely, Irving Fisher, Arthur Holcombe, Jeremiah Jenks, W. Jett Lauck, Richmond Mayo-Smith, Royal Meeker, Simon N. Patten, and Henry R. Seager.
>
> They were joined by the founders of American sociology, Charles Horton Cooley, Charles Richmond Henderson, and Edward A. Ross; pioneering social-work professionals, such as Edward Devine, Robert Hunter, and Paul U. Kellogg; and leading Protestant social gospelers, such as Walter Rauschenbusch and Josiah Strong. University presidents, such as the University of Wisconsin's Charles Van Hise and Stanford's David Starr Jordan, vigorously advocated exclusion of hereditary inferiors, as did such political journalists as [*New Republic* founder] Hebert Croly, [and] jurists [such] as Oliver Wendell Holmes, Jr., and many other progressive luminaries, not least U.S. Presidents Theodore Roosevelt and Woodrow Wilson.[73]

Leonard copiously documents the Progressive economic, sociological, social, university, journalistic, and political agendas of these American elites, wherein they called for exclusion "of immigrants, African Americans, women, and the disabled."[74]

The Progressives and Socialists were led by those who viewed immigrants from Eastern and Southern Europe, Africa, Asia, and South America as threats to a presumed "pure" white race of Anglo-Saxons or Nordic stock. They viewed disfavored ethnicities as ones who through breeding with whites would dilute or "poison" presumed "pure" white bloodlines. Many openly condemned non-white, immigrant, and uneducated white laborers as "degenerates" who had to be contained and controlled.

Based principally on interpretive reading of selective hereditary principles loosely derived from Charles Darwin's theories on evolution in *On the Origins of Species* (1859) and *The Descent of Man and Selection in Relation to Sex* (1871) and from Gregor Mendel's theories on pea cross-breeding in *Experiments on Plant Hybridization* (1865), many Progressives and Socialists regarded those who engaged in paid labor as genetically ill-bred and inferior, beneath their social status. They believed these "inferiors" had to be strictly controlled to avoid their population growth and their interbreeding with whites, which risked dilution of superior white "stock," thereby downgrading a presumptively elite lineage. The Progressive and Socialists' prejudice in favor of their "own kind" found a convenient pseudo-scientific cover for bigotry in the works of the so-called "social Darwinists." The social Darwinists weaponized bigotry by endorsing "eugenic" sterilization of tens of thousands of Americans deemed "undesirable."

The almost universal endorsement of eugenics by Progressive and Socialist leaders reveals how fundamentally and fully they accepted authoritarianism in place of natural rights theory. Consistent with their support for unconstitutional government, Progressive and Socialist leaders believed that the "social good" they desired ought not be encumbered by individual rights and constitutional constraints on government. Indeed, they believed the goals they defined as the "common good" outweighed the rights of dissenting individuals, even to the extent of justifying incarcerating "undesirables" and forcibly sterilizing them. They believed those goals ought to be attained by commissions operating outside of the system of constitutional checks and balances.

There is perhaps no greater assault on individual liberty and life than arrest, incarceration, and forced sterilization, and yet most Progressives and Socialists favored that recourse for those they deemed "unfit" without the slightest concern for the rights of those affected. They bemoaned the need for judicial commitment proceedings and sought liberal deference by the courts to the rule of "experts" whom they trusted to make sterilization decisions based on their subjective view of the "fitness" of anyone suspected of being inferior.

The prolific novelist and half-cousin of Charles Darwin, Francis Galton, was a major advocate of eugenics to rid society of inferiors. He coined the term "eugenics." The father of so-called "social Darwinism," he argued that eugenics should become a secular religion, insisting it "must be a religion."[75] In Galton's then popular novel depicting his ideal society, entitled *Kantsaywhere*, each individual's hereditary worth was measured by tests and "[g]enetic failures were shunted off to labor colonies, where enforced celibacy was the rule" and "childbirth for the 'unfit' was a crime."[76]

Many Progressives and Socialists believed the state in *Kantsaywhere* epitomized the best form of governance, a form that would accelerate the advance of society to a higher level, believing that those variously classified by the state as "undesirable" ought to be placed in labor and indoctrination camps, and then forcibly sterilized. Indeed, some, like former Supreme Court Justice Oliver Wendell Holmes, Jr., went beyond forced sterilization, advocating infanticide for children who did not make an acceptable grade on intelligence tests given in their first years of life. [77]

The Progressive Era eugenicists' "agenda appealed to reformers of every political stripe: from suffragists to 'social purity' moralists, from temperance workers and fire-and-brimstone preachers to natural resource 'conservationists.'"[78] Progressive academics made eugenics a course of study, indoctrinating thousands of college students and would-be Progressive and Socialist reformers. From 1914 to 1928, American university courses in eugenics rose from forty-four to 376[79], revealing widespread academic acceptance of the idea that the "unfit" ought not be allowed to procreate.

The list of eugenicists (i.e., those who advocated sterilization to prevent reproduction of "undesirables," the "feeble-minded," and "imbeciles" (or to preserve a master white race from racial dilution, called "race suicide")) reads like a Who's Who of Progressive reformers dominant in the fields of economics, sociology and law (indeed, of those who advocated unconstitutional government in America and the administrative state). Progressives and Socialists wrapped their call for the elimination of "undesirables" in social Darwinist pseudo-science, which convinced many who otherwise opposed Progressive reforms to join in support of institutions for the forced sterilization of "undesirables." "Hundreds, perhaps thousands of Progressive Era scholars and scientists proudly called themselves eugenicists," records Leonard.[80] They believed alcoholism, promiscuity, low intelligence, lethargy, shiftlessness, mental illness, criminal behavior, and all manner of "anti-social" conduct were inherited characteristics and presumed that by denying procreation to those possessed of one or more of those proclivities society would be improved, progress achieved, and the white race protected.

Progressives and Socialists viewed eugenics as a means of achieving two prime social objectives: elimination of individuals possessed of what they falsely presumed to be unfortunate heritable characteristics (like the propensity to engage in crime, prostitution, and addiction) and reduction of immigrant populations, which they feared would replace white laborers and would "dilute" Anglo-Saxon blood lines. Both objectives operated under the cover of pseudo-scientific social Darwinism but arose not simply from bigotry but more fundamentally from prime motivations that rejected individual rights and constitutional government in favor of authoritarianism that would create by force a society Progressives considered ideal. That ideal society they insisted was urgently needed, a quest that necessarily demanded liberal tolerance for the suppression of all dissenters' rights and abandonment of constitutional constraints on the exercise of government power.

President Theodore Roosevelt believed in eugenics, denouncing, "the unrestricted breeding of [a] feebleminded, utterly shiftless, and worthless family." In a letter to Charles Benedict Davenport, one of the founders of the American eugenics movement, Roosevelt wrote: "Society has no business to permit degenerates to reproduce their kind. . . . Someday, we will realize that the prime duty, the inescapable duty, of the good citizen of the right type, is to leave his or her blood behind him in the world; and that we have no business to permit the perpetuation of citizens of the wrong type."[81]

New Jersey Governor Woodrow Wilson (who later became President) also supported eugenics. He signed into law a eugenics bill that appointed a Board of Examiners comprised of a surgeon and a neurologist who determined whether "procreation was inadvisable" among those deemed feeble-minded (including, "Idiots, imbeciles and morons"), epileptics, rapists, certain criminals and other "defectives" who had been committed to New Jersey institutions. Once approved by the Board, the "most effective" remedy, forced sterilization, could be applied.[82]

Presidents Warren Harding, Calvin Coolidge, and Herbert Hoover each supported "eugenic reforms."[83]

Governor of New York and Chief Justice of the United States Supreme Court Charles Evans Hughes advocated eugenics.[84]

President and Chief Justice of the United States Supreme Court William Howard Taft advocated eugenics and was "an active member of the national eugenics movement."[85]

Justice Oliver Wendell Holmes, Jr. (said to have "more than any other individual, shaped the law of the twentieth century"[86]) reveled in the idea of taking the lives of those he considered of low intelligence, even advocating infanticide, professing that through eugenics the nation could "take control of life, and condemn at once with instant execution what is now left to nature to destroy."[87] The man heralded as among the leading American jurists of all time, Holmes favored "putting to death the inadequate" and "restricting propagation by the undesirables and putting to death infants that didn't pass the examination."[88]

Sociologist Henry Laughlin, the Superintendent of the Eugenics Record Office, advocated eugenic sterilization for the "socially inadequate," i.e., all those the state held to be "defective, dependent, and delinquent . . ."[89]

Sociologist Charles Horton Cooley, Professor of Sociology and Economics at the University of Michigan, founding member and President of the American Sociology Association, recommended against health care and nutrition for African Americans because it "would lower black death rates, raising the dysgenic specter of the black population 'overwhelming' the white." In addition to starving blacks and denying them adequate medical care, he favored "eugenic measures . . . to reduce the quantity and improve the quality of black births."[90]

Sociologist Edward A. Ross repeatedly warned that the Anglo-Saxon race could never reach its potential, and faced loss of racial integrity, if "inferior heredity" was not checked with limitations on procreation by undesirables.

Co-Founder of the American Judicature Society and President of the Eugenics Research Association Harry Olson believed criminality inheritable and advocated forced sterilization of alcoholics, those with "mental defects," and sex offenders. He preferred "segregating 'human derelicts' in farm colonies" where sterilization could be performed.[91]

The famed founder of the American environmental movement and of methods for wildlife management, zoologist Madison Grant wrote, in his 1916 *The Passing of the Great Race*, that eugenics was essential to ensure the superiority of Nordic bloodlines.[92]

Economist and Statistician Irving Fisher (heralded by economists Joseph Schumpeter, Milton Friedman, and James Tobin, as among the greatest, and perhaps the greatest, U.S. economist) advocated eugenics, was one of the original directors of the Eugenics Record Office, and helped organize the American Eugenics Society.[93] Fisher celebrated Indiana's first in the nation forced sterilization law, explaining that by it "[w]e insure certain of these classes are not permitted to propagate their kind."[94] Eugenics, Fisher counseled, was a moral imperative; indeed, it was "the foremost plan of human redemption."[95]

Economist, Chair of the Wharton School of Business at the University of Pennsylvania, and founder of the American Economic Association and the American Academy of Political and Social Science Simon Nelson Patten wrote in 1915 that, "eugenics is giving us a stronger man and a vigorous woman." By culling inferiors from society, the way was paved to a hardier race.[96]

Economist and labor historian John R. Commons believed "an enlightened society" depended on "displace[ment of] the baser elements,"[97] by which he meant limits on procreation by "undesirables."

Economist, Sociologist and Socialist Scott Nearing, a lecturer at the Socialist Party's Rand School of Social Science, who applauded communist reforms following a 1925 visit to the Soviet Union, understood eugenics to be indispensable to creating a socialist utopia. He wrote, "persons with transmissible defects have no rights to parenthood and a sane society in its efforts to maintain its race standards would absolutely forbid hereditary defectives to procreate their kind."[98]

Fabian socialist George Bernard Shaw agreed, favoring eugenics, as did socialists Sidney and Beatrice Webb.[99]

University of Wisconsin President and Geologist Charles R. Van Hise joined Edward A. Ross in supporting passage of Wisconsin's 1913 forcible sterilization law under the slogan "Sterilization or Racial Disaster."[100]

English modernist writer Virginia Woolf supported eugenics, explaining in her diary that imbeciles "should certainly be killed."[101]

Poet, playwright, and social critic T. S. Eliot supported eugenics, believing that we should segregate and then sterilize all "defectives."[102]

Poet and writer D. H. Lawrence thought it best to exterminate "the sick, the halt, and the maimed" in gas chambers, presaging what would become reality in Hitler's Third Reich.[103]

There is in the assumptions that the state may take away the liberty of thousands deemed "undesirable" and the lives of their future off-spring, a cruel embrace of unlimited authoritarian state power. Certainly the overt call for eugenics by Progressives and Socialists spanning academia, journalism, and government in this era reveals a contempt for individual rights so profound that it should come as little wonder that these same Progressives and Socialists became instrumental in the creation of an administrative state which, through agencies, commissions, and boards, could run roughshod over individual rights and rule over the private sector without constitutional limits.

Through these unconstitutional agencies, boards, and commissions governing elites trampled the rights of disfavored minorities in the service of a "public interest" they defined and urgently demanded be fulfilled. Although many leaders of eugenics reform were atheists and agnostics, many others regarded themselves as Christian crusaders and viewed eugenics as a moral undertaking. Many religious Progressives and Socialists believed eugenics urgently needed to cleanse society of people regarded as defective and hasten the creation of a white utopia founded on Protestant values.

The Progressive and Socialists' demand for authoritarian control is the very antithesis of America's founding principles and of constitutionally protected rights against majority tyranny, yet the leaders of Progressive and Socialist reform achieved that rule in over half of the states without uttering a peep about whether such drastic change in the relationship between the state and the individual should be instituted only after constitutional amendment. Based on visceral prejudices masked by the false pseudo-science of social Darwinism, Progressives and Socialists brutally denied individuals they deemed unfit the right to procreate in a concerted effort to end "their kind." They succeeded in making forced sterilization an institution in thirty states, and they forcibly sterilized over 60,000 American citizens between 1907 and 1981.[104]

The high-water mark for Progressive and Socialist eugenics reform came immediately after a 1927 Supreme Court decision written by Progressive eugenicist and juristic powerhouse Oliver Wendell Holmes, Jr. Justice Holmes' *Buck v. Bell* majority opinion gave a strong national endorsement to the cause of forced sterilization precisely at a time when enthusiasm for eugenics was waning.

Holmes believed in rule by the dominant majority, in legislative contests where the more powerful forces would come to the fore. He favored judicial protection for decisions of the majority, even if it sacrificed individual rights.[105] He did not favor the classical liberal concept of individual rights, and he had no sympathy for the underdog, whom he regarded as weak and unworthy of support. He wrote, "wise or not, the proximate test of a good government is that the dominant power has its way."[106]

University of Chicago Law Professor Albert W. Alschuler summed up Holmes by reference to his desired epitaph:

> Holmes suggested that his epitaph should read, "Here lies the supple tool of power," and he wrote, "[i]f my fellow citizens want to go to Hell I will help them. It's my job." He viewed democracy as Darwinian struggle and, perhaps, as spectator sport.[107]

HOLMES' ENDORSEMENT OF FORCED STERILIZATION: *BUCK V. BELL*

On June 4, 1924, seventeen-year-old Carrie Buck was committed to the Virginia Colony for Epileptics and the Feeble-minded by an order of the Juvenile and Domestic Relations Court of Charlottesville, Virginia. Her baby, Vivian, born on March 28, 1924, was taken from her and placed in the custody of Carrie's foster parents, John and Alice Dobbs. Pregnant out of wedlock (a circumstance viewed at the time as *per se* evidence of a lack of social fitness), Carrie became a source of shame and embarrassment for the Dobbs who resolved to have her put away.

Far from the product of consensual sexual relations, Carrie's pregnancy appears to have been the result of rape by Clarence Garland, Alice Dobbs' nephew. Carrie said Clarence "forced himself on me" and "took advantage of me." Those allegations did not dissuade the Dobbs from having Carrie institutionalized and may have made them more desirous for that end. Without reference to the Garland rape, the Dobbs presented their case for commitment to Justice of the Peace C. D. Shackleford in the Juvenile and Domestic Relations Court, variously arguing that Carrie's pregnancy was proof of her "moral delinquency," that over the course of her life she had "some hallucinations" and "some outbreaks of temper," and that she was "dishonest."[108]

With no proof of rape in the record, the plain suggestion was that Carrie's pregnancy arose from promiscuity. The record lacked any proof that promiscuity was heritable. With no evidence concerning Carrie beyond subjective belief, the Dobbs' family physician, Dr. J. C. Coulter, and another Charlottesville doctor, J. F. Williams, proclaimed Carrie "feeble-minded within the meaning of the law," and the court ordered her committed to the Virginia Colony for Epileptics and the Feeble-minded.[109] Judge Shackleford reached his conclusion despite the fact that Carrie was an able student during the years she was allowed to attend school (her daughter Vivian likewise performed well in school, including honor roll status, until her death from enteric colitis at the age of eight).

In 1920, Carrie's mother Emma had been committed to the Colony following charges that she was immoral, syphilitic, and a prostitute. Although previously married to Frank Buck, Colony records described Emma as a widow lacking "moral sense and responsibility," as "notoriously untruthful," as having been arrested for prostitution, as having had illegitimate children, and as having been "untidy" in her housework.[110]

Once an inmate at the Virginia Colony, Carrie Buck soon figured prominently in the Colony Board's efforts to build a test case for the Virginia Eugenical Sterilization Act of 1924. That law was based on the entirely unproven (and indeed false) supposition "that defects—criminality, poverty, illegitimacy, and the like—were passed down"[111] through the "germ plasm" from generation to generation. The law aimed to remedy presumed threats to the "race" (meaning white race) by authorizing the Colony's Superintendent (Dr. Albert Priddy and thereafter Dr. John Bell) to sterilize any Colony inmate deemed "afflicted with hereditary forms of insanity that are recurrent, idiocy, imbecility, feeble-mindedness or epilepsy" upon the approval of the Colony Board. Declaring Carrie "feeble-minded," the Board authorized the Superintendent to sterilize her.

In cahoots with the Colony Board, of which he was a founding member (and a staunch proponent of sterilization of "undesirables"), the conflicted attorney Irving Whitehead volunteered to defend Carrie Buck and then betrayed her by offering virtually no substantive defense to the charges against her, indicative of his clandestine agreement with the prosecution to stage a test case.

Law Professor George A. Lombardo explains that Whitehead "betrayed his client" and "defrauded the court," concluding that Whitehead's case was a "legal sham."[112] Whitehead "secretly met with [the Colony's superintendent] Priddy and the Board and voiced satisfaction that the case was proceeding as planned."[113]

At trial, the evidence against Carrie went unrebutted. Whitehead presented no counter to the state's case for surgery and no expert witness to contradict the testimony of the Board's experts. He did not reveal that Carrie had been raped. He offered no serious objection to, and no witness to contradict, the accusations that Carrie lacked intelligence and was irresponsible, immoral, incorrigible, and dishonest. His inaction mightily aided the prosecution case that rested on authoritatively sounding (yet entirely inept) psychobabble from, among others, eugenicists Arthur H. Eastabrook, Ph.D., formerly of the infamous Eugenics Record Office at Cold Spring Harbor, New York (and, at the time of the trial, at the Eugenics Record Office of the Carnegie Institution in Washington) and Dr. Joseph Dejamette, an "alienist" (i.e., forensic scientist in the field of mental health) and crusader against procreation by "the syphilitic, epileptic, imbecile, drunkard and unfit."[114]

Eastabrook had brief verbal encounters with Carrie and with her daughter Vivian, after which he presumed himself fully competent to declare it his "expert" opinion that both were "feeble-minded."[115] He explained that Emma Buck was also feeble-minded and, so, he concluded that the Bucks had bad "germ plasm" passed on from generation to generation, warranting the sterilization of their kind. The Amherst County Court Judge Bennett Gordon upheld the order to sterilize Carrie Buck. The Virginia Supreme Court of Appeals affirmed, paving the way for one of the most notorious decisions ever handed down by the United States Supreme Court, *Buck v. Bell* (1927), authored by Justice Oliver Wendell Holmes, Jr. and joined by every Justice then sitting (Justices William Howard Taft, Willis Van Devanter, James Clark McReynolds, Louis Brandeis, George Sutherland, Edward T. Sanford, and Harlan Fiske Stone) with the sole exception of Justice Pierce Butler, a Catholic, who dissented without opinion (but was said by Holmes to have done so because he was "afraid of the Church").[116]

Buck v. Bell[117] is but one brutal example of the High Court's overall propensity in the Progressive Era to favor state power in furtherance of an expert-divined "common good" or "public interest" against individual rights. During that era, the Court repeatedly held the Fourteenth Amendment no barrier to state action in pursuit of state objectives, even where under that rubric the state created monopolies, segregated the races, deprived people of property, compelled people to be vaccinated, punished publishers for content critical of state officials and judges and, in the *Bell* case, compelled sterilization. The following is a non-exhaustive listing of cases from the era where state actions depriving individuals of their lives, liberties and properties were upheld in defense of the "common good," consistent with Progressive aims at the expense of individual rights. The common strain in the cases is a preference for authoritarian rule over individual right.

PROGRESSIVE INFLUENCES ON THE SUPREME COURT

Although most of the Justices on the Court during this period have been referred to as "conservatives," they are in fact more aptly described as "statists." Whether supporting what may be termed a politically conservative outcome or not, they favored the state over the rights of individuals to liberty and property. In that overall characteristic of Supreme Court decisions in the Progressive Era we may see a sometimes explicit but often implicit defense of authoritarianism antithetical to the core principles of the Constitution (more particularly at odds with the limited government, rights centric foundation of the Constitution).

In the *Slaughter-House Cases* (1873)[118], a narrow 5–4 majority of the Supreme Court upheld a Louisiana statute that granted a twenty-five year state-sponsored monopoly to a single slaughterhouse (owned by seventeen people) for the parishes of Orleans, Jefferson, and St. Bernard, compelling the closure in those parishes of all competing concerns (destroying approximately 1,000 people's livelihoods). The plaintiffs argued that property and livelihoods were taken by the statute in contravention of the Thirteenth Amendment's prohibition on involuntary servitude (which they interpreted broadly to impose a barrier against discrimination between classes of people) and the Fourteenth Amendment's prohibitions against deprivation of privileges or immunities and of property without due process of law.

Every Justice of the Court rejected the plaintiffs' Thirteenth Amendment argument on the basis that the prohibition on "involuntary servitude" was solely meant to protect human beings, like the newly freed slaves, from forced labor. The Court split on the question of whether the statute violated the Fourteenth Amendment. Justice Samuel Freeman Miller, writing for the majority, reasoned that the statute was in line with police powers "always conceded to belong to the States," accepting without serious question that the state's interest underlying the statute was to ensure the public health and convenience, stating: "It cannot be denied that the statute under consideration is aptly framed to remove from the more densely populated part of the city, the noxious slaughter-houses, and large and offensive collections of animals necessarily incident to the slaughtering business of a large city . . . And it must be conceded that the means adopted by the act for this purpose are appropriate, are stringent, and effectual." The majority did not explain whether less restrictive alternatives, such as enforcement of nuisance or health statutes against specific slaughterhouse practices would have been a less draconian alternative to shutting down all competing slaughterhouses. Nor did the majority explain how allowing one enormous monopoly slaughterhouse to operate would end the allegedly adverse public health effects.

Decided before the Supreme Court incorporated most of the first ten constitutional amendments to the States, the decision of the majority held the Fourteenth Amendment applicable only to a narrow set of national rights guaranteed by the United States. The decision of the majority thus embraced state-sponsored monopoly as constitutional against the pleas of individuals whose property and livelihoods were destroyed by the state's action. Consistent with the thinking of leading Progressives, pursuit of public health justified deprivations of individual rights.

In a dissent to which three other Justices concurred, Justice Stephen J. Field rejected the majority's reasoning. Justice Field explained that the only police powers in support of health furthered by the statute were those governing the location of animal landing and slaughter and the inspection of animals before slaughter. "When these requirements are complied with," he wrote, "the sanitary purposes of the act are accomplished." The monopoly provisions of the statute, however, were, according to Field, "a mere grant to a corporation created by it of special and exclusive privileges by which the health of the city is in no way promoted." Field believed the statute's monopoly grant violated the Privileges or Immunities Clause of the Fourteenth Amendment. He reasoned:

> If exclusive privileges of this character . . . may be granted for twenty-five years they may be equally granted for a century, and in perpetuity. If they may be granted for the landing and keeping of animals intended for sale or slaughter they may be equally granted for the landing and storing of grain and other products of the earth, or for any article of commerce. If they may be granted for structures in which animal food is prepared for market they may be equally granted for structures in which farinaceous or vegetable food is prepared. They may be granted for any of the pursuits of human industry even in its most simple and common forms. Indeed, upon the theory on which the exclusive privileges granted by the act

in question are sustained, there is no monopoly, in the most
odious form, which may not be upheld.

Field understood that the Fourteenth Amendment was designed "to
place the common rights of American citizens [to life, liberty, and property]
under the protection of the National government." Following adoption of the
Fourteenth Amendment, Field reasoned, "[t]he fundamental rights, privileges,
and immunities which belong to [a citizen of the United States residing in
a state] now belong to him as a citizen of the United States, and are not
dependent upon his citizenship" in any state. He explained that the privileges
and immunities secured against state abridgment had been enumerated at
least to some extent in the Civil Rights Act of 1866 as rights "to make and
enforce contracts, to sue, be parties and give evidence, to inherit, purchase,
lease, sell, hold, and convey real and personal property, and to full and equal
benefit of all laws and proceedings for the security of person and property." He
found "the right of free labor" to be a "sacred and imprescriptible" right against
which discriminatory legislation, which here created a monopoly, abridged "the
privileges or immunities of citizens of the United States."

In the advent of the *Slaughter-House Cases,* there stood no constitutional
barrier to the enactment of legislation, which cartelized industry, enabling
politicians to secure a set of promises from industry leaders in exchange for
granting them monopolies at the expense of all competing concerns (and
consumers).

In *Plessy v. Ferguson* (1896)[119], the Supreme Court reviewed a Louisiana
statute that forbad "white" and "colored" people from occupying the same
railway coaches, mandating that "all railway companies carrying passengers in
their coaches in this state, shall provide equal but separate accommodations
for the white, and colored races . . ." The Court described Homer Plessy
as a state resident of "mixed descent" "seven-eighths Caucasian and one-
eighth African blood" who, despite those proportions, was declared by
the conductor to be "colored" within the meaning of the Louisiana law.
Plessy purchased a first-class ticket on the East Louisiana Railway, entered
the train, and sat down in a vacant seat reserved for whites in the coach
section. He was ordered by the conductor to move to the section reserved

for "coloreds." He refused. He was then forcibly removed from the train by a police officer, arrested, and incarcerated in the New Orleans parish jail under the criminal penalty provisions of the statute. The issue before the Supreme Court was whether the Louisiana statute violated the Thirteenth and Fourteenth Amendments to the United States Constitution.

Writing for the majority, Justice Henry Billings Brown rejected the Thirteenth Amendment challenge, finding the case not to involve "a state of bondage; the ownership of mankind as a chattel, or, at least, the control of the labor and services of one man for the benefit of another; and the absence of a legal right to the disposal of his own person." Justice Brown and the majority perceived a distinction to be drawn between equal justice under law, which they understood to be required by the Fourteenth Amendment, and the social equality of the races, an effect they believed achievable only by the preferences of those of one race in their dealings with another.

Justice Brown reasoned that the state's "police power" permitted the state to require a separation of the races in education, marriage, transportation, and theaters so long as the separate accommodations were equal. Wrote Brown: "[W]e think the enforced separation of the races, as applied to the internal commerce of the state, neither abridges the privileges or immunities of the colored man, deprives him of his property without due process of law, nor denies him the equal protection of the laws, within the meaning of the fourteenth amendment." Consistent with Progressive reasoning of the time, Brown lauded the law as serving a "common good," viewing that end superior to individual right. ". . . [T]here must necessarily be a large discretion on the part of the legislature," he wrote. "It is at liberty to act with reference to the established usages, customs, and traditions of the people, and with a view to the promotion of their comfort, and the preservation of the public peace and good order. Gauged by this standard, we cannot say that a law which authorizes or even requires the separation of the two races in public conveyances is unreasonable . . ." Justice Brown thought laws that "enforced separation of the two races" did not stamp "the colored race with a badge of inferiority." Rather, if that notion had any validity at all, Brown believed it was entirely the fault of "the colored race" which, he said, "chooses to put that construction upon it."

Without regard to the quality of accommodations at issue, the law was premised on race conscious discrimination. It thus burdened travelers whether white or non-white by denying them the freedom to sit next to spouses, family members, and friends of a different race. The law compelled racial separation against individual freedom of association (a First Amendment right), doing so to reinforce Jim Crow vestiges of slavery from Louisiana's confederate past. The majority was unpersuaded by those realities, but Justice John Marshall Harlan, writing in dissent, was not. He foresaw that the ruling would beget all manner of race-conscious laws, laying a solid legal foundation for the Jim Crow era.

Harlan recognized the lack of equal protection to be at the heart of the law's compelled segregation. He understood the Thirteenth Amendment not only to abolish slavery but also "the imposition of burdens or disabilities that constitute badges of slavery or servitude." Concerning the Fourteenth Amendment, Justice Harlan explained that "[i]f a white man and a black man choose to occupy the same public conveyance on a public highway, it is their right to do so; and no government, proceeding alone on grounds of race, can prevent it without infringing the personal liberty of each." Harlan perceived that the feeble principle of distinguishing among people based on skin tone would likewise justify distinctions based on nativism, naturalization, and faith, writing: "[I]f this statute . . . is consistent with the personal liberty of citizens, why may not the state require the separation in railroad coaches of native and naturalized citizens of the United States, or of Protestants and Roman Catholics?"

He then articulated what would later become a central constitutional doctrine: "Our constitution is color-blind, and neither knows nor tolerates classes among citizens." Far-sighted, Justice Harlan predicted, rightly, that *Plessy v. Ferguson* would come to be regarded "as pernicious as" the Court's decision in *Dred Scott* (upholding the Fugitive Slave law by holding slaves not entitled to any protections the Constitution afforded to citizens but, instead, to leave them with the status of chattel, like farm animals). Justice Harlan wrote:

[I]t seems that we have yet, in some states, a dominant race—a superior class of citizens—which assumes to regulate the enjoyment of civil rights, common to all citizens, upon the basis of race. The present decision, it may well be apprehended, will not only stimulate aggressions, more or less brutal and irritating, upon the admitted rights of colored citizens, but will encourage the belief that it is possible, by means of state enactments, to defeat the beneficent purposes which the people of the United States had in view when they adopted the recent amendments of the Constitution, by one of which the blacks of this country were made citizens of the United States and of the states in which they respectively reside, and whose privileges or immunities, as citizens, the states are forbidden to abridge. . . . The destinies of the two races, in this country, are indissolubly linked together, and the interests of both require that the common government of all shall not permit the seeds of race hate to be planted under the sanction of law. What can more certainly arouse race hate, what can more certainly create and perpetuate a feeling of distrust between these races, than state enactments, which, in fact, proceed on the ground that colored citizens are so inferior and degraded that they cannot be allowed to sit in public coaches occupied by white citizens? That, as all will admit, is the real meaning of such legislation as was enacted by Louisiana.

Thus, in line with Progressive racial animus and preference for use of state power to achieve a supposed "common good," the Supreme Court's majority refused to strike down laws compelling separation of the races in public accommodations. The decision thus gave impetus to Jim Crowism, helping to extend its reach into the twentieth century.

While we may credit Justice Harlan for refusing to follow the Progressive direction of the majority in upholding separate but equal in Plessy, we should not define him as an enemy to the Progressive cause, far from it. In

Mugler v. Kansas (1887)[120], the Supreme Court evaluated whether Kansas constitutional and statutory prohibitions against the manufacture and sale of intoxicating liquors (except for medical, mechanical, and scientific purposes) violated the privileges or immunities and due process clauses of the Fourteenth, and the takings clause of the Fifth, Amendments. In holding that the laws did not violate the Constitution, the Court broadly defined all manner of state actions in pursuit of the "common good" as constitutional, even when applied, as here, to private property that was used for a lawful purpose before enactment of the state laws. Justice Harlan, writing for the Court's majority, reasoned that "rights are best secured, in our government, by the observance, upon the part of all, of such regulations as are established by competent authority to promote the common good." Laws to promote the common good were rightful across a broad expanse, explained Justice Harlan, writing that nothing in the Constitution stood as a barrier against the state prescribing "regulations to promote the health, peace, morals, education, and good order of the people, and to legislate so as to increase the industries of the state, develop its resources, and add to its wealth and prosperity."

In *Jacobson v. Massachusetts* (1905)[121], the Supreme Court decided whether a Cambridge, Massachusetts' ordinance, requiring all persons in that city to be vaccinated for smallpox or face a fine, was constitutional under the Fourteenth Amendment. Writing for the Court's majority, Justice Harlan upheld the ordinance as applied against an adult citizen who refused vaccination. In so doing, Harlan weighed a general government interest in health and safety, enforced through the police power, against the rights of an individual. While professing that if in future the Court were presented with facts sufficient to establish that an individual was medically unfit for vaccination, it might rule otherwise, he found no such facts present before the Court (despite a record which included uncontroverted representations that the defendant had experienced a prolonged illness as a child following vaccination and that his son, too, had an apparent adverse reaction to vaccination).

Harlan minimized the significance of those experiences, reasoning without proof that it was conceivable that as an adult the defendant had *ipso facto* become a fit subject of vaccination, even if he had not been as a child. Overall, *Jacobson* stands for the proposition that the state's mere recitation that its actions are in furtherance of the general welfare constitutes a sufficient basis for the state to take extraordinary measures against citizens, including deprivation of their right to refuse unwanted medical treatment, here vaccination.

Consistent with the Progressive position in favor of virtually unlimited state power in the service of an amorphous "common good," the Court repeatedly asserted that no private right could stand in the way of achieving majoritarian goals except in the most extraordinary circumstances. "There are manifold restraints to which every person is necessarily subject for the common good," wrote Harlan. "This court has more than once recognized it as a fundamental principle that 'persons and property are subjected to all kinds of restraints and burdens in order to secure the general comfort, health, and prosperity of the state . . .'" quoting *Hannibal & St. J. R. Co. v. Husen* (1878)[122]. "The possession and enjoyment of all rights are subject to such reasonable conditions as may be deemed by the governing authority of the country essential to the safety, health, peace, good order, and morals of the community," he recited, quoting from *Crowley v. Christensen* (1890)[123]. Indeed, Harlan adopted the Progressive view of state power, even to the extent of demanding no proof from the state of the truthfulness of its assertions about the gravity of its interest in acting: "[W]hat the people believe is for the common welfare must be accepted as tending to promote the common welfare, whether it does in fact or not." That view that majority will prevails regardless of individual right echoed Justice Holmes' view underlying his later decision in *Buck v. Bell.*

In short, the *Jacobson* decision imposed no burden of proof on the state to establish that, in a particular case, the dangers it recited were real, and no burden on the state to establish that it could not avail itself of less liberty intrusive alternatives to achieve its objectives. Harlan did not require that the state prove there to be no alternative by which it could protect the community from the danger of smallpox than by forcibly vaccinating one of its citizens. There were, even in 1905, obvious alternatives to compelling vaccination that may have sufficed to reduce to near zero the risk of smallpox spread that did not involve vaccination (such as self-quarantine, donning of face masks, and avoiding close proximity with others). The deadly Spanish flu pandemic of 1917, which killed between fifty and one hundred million people worldwide, raged across the nation, yet the donning of masks became a commonplace used in the cities because a proven vaccine did not exist.

Why then, in a nation founded on the principle that the rights of the governed were paramount, would it not be an essential defense of liberty to demand the state prove less intrusive alternatives incapable of affording protection against the alleged injury before commandeering the body of a person and compelling him to receive an unwanted treatment? Moreover, by the time the matter reached the Supreme Court, there was no longer a smallpox outbreak in Cambridge. Why then did the Court not recognize that fact and dismiss the matter as lacking requisite Article III standing, there no longer being a ripe case or controversy? The unvaccinated defendant had not been shown to have endangered the community because, in fact, his refusal to be vaccinated did not provably contribute to the spread of smallpox. The strength of the Progressive cause thus dictated the outcome, overruling Jacobson's rights and even the Article III requisite of standing. In an area so closely associated with liberty as personal autonomy, the Progressive court bowed greatly to the power of the state and gave no protection to the liberty rights of the defendant. This same disdain for individual rights arose in an area of greater sensitivity for Justice Harlan, but not, initially, for Justice Holmes, when it occurred in the context of the freedoms of speech and press.

In *Patterson v. Colorado* (1907)[124], the plaintiff had been held in contempt by the Supreme Court of Colorado for publishing articles and a cartoon protesting alleged acts of corruption that thwarted the election of Democrats to certain state offices, including that of Governor, enabling Republicans to assume the seats of those Democrats. Among the plaintiff's arguments to the Court were those alleging that under the Constitutions of Colorado and the United States, the plaintiff had a right to present proof of the truthfulness of the publications against the contempt charge. In particular, the plaintiff argued that the Fourteenth Amendment prohibition against state action to deprive a citizen of his or her privileges and immunities and liberty without due process essentially incorporated to the states as a right of national citizenship the First Amendment protections against deprivation of speech and press. Writing for the Court's majority, Justice Oliver Wendell Holmes, Jr. rejected the plaintiff's arguments. He held the public welfare best served by the orderly administration of the courts even if that meant trenching on truthful speech. Indeed, he essentially ruled that any criticism of those in power that might interfere with their performance of duties could lawfully be punished, even if the facts in the criticism were true. That revivified the Blackstonian law of England, which had been rejected with the adoption of the First Amendment.[125] Holmes wrote in pertinent part:

> We leave undecided the question whether there is to be found in the 14th Amendment a prohibition similar to that in the 1st. But even if we were to assume that freedom of speech and freedom of the press were protected from abridgments on the part not only of the United States but also of the states, still we should be far from the conclusion that the plaintiff in error would have us reach. In the first place, the main purpose of such constitutional provisions is 'to prevent all such previous restraints upon publications as had been practiced by other governments,' and they do not prevent the subsequent punishment of such as may be deemed contrary to the public welfare.

Having reasoned in line with Progressive thought that the "public welfare" outweighs the individual right to freedom of speech and press, Holmes insisted upon the pre-First Amendment, Blackstonian law: that even if the publications at issue were demonstrably true, that would be no defense to contempt for libel. Holmes wrote, "[t]he preliminary freedom extends as well to the false as to the true; the subsequent punishment may extend as well to the true as to the false."

Unable to accept that the First Amendment was not incorporated to the states by the Fourteenth Amendment (an incorporation ultimately adopted by a majority of the Court eighteen years later in *Gitlow v. New York* (1925)[126]) or that general reference to the "public welfare" was enough of a justification to allow the state to suppress truthful speech, Justice Harlan distinguished himself again, as he had in *Plessy*, with a famous dissent. Harlan thought the Fourteenth Amendment Privileges and Immunities Clause "necessarily prohibited the states from impairing or abridging the constitutional rights . . . to free speech and a free press." He also thought the liberty component of the Fourteenth Amendment Due Process Clause made freedom of speech and press "essential parts of every man's liberty" and thus protected against state and federal action that impaired or abridged those freedoms. He could not "assent to [the] view" that the First Amendment did not "prevent the subsequent punishment of such as may be deemed contrary to the public welfare." Indeed, "[t]he public welfare cannot override constitutional privileges," he wrote, "and if the rights of free speech and of a free press are, in their essence, attributes of national citizenship, as I think they are, then neither Congress nor any state, since the adoption of the 14th Amendment, can, by legislative enactments or judicial action, impair or abridge them."

Holmes' decision thus gave legal sanction to the notion that a general recitation of the "public welfare" in defense of state action depriving individual rights to speech and press was sufficient to justify prosecution for seditious libel. That reasoning would necessarily enable the states to suppress publications critical of government, defeating a core purpose of the First Amendment and its state analogues.

In *Schenck v. United States* (1919)[127], the Supreme Court determined whether the First Amendment stood as a bar to prosecution under the federal Espionage Act of 1917, as amended, of U.S. Socialist Party General Secretary Charles T. Schenck for attempting to "obstruct the recruiting or enlistment service." The Socialist Party under Schenck's direction published about 15,000 copies of a leaflet that condemned the United States military draft during World War I. As Holmes summarized in his opinion for a unanimous Court: "In impassioned language it intimated that conscription was despotism in its worst form and a monstrous wrong against humanity in the interest of Wall Street's chosen few." The Court recited no evidence that the leaflets caused any draftee to avoid service. Instead, the Court presumed the leaflets might inspire certain recipients to resist the draft. Holmes equated that risk with the risk to life and limb brought about when a person falsely cries fire in a crowded theater. He did not perceive any distinction between the two circumstances despite the obvious difference in imminent apprehension of injury (and the absence of time to evaluate risk in the theater context versus a fulsome opportunity to evaluate the leaflet). He likewise had no difficulty in ascribing culpability for refusal to enlist to Schenck, albeit that decision would, of course, be the draftee's to make in any event.

The test developed by Holmes that became the standard in precedent applied during the age arises from this passage: "The question in every case is whether the words used are used in such circumstances and are of such a nature as to create a clear and present danger that they will bring about the substantive evils that Congress has a right to prevent." Consistent with his predisposition to diminish the significance of individual rights to dissent from majoritarian preferences, Holmes at once admitted that the speech was of a kind ordinarily protected by the First Amendment; nonetheless, he had little difficulty dismissing the First Amendment in war time, giving a broad license to censorship: "We admit that in many places and in ordinary times the defendants in saying all that was said in the circular would have been within their constitutional rights . . . When a nation is at war many things that might be said in time of peace are such a hindrance to its effort that their utterance will not be endured so long as men fight and that no Court could regard them as protected by any constitutional right."

Holmes suffered considerable criticism for his broad dismissal of Schenck's right to dissent, which criticism led him to a *volte-face* in *Abrams v. United States* (1919). Ironically, the decision condemning Schenck's leafleting had the substantive effect of increasing state power to censor speech critical of government, a common authoritarian power of socialist states that Charles T. Schenck, General Secretary of the U.S. Socialist Party, wanted for the United States.

Decided eight months after *Schenck*, *Abrams v. United States*[128] involved a prosecution for seditious libel under the Espionage Act of 1917, as amended, for speech deemed disloyal to the United States and speech that encouraged resistance to United States involvement in World War I. Uncharacteristically, Holmes who wrote for the majority in *Schenck* chose to attack the majority in *Abrams*, revealing that he, like Harlan, could be moved from a more typical acceptance of Progressive state power. Moreover, although most of his decisions favored majoritarian rule over individual rights, in *Abrams,* Holmes wrote eloquently in defense of individual free speech against majoritarian demands for censorship, even in time of war. He wrote in language that has endured in modern First Amendment decisions protective of speech critical of state censorship. Justice Louis Brandeis joined Holmes in dissent.

The five *Abrams'* defendants were Russian natives, three of whom admitted they were "rebels," "revolutionists," and "anarchists" and one admitted he was a "socialist." The five printed and distributed about 5,000 circulars to the public and, apparently, to port side pedestrians while soldiers were embarking and disembarking from ships and while war munitions were being supplied for shipment overseas. The circulars did not specifically advocate draft evasion or any acts of sabotage; rather, the circulars were filled with philippics against President Wilson, the United States, and American allies in World War I. The circulars also praised the Russian communist revolution and called for "workers of the world" to unite against capitalism, the United States and other "enemies" of workers. Writing for the majority, Justice John Hessin Clarke interpreted the circulars to convey advocacy of a general strike, declaring: "[T]he manifest purpose of . . . publication was to create an attempt to defeat the war plans of the government . . . by bringing upon the country the paralysis of a general strike, thereby arresting the production of all munitions and other things essential to the conduct of the war."

After endeavoring to distinguish *Schenck* on the basis of the immediacy of the threat posed, Holmes in dissent argued that the First Amendment was intended to permit a contest of ideas, free of censorship. His reasoning, if accepted, would most certainly result in an end to seditious libel, the very Espionage Act provisions he had defended in *Schenck*. Holmes wrote that "Congress certainly cannot forbid all effort to change the mind of the country," revealing a solicitousness for minority dissent atypical in his decisions. Defining the very "theory of our Constitution" to be free trade in ideas, Holmes abruptly veered into a substantive ideological defense of the First Amendment in a manner supportive of the Framers' intent, writing:

> But when men have realized that time has upset many fighting faiths, they may come to believe even more than they believe the very foundations of their own conduct that the ultimate good desired is better reached by free trade in ideas—that the best test of truth is the power of the thought to get itself accepted in the competition of the market, and that truth is the only ground upon which their wishes safely can be carried out. That at any rate is the theory of our Constitution.

Returning to his point of distinction, Holmes also shifted, heightening the degree of close connection to imminent harm that he would deem sufficient to overrule speech freedom. He wrote: "I think that we should be eternally vigilant against attempts to check the expression of opinions that we loathe and believe to be fraught with death, unless they so imminently threaten immediate interference with the lawful and pressing purposes of the law that an immediate check is required to save the country." Surely that kind of immediacy did not exist in the context of Schenck's leafleting. Holmes rejected seditious libel as inconsistent with the First Amendment, writing: "I wholly disagree with the argument of the Government that the First Amendment left the common law as to seditious libel in force." Rather he would make no exception to the First Amendment's "sweeping command, 'Congress shall make no law abridging the freedom of speech,'" in the absence of an "emergency that makes it immediately dangerous to leave the correction of evil counsels to time." He thus departed from his earlier logic in *Schenck*, recognizing as had James Madison and Thomas Jefferson, that the First Amendment's purpose not only embraced an end to prior restraint but also an end to seditious libel.

But, alas, Holmes departed from authoritarianism in the Progressive tradition only for a moment. Indeed, in a decision infamous for its brutal deprivation of individual liberty, *Buck v. Bell*, Holmes wrote a cruelly uncompassionate and terse majority opinion. In *Buck v. Bell* (1927), the Supreme Court evaluated whether the Fourteenth Amendment Due Process Clause prohibited the State of Virginia from compelling a person deemed "feeble-minded" to be sterilized. Writing for all Justices but one (Justice Pierce Butler), Holmes ruled that the "welfare of society" achieved by forcible sterilization of the "unfit" superseded the rights of an individual to procreate. Holmes, a eugenics advocate, reasoned that if the state could draft citizens to serve and die in battle to defend the United States, "it would be strange if it could not [also] call upon those who already sap the strength of the State for these lesser sacrifices [sterilization]. . . in order to prevent our being swamped with incompetence." Holmes did not question the record before him; he accepted the state's justifications unhesitatingly. An advocate of eugenics, he accepted without scientific proof (yet consistent with Progressive views of the day and his own physician father's misconceptions) that those who committed crimes or were impoverished were genetically pre-disposed to do or be so and would bear offspring likewise pre-disposed. By Holmes way of thinking, "[i]t is better for all the world, if instead of waiting to execute degenerate offspring for crime, or to let them starve for their imbecility, society can prevent those who are manifestly unfit from continuing their kind." Citing as his sole authority the *Jacobson* vaccination decision which had earlier overruled the liberty right of an individual to dissent from vaccination, Holmes reasoned, brutally, "[t]he principle that sustains compulsory vaccination is broad enough to cover cutting the Fallopian tubes." Accepting without question the false assertions in the record that defendant Carrie Buck, her mother Emma, and her daughter Vivian were all ignoramuses, Holmes infamously declared, "Three generations of imbeciles are enough." In one of the shortest substantive decisions ever written by the Court, Holmes did not remand the case to fill in the enormous factual holes in the record (including the utter absence of competent evidence of Carrie Buck's imbecility and of the inheritability of imbecility, and the false pseudo-science "germ plasm" theory of the prosecution). Instead, Holmes ordered the sterilization of Carrie Buck forthwith and ushered in an era of state laws resulting in the sterilization of approximately 60,000 American citizens from 1927 to 1981.

Holmes' rush to judgment in *Buck v. Bell*, his unequivocal embrace of the state's case and summary rejection of the arguments against it, left in place questions that should have been asked and that would have revealed the suit to have been a complete sham. As Albert W. Alschuler explains:

> Holmes could not have known it, but . . . [n]either Carrie Buck nor her daughter was mentally defective, at least not by today's standards. The daughter, who died . . . after completing the second grade, was in fact reported to have been "very bright." She was listed on her school's honor roll.

> Holmes might have noted that the record contained no evidence of the daughter's mental condition. . . . Without evidentiary support, a lower court opinion . . . described the daughter as "apparently feeble minded."

> [Holmes] could not have known that two eugenics enthusiasts, the author of the Virginia sterilization law and the superintendent of the State Colony for Epileptics and Feebleminded, had chosen Buck as a bit player in a test case that they had devised . . .

> Holmes also could not have known that a friend of the law's author had agreed to serve as Buck's counsel.[129]

Alschuler reports that following the decision, Carrie Buck's sister, Doris Buck, was also sterilized but "without her knowledge after being told that she needed an appendectomy."[130]

The authoritarian philosophy the Progressives adopted to justify the horror of forced sterilization was studied by the Nazis and then employed to justify sterilization of some 375,000 people, "most for congenital feeblemindedness," but also for "blindness and deafness."[131] The notion of state power superior to private right to pursue what the state defined as a "common good" was a hallmark of national socialism. The theories of nineteenth-century German scholars supporting an all-powerful administrative state begat systematic state by state forced sterilization in the

United States, which in turn, educated the Nazis in Germany and led to their redeployment of comparable eugenics practices in the Nazi controlled countries of Europe. Indeed, during the Nuremberg trials, Nazi defendants repeatedly cited *Buck v. Bell* in defense of their extermination of the Jews and others deemed "unfit." The Hegelian-derived idea that the collective right of the state to pursue a presumed common good trumps the individual right to dissent had been practically applied to achieve a state-defined "common good," destruction of "inferiors" to advance the "master race."

PROGRESSIVES GERMINATE THE AUTHORITARIAN SEED PLANTED BY FRIEDRICH HEGEL

The authoritarianism so apparent in the eugenics context was, in fact, a subset of a broader authoritarianism that infused nearly every state action supported by the Progressives and Socialists during the period between the end of the Civil War and the First World War. In his *Elements of the Philosophy of Right* (1821), Georg Wilhelm Friedrich Hegel described the state as an "organism" having interests paramount to those of the individual. An individual's "highest duty," Hegel wrote, was to be a "member of the state."

"The state in and for itself is the ethical whole, the actualization of freedom, and it is the absolute end of reason," wrote Hegel. "[I]t is only through being a member of the state that the individual himself has objectivity, truth, and ethical life," he wrote. Indeed, human worth is valued by its contribution to the state or, as Hegel explains, "[a]ll the worth which the human being possesses—all spiritual reality, he possesses only through the State."[132] The interests of civil society and those of the family were to be "subordinate" to the "higher power" of the state "on which they depend." Indeed, the individual was subordinate in all respects to the state, such that "if the state claims life, the individual must surrender it."[133] Hegel deemed a constitutional monarch as the proper and highest authority of the state and the monarch's civil administrators as appropriately assigned to "look after" the interests of private property, which interests were also to be "subordinated to the higher interests of the state."[134]

Hegelian philosophy in the nineteenth century played a major part in the development of schools of "political economy" in Germany and of German teachings supportive of the administrative state. Many American Progressive and Socialist scholars who yearned for extra-constitutional justification for state intervention into the economy and society of the Industrial-age United States attended the German schools.

In the 1870s and 1880s, American academics in law, economics, philosophy, and history from Harvard, Yale, Princeton, Cornell, Columbia, Johns Hopkins, the University of Pennsylvania, the University of Wisconsin, and the University of Michigan, among others, originally educated in classical liberalism, flocked to universities in Berlin, Halle, and Heidelberg to study the new schools of historicism and political economy.[135] "[B]etween the mid-1870s, when the first Americans began to find their way to Germany for postgraduate education in economics, and the student migration's peak in the late 1890s, a generation of young progressive intellectuals" came to be taught that laissez-faire economics and individualism were archaic barriers to creation of a new, superior state dependent on collectivism.[136] The Americans so taught came back with, at a minimum, "massive doubts about laissez-faire but also sweeping, still inchoate visions of radical change."[137] Daniel T. Rodgers explains:

> From the University of Pennsylvania's Wharton School of Finance and Economy, Edmund J. James sent a stream of graduate students back to {Johannes] Conrad's [economics] seminar in Halle where, by the early 1890s, ten to fifteen Americans were regularly to be found. James helped fill the Wharton School faculty with German-trained economists: Simon Patten, Roland P. Falkner, Samuel M. Lindsay, Leo S. Rowe, Henry R. Seager, Emory R. Johnson, and Joseph F. Johnson. Columbia was another center of German-trained economists, and it, too, regularly sent graduate students to Germany to cap their economics studies. . . . In Berlin where, sooner or later, the vast majority ended up, Mary Kingsbury in 1895 and 1896 found herself in the middle of a circle of American students that included Walter Weyl (who would be one of the cofounders [of] the *New Republic),* Emily Greene Balch (later a professor of economics at Wellesley and

a prominent figure in the international women's networks), Robert A. Woods (now of the South End Settlement in Boston), and Franklin H. Dixon (soon to become a Dartmouth professor and expert on railway legislation)."[138]

They soon transformed academia in America by regurgitating these state interventionist teachings into their respective fields of economics, sociology, history, political science, and law. But the socialist teachings they had learned were more than simple academic concepts, they were a call to action, bidding them to leave the college office and classroom and translate the concepts into interventionist state policies across the United States. Daniel T. Rodgers records: "They wrote for popular outlets. Several reached out for labor union contracts. By the middle of the decade [i.e., the 1880s], [Richard T.] Ely, the boldest of his generation, was deep into studies of [the] working-class socialist . . ."[139] The "most prominent of them labored to promote a transformation of values deep and thorough to hollow out the system of competitive and individualistic economics at its ethical core."[140]

The leading German scholars taught these pupils that classical liberalism was passé and had no place in the Industrial Age with its wealthy corporate structures, urban societies, material abundance, and large labor force. They drew principally from the philosophy of Hegel[141] who taught that classical liberalism was based on a false original conception of the relationship between man and the state. There never had been a pre-political state of nature, Hegel taught; that was Locke's fiction. Rather, there always was a collective which begat action through the state. Hegel taught that man and the state were not antagonistic as Locke and the Founding Fathers understood them. Far from it, they were harmonious parts of a collective whole, which collective was the organism of the state. Drawing from biological science, he taught that individuals were like cells within the state organism.

Under the classical liberal view, man is endowed by his creator with unalienable rights, and just governments are based on the consent of the governed and are instituted among men to protect the rights of the governed. In addition, laws are just only if adopted by the elected representatives of the people and, even then, pure democracy would tend toward tyranny unless government power was limited and checked to avoid deprivations of rights, which encroachments were the inherent risk of governors ever prone to abuse their power in pursuit of self-interest. Moreover, government was understood to be tyrannical if its legislative, executive, and judicial powers were ever combined in single hands rather than dispersed in separate departments, and each department needed to be the jealous guardian of its own authority and possess the power to check the other, so as to prevent precipitous action and defeat abuse.

By contrast, under the philosophy professed by the leading German scholars (such as Adolph Wagner of the University of Berlin), individual rights were a primitive concept inapplicable in the Industrial age; rather, collective rights possessed by the government for use in pursuit of a common good were the only rights worthy of legal recognition and furtherance. It was the duty of citizens to pursue the common good as defined by the state; dissent from that pursuit was unlawful. Rights did not exist from God independent of, and preceding the existence of, government but were said to be derived from government and, thus, legitimate only if in service to state ends. Moreover, governmental powers were not limited but were limitless; rather individuals were appropriately limited by all-powerful governments to ensure their pursuit of the collective good. Far from posing a threat to liberty, governments were understood to be organisms with power sufficient to alter society in service to, and for the betterment of, all mankind. Governments could only address the common good properly if societal elites in the form of experts, relying on objective facts, defined that good and guided government leaders in pursuit of it. In that regard, an administrative state possessed of near absolute power, as postulated by Rudolf von Gneist, was necessary to supervise and direct government officials to enforce laws the experts deemed best. Indeed, private claims were viewed as products of self-interest at odds with the collective good.

As law professor Philip Hamburger explains, the German school of political economy was in many respects an updated version of earlier European continental defenses of absolute monarchy.[142] There was little difference between the consolidated power of an absolute monarch and the consolidated power of the new administrative state favored by the Hegelian

Progressives and Socialists. Both presumed the state better able to discern what was in the best interest of society than the individual him or herself. In this way classical liberalism could be turned on its head with the individual being powerless and the state being all-powerful, with the individual lacking sovereignty and the state possessing it exclusively.

The American Progressives embraced the German school to escape the limits on power prescribed by the Constitution, which they viewed as obstacles to progress. Mainly from the Germans, the American scholars "imbibed an academic idealization of administrative power and a corresponding contempt for power exercised through and under law, including a contempt for many of the formalities of constitutional law."[143] Back on American shores, leading academics in all major schools endeavored to adapt German theories of political economy to American government, insisting on the creation of unconstitutional commissions and agencies, which eschewed classical liberalism in favor of an all-powerful and efficient administrative state run by experts.

Among those responsible for laying the foundations for the administrative state in America was Columbia University Professor of Law and Political Science Frank Goodnow, who studied Hegelian and socialist philosophies in Berlin. Goodnow's writings, including *Municipal Problems* and *Comparative Administrative Law*, borrowed heavily from the German school and became a bible for municipalities seeking to establish new government entities outside of the old and without constitutional constraints.[144] Reflective of Hegelian principles explained in *Elements of the Philosophy of Right*, Goodnow taught that society, or more particularly, the state, possessed rights and needed to channel human behavior to serve a common good. Rights were not God-given to individuals, the principal tenet of the Declaration of Independence that underlay the Constitution. Bestowed by the state, rights were fungible, meaning that "[s]ocial expedience, rather than natural right, . . . determine[d] the sphere of individual freedom of action." Consequently, as modernization begat greater governmental action, "the actual content of individual rights [would] increasingly [be] narrowed," wrote Goodnow.

Goodnow rejected the American conception of individual liberty where citizens could resort to the courts to protect them from the state, finding "the rule in Europe" preferable. There, the parliament, not the courts, determined the scope of allowable freedoms and, thus, the extent to which they could be constricted for the pursuit of an officially prescribed "common good."[145] Many Progressive scholars echoed Goodnow's sentiments. For example, Johns Hopkins Professor of Political Science Westel Willoughby wrote, "private rights and property are not to be allowed to stand in the way" of efficient government administration.[146] One of the most influential academics of the age, socialist economist Richard T. Ely taught in line with Hegel that "the State is [a] moral person." Another prolific eugenicist writer of the time, sociologist Edward A. Ross defined the collective embodied in the state as "a living thing." President Woodrow Wilson likewise adapted the Hegelian organism language to support his vision of the ideal state, declaring government "not a machine, but a living thing."

The transformation wrought from laissez-faire economics to state-directed economies along the model of German Chancellor Bismarck could not have been more complete in the American universities. Daniel T. Rodgers explains that "[o]f the initial 6 officers of the American Economic Association in 1885, 5 had studied in Germany; of its first 26 presidents, at least 20 had done so. In 1906, when Yale's Henry Farnam polled what he took to be the 116 leading economists and sociologists in the United States and Canada, 59 had spent a student year or more in Germany."[147]

By anthropomorphizing the state into a living creature, the notion that the state had a right and a will independent of the people became comprehensible. In the bold, state-centric world of the Progressives and Socialists, governments are not instituted among men to protect the rights of the governed, governments are themselves alive, instituted to ensure efficient administration as dictated by "experts" who goad the public in the direction of what the experts perceive to be a "common good," which movement is declared "progress." Moreover, as Louis D. Brandeis insisted along with Wilson (both tapping into Hegel), the Constitution was a dead letter unless it adapted and grew to meet each new exigency.

If the Progressives were honest, they would have to admit that the administrative state they envisioned was beyond the government defined by the Constitution, requiring constitutional amendment. But they were not honest. To appease popular concerns against radical change, they reinterpreted the Constitution meant to limit power and deny authority to invade private rights such that its limits on power were deemed inapplicable or non-existent and its authority was deemed to reach private actions.

Hamburger writes that the German vision "of the state's unity, functions, and rights . . . displaced the American vision of federalism, separation of powers, and rights reserved by the people."[148] Indeed, American scholars in the fields of economics, history, and law obtained a comparatively inexpensive graduate education abroad, an education that condemned laissez-faire capitalism, individual rights, private property, and America itself and called for all governments to be replaced with socialist states either directly or through regulation. Those scholars trained in the German school commonly assumed prominent teaching positions in every major graduate and law school in the United States. In those schools, they established programs and curricula akin to those in Germany.

Daniel T. Rodgers explains "the German university connection had . . . lasting historical consequences . . . [Edmund J.] James [of the Wharton School of Finance and Economy] helped fill the Wharton School faculty with German-trained economists: Simon Patten, Roland P. Falkner, Samuel M. Lindsay, Leo S. Rowe, Henry R. Seager, Emory R. Johnson, and Joseph F. Johnson. Columbia was another center of German-trained economists, and it, too, regularly sent graduate students to Germany to cap their economic studies."[149]

German academics who championed socialism bore intellectual offspring in the form of Americans who, under their tutelage at the then famous German schools, also became enthralled with socialism, returning home to universities intent on teaching it, and then came to influence heavily, if not dominate entirely, the new fields of economics, sociology, political science, psychology, public education, and law, which they molded to embrace socialism. By 1885, five of the six officers of the American Economic Association were German-trained, and at least twenty of the first twenty-six presidents of the AEA were German-trained.[150] "In 1906, when Yale's Henry Farnam polled what he took to be the 116 leading economists and sociologists in the United States and Canada, 59 had spent a student year or more in Germany."[151] A lecturer at Johns Hopkins University (1880 to 1882), then at Cornell University, and then a Professor at the University of Michigan where he worked with the socialist John Dewey, Henry Carter Adams went to Berlin in 1878 where he "read as much of the socialists' literature as he could acquire."[152] The American socialist W. E. B. DuBois performed his graduate work at the University of Berlin and at Harvard. In Berlin in the 1890s, DuBois was delighted by the socialism that pervaded William II's German Empire, permeating academia, government, and society. DuBois wrote, "the German professors have preached socialism, German popular leaders have deified it, and the German state has practiced it, until all German reform movements take on a more or less socialistic form."[153]

It was while pursuing his Ph.D. in Economics at the University of Heidelberg in 1879 that Richard T. Ely first met Berlin scholar Adolph Wagner, an ardent socialist, who taught him to despise as immoral a supposed ego-centrism unique to capitalism. Ely, who became the founder and first Secretary of the American Economic Association, and would serve on the faculty of Johns Hopkins University, the University of Wisconsin, and Northwestern University, later described Wagner as "[o]ne of the great economists of his age." A socialist since at least his Ph.D. studies in Germany, Ely went on to teach his American students to deplore capitalism and to idolize Wagnerian state socialism. Wagner professed the need for the state to replace the private sector in the "railroads, canals, banking, insurance, utilities, mining, and housing" and to assume ownership of all urban lands.[154] Wagner wanted to move the German economy "more and more out of private and into public organizational forms."[155] The Berlin economists taught their American students to reject American culture, revere authoritarianism as exemplified by the German emperor and state, and despise capitalism. Indeed, they taught American students to harbor "contempt [for] everything American."[156]

Ultimately translated into American scholarship, the German-trained professors of economics, law, and history created a new American scholarship that "delegitimized American constitutional principles that stood in the way of administrative law."[157] Richard A. Epstein explains the underlying emphasis: "The Progressive view of social progress equated active government with good government. . . . Thus, any constitutional doctrine that stood in the way of comprehensive reforms had to be rejected or circumvented."[158] While having little to no confidence in classical liberalism, in the Constitution, and in free markets, the Progressives and Socialists who predominated in Progressive era education professed unquestioning confidence in state power to achieve an ever more amorphous "common good." "The progressives combined their extravagant faith in science and the state," writes Thomas C. Leonard, "with an outsized confidence in their own expertise as a reliable, even necessary, guide to the public good."[159]

"[A]fter late-nineteenth century American scholars of political science and sociology became fascinated with German scholarship," writes Hamburger, "they taught generations of students [in the United States] the Germanic skepticism about constitutional limitations, consent, and the separation of powers, and the Germanic love of the state and administrative authority."[160] Quoting British Democratic socialist Bernard Crick, Donald J. Pestritto explains that following the Civil War, "there was a considerable influx of German-trained thinkers into American academic circles at the same time that resources for higher education were being expanded."[161] Leonard meticulously documents how those so educated dominated the new field of economics and endeavored successfully to be recognized as "experts" worthy of defining the agendas of, and running, the new extra-constitutional agencies, commissions, and bureaus in the state and federal governments.

Indeed, as Daniel T. Rodgers explains, the students who learned the German scholarship antagonistic to individual liberty and free enterprise found employment in "many of the key agencies" and "left the marks of their German encounter across a broad spectrum of social-political endeavor."[162] Those scholars re-created the American graduate school in line with the German model, and they filled the curricula with the popular German collectivist educational courses, forming the new schools of sociology, economics, and labor. Daniel T. Rodgers summarizes:

> The first act of the German-trained American students, as they began to take up professorships of their own in the 1880s, was a rush to re-create the forms of academic life into which they had been initiated abroad. Into the curricula they

shoved the defining marks of German university scholarship: lecture, seminar, research paper, monograph, scholarly journal, graduate education, and the Ph.D. degree. . . . They began to sprinkle the catalog offerings with new courses—social politics, social economics, public finance (Wagner's special province), the problems of labor and capital—and ventilated the old textbook pedagogy with new readings.[163]

In the latter half of the 1880s, the German-trained economists, sociologists, historians, political scientists, and historians along with their most loyal students were not content just to teach socialism in universities. They wanted to turn their teachings into a new administrative state that would achieve an end-run around the Constitution. "Through this intellectual route the German-trained economists made their way back, in the end, to the role of legislation and the state," explains Daniel T. Rodgers. By the late 1880s, supported by a cadre of other German-trained economists, Richard T. Ely reached beyond academia, demanding that the state acquire ownership, operation and control of the "railroads, telegraphs, streetcar lines, and city electric, gas, and waterworks—if not immediately, at least slowly and inexorably."[164]

CHAPTER 2

THE PRESIDENTS WHO EMBRACED AUTHORITARIANISM

From the 1880s to the 1930s, leaders of the parties were swayed by a desire variously to placate, capitalize upon, or champion causes of Progressives. The moderate President Grover Cleveland bent to the wishes of Progressives (and the leading railroads) who demanded fixed rates, elimination of subsidies, and regulation of rail services and business practices, signing into law the first legislation creating a federal regulatory commission, the Interstate Commerce Commission, in 1887. Self-avowed Progressive Presidents Theodore Roosevelt, Woodrow Wilson, and Franklin Delano Roosevelt all drank heavily from the well of disdain for limited government, individual rights, and free enterprise, variously using their political clout to favor sustained government intervention into the market beyond constitutional limits. But even Herbert Hoover revealed an authoritarian side, helping, among other government interventions, to engineer the collapse of voluntary radio self-regulation, thus engendering a cacophonous collision of voices on the airwaves to serve as a catalyst to federal ownership of the ether and regulation of radio. It was also Hoover who signed into law the Smoot-Hawley tariff, which helped trigger the

Great Depression, and raised taxes in the economic contraction following the Great Crash of 1929, causing a massive wave of unemployment.

In 1887, Wilson professed his admiration for the German model and dedicated himself to defeating the Constitution's separation of powers and non-delegation doctrines so that an authoritarian administrative state could take root in America.[165] In 1910, Theodore Roosevelt advocated sterilization by order of state boards to prevent dilution of a master race of white Americans, a dilution he called "race suicide,"[166] and when he finally bolted from the Republican Party and formed his own Progressive "Bull Moose" Party, he had been so overtaken with authoritarian sentiments that he endeavored to lure socialists away from Socialist Party of America candidate Eugene Debs to his Progressive Party. In his 1912 presidential campaign, Roosevelt repeatedly endorsed administrative power as the best means to govern efficiently and expertly. He also joined Louis Brandeis in calling for taxpayer funded "comprehensive" social insurance that would pay for the costs of "sickness, accident, invalidity, unemployment, and old age." The promise of comprehensive social insurance was included in Teddy Roosevelt's 1912 Progressive Party platform.[167] He was unable to deliver on that pledge, but his distant cousin and nephew-in-law Franklin D. Roosevelt did deliver upon it, signing the Social Security Act into law in 1935.

With the advent of state, and then federal, administrative agencies in America, governments drew Progressive scholars out of academia who harbored disdain for limited government, individual rights and free enterprise and placed them in the administrative state, assigning them the task of leading reforms beyond constitutional limits. As Philip Hamburger records, Progressive students "soon became bureaucrats, lawyers, and judges, and in these positions eventually swept away the constitutional impediments."[168]

The Progressives who created the administrative state in America were elitists, coming from America's most respected colleges and universities. Those institutions were increasingly dominated by young professors trained in the German school from the 1860s forward, embracing denunciations of the Constitution as a historic relic inapplicable to the demands of the modern industrial society and calling for collectivism to conform capitalism to conceptions of the "common good." They presumed their own prejudices and their own economic and social preferences synonymous with that "common good" which they demanded become law to which all would be forced to comply. They construed the need for an appeal to the legislatures, to the courts, or to the amendment process a waste of precious time that could only encumber the "rule of experts." Indeed, they rejected the need for involvement of any constitutional branch of government. They initially sought, then obtained, and then enforced authoritarian powers to break apart or regulate big businesses they disliked; control the manner in which businesses operated; redistribute income selectively (excluding from government largess disfavored minorities); bar immigration from Southern and Eastern Europe, Africa, and Asia (regions the Progressive elites viewed as producing social inferiors of Anglo-Saxons); limit the hours women could work on the sexist predicate that women were too delicate for strenuous labor and needed to be devoted to domestic chores and child bearing and rearing; institutionalize or forcibly sterilize people deemed "undesirable;" ban alcohol; enact Jim Crow laws in the South to keep blacks, deemed inferior, away from work competitive with whites, venues favored by whites, and the polls; and favor a minimum wage to prevent non-Anglo-Saxons from undercutting the "living wage" demanded by whites.

The Progressives found *laissez-faire* unacceptable in large measure because it failed to contribute consistently and directly to the utopian society they desired; rather, free enterprise created its own economic successes with independent powers not subject to the control of these elites. They resented the way in which free market economics elevated people from lower socio-economic classes to the upper classes, raising to prominence those who were immigrants or minorities, who lacked college educations, who had no familial connection with traditional "blue blood" families, or who were related to people involved in criminal activities. They were envious of the wealth and clout exercised by these social upstarts. They particularly resented those instances in which their own families of established stock lost power in their own regions and were uprooted by industrialists who climbed the social ladder and displaced them in local, state, and national influence.

They were especially unsettled by the reality that some of lower socio-economic standing who were from categories they thought inferior, such as Jews, Catholics, Irish, and Italians, could rise to great wealth, could redirect the course of public policy, and could gain notoriety and exercise considerable influence beyond their original stations in life and in place of the old political dynasties. They complained that some of "low class" or immigrant stock had attained fabulous riches in the Industrial Age, had become more wealthy by far than the federal government itself. Many Progressives feared a loss of control to those they presumed their "inferiors."

For example, they were appalled that immigrants like the Irish Catholic Joseph P. Kennedy could make a fortune illegally from selling bootleg scotch whiskey and could translate that wealth into political power. They aimed to right those wrongs through the exercise of administrative power, regulating free enterprise in ways that would influence who succeeded in the market, would protect white domestic labor from immigrant competition, would eliminate sale of products deemed immoral, and would channel market activity into pursuits they deemed beneficial for society. According to Economic Historian Thomas C. Leonard:

> When progressives condemned natural selection [as opposed to artificial selection] as indifferent to progress, they had in mind not only improved efficiency but also moral improvement. Henry Carter Adams's landmark indictment of laissez-faire, *The Relation of the States to Industrial Action* (1887), justified regulation on the grounds that economic competition, like competition in nature, was amoral and inhumane. Because markets rewarded the unscrupulous, and good people had to compete with the unscrupulous, markets tempted good people into bad behavior. The solution, said Adams, was regulation of industry. Adams' framing of regulation as a defense of Christian morality, protecting the upright from the corrupting effects of market competition, proved irresistible to progressives.[169]

The founding editor of the *New Republic*, eugenics advocate Herbert Croly was among early Progressives who pushed for the creation of a heavily regulatory administrative state and helped form Theodore Roosevelt's New Nationalism and Franklin D. Roosevelt's New Deal platforms. He called for "the eventual assumption by the state of many functions now performed by individuals,"[170] professing that "reform is both meaningless and powerless unless the Jeffersonian principle of [state] non-interference [with private life] is abandoned."[171] In particular, he called for the state to dissolve market concentration and institute forms of socialism, explaining that "[i]n all such cases [of industry centralized control], some system of public ownership and private operation should, if possible, be introduced."[172]

Progressives like Louis D. Brandeis and Felix Frankfurter shared many of Croly's views. Like Croly, Brandeis despised big business, looking back nostalgically to America's decentralized, less prosperous and, what he regarded as, more virtuous agrarian past. In the cities, newly visible disparities in wealth, public drunkenness and licentiousness, and dynamic capitalist economies where individuals rose from poverty to wealth and fell back to poverty again, caused many elites who witnessed the dizzying changes to seek control over the dynamics through government and, ultimately, through imposition of their socio-economic preferences via regulation. Some, like the Grangers, aimed at controlling rail transportation costs, to promote farmers' interest in profitably supplying urban demand for agricultural products. Others, like the Prohibitionists, aimed at ridding the cities of alcohol and leading those in vice to salvation. For many Progressive reformers, government power was increasingly viewed as the only way to force a remolding of the economy and society by overruling private choice and substituting for it their own preferences backed by the force of law. While their forebears clamored for liberty, Progressives of all stripes clamored for control, beginning in the late nineteenth century and continuing to the present.

THEODORE ROOSEVELT AND THE ESTABLISHMENT OF PROGRESSIVE GOVERNANCE

Theodore Roosevelt was catapulted into the presidency and acquired a like for executive power. For 194 days, he served as President William McKinley's Vice President. That changed on September 14, 1901. On September 8, McKinley attended the American Exposition at the Temple of Music in Buffalo, New York. A presidential receiving line formed inside the

Temple. As he stood to shake hands, Leon Frank Czolgosz (a self-proclaimed anarchist), approached shortly after 4PM, with his right hand wrapped in a handkerchief. Believing Czolgosz's wrapped right hand injured, the President reached for and touched Czolgosz's left hand, whereupon Czolgosz lifted his right, revealing a .32 caliber revolver, and fired two shots at point blank range at the President. One ricocheted off McKinley's metal coat button but the other entered and exited his stomach, causing McKinley to lurch forward and then stagger. The President was aided to a chair. Czolgosz was beaten and subdued by the crowd (with the President requesting that the beating stop). When it became clear that the President had suffered a serious wound to the stomach, he was transported by electric ambulance to the Exposition hospital and then to the hospital's operating room for surgery. Police apprehended Czolgosz and jailed him in the Auburn Correctional Facility. McKinley's stomach wound turned gangrenous, and he succumbed to the infection in the Milburn House in Buffalo on September 14, 1901. His death elevated Roosevelt to the presidency. Following a trial on the merits, Czolgosz was found guilty of murder. He was sentenced to death by electrocution, which sentence was imposed on October 29, 1901.[173]

McKinley was a Republican, as was Theodore Roosevelt, until he left the Republicans to form the Progressive "Bull Moose" Party in 1912. Roosevelt completed McKinley's term. He distinguished himself by fashioning a new set of interventionist domestic policies against "trusts" (i.e., presumed monopolies), which policies he called the "Square Deal." In 1902, Roosevelt followed the lead of progressives in his party by selectively attacking concentrations of wealth, not all concentrations but those he presumed indicative of "bad" companies. That same year, he urged Congress to pass legislation creating the U.S. Department of Commerce and Labor, which included a Bureau of Corporations, the immediate predecessor of the Federal Trade Commission (established in 1915). Congress enacted the legislation, including nearly all provisions Roosevelt wanted, and he signed the legislation into law on February 14, 1903. The Bureau of Corporations studied and reported on American industry and, particularly, those companies suspected of market concentration. The Bureau's 1906 report on the petroleum industry led to key provisions in the Roosevelt endorsed Hepburn Act of 1906. The

Hepburn Act gave the Interstate Commerce Commission authority to set "reasonable" maximum railroad rates; compel reliance on a uniform system of accounts and on inspection of railroad accounting records; and "through routes" around city centers. It also expanded ICC jurisdiction over several industries, including the oil pipeline industry. The Elkins Act, signed into law by Roosevelt in 1903, gave the ICC authority to impose heavy fines on the railroads if they offered rebates and upon shippers if they accepted them. Rebates were commonly used to induce loyalty to a specific railroad and, thus, encouraged competition. By banning rebates, the Elkins Act encouraged fixed, above market rates.

In reliance on the Sherman Act and the Hepburn Act's pipeline provisions, Roosevelt's Department of Justice pursued a case through the Circuit Court against John D. Rockefeller's Standard Oil Company of New Jersey. Three years after Roosevelt left the presidency, in 1911, the Supreme Court upheld Roosevelt's position in *Standard Oil Company of New Jersey v. United States*[174], ruling that Standard Oil violated the Sherman Act by monopolizing the petroleum industry and ordering the company to be split into thirty-four independent, competing companies.

Running as a Republican, Roosevelt succeeded in winning election in 1904, during which time he endorsed several major pieces of reform legislation. On June 30, 1906, following public outrage against the meatpacking industry inspired by Upton Sinclair's fictional work, *The Jungle*, President Roosevelt signed into law the Meat Inspection Act (making it unlawful to sell adulterated meat and misbranded meat products and mandating standards for the sanitary slaughter and processing of livestock) and the Pure Food and Drug Act (prohibiting the interstate distribution and sale of adulterated and misbranded foods and drugs, requiring label disclosure of active drug ingredients, and requiring minimum purity levels for drugs). Both laws were assigned to the Bureau of Chemistry under the Department of Agriculture for implementation. That Bureau was renamed the Food and Drug Administration in 1930 and became an independent regulatory agency with a substantial increase in scope and power in 1938 upon passage of the Food, Drug, and Cosmetic Act.

Having campaigned in 1904 primarily on the promise that he would break up large corporations that restricted competition, Roosevelt made good on that promise in selective instances. During the Roosevelt Administration, some forty-four anti-trust actions were brought against companies.

Over the course of his political career, Theodore Roosevelt veered ever leftward. He served out McKinley's remaining term in office and was then re-elected in 1904 as a Republican for a second term, ending in 1908. In his second term, he became increasingly convinced that the federal government needed to intervene in all manner of economic and social affairs. At first, while he completed McKinley's term, he advocated economic intervention in the form of "trust-busting" via enforcement of the Sherman Act of 1890. After he left the White House and following a tour of Europe, he returned convinced that greater, more radical, government interventions were required. Although he initially declined the invitation to seek the Republican nomination for President in 1912, deferring to the sitting Republican President William Howard Taft (whom he had endorsed for the presidency following his decision not to run for re-election in 1908), Roosevelt had a change of heart and challenged Taft for the Republican nomination. By the time of the convention, Roosevelt suspected that he could not prevail against the dominant faction favoring Taft, so he withdrew his nomination. Rallying the progressives from within and outside the Republican Party, Roosevelt then formed a third party, the Progressive "Bull Moose" Party.

By 1912, Roosevelt had whipped himself into a lather that increasingly favored policies advocated by the Socialist Party of America's candidate for President Eugene V. Debs.[175] Doing so placed him to the effective left of the Democratic Party's standard-bearer, the Progressive Woodrow Wilson. To bolster his prospects for presidential election, Roosevelt aimed to cause members of the Socialist Party of America to shift their allegiance to his Progressive Party. He even wore a red bandana indicative of the communist red flag favored by the socialists. He made that bandana his campaign's symbol. As University of Virginia Professor of Politics Sidney M. Milkis explains:

Invoking the red flag of socialism, Roosevelt chose the crimson bandana handkerchief as the symbol of his campaign, thus hoping to signal to potential Debs supporters that the Progressives represented an alternative form of radicalism . . . The Progressive Party platform, especially the plank on "Social and Industrial Justice," endorsed many of the objectives championed by the Socialist Party . . . As Fred Warren, the managing editor of *Appeal to Reason,* wrote Debs after the Progressive Party convention, "My prediction that Roosevelt would steal our platform bodily has been fulfilled."[176]

Roosevelt had become a lightning rod for Progressive causes, favoring federal government intervention across a wide range of matters from wage and hour limits to a broad social security platform including federal retirement payments, socialized medicine, and unemployment compensation. He favored a strong executive who would be "empowered to regulate social and economic conditions in the public interest,"[177] acting through an administrative state excused from constitutional restrictions on power. As he explained during his heralded European tour immediately preceding his decision to run for President in 1912, the United States must abandon its commitment to "unalienable rights" and, instead, act against owners of corporations in favor of the public. He explained his animus against propertied interests in his autobiography:

The men who first applied the extreme Democratic theory in American life were, like Jefferson, ultra-individualists, for at that time what was demanded by our people was the largest liberty for the individual. During the century that had elapsed since Jefferson became President the need had been exactly reversed. There had been in our country a riot of individualistic materialism, under which complete freedom for the individual—that ancient license which President Wilson a century after the term was excusable has called the

"New" Freedom—turned out in practice to mean perfect freedom for the strong to wrong the weak. The total absence of governmental control had led to a portentous growth in the financial and industrial world both of natural individuals and of artificial individuals—that is, corporations. In no other country in the world had such enormous fortunes been gained. In no other country in the world was such power held by the men who had gained these fortunes; and these men almost always worked through, and by means of, the giant corporations which they controlled. The power of the mighty industrial overlords of the country had increased with giant strides, while the methods of controlling them, or checking abuses by them, on the part of the people, through the Government, remained archaic and therefore practically impotent.[178]

Roosevelt's 1912 "New Nationalism" campaign called for the President to serve "as the steward of the public welfare." He wanted to employ executive power to intervene in all aspects of American life, wherever he perceived something remiss. Quoting Roosevelt, Sidney M. Milkis explains:

The time had come, Roosevelt argued, for a "policy of a far more active governmental interference with social and economic conditions in this country than we have yet had." Calling for reforms such as the enactment of graduated income and inheritance taxes, Roosevelt argued that a national state had to be formed that could push back against jealous advocates of property rights. "The man who wrongly holds that every human right is secondary to his profit must now give way to the advocate of human welfare, who rightly maintains that every man holds his property subject to the general right of the community to regulate its use to whatever degree the public welfare may require it."[179]

He also proposed to create a popular veto power to overrule Supreme Court interpretations of the Constitution, thus defeating the Constitution's independent federal judiciary, constricting the courts' power to check constitutional excesses of the popularly elected branches. On February 21, 1912, Roosevelt told an assembly gathered at the Ohio Constitutional Convention in Columbus:

> If any considerable number of people feel that the [Supreme Court's] decision is in defiance of justice, they should be given the right by petition to bring before the people at some subsequent election, special or otherwise, as might be decided, and after opportunity for debate has been allowed, the question whether or not judges' interpretation of the Constitution is to be sustained. If it is sustained, well and good. If not, then the popular verdict is to be accepted as final; the decision is to be allowed to be reversed, and the construction of the Constitution definitely decided; subject only to action by the Supreme Court of the United States.[180]

The radical agenda endorsed by Roosevelt did not gain enough popular support to return him to the White House. Wilson won an Electoral College landslide with the votes breaking down as follows: Wilson, Democrat (435 electoral votes; 6,293,454 popular votes); Roosevelt, Progressive (88 electoral votes; 4,119,207 popular votes); Taft, Republican (8 electoral votes; 3,483,922 popular votes); and Debs, Socialist (0 electoral votes; 901,551 popular votes).[181] Debs' showing, fully 6% of the voting populace, revealed that the nation had become far more accepting of socialism, a degree of popularity that would not be surpassed until the presidential candidacy of Democratic Socialist Bernie Sanders in 2019.

WOODROW WILSON AND THE DOCTRINE OF NO CONSTITUTIONAL LIMITS

After attending the University of Virginia's "law department" and practicing law for a short time, future president of the United States and leading Progressive Woodrow Wilson gained admission to Johns Hopkins

University and graduated with a Ph.D. in political science in 1886. His graduate program of study followed the teachings of the German school taught by economist Richard T. Ely (who was a socialist predisposed against private property rights) and historian Herbert Baxter Adams. As Wilson biographer Ronald J. Pestritto explains:

> Wilson's teachers at Hopkins were all educated in Germany and in the tradition of German state theory and philosophy of history. The professors who seem to have influenced Wilson most were Richard T. Ely and Herbert Baxter Adams. Ely and Adams had both been hired in 1881, four years after the university's opening, as the university's first full-time professors of social science. Both Ely and Adams had studied at the University of Heidelberg and received their doctorates there in the 1870s, and both studied under Johann K. Bluntschli. Bluntschli was a prominent Hegelian state theorist . . .[182]

In the 1880s and 1890s, Wilson variously taught political economy and jurisprudence, public administration, English law, international law, and constitutional law as a professor at Bryn Mawr College, Wesleyan University, and Princeton. In his academic writings, Wilson rejected classical liberal thinking and constitutional limits on power, believing they blocked reforms needed to meet the challenges of the Industrial Age. Wilson was a Hegelian. As his biographer Ronald J. Pestritto records, Wilson adopted a historicism "most directly attributable to Hegel."[183] Indeed, "[a]ll of the criticisms of social compact theory, abstract liberty, and the checking of government through the separation of powers are employed, in precisely the same terms [as Hegel] by Wilson in [his book] *The State*, as well as other works."[184]

In line with Hegel (and indeed in line with slavery apologists in the antebellum South), Wilson rejected the embodiment of natural rights theory contained in the preamble to the Declaration of Independence. Of the Declaration, Wilson wrote:

> No doubt a great deal of nonsense has been talked about the
> inalienable rights of the individual, and a great deal that was
> mere vague sentiment and pleasing speculation has been put
> forward as fundamental principle. . . . Such theories are never
> "law" . . . Only that is "law" which can be executed, and the
> abstract rights of man are singularly difficult to execute.[185]

Wilson insisted that "[i]f you want to understand the real Declaration of Independence, do not repeat the preface." In other words, exclude the preamble wherein the unalienable, God-given rights of man are referenced, and the fundamental duty of government to protect those rights, is explained. Shorn of its Lockean preamble, the Declaration is a historical document lacking eternal principles. It is a recital of abuses by the Crown and its ministers, of ignored entreaties from the colonies to end the abuses, and of a declaration of colonial independence without the timeless philosophy supporting the move for independence. Wilson rejected those principles as fictive, abstract, and unrealistic.

Wilson rejected as a falsehood John Locke's "social compact" theory of government, supplied, *inter alia*, in Sections 88 and 89 of Locke's *Second Treatise on Government*, stating that the compact never actually existed in history (to which Locke may well have agreed, it being his hypothetical construct or theory in logic for the creation of good government, not his recitation of historical fact) and was not indicative of the true origin of societal organization, which Wilson said was the patriarchal family unit, not the individual. Under Locke's compact theory, man is endowed at birth by God with unalienable rights to life, liberty, and property and exists in a pre-political state of nature, which state has a natural law of its own wherein no man may rightfully deprive another of life, liberty, or property, without suffering the other's exercise of the right of self-defense. To relieve themselves of the need to resort to that self-defense, individuals consensually agreed to relinquish the right to punish others for rights' transgressions in exchange for the government protecting all rights of the governed. The right to self-defense was retained, only the right to adjudicate and punish rights' transgressions was conveyed to the state. So long as government honored its obligation to protect the rights of the governed, it could govern, but if it did not protect those rights (as indeed the American revolutionaries contended the Crown did not), it would become the right of the people to alter or abolish the government and erect a new one consistent with the original social compact.

In *The State; Elements of Historical and Practical Politics*, Wilson wrote that the social compact theory "has no historical foundation." Rather, Wilson argued that "the family was the original . . . basis of primitive society" with "the individual count[ing] for nothing; society—the family, the tribe, count[ing] for everything." He insisted, "individuals that were drawn together to constitute the earliest communities were not individual men, as Locke and Locke's co-theorists would lead us to believe, but individual families; and the organization of these families, whether singly or in groups, furnished the ideas in which political society took its root."[186] Of course, Wilson had no proof of the historical "fact" of his family unit foundation of original government, as opposed to it arising from individual family members forming such organization. Nor did he provide any explanation for why families even if the well-spring of government, rather than individuals, ought logically lead to the conclusion that individuals have no rights, yet he reached precisely that epistemologically unsound conclusion. Untethered from Locke's social compact theory, the Constitution forms no barrier to the creation of a state at odds with its literal text. As Ronald J. Pestritto explains, if the federal government is, as Wilson posited, merely a reflection of the current historical spirit, then the Constitution does not control and is irrelevant. Pestritto writes, "as Hegel suggests that the current state is always just because it is what has been brought about by history, so too Wilson argues that the state is grounded in historical development, and not in human choice, or contract."[187]

Wilson understood the institution of slavery, as did Hegel. For Wilson, abolition of slavery did not bring about a change in the historical facts he regarded as evident: the superiority of the white race to the black. Wilson viewed the enslavement of blacks in America in the same way Hegel viewed slavery: as beneficial for whites and blacks, enabling whites to progress and enabling blacks to associate with a superior white race and thereby improve their station. Wilson's racism is entirely Hegelian. He detested post-Civil War reconstruction policy because it placed an "inferior [black] race" in government positions over a "superior [white]" one, thereby upsetting the Hegelian dialectic order of history and disserving both white advancement and black acclimation to the higher refinements of whites.[188]

Rather, like Hegel, Wilson believed in an evolution of government reflective of the relative power wielded by one race over another in inevitable historic struggles. Like Hegel, Wilson viewed the conquest of an "inferior race" by a "superior" one indicative of an unfolding historical dialectic, the outcome of which was the very source of progress. Pestritto writes:

> For Wilson . . . [p]rogress in history is based upon the advance of certain races. Individuals advance as part of particular races, peoples, or civilizations. In *The State,* Wilson explained that certain races had been 'progressive,' and that all governments must have had their historical foundations in the beginnings of these 'progressive races.' He traced the roots of modern government to the development of these races in particular: Aryan, Semitic, and Turanian . . . Wilson perceived "the historical superiority of some races over others."[189]

Wilson's Hegelian racism expressed itself in the following logic: that but for black enslavement white advancement would be lessened and black adaptations to superior white refinements would be impossible. History is replete with evidence that refutes the Hegelian view. That evidence comes from plantation slavery in the United States, revealing the system failed uniformly to advance the economic status of whites and confounded slave owner controls through sophisticated, multi-faceted acts of resistance. The evidence reveals that the enslaved were oftentimes purposefully less efficient and productive than those who labored for pay in the North and advanced rapidly once freed from bondage, as in the case of abolitionist orator, author and human rights advocate Frederick Douglass, who escaped slavery. That stands to reason as one deprived of freedom and compelled to work solely for the benefit of another must invariably endeavor to reduce the burdens of that work by doing less of it and has no incentive to increase profit for the slaveowner because no part of that profit is directly returned to the slave. Several historians have documented a sophisticated, widespread resistance by slaves to their captivity, involving repeated instances of destruction of farm equipment, work slowdowns, feigned illnesses, acts of sabotage, formation of highway marauding parties, coordination with abolitionists to escape to freedom, and hundreds of slave revolts.[190] Keeping the slave in subjugation taxed productivity and was costly and burdensome for most slaveowners. The South advanced much more slowly than the North; concerning efficiency and productivity, levels of both were far higher in the North.

Consistent with Hegelian philosophy, Wilson conceived of man not as an individual but as part of a community, writing, "[m]an was merged in society."[191] The collective is thus given rights denied the individual. Yet, while criticizing Locke's social compact theory for lacking a historical basis, Wilson likewise lacked any proof of man giving up his individuality to "merge" with society. Moreover, outside the experience of war or direct intra-familial aid, he had no proof that individuals voluntarily sublimated their individual wants and needs on a consistent basis to satisfy those of the collective. Ironically, while condemning the "social compact" as fictive, he cleaved to another fiction as the basis for administrative government: that on all questions of governance there is a clearly identifiable "view of society" ascertainable to experts uniquely equipped to translate that view into regulation. In fact, beyond broad generalizations of public opinion, "experts" cannot identify a majoritarian consensus on most of the granular aspects of regulation. While invariably said to be in the "public interest," regulation is never dependent on a popular vote and is commonly reflective of the private interests of the unelected bureaucrats with authority to promulgate legislative rules without suffering any popular check on the exercise of their discretion.

Having a blind faith in "expert" regulation of private enterprise, Wilson did not believe in individual liberty nor think the state ought to defend individual rights. Rather, Wilson understood "liberty" not to be an individual's freedom from state action but instead to be a community's obedience to state action. He believed the law "the external organism of human freedom" because, for Wilson as for Hegel, the "manifestation of the free will of the people" is the law, so obedience to it "is the fulfillment of true freedom."[192] On this fiction, Wilson understood there to be collective rights, but no individual rights and no rights of the minority against the majority. In Wilson's revision of the American republic, the majority rules, and there is no legal protection for dissent. Minorities are, by Hegelian definition, on the losing side of history; were they not, they would be the majority. As such, they can have no rights because the exercise of such rights retards human progress, which is the bailiwick of the majority. Wilson wrote: "The bayonets of a minority cannot long successfully seek out the persistent disobediences of the majority."[193] Rather, majorities would, of historic necessity, rule whether morally right or wrong. This too is the view of Oliver Wendell Holmes, Jr.

Wilson believed there to be no limit to state power. "Government does not stop with the protection of life, liberty, and property," he wrote. "[I]t goes on to serve every convenience of society."[194] Pestritto writes of Wilson: "[T]he most important consequence of his conception of government as the mere extension of society's organic will is that it makes no sense to place formal limits on the power of the state."[195] Wilson understood that the Founding Fathers viewed government as a necessary evil (necessary in the sense that it was required to provide defense against wrongful deprivation of life, liberty, and property and evil in the sense that it invariably would abuse power to achieve the self-interested, corrupt ends of governors, requiring eternal public vigilance to cabin that power). Wilson rejected the Founders' premise; instead viewing government as a necessary good, as a wholesome and beneficent *socialism*. He wrote:

> It by no means follows . . . that because the state may unwisely interfere in the life of the individual, it must be pronounced in itself and by nature a necessary evil. It is no more an evil than is society itself. It is the organic body of society: without it society would be hardly more than a mere abstraction. If the name had not been restricted to a single, narrow, extreme, and radically mistaken class of thinkers, we ought all to

regard ourselves and to act as *socialists,* that is, believers in the wholesomeness and beneficence of the body politic.[196]

Pestritto draws from Wilson's diary a more direct statement of the future President's detestation of America's limited, individual rights-centric republic. Wilson's July 4, 1876 diary entry reads: "How much happier [America] would be now if she had England's form of government instead of the miserable delusion of a republic. A republic too founded upon the notion of abstract liberty!"[197] In other words, Wilson yearned from his youngest years for a parliamentary monarchy without a written constitution, without a system of checks and balances, and without a bill of rights. In short, he wanted government without limits.

We may aptly describe Wilson as a socialist because he very clearly favored a degree of government regulation over all private enterprise, and he thoroughly subscribed to the Hegelian view that man's most noble pursuit was to be a supple instrument of the state, unbound by any tether to his own self-interest and dedicated to furtherance of the state's objectives. Wilson wrote: "Every means, therefore, by which society may be perfected through the instrumentality of government, every means by which individual rights can be fitly adjusted and harmonized with public duties, by which individual self-development may be made at once to serve and to supplement social development, ought certainly to be diligently sought, and, when found, sedulously fostered . . ."[198]

To describe Wilson as a socialist is not to engage in editorial license. Wilson openly admitted his fondness for socialism, albeit he harbored disdain for some socialist tactics. He fundamentally believed socialists right when they insisted, as did Hegel, that man's highest pursuit and achievement lay in serving the dictates of state masters. Wrote Wilson:

> It is possible . . . to understand and even in a measure to sympathize with the enthusiasm of those special classes whom we have dubbed with the too great name of 'Socialists.' The schemes of social reform and regeneration which they support with so much ardor, however mistaken they may be,

have the right end in view: they seek to bring the individual with his special interests, personal to himself, into complete harmony with society with its general interests, common to all. Their method is always some sort of cooperation, meant to perfect mutual helpfulness. They speak [to] a revolt from selfish, misguided individualism; and certainly modern individualism has much about it that is hateful, too hateful to last.[199]

Wilson's theory of democracy was closely analogous to socialism.[200] In Wilson's essay "Socialism and Democracy," he explains:

In fundamental theory socialism and democracy are almost if not quite one and the same. They both rest at bottom upon the absolute right of the community to determine its own destiny and that of its members. Limits of wisdom and convenience to the public control there may be: limits of principle there are, upon strict analysis, none.[201]

Wilson advocated government by regulatory agency as an alternative to government by United States Constitution, viewing the latter as too anachronistic to address modern problems. He rejected all power limiting doctrines that stood in the way of the administrative state, thus condemning the Constitution's separation of powers and non-delegation doctrines.[202] The "commission form" popular among individual Progressive states had much that Wilson admired. "Its merit lies in the concentration of powers in the hands of a few men whom it is easier to hold responsible than was formerly the case when authority was divided and parceled out among many," he wrote.[203]

For Wilson, the Constitution was a rusty anchor that had to be cut loose to permit the ship of state to move forward. To ensure outcomes he desired without need for convincing the people's representatives in Congress, or the people themselves, Wilson advocated giving new meaning to the Constitution, neutering its power limiting provisions. He rejected the notion that the Constitution should be understood to mean what it was intended by the Founders. Rather, consistent with Hegelian philosophy, he believed the Constitution needed to be interpreted flexibly to address the unique social and economic conditions that concerned him in the ways he thought fit. Wilson wanted government to regulate the market extensively, to eliminate what he called "unfair competition,"[204] a term that suffers from inherent definitional incoherence and subjectivity. It is a truism that market transactions of every kind may be deemed unfair by some metric; thus regulation of "unfair competition" invites unbridled official discretion over all market transactions. In short, whatever Wilson or those regulators he empowered thought unfair in the market would invite the label "unfair competition."

In addition to redirecting markets through federal regulatory coercion, Wilson meant to use government as a force not so much to eliminate concentrations of wealth as to coopt them into government service, compelling them to be agents of the state. He wrote:

> All combinations which necessarily create monopoly, which necessarily put and keep indispensable means of industrial or social development in the hands of a few, and those few, not the few selected by society itself, but the few selected by arbitrary fortune, must be under either the direct or the indirect control of society. To society alone can the power of dominating by combination belong. It cannot suffer any of its members to enjoy such a power for their own private gain independently of its own strict regulation or oversight.[205]

To arrest the other aspects of industry that more broadly irritated him, Wilson favored an overbearing regulatory presence in the market. He explained that there were two options available to the state, either to allow private ownership and management of enterprise under government regulation or have government own all enterprise. Wilson thought, "[g]overnment regulation may in most cases suffice," but he did not rule out the prospect of direct government ownership. Rather, "such are the difficulties in the way of establishing and maintaining careful business management on the part of government, that control ought to be preferred to direct administration in as many cases as possible—in every case in which control without administration can be made effectual."[206] So, Wilson conceived of direct government ownership of private enterprise when he found regulation insufficient to achieve government ends.

To reconfigure government to intervene in the market beyond assuring the free flow of interstate commerce pursuant to Article I, Section 8, Clause 3 of the Constitution, Wilson needed to eliminate its legal barriers to state action. He preferred reinterpreting the Constitution to amending it, ignoring the requirements of the amendments clause in Article V. As Wilson biographer Pestritto explains it, Wilson eschewed "a fixed view of the U.S. Constitution's meaning and instead suggest[ed] that the Constitution must mean what the times require of it"[207] and "constantly referred to government as something that is living and must adapt and grow in accord with the progress of history."[208] Consequently, Wilson rejected the power-limiting doctrines of the Constitution, such as the Founders' concept of unalienable, God-given rights, which defined a private sphere protected against state action.

Consistent with his insistence that neither the Constitution nor individual right stand in the way of efficient reform, Wilson urged Congress to drop its demand for legislating solutions to socio-economic problems and, instead, delegate legislative, executive, and judicial powers to federal bureaus and agencies, thus uncoupling the elected representatives of the people from the exclusive Article I power to make the law and the federal judiciary from the exclusive Article III power to adjudge the law, while simultaneously expanding the President's Article II powers beyond those prescribed in the Constitution (by placing these law-making and adjudicatory bureaus and agencies under the executive branch). This was a tectonic shift because it created an administrative state outside of the Constitution's three branches by defeating three constitutional bulwarks: the separation of powers doctrine; the non-delegation doctrine; and the independence of the judiciary. It also laid the foundation for a deprivation of individual rights guaranteed by the Bill of Rights, including the Fifth Amendment right to due process of law within an Article III court and the Sixth and Seventh Amendment rights to trial by jury in criminal and civil cases, respectively. Access to the courts would be restricted or eliminated in favor of administrative adjudication in which the lawmaker, prosecutor, and judge would be one and the same: the agency itself. Access to a jury trial would be eliminated entirely along with access to the courts.[209] Several Founders, including James Madison, Thomas Jefferson, Alexander Hamilton, and George Washington defined this colocation of legislative, executive, and judicial powers in single hands as the very definition of tyranny because there could be no impartial justice when the party that prosecuted the accused also judged the accused.

A friend of the Interstate Commerce Commission, the first major federal regulatory commission, created in 1887 during the administration of Grover Cleveland, President Woodrow Wilson signed several pieces of legislation to ensure greater federal regulatory control over the marketplace. In 1913, he signed the Federal Reserve Act, creating a national central banking system. Under the Act, a Federal Reserve Board was created to oversee monetary policy. Among its powers, the Board could adjust the discount and federal funds rates and could order the purchase and sale of United States treasuries. The Act established regional federal reserve banks, of which there were twelve, empowered to print money and manage the money supply under the direction of the Federal Reserve Board. All nationally chartered banks were required to become members of the Federal Reserve System, and a new uniform United States currency was established, Federal Reserve Notes, denominated in United States dollars.

In 1914, Wilson signed into law the Clayton Antitrust Act. The Clayton Act expanded the government's power to regulate restraints of trade. While the Sherman Antitrust Act of 1890 operated after the fact, making it illegal to monopolize, cartelize, and form trusts to restrain trade, the Clayton Act operated before market concentration took place, enabling the Federal Trade Commission and the Department of Justice upon required notice of planned mergers to disapprove and disallow them. In addition, the Clayton Act prohibited: price discrimination between purchasers that substantially lessened competition or tended to create a monopoly; exclusive sales agreements that prohibited a buyer or lessee from engaging in transactions with the buyer or lessee's competitors; tying agreements whereby a buyer would agree to purchase a second kind of product from a seller on the condition that the seller engage in acts or practices that lessened competition; and multiple directorships in two or more companies when a merger of the companies would violate the anti-trust laws.

In 1914, Wilson signed into law the Federal Trade Commission Act, establishing a federal governmental agency with broad authority to prohibit unfair methods of competition and unfair acts and practices that affect commerce. Louis D. Brandeis was instrumental in drafting the Federal Trade Commission Act, seeking to compel reformation of industry to favor competitive smallness.[210] The Act gave the Commission broad authority to define unfair and deceptive acts and practices in commerce and to seek monetary redress for conduct deemed injurious to consumers. The Act gave the Commission extremely broad powers to conduct investigations "relating to the organization, business, practices, and management of entities engaged in commerce." The Commission was empowered to prosecute companies that violate the anti-trust laws, the Sherman and Clayton Acts.

Until 1917, American socialists were largely dismayed at the extent and pace of Wilson's pursuit of means to intervene into and regulate the market, as reflected in this quote from an editorial by the socialist Walter Lippmann in Croly's *New Republic* of March 1917, a month before the United States entered the war: "The United States trundles along without nationalized railroads or shipping, its mineral resources unsocialized, its water power exploited, its fundamental industries whipped into competition, its food distribution a muddle, its educational system starved, its labor half organized, badly organized, and unrecognized in the structure of society."[211] American socialists took heart when Congress declared war, and Wilson did not disappoint them when he used that opportunity to draw from Progressive and Socialist circles zealots to create new government projects. Several agencies designed to support the war effort continued long after the war came to an end. Daniel T. Rodgers explains:

> In the United States, the social progressives were brought
> en masse into government and quasi-government service.
> The army's need for experts on hygiene, morale, and welfare

absorbed many of them. Others were recruited as labor relations experts, mediators, industrial welfare specialists, or labor standards constructors. Much of the National Consumers League staff was drafted to oversee the treatment of the new wartime women workers. Hull House's Grace Abbott directed the War Labor Policies Board's enforcement of the wartime child labor code. Josephine Goldmark served on the Council of National Defense as an expert on fatigue; her sister Pauline Goldmark was tapped to be manager of the Railroad Administration's special section for women workers. Florence Kelley herself sat on the War Department's Board of Control of Labor Standards. The Russell Sage Foundation's Mary Van Kleeck became head of the Labor Department's Women in Industry division. Henry Seager signed on as secretary to the Shipbuilding Labor Adjustment Board. Lee Frankel and the U.S. Children's Bureau's Julia Lathrop joined forces in drafting the government's war-risk insurance act—a voluntary federal soldiers' and sailors' life and disability insurance program, designed in deliberate contrast to the Civil War pension system and widely heralded as a breakthrough for the principle of social insurance.[212]

After the first world war, Progressive and Socialist academics and politicians, like the socialist educator John Dewey, the socialist sociologist and historian W.E.B. Du Bois, Progressive politician Robert La Follette, communist labor leader Sidney Hillman, and advocate of government-planned economies Rexford Tugwell, among others, became infatuated with the Russian Revolution and made a beeline to Moscow in large numbers. Following their visits, they wrote glowing appraisals of Russian communism, ignoring its mass genocide, selective and brutal executions of political opponents, religious intolerance, labor camps, and absence of free speech and marveling instead at its party discipline, planned economies, and unified public voice, albeit variously conceding that Russia was in a primitive stage of communist development. Daniel T. Rodgers explains:

No one looking for the cutting edge of change in 1920s Europe could ignore the new Soviet experiment. Lillian Wald, John Dewey, W.E.B. DuBois, Robert La Follette, Sidney Hillman, Rexford Tugwell, Paul Douglas, and Lincoln Steffens all visited the Soviet Union in the 1920s. By 1926 the American Russian Institute [listed by U.S. Attorney General Thomas C. Clark as a communist front group in 1947] was in the business of promoting Russian-American exchanges, with Wald and Dewey among its honorary vice presidents . . . Reports from the Soviet Union were the hottest items of international social reportage in the 1920s; they crowded out some of the space prewar Germany and Britain had occupied in American progressives' minds.[213]

Amity Shlaes writes of the travelers' response to this first trip to the Soviet Union in 1923. She explains that Lincoln Steffens gushed upon his return, writing, "I have been over to the future and it works" and "I would like to spend the evening of my life watching the morning of a new world."[214] Lillian Wald likewise was effusive in her praise, heralding "the vast promise of the Soviet government and the strength and wisdom and social passion of Lenin."[215] As Shlaes explains, most of the travelers on this 1923 trip harbored grave doubts about the American republic, writing "[t]heir progressivism went beyond the progressivism of, say, Theodore Roosevelt, . . . for they believed specifically that ideas should be collected abroad and then used at home to improve the country." One of the academics who believed fundamentally in government-planned economies along the Soviet model was Rexford Guy Tugwell. In 1915, as the Russian Revolution began to emerge, Tugwell wrote a low quality poem for a student publication, the *Intercollegiate,* reflecting his dislike of America. He wrote: "I am sick of a nation's stenches, I am sick of propertied czars . . . I have dreamed my great dream of their passing . . . I shall roll up my sleeves—make America over!"[216]

The first heralded trip to the Bolshevik's Soviet Union by these prominent American figures was followed by another, on the steamship *President Roosevelt* in 1927. Shlaes writes of that trip which, like the first, brought

Progressives, socialists, communists, and labor leaders to the Soviet Union, this time under Joseph Stalin's communist dictatorship, where again the leftist travelers became enthralled with the "wonders" of communism. Those on the second trip included, among others, Rexford Guy Tugwell (again), Tugwell's fellow academic John Bartlet Brebner, Certified Public Accountant and consumer activist Stuart Chase, Columbia law student Carlos Israels, Seamen's Union attorney Silas Axtell, the aging socialist labor leader James Hudson Maurer, editor of the *Brotherhood of Locomotive Engineers Journal* Albert Coyle, labor scholar Paul Douglas (again), educator George Counts, government finance expert Alzada Comstock, labor researcher and American Civil Liberties Union staffer Robert Dunn, and peace activist and ACLU founder Roger Baldwin.[217] As Shlaes recounts, Stalin's henchmen strictly controlled the agenda and kept from the travelers view the many scenes of communist oppression, sharing with them staged events depicting happy factory workers, happy farm laborers, as well as uniformed, well-groomed communist youth pre-programmed to answer questions to awe the American spectators. From this experience, the left leaning travelers returned to the United States with compliments galore for the Soviet experiment. "The travelers' positive reports validated the admiring view presented nearly daily in the *New York Times* by the paper's Walter Duranty," notes Shlaes.[218] So enthralled with communism did James Hudson Maurer become that he ran on the Socialist Party's ticket for Vice President.[219] Douglas, too, did his part, endorsing Socialist candidates for elective office.[220]

Socialism had little currency among the American people, particularly during the economic boom of the 1920s. Republican Presidents maintained control with Warren G. Harding succeeding Woodrow Wilson in 1920 but dying in 1923 of apparent heart failure during a cross-country tour. Harding's Vice President, Calvin Coolidge, a strong advocate of limited government and free enterprise, filled Harding's remaining term through 1924 and was elected directly thereafter, serving from 1925 through 1929. Herbert Hoover succeeded him, holding office from 1929 through 1933. The stock market crash on Black Tuesday, October 29, 1929, presaged the major global economic downturn known as the Great Depression and brought an end to Republican control of the executive branch for almost two decades, from 1933 to 1952. That economic downturn, the worst to that point in American history, caused Hoover to be vilified and enabled the Democratic Governor of New York, Franklin Delano Roosevelt, to win the November 8, 1932 presidential election and remain in office for four consecutive terms until 1945. He died in office on April 12, 1945.

HERBERT HOOVER AND THE TEMPTATIONS OF POWER

Herbert Hoover is often portrayed as a laissez-faire capitalist. He was not. He did more to involve government in the take-over and regulation of private enterprise than any prior president. He believed in the administrative state and government power as a counterweight to private enterprise, and he had no hesitation in using government power to alter private practices he questioned. In that sense, he was in his heart of hearts a Progressive. During his four years in office, federal spending rose by over 48%, and as unemployment levels mounted, he turned repeatedly to the machinery of government for solutions, not reducing regulation but expanding it, not eliminating taxation but raising it substantially, and not eliminating barriers to free trade but erecting the highest and most extensive barriers to trade in American history.

On October 22, 1928, in his presidential acceptance speech, Herbert Hoover confidently proclaimed: "We are nearer today to the ideal of the abolition of poverty and fear from the lives of men and women than ever before in any land." Within seven months of that March 4, 1929 start of Hoover's presidency, the economic boom of the Roaring Twenties, celebrated by the decidedly laissez-faire President Calvin Coolidge, went bust with the great stock market crash of October 24, 1929. Mass poverty, unemployment and fear arose in its wake. The crash signaled the start of the Great Depression and doomed Hoover's presidency, but not because he refused to rely heavily on government programs. Indeed, it was Hoover, as Rexford Tugwell would later concede, who effectively adopted his own "New Deal" to combat the crash. It, like Roosevelt's larger, more comprehensive version, failed miserably.

The Federal Reserve created in the Wilson Administration proved itself an enemy of liquidity precisely at a time when banks needed funds to avoid panic, businesses needed funds to stem their losses, and consumers needed loans. The Fed raised interest rates from 3.5% to 6% in a single year from 1928 to 1929. That dramatic rise in rates "contributed to the October 1929 stock market crash, the race by consumers to get their money out of their banks, and the closing of many banks."[221]

Hoover's reflexive turn to government in a crisis is deeply revealing of Hoover's true predilections, confirming that he was no reliable friend of laissez-faire capitalism but was in close alignment with the Progressives. Rather than dramatically reduce government regulation, federal taxation, and tariff barriers to help alleviate the crisis, Hoover did the opposite, increasing government regulation, increasing federal taxation, and increasing tariff barriers, all of which exacerbated, rather than lessened, the Great Depression. Given Hoover's public service history before entering the White House, it is unsurprising that he would place faith in government to engineer a solution and not in the private sector to reverse the crash through private direction of capital.

Hoover believed a well-made government plan would assure positive results. He became a federal government Mr. Fixit, beginning with his public service in the Wilson administration. He continually brought industry leaders together to impart his plans for solving their problems, providing pathways to direct and smooth industry's journey. Among the many interventions Hoover made to fix the workings of the market are the following recorded by Hoover biographer Kenneth Whyte:

> [Hoover] became [the Harding and, thereafter, the Coolidge] administration's point man for distinctly modern problems. When the millions of automobiles spit out from Detroit's production line at a rate of one every ten seconds produced a disturbing increase in highway carnage, Hoover stepped forward with a plan to coordinate national traffic safety standards. When a nascent airline industry suffered from a lack of public confidence in the safety of air travel. . . Hoover asserted a broad federal authority to improve navigation systems and runways, inspect planes, and license pilots. His

Aeronautics Branch would produce dependable commercial aviation by the end of the decade and evolve over time into the Federal Aviation Administration (FAA).

* * * *

As many as one-third of Americans lived in crowded and ill-equipped rental properties. Hoover worked with the American Institute of Architects to produce plans for standardized houses made of standardized building materials with the aim of reducing the cost of building by a third . . . Hoover also succeeded in promoting improved mortgage terms for consumers. He produced model zoning ordinances and municipal building codes to support best practices among developers and local administrators, literally shaping the houses and neighborhoods that generations of twentieth-century Americans would dream about and live in.[222]

In *Freedom, Technology, and the First Amendment*, I explained that Secretary of Commerce Herbert Hoover played an instrumental role in helping the radio industry enter private agreements to avoid signal interference between 1922 and 1925. He did this through annual radio conferences at which broadcasters would negotiate operating parameters to avoid interference, achieving signal protection through private agreement. Of this period, Secretary of Commerce Hoover remarked, "We have not only developed, in the conferences, traffic systems by which a vastly increasing number of messages are kept upon the air without destroying each other, but we have done much to establish the ethics of public service and the response of public confidence." Hoover was very much concerned with the "ethics" of radio. He was an early advocate for public ownership of what was, at the time, a thriving private enterprise. He was deeply concerned that "low brow" music and entertainment kept cropping up on radio channels, offending his ears. He wanted government to ferret out of radio through content controls Jazz music, a relatively new form popular with youth, including, to Hoover's profound chagrin, his own son.

At the start of the First National Conference on Radio Telephony in February of 1922, Hoover insisted that the field of radio communication was "one of the few instances that I know of in this country where the public—all of the people interested—are unanimously for an extension of regulatory powers on the part of the Government." He professed there to be a "public right over the ether roads" and warned that without federal regulatory control of that "public" resource there would be "regret that we have parted with a great national asset into uncontrolled hands." He then helped lead the charge, working with cooperative radio industry leaders who sought federal regulation to help cartelize the radio business, culling from the field all manner of small broadcasters in favor of the major network broadcasters. Hoover established his credentials as a crony capitalist. He joined with members of Congress who shared his view that the government, not the private sector, ought to own and control the only electronic medium of mass communication then in America.[223]

Failing to garner enough support for passage of a Radio Act to commandeer control of the airwaves, Hoover's congressional allies looked to him for help. Hoover hastened the arrival of a change in circumstances that would beget a popular reaction. In late 1925 and early 1926, Secretary Hoover stopped issuing radio licenses altogether, proclaiming that there were "no more channels." In *United States v. Zenith Radio Corporation*[224], the United States District Court for the Northern District of Illinois held his action unlawful, explaining that under the Radio Act of 1912, the Secretary of Commerce had no power to deny radio licenses. With that decision in hand, and an opinion from the Acting Attorney General William Donovan on the correctness of the Court's decision, Hoover then abandoned the industry conferences and issued licenses to every applicant, predictably precipitating interference wars across the country. That laid the foundation for passage of the Radio Act of 1927, which placed the radio waves in government ownership and established a Federal Radio Commission. The FRC achieved cartelization of what was a highly competitive industry by revoking the licenses of hundreds of independent broadcasters in favor of the major networks and their affiliates.[225]

Hoover's predilections in favor of government came from his decades in public service. Trained as an engineer, he liked to think engineered solutions to problems superior and, so, he was no consistent enemy of government planning, at least not until he lost his re-election bid to Franklin Delano Roosevelt. He thus had no problem serving as a United States Food Administration bureaucrat in Progressive Woodrow Wilson's administration during World War I. Indeed, as Kenneth Whyte records, as Wilson's Food Administrator, Hoover shared Progressives' ideals and supported a "positive role for the state" in directing business and Americans to adhere to his prescriptions for a better life:

> Hoover demonstrated daily his confidence in cooperative action, his belief in a positive role for the state, and his willingness to stamp out predatory business practices. Progressives were [enthralled with] expert administrators promising a more rational, efficient, and scientific approach to government; Hoover was the great engineer, rationalizing an entire sector of the economy and teaching Americans to live more efficiently for their own good.

> Hoover was progressivism incarnate, and he was pleased to carry the movement's banner. He was conscious of leading a noble experiment in social engineering, one that he hoped would outlast the war.[226]

With a sense of confidence buoyed by years of success in public life, Hoover pursued several initiatives following the Great Crash that worsened it, contributing to destruction of business and unemployment. It is thus no wonder that he faced such strong public derision at the end of his term, albeit encouraged by the Democratic Party.

Most notably, on June 17, 1930, Hoover rejected the recommendation of 1,028 economists[227] and signed into law the United States Tariff Act, also known as the Smoot-Hawley Tariff. That law raised to the limit 890 tariff rates, making it too costly for foreign buyers to purchase and import many American goods. The economists warned the President that the bill would cause a loss in domestic manufactures and an increase in unemployment. They also warned him that it would lead to retaliatory tariffs from the affected foreign states. The President professed sympathy with those who urged him to veto the bill, but said he must sign it, reciting that he had promised to raise tariff rates during the presidential campaign. While the tariffs remained in place from 1927 to 1930, U.S. exports dropped catastrophically from $7 billion to $2.4 billion.

While he initiated federal public works projects and encouraged states to do the same, those make work programs failed to stem the tide of unemployment. For example, in July of 1932, Hoover signed into law the Emergency Relief and Construction Act to finance state and local public works projects. He endeavored unsuccessfully to reduce bank closures, which reached some 5,000 by the end of his presidency. He signed into law a bill that created the federal Reconstruction Finance Corporation to provide financing for failing banks and businesses, but it was not enough.

In addition to the devastating economic effects of the Smoot-Hawley Tariff, Hoover signed into law a massive tax increase, the Revenue Act of 1932, which hit the fallen economy hard. Against the golden rule that one ought never raise taxes in an economic contraction, Hoover did just that, believing it all-important to balance the budget. He did not subscribe to the view that government revenues were more likely to rise if taxes were reduced. Instead, he signed into law a bill that raised taxes across the board. The Revenue Act of 1932 raised the corporate tax rate by almost 15%; doubled the estate tax; hiked the top personal tax rate from 25% to 63%; and imposed a new gift tax.

Before the Smoot-Hawley tariff became law, the unemployment rate stood at 3.2% with 1,550,000 unemployed. Following the tariff law's implementation, the unemployment rate jumped from 5.5% to 8.7%, equaling 4,340,000 unemployed. While the Smoot-Hawley tariff is not solely responsible for the losses in businesses and jobs, it certainly made a significant contribution. In another misfortune, agricultural practices that failed to employ crop rotation and dryland farming techniques, along with severe draughts, caused the "Dust Bowl" in 1931, depleting topsoils and leading to extensive crop losses. In 1931, the continuing market contraction combined with the Dust Bowl to yield another major uptick in unemployment with 15.9% unemployed, equaling 8,020,000 people.

The massive Hoover tax hike, however, pushed the economy over the edge. Following enactment of the Revenue Act of 1932, unemployment levels jumped from 15.9% to 23.6% as 12,060,00 were out of work and shanties ("Hoovervilles") appeared in urban areas across the country. During Hoover's few short years in office, unemployment rose from 3% to 24.9%, credit dried up, and banks failed in ever increasing numbers with a total of some 5,000 shuttered by the end of 1933.

Ironically, given what Roosevelt would command the government to spend during his multiple terms, candidate Roosevelt condemned Hoover for extravagant federal spending and for not balancing the federal budget. Roosevelt's running mate, John Nance Garner, said Hoover was "leading the country down the path of socialism" with his attempts to gain control over the market. To be sure, Hoover had revealed his trust in authoritarian alternatives to free markets, but his movement in the direction of government control was anemic compared to Roosevelt's drive to acquire total government control of American enterprise.

FRANKLIN DELANO ROOSEVELT AND LIMITLESS GOVERNMENT

In between the November 8, 1932 presidential election and Franklin Delano Roosevelt's inauguration on March 4, 1933, an event took place that reflected the hopelessness and despair that gripped the nation as the Great Depression reached its apex, a crisis begging the country to choose between far less government and far more free enterprise (an option no candidate, not even the incumbent Herbert Hoover, offered) or far more government and far less free enterprise (an option only the Socialist Party of America candidate Norman M. Thomas offered, but which Roosevelt actually delivered). Indeed, Roosevelt campaigned on a platform of fiscal restraint and a balanced budget, precisely the opposite of what he delivered as president.

Progressives had argued against unregulated capitalism since the antebellum South but those arguments turned into action during the Great Depression with many entering the Roosevelt administration favoring the socialist view that business was inherently evil, that the market had failed, and that government had to assume direct control over the market, determining every detail: supply, price, distribution, wages, hours, and labor relations.

Roosevelt was a peculiar Progressive who harbored capitalist and anti-capitalist sentiments, a confused, even contradictory set of directions suggesting no true ideological core; indeed, he admitted as much. The socialist Frances Perkins, who served as Roosevelt's Labor Secretary, recalled an interaction between Roosevelt and a young reporter:

"Mr. President, are you a communist?"

"'No,' said Roosevelt."

"Are you a capitalist?"

"No."

"Are you a socialist?"

"'No.'"

When the reporter then asked Roosevelt what his philosophy was, Roosevelt replied, "'Philosophy? . . . Philosophy? I am a Christian and a Democrat—that's all.'"[228] A Democrat in the 1930s was a Progressive.

Whatever he wished to call himself, Roosevelt consistently governed like a socialist, allowed many socialists and some communists into his administration, and courted favor with the national socialist Benito Mussolini.[229] He did not abolish the Constitution, other political parties, arrest political opponents *en masse*, or nationalize industry, but he did control production, price, and distribution of all goods and services in America. Indeed, he and *Il Duce* professed mutual admiration for one another and for one another's policies, albeit Mussolini's went farther than Roosevelt's, but not by much.

One look at the platform of the Italian socialists reveals the extraordinary similarities between Italy's national socialism and Roosevelt's New Deal. As Dinesh D'Souza explains, the *Fasci di Combattimento* of 1919 "included . . . mandating an eight hour workday, a massive public works program, worker participation in industrial management, nationalization of defense-related industries, old age and sickness insurance for all citizens, state confiscation of uncultivated land, steeply progressive taxation, an 85 percent tax on war profits, and strong anti-clerical policies including no religion instruction in schools and government appropriation of the property of religious institutions." With the exception of the anti-clerical policies, the National Recovery Administration, the Agricultural Adjustment Administration, and Roosevelt's public works programs, such as the Works Progress Administration, achieved many of these same ends.

New York Times' reporter Anne McCormick, a fan of Italian socialism, who had recently returned from Rome, lauded Roosevelt for his plans proceeding along the lines of Mussolini's national socialism. Referring to congressional passage in Roosevelt's first one hundred days of a massive expansion in executive branch control over all market production, prices, distribution, wages, and labor relations through gargantuan new federal agencies such as the National Recovery Administration and the Agricultural Adjustment Administration, McCormick praised Roosevelt for establishing "a federation of industry, labor and government after the fashion of the corporative State as it exists in Italy."[230] She heralded the new laws because they gave the president "the authority of a dictator."[231] The comparison was not coincidental. Roosevelt and Mussolini carried on correspondence in which they each praised the other for national socialism. In a June 1933 letter to Italian Ambassador Breckinridge Long, Roosevelt wrote, "There seems no question [Mussolini] is really interested in what we are doing and I am much interested and deeply impressed by what he has accomplished and by his evidenced honest purpose in restoring Italy."[232] Mussolini was also a fan of Roosevelt. In a review of Roosevelt's 1933 book, *Forward Looking*, Mussolini found Roosevelt's plans for a new America "reminiscent of Fascism." He was not alone, the primary Nazi newspaper, *Volkischer Beobachter*, praised "Roosevelt's adoption of National Socialist strains of thought in his economic and social polices" and his "development toward an authoritarian state" predicated on "demand that collective good be put before individual self-interest."[233]

Among those whom the President and indeed nearly all Progressives admired was *New Republic* editor Herbert Croly. The magazine lauded

Roosevelt for following Mussolini's example. George Soule, another editor of the publication, wrote of the administration's efforts: "We are trying out the economics of fascism."[234]

So taken was he with Mussolini's national socialism that Roosevelt sent top advisors to Rome to learn lessons from the fascists that might be applied in the United States. Among those who visited the fascist state was Roosevelt advisor and confidante Rexford Guy Tugwell. Tugwell came back renewed in his pre-existing commitment to government-planned economies, writing that fascist Italy "is the cleanest, neatest, most efficient operating piece of social machinery I've ever seen. It makes me envious."[235]

More than anything else, Roosevelt was a consummate progressive politician. He bore a broad smile and spoke in a voice that exuded self-confidence, precisely the kind of calming influence a nation in dire straits needed to receive. His long tenure as President, including four terms, the last ending in his death, spanned an extraordinary twelve years and thirty-nine days. During that time, he tried various interventionist strategies, but they all failed to reduce unemployment. Those strategies were hostile to free enterprise. They benefited large firms, enabling cartelization, and were particularly destructive to small firms, the engine of employment and innovation.

For an instant on February 15, 1933, weeks before his inauguration, Roosevelt had an encounter with an anti-capitalist that might have caused another person of perhaps greater perspicacity to reconsider the prudence of stoking anti-capitalist sentiment, which might tend to excite the violent propensities of anarchists and Marxists, leaving no head of government, not even Roosevelt, unscathed.

The anti-capitalist who approached Roosevelt came from a walk of life entirely unlike the Roosevelts of Hyde Park, a "scion of Hudson Valley landowners descended from pre-Revolutionary Dutch patrons,"[236] and "the stable Knickerbocker society of Edith Wharton."[237] That anti-capitalist was an unemployed Italian immigrant bricklayer. He perceived Roosevelt as an enemy when, in fact, Roosevelt was about to pursue policies that this anti-capitalist might have admired. Roosevelt harbored a progressive's disdain for capitalism, a disdain that would repeatedly reveal itself in the form of New

Deal policies he relentlessly pursued that placed unprecedented restrictions on American business and liberty.

In a twist of fate, the two men, each one ravaged by disease, one crippled and the other in chronic pain, came together in a near collision that could have cost Roosevelt his life. Roosevelt was spared by a wobbly folding chair and a deftly swung handbag.

On February 15, Roosevelt arrived in a yacht at the Miami, Florida pier. William Vincent Astor owned the yacht. He and Roosevelt were close family friends. Astor attended boarding school at St. George's and Harvard University (dropping out before graduating). Roosevelt attended boarding school at Groton, graduated from Harvard College, and attended Columbia Law School (dropping out after he passed the New York bar). The Roosevelt farm at Hyde Park near the Hudson River was only ten miles from the Astor estate at Rhinebeck, New York. The two enjoyed largely the same elite social circles, fraternizing with, among others, the Delanos, the Rockefellers, and the Vanderbilts. Astor was the owner of *Newsweek* magazine and served on the boards of Western Union, Chase Manhattan Bank, and The United States Lines (an American transatlantic shipping company). Astor also owned what was considered the finest private yacht of the era, the *Nourmahal*, a 3,200-ton, 263-foot German built motor ship, which Roosevelt boarded each year of his presidency. It was the *Nourmahal* that housed Roosevelt as he prepared to disembark that February afternoon.

It was seventeen days before Roosevelt's inauguration. Roosevelt had just completed a two-week Caribbean fishing trip on the *Nourmahal*. That evening, he planned to deliver a short speech in Miami's Biscayne Bay Park before returning to New York by private rail car. He also planned to confer with Chicago Mayor Anton Cermak whom he would meet at the park. Cermak asked for a chance to speak with the President-elect about depression relief for his city.

Roosevelt left the pier at nine o'clock escorted by two secret service agents. He was lifted from his wheel chair and placed in the back seat of a chauffeur-driven, open touring car, a light blue Buick. A dozen police motorcycles assembled in two lines of six to drive ahead of the president-elect's car. Three aides followed in a pursuit vehicle. With police sirens blaring, the motorcade sped down Biscayne Boulevard on the way to Biscayne Bay Park. Entering the park at a slow speed, Roosevelt's car came to a stop in an area cordoned off from the crowd and directly in front of a band shell that had been converted into a reviewing stand. There, some one hundred dignitaries stood and applauded the President-elect. A crowd also sat on folding chairs opposite the reviewing stand and came to rise in applause as the President-elect's car approached.

When the car came to a complete stop, Roosevelt, who had been rendered permanently paralyzed from the waist down at age thirty-nine from either polio (most likely) or from Guillain-Barré syndrome, maneuvered himself to the roof adjacent to the back seat, so he could be seen by the crowd. A corded microphone was handed to him. He delivered the following one-minute impromptu remark at approximately 9:35 p.m.:

> Mr. Mayor, my friends of Miami, I am not a stranger here because for a great many years I used to come down here. I haven't been here for seven years, but I am coming back. I have firmly resolved not to make this the last time. I have had a very wonderful rest and we have caught a great many fish. I am not going to attempt to tell you any fish stories and the only fly in the ointment has been that I have put on about 10 pounds. So that among other duties which I shall have to perform when I get North is taking those 10 pounds off. I hope much to come down here next winter and to see all of you and to have another wonderful 10 days or two weeks in Florida waters. Many thanks.[238]

The crowd roared. Roosevelt then signaled for Mayor Cermak to come to the car from the reviewing stand. Cermak moved to the Buick's running board and shook hands with Roosevelt. Cermak spoke with the President-elect for a few minutes and then moved away from the convertible.

Shots rang out. From about twenty feet away in between the fifth and sixth audience rows, the thirty-three-year old anti-capitalist anarchist, Giuseppe "Joe" Zangara, fired one shot and then five more in rapid succession. At 5 feet, one inch, Zangara could not see the President-elect at first, so he stood on a wobbly folding chair and took aim at Roosevelt with his .32 caliber revolver. As he aimed, two spectators standing next to him, Lillian Cross and Tom Armour, noticed the gun and tried to knock it out of Zangara's hand. As Zangara shot, Cross hit his arm either with her purse or with her own arm, deflecting his aim. A policeman standing nearby who heard the shot ran and lept on Zangara, hitting Zangara and knocking two others to the ground, including Mrs. Cross. Several people then piled on. Another policeman with a blackjack beat Zangara repeatedly. As Zangara flailed, he managed to pull the trigger repeatedly and dislodge all remaining rounds, hitting spectators. The President was not struck, but Chicago Mayor Cermak was. The bullet traversed Cermak's right lung, right diaphragm and grazed his liver. It traveled posterior and downward, lodging in Cermak's eleventh thoracic vertebrae.

Upon realizing that the popping sound heard was gunfire and not flash bulbs from journalists' cameras, Roosevelt looked for the source in the direction of Zangara, and his chauffeur slowly began to move the car. Whereupon Chicago Alderman James Bowler, who stood helping Cermak remain standing, said, "Mr. Roosevelt, Mayor Cermak is shot. Wait." Roosevelt then ordered his driver to stop and asked Miami City Manager L. L. Lee and Alderman Bowler to move Cermak into the car. The car then drove to Jackson Memorial Hospital in Miami, with Cermak leaning on Roosevelt's shoulder. They traveled some twenty city blocks to the hospital where Cermak was attended by physicians. After staying with the shooting victims for several hours, Roosevelt left the hospital and returned to the *Nourmahal*. The next day, he visited the shooting victims again in the morning. Thereafter, he returned to New York by private rail car.

Cermak initially appeared to be recovering but took a turn for the worst and died of peritonitis nineteen days after the shooting, on March 6, 1933, just two days after Roosevelt's inauguration. Following Cermak's death, Zangara was charged with first degree murder under the doctrine of transferred intent, pled guilty, was convicted and then sentenced to the electric chair by Miami Circuit Court Judge Uly Thompson. Zangara offered little to explain his actions but did say that he meant to kill capitalists and government leaders. Zangara's death sentence was carried out by electrocution on March 20, 1933 at the Florida State Prison in Raiford, Florida. Ironically, Roosevelt would harm many capitalists during his four terms of office, an occurrence that might have pleased Zangara had he lived to see it.

Elected as 12.8 million remained unemployed (24.75% of the labor force), Franklin Delano Roosevelt assumed tremendous executive powers in his first one hundred days and used those powers to expand the administrative state substantially, creating over sixty-nine federal agencies and bureaus during his first four years and over one hundred by the time of his death in his fourth term, which agencies and bureaus collectively exercised control over all wages, labor, and industry in the United States. The following includes a partial listing of the government agencies and bureaus created during the New Deal, a veritable explosion in the size, scope, and cost of government, exceeding in a decade the combined budgets of the federal government from 1787 to 1933:

Federal Works Agency (FWA)
National Recovery Administration (NRA)
United States Maritime Commission (USMC)
Home Owners Loan Corporation (HOLC)
Agricultural Adjustment Administration (AAA)
Drought Relief Service (DRS)
Subsistence Homesteads Division (DSH)
Civilian Conservation Corps (CCC)
National Youth Administration (NYA)
Social Security Board (SSB)
Board of War Communications (BWC)
Federal Deposit Insurance Corporation (FDIC)
National Labor Relations Board (NLRB)
National Historical Publications Commission (NHPC)
National Mediation Board (NMB)
United States Housing Authority (USHA)
United States Employment Service (USES)
Federal Insurance Corporation (FIC)

Civil Works Administration (CWA)
Resettlement Administration (RA)
Federal Public Housing Authority (FPHA)
Federal Emergency Relief Administration (FERA)
Federal Housing Administration (FHA)
Commodity Credit Corporation (CCC)
Federal Crop Insurance Corporation (FCIC)
Farm Security Administration (FSA)
Soil Conservation Service (SCS)
Agricultural Marketing Administration (AMA)
Federal Real Estate Board (FREB)
Committee on Economic Security (CES)
Works Progress Administration (WPA)
Federal Communications Commission (FCC)
Office of Bituminous Coal Consumer Council (OBCCC)
Railroad Retirement Board (RRB)
Securities and Exchange Commission (SEC)
Tennessee Valley Authority (TVA)
Board of Investigation and Research-Transportation (BIR-T)
Civil Aeronautics Authority (CAA)
National Investors Council (NIC)
Defense Plant Corporation (DPC)
Rubber Reserve Company (RRC)
Metals Reserve Company (MRC)
Defense Supplies Corporation (DSC)
War Damage Corporation (WDC)
Disaster Loan Corporation (DLC)
Federal National Mortgage Association (FNMA)
Regional Agricultural Credit Corporation (RACC)
Combined Food Board (CFB)
United Nations Relief & Rehabilitation Administration (UNRRA)
Commodity Exchange Administration (CEA)
Surplus Marketing Administration (SMA)
Federal Surplus Commodity Corporation (FSCC)

Foreign Funds Control (FFC)
Production Requirements Plan (PRP)
Combined Raw Materials Board (CRMB)
Combined Munitions Board (CMB)
Combined Shipping Adjustment Board (CSAB)
Combined Production and Resources Board (CPRB)
Combined Chiefs of Staff (CCS)
Public Works Administration (PWA)
Administration of Operation Activities (AOA)
Export-Import Bank of Washington (EIBW)
Electric Home and Farm Authority (EHFA)
Council of Personnel Administration (CPA)
Public Roads Administration (PRA)
Emergency Price Control Act (EPCA)
Food Production Administration (FPA)
Office of Economic Stabilization (OES)
Petroleum Administration for War (PAW)
Small War Plants Corporation (SWPC)
Petroleum Industry War Council (PIWC)
National Resources Planning Board (NRPB)
Liaison Office for Personnel Management (LOPM)
Office of Emergency Management (OEM)
Selective Service System (SSS)
National War Labor Board (NWLB)
Office of Civilian Defense (OCD)
Office of Coordinator of Inter-American Affairs (OCIAA)
Office of Defense and Health Welfare Services (ODHWS)
Office of Defense Transportation (ODT)
Office of Lend-Lease Administration (OLLA)
Office of Scientific Research and Development (OSRD)
Office of War Information (OWI)
War Manpower Commission (WMC)
War Production Board (WPB)
War Relocation Authority (WRA)

War Shipping Administration (WSA)
Office of Price Administration (OPA)
Board of Economic Warfare (BEW)
National Housing Authority (NHA)
Farm Credit Administration (FCA)
Farm Security Administration (FSA)
Rural Electrification Administration (REA)
Sugar Agency (SA)
Petroleum Conservation Division (PCD)
Office of Petroleum Coordinator for War (OPCW)
War Emergency Pipe Lines, Inc. (WEPL)
Bituminous Coal Division (BCD)
Puerto Rico Reconstruction Administration (PRRA)
Bonneville Power Administration (BPA)
National Power Policy Committee (NPPC)
Office of Censorship (OC)
Facilities Review Committee (FRC)
President's War Relief Control Board (PWRCB)

The new administrative state was staffed with Progressives, Socialists and even Communists drawn from academia and educated in Hegelian philosophy. Many who would lead the most powerful agencies were recommended to their positions by Harvard Professor Felix Frankfurter. A disproportionate number of those viewed capitalism as having reached its predicted collapse and the nation as in an inevitable transition to socialism. They hoped to see the nation get to socialism under their leadership. The "New Deal" pursued three substantive objectives, to raise taxes, yet again, on the middle and upper classes and redistribute the revenues to achieve social and economic reforms; to reverse the economic downturn by expanding certain industries; and to gain regulatory control over the market. The New Deal succeeded in raising taxes but failed to reverse the economic downturn, which persisted until America's build-up and entry into World War II in 1941. The New Deal did alter fundamentally the relationship between the government and the private sector such that from the New Deal forward the federal government has influenced to a greater or lesser degree almost every important economic decision made by private businesses.

In March of 1933, President Roosevelt set the tone for what was to come. Following in the footsteps of his Progressive predecessors, Theodore Roosevelt and Woodrow Wilson, Franklin Roosevelt explained that he was "unafraid of power" and intended to exercise it vastly in excess of any prior president. "This Nation asks for action, and action now," he said. "I shall ask the Congress for the remaining instrument to meet the crisis—broad Executive power to wage a war against the emergency, as great as the power that would be given to me if we were in fact invaded by a foreign foe . . ."[239] He relied heavily on advice from Hugh S. Johnson, Raymond Moley, Rexford Tugwell, Jerome Frank, and Bernard Baruch. In addition, Roosevelt took regular counsel from Harvard Law Professor Felix Frankfurter and Louis Brandeis. Tugwell, Frankfurter, and Brandeis were highly critical of free markets and believed the Great Depression caused by "unrestrained competition." They meant to tame the markets through an aggressively interventionistic administrative state, one that would remain in place forever, not just during the crisis.

Under the New Deal, America would indeed be largely transformed into a socialist state with wage, price, production, and labor controls set by the federal government on every business in the country. Egged on by his cadre of academics from Columbia University, Professors Rexford Tugwell, Lindsay Rogers, Joseph D. McGoldrick, and James W. Angell, along with influential attorney Adolf Berle (collectively referred to as Roosevelt's "brain trust"[240]), the President set out to impose the government's will on the entire market. On "an amazing scale [Roosevelt] undertook to organize every profession, every trade, every craft under [federal government] supervision and to deal directly with such details as the volume of production, the prices, the means and methods of distribution of every conceivable product."[241] The primary government entity that would direct the entire market was the National Recovery Administration (NRA), a massive new federal regulatory agency created by the National Industrial Recovery Act of 1933. The NRA's national headquarters in Washington, D.C. housed an army of six thousand bureaucrats with thousands more who served as local code authorities.[242]

The NRA became the hallmark of President Roosevelt's first one hundred days. It was "the Roosevelt Administration's chief weapon in the war against the Depression."[243] That Act vested in the President the power to engage in industry wide price-fixing, wage setting, production quotas and working hour limits, fundamentally altering the nature of business in America and bringing it, as never before, under direct federal government control. Roosevelt said it would end "cut throat competition" by imposing industry "codes of fair practices" and "codes of fair competition." The NRA proceeded on an aggressive and hostile anti-free market premise. The NRA "essentially spelled the death knell for the free market in the United States. It empowered the federal government to establish coalitions of labor and management in every industry to set production targets, wages, prices, and even minimum and maximum working hours."[244] Tugwell explained that the NRA aimed "to eliminate the anarchy of the competitive system."

NRA parallels to the Italian corporatist state were many and quite familiar at the time. Writes Dinesh D'Souza: "The NRA was widely recognized across the political spectrum at the time as a fascist project. The progressive writer Roger Shaw, writing in *North American Review*, stated the NRA was 'plainly an American adaptation of the Italian corporate state.' The Marxist writer Victor F. Calverton seconded this in *Modern Monthly*, noting, "'The NRA is doing part of the job that European fascism has set out to accomplish.'" When he heard of the NRA, Mussolini was impressed, purportedly declaring of Roosevelt: "Ecco un ditatore!" ("Behold a dictator!").[245]

The NRA was initially directed by General Hugh Johnson whose enormous staff, largely composed of young college graduates of universities with a Hegelian curriculum, proposed codes to govern industries with which they had no meaningful familiarity. Academic youth with little real world experience, these new code creators and enforcers frequently had little, if any, comprehension of the likely effect the codes would have. They generally favored the direction desired by industry leaders, thus supporting cartelization. Industry leaders would set the codes to yield anti-competitive results in their favor, causing many to complain that the codes created industry monopolies that drove smaller firms out. The proposed codes would be reviewed and approved by Johnson for the President's ultimate approval, whereupon the set prices, wages, and working hours would immediately go into effect without the passage of any legislation. Any transgressor could be fined or prosecuted, or both.

Under the NRA, Roosevelt replicated the Mussolini model. Roosevelt admired Mussolini, as did Rexford Tugwell and several other members of the Roosevelt Administration and of Congress.[246] Mussolini had organized every trade, industrial group and profession into an entity he called a "corporative" which operated under state supervision, responding to state plans which set "production, quality, prices, distribution, labor standards" and other details ordinarily determined by free enterprise. Long since his two trips to Moscow and since his more recent trip to Rome, Assistant Secretary of Agriculture Tugwell prized the examples of government planning he saw in the communist and fascist states. Indeed, he was obsessed with implementing government-planned economies, i.e., socialism, as a permanent replacement for American free enterprise. He strongly supported Roosevelt's move to build a planned economy through the NRA. Roosevelt, Tugwell, and Johnson meant for the change to a planned economy under NRA direction to last in perpetuity, long past the time when the Great Depression was over.

The head of the NRA, General Johnson, was a retired Army general with a bad drinking habit and a foul mouth. Johnson loved fascism; even mention of the word "Mussolini" delighted him. He called it a "shining name." With religious intensity, Johnson kept with him an English translation of an Italian propaganda pamphlet lionizing national socialism entitled, *The Structure of the Corporate State*. Johnson's NRA produced a pamphlet of its own entitled *Capitalism and Labor Under Fascism*, which explained that "fascist principles are very similar to those which have been evolving in America."[247] Johnson worked feverishly to put in place the NRA regulatory behemoth and then coerce and cajole American business to enter into "voluntary" agreements authorizing the NRA to control prices, wages, production, distribution, and labor relations, sporting the NRA's "Blue Eagle" symbol in a prominent entry to each business that so complied. Johnson and the bureaucrats working with him set up local NRA Code Authorities to inspect code compliance and enforce the codes. The hired "authorities" oftentimes relied on intimidation and violence to cow business people into compliance.

An early supporter of Roosevelt who later became a chief critic, John T. Flynn records an example of the NRA code authority at work in the Chicago garment district, then controlled by labor leader Sidney Hillman of the Amalgamated Clothing Workers of America, a strong backer of Roosevelt and founder of the socialist Congress of Industrial Organizations:

> Only the most violent police methods could procure enforcement. In Sidney Hillman's garment district the code authority employed enforcement police. They roamed through the garment district like storm troopers. They could enter a man's factory, send him out, line up his employees, subject them to minute interrogation, and take over his books on the instant. Night work was forbidden. Flying squadrons of these private coat-and-suit police went through the district at night, battering down doors with axes looking for men who were committing the crime of sewing together a pair of pants at night.[248]

The strong-armed tactics of the NRA caused objecting parties to sue in federal court, challenging the constitutionality of the regime. As New Deal supporter Ernest Lindley put it, "NRA was an administrative failure and it evoked a wide range of unfavorable public reactions,"[249] and yet it was the heart and soul of the New Deal in Roosevelt's first term.

Few were courageous enough to oppose the NRA codes despite tremendous pressure placed upon them, including boycotts advocated by Johnson. Indeed, Burton Fulsom, Jr. records that Johnson used "the arm of the law to jail many men who refused to jeopardize their businesses by complying with NRA codes."[250] One such opponent was Henry Ford, owner of the Ford Motor Company. Ford refused to agree to implement the NRA codes despite direct and substantial pressure from Johnson and Roosevelt, and despite virtually every other automobile industry titan signing on in response to Johnson's demands.

Unhappy with Ford's insistence on free enterprise, Johnson and Roosevelt cut Ford off from all government contracts and signed those contracts with Ford's competitors. Johnson called on the public to boycott Ford automobiles, and he ceased traveling in his Lincoln. Those actions did not work, so Johnson upped the ante, threatening that he would shut down the Ford plant. Ford still refused to budge and called Johnson's bluff. Restrained by the President, Johnson did not make good on his threats. Despite repeated entreaties, even from the President himself, Ford remained resolute that his company would remain free from government constraints. His opposition was not because he sought to employ workers at a low wage or for excessive hours. He maintained rates and hours equal to those required under the industry code. The public largely favored Ford's position and courage. Johnson's demand that the public boycott Ford backfired with Ford selling more automobiles than before the code fight. Roosevelt eventually backed down and allowed Ford to be the only auto manufacturer in the country to escape the NRA codes.[251]

Johnson and his agents met with leaders in every industry in the country to fix wages and prices and production quotas. The effect was ordinarily to set prices that made competition difficult, if not impossible, to the injury of small firms and the benefit of large firms, cartelizing industries. The fixed prices greatly enhanced the market power of larger firms and threatened the survival of smaller firms. The cartelization suited the Administration, whose members, Johnson and Tugwell particularly, believed that combinations in restraint of trade brought about by the codes would ultimately redound to the benefit of labor with better working conditions. Ironically, Teddy Roosevelt's campaign to break up the trusts, a campaign endorsed by Brandeis, was turned on its head by his cousin Franklin, who now embraced direct cartelization. That change also offended Brandeis, now a Justice on the Supreme Court, who would reveal his wrath during the court battles over the constitutionality of the New Deal agencies.

The brutish tactics and extensive market controls that drove under many small firms ultimately led even President Roosevelt to express regrets. His Labor Secretary, the avowed socialist Frances Perkins, recorded Roosevelt as having said of the NRA, "You know the whole thing has been a mess. It has been an awful headache. Some of the things they have done are pretty wrong."[252] The disaster that was the NRA ultimately met its match at the Supreme Court.

In a first major test of the NIRA, representatives of the petroleum industry, Panama Refining Company and American Petroleum Corporation, among others, challenged the constitutionality of the NIRA's Section 9(c), permitting the Roosevelt Administration to prohibit trade in petroleum goods in violation of state quotas, so-called "hot oil." Secretary of the Interior A. D. Ryan implemented an August 19, 1933 presidential executive order establishing a "Code of Fair Competition for the Petroleum Industry." Under the Petroleum Code, federal agents descended unannounced on the facilities of those accused of exceeding state quotas and gauged their petroleum tanks and dug up their pipelines. In response, the plaintiffs in *Panama Refining Company v. Ryan*[253] sued to invalidate Section 9(c). Among other grounds, the plaintiffs argued that Section 9(c) constituted an unconstitutional delegation of legislative power to the executive. In an 8–1 decision, authored by Chief Justice Charles Evans Hughes, the Court held the Roosevelt Administration's prohibition on interstate and foreign trade in petroleum goods that exceeded state quotas to be unconstitutional in violation of the non-delegation doctrine. Justice Benjamin Cardozo of the liberal wing of the party dissented. The Court took umbrage at the legislative grant of unbridled discretion to the executive in stemming the production of "hot oil," holding NIRA Section 9(c) invalid.

The *Panama Refining Company v. Ryan* decision reinforced the view held by several key advisors to the President that every effort should be made by the administration to avoid court prosecution of NIRA violators until an ample record of administrative prosecution had been established. They thought this approach more in line with the legal thinking of Justice Louis D. Brandeis, lowering the risk of a precipitous High Court decision ruling the NIRA unconstitutional. Felix Frankfurter, Thomas Corcoran (formerly an attorney in the Solicitor General's office but presently an aide to President Roosevelt) who studied law at Harvard under Frankfurter, Solicitor General Stanley Reed, and others within the Administration, urged NRA Administrator Hugh Johnson and the NRA legal office to avoid prosecuting code breakers in federal court because they feared the Supreme

Court might strike down the NIRA. They believed the law to have been drafted in haste and to be on shaky ground, particularly due to its transfer of legislative power over making the codes to the executive branch in violation of the non-delegation doctrine, whereby the Constitution vests Congress with the exclusive power to make law. They also questioned whether the Commerce Clause permitted the law to be applied to what were wholly intrastate sellers. They thus predicted that if the NIRA were rapidly brought before the High Court, it would not survive constitutional muster. If lost solely on Commerce Clause grounds, the law could remain applicable in those instances where there was interstate trade, but if struck for violation of the non-delegation doctrine, the entire law would be invalidated. They hoped Congress would revamp the statute and correct its deficiencies before it reached the Court.[254]

The zealous enforcement efforts of a young talented Justice Department lawyer, Walter L. Rice, dashed their plans for delay, however. That prosecution delighted attorneys Donald Richberg and Blackwell Smith of the NRA legal office. They disagreed with Frankfurter and Corcoran and thought a "sick chicken" case a good factual premise, likely to induce widespread public support for the prosecution and persuade the Justices of the need to keep the NIRA in place. To the chagrin of the Frankfurter faction, the Richberg faction reached Roosevelt first; he was then vacationing, and the President okayed an appeal to the High Court.

Walter L. Rice was known and feared by New York City's poultry industry because he had successfully prosecuted members of the industry for racketeering. Rice brought a Live Poultry Code violation case in the United States District Court for the Eastern District of New York against the owners of a slaughterhouse in Brooklyn, the Schechter family. He won a nineteen-count conviction against them in 1934.[255] The year following, Judge Martin Thomas Manton writing for the United States Court of Appeals for the Second Circuit struck down the Schechters' conviction on the two counts related to their alleged violation of the wage and hour provisions of the Live Poultry Code, but upheld the Schechters' conviction on the seventeen remaining counts, including those for the alleged sale of a chicken "unfit for human consumption;" the alleged failure to abide by a peculiar code provision requiring "straight killing" (defined by the Supreme Court in *A.L.A. Schechter Poultry Corp. v. U.S.* as "the practice of requiring persons purchasing poultry for resale to accept the run of any half coop, coop, or coops, as purchased by slaughterhouse operators, except for culls."); and the alleged concealment of the law violations.[256] In the chicken slaughter trade, "culls" were removals of chickens unfit for human consumption. Under the code, culls were to be performed in advance of the sale by the slaughterhouse operators and not by customers preferentially making selections.

Joseph Schechter ran Schechter Live Poultry Market and his sons Martin, Alex, and Aaron ran A.L.A. Schechter Company. Both businesses were small family owned slaughterhouses that sold chickens in Brooklyn's kosher markets to retail poultry dealers and butchers.[257] Before antibiotics, chickens remained at risk of contracting tuberculosis and becoming vectors for the transmission of the disease to humans. The Schechters hired Shochtim (persons trained to perform "shechita," the kosher slaughtering and food preparation of animals). The Schechters were inspected numerous times until they finally ordered the inspectors to leave. They were thereafter charged with and convicted of violating the Live Poultry Code, which Roosevelt signed on April 13, 1934. The Code bore the formal title: "Code of Fair Competition for the Live Poultry Industry of the Metropolitan Area in and about the City of New York." It was the law in the five boroughs of New York City; in Rockland, Westchester, Nassau, and Suffolk Counties, New York; Hudson and Bergen Counties, New Jersey; and Fairfield County, Connecticut. The Schechters were Roosevelt supporters,[258] but they and other small slaughterhouse operators in the city found it difficult to abide by the Live Poultry Code. Among its many provisions, the code required that employees not work more than forty hours per week; be paid not less than fifty cents per hour; not be under sixteen years of age; and be allowed to join a union and engage in collective bargaining. The code also set the minimum number of employees required for business and the specific contents of required records of account and filings with the code authorities in proof of compliance.

Controversy presently surrounds whether kosher customs of Kashruth required the Schechters to allow buyers to reject individual birds those buyers questioned under the Jewish religious dietary laws. Amity Shlaes believes the operative rabbinical customs did in fact call for Jewish customers to be given the right to make their own culls, and she suggests as much in her book, *The Forgotten Man*,[259] and in her defenses of the book.[260] Justice Neil Gorsuch, whose dissent calling for a revivification of the non-delegation doctrine in *Gundy v. United States*[261] cited in passing Shlaes' *Forgotten Man* reference, likewise takes the view that those customs were implicated, writing "Kosher butchers such as the Schechters had a hard time following" the Live Poultry Code. Harvard Law Professor Mark Tushnet and Michigan Law Professor Richard Primus are among academics who challenge the Shlaes and Gorsuch interpretation. Regardless, the rule plainly interfered with customer choice, thus diminishing prospects for sale in those instances where customers who did not agree with the adequacy of culling were forced either to buy half or whole coops of chickens they did not want or forego a purchase. The imposition of the rule thus likely increased distrust between buyers and sellers and may also have interfered with Shochtim practices.

A unanimous Supreme Court held the centerpiece of the New Deal, the NIRA, unconstitutional in *A.L.A. Schechter Poultry Corp. v. United States*[262]. Chief Justice Charles Evans Hughes wrote the opinion for the Court, which also included the four conservative justices labeled by the press, "The Four Horseman" (Willis Van Devanter, Pierce Butler, James Clark McReynolds, and George Sutherland), the three liberal justices labeled by the press, "The Three Musketeers" (Louis Brandeis, Benjamin Cardozo, and Harlan Stone); and Owen Roberts. Justices Cardozo and Stone wrote concurring opinions. The press's "Four Horsemen" nickname for the conservative justices played on the "four horsemen" of the scriptures, mentioned in New Testament Revelations and the Old Testament Books of Zechariah and Ezekiel, as an apparent reference to pestilence, war, famine, and death.

Counsel for the Schechters argued that the Live Poultry Code was an unconstitutional delegation by Congress of legislative power to the President; an unconstitutional regulation of intrastate transactions outside the authority of Congress; and a violation of due process under the Fifth Amendment. The Court reached two of the three arguments, holding the code a violation of both the non-delegation doctrine (forbidding Congress from delegating the legislative function to the executive branch) and the Commerce Clause (requiring that transactions affect interstate commerce to be regulated by act of Congress).

Section 3 of the NIRA authorized the President to approve "codes of fair competition." The Live Poultry Code was approved by Roosevelt through an executive order dated April 13, 1934. The NIRA did not define "fair competition," leaving the definition of it wholly within the President's discretion. The bulk of the counts against the Schechters concerned an alleged violation of the trade practice provision of the Live Poultry Code, which forbade "straight killing." The term is a misnomer because it concerned what was a sales requirement. As Chief Justice Hughes related, under it persons "purchasing poultry for resale" were required "to accept the run of any half coop, coop, or coops, as purchased by slaughterhouse operators, except for culls." The Schechters were alleged to have sold "selections of individual chickens taken from particular coops and half coops," which violated the "straight killing" practice requirement. They were also alleged to have sold to a butcher one "unfit chicken," a code violation, thus begetting the popular name of the case, the "sick chicken case." They were charged with three counts of making sales without having poultry inspected and approved by New York City authorities and of making sales to unlicensed slaughterers or dealers. They were charged with two additional counts of making false reports or failing to make report on the range of daily prices and volume of sales for certain periods.

The government argued that the extraordinary circumstance of the Great Depression justified Congress's NIRA delegations to the executive, inviting a judicially created "emergency" exception to the Constitution. Chief Justice Hughes rejected that justification, writing "[e]xtraordinary conditions do not create or enlarge constitutional power." Rather, "[t]hose who act under [the Constitution] are not at liberty to transcend the imposed limits because they believe that more or different power is necessary. Such assertions," he wrote, "were anticipated and precluded by the explicit terms of the Tenth Amendment."

The Court understood the codes of fair competition to be laws indistinguishable from Congressional enactments because "they placed all persons within their reach under the obligation of positive law, binding equally those who assent and those who do not . . ." Violators were being punished as criminals.

It was not enough for Congress to declare a need for codes to be fleshed out at the whim of the executive. As laws, the codes were themselves within the province of the legislature and could not be delegated for substantive creation to the executive. Rather, the power to create laws is squarely vested in Congress by Article I, Section 1 of the Constitution, the Court held. "Congress is not permitted to abdicate or to transfer to others the essential legislative functions with which it is thus vested," wrote Hughes.

The constitutional violation consisted in the fact that Congress had not "itself established the standards of legal obligation." Rather, it had transferred that essential legislative function to the President. "Fair competition," wrote Hughes, was "used as a convenient designation for whatever set of laws the formulators of a code for a particular trade or industry may propose and the President may approve . . . or the President may himself prescribe . . ." The President's discretion to craft each code was entirely unfettered by the statute, Hughes wrote. There was in the language of the statute not even an attempt to suggest the delegation was less than complete. "Congress cannot delegate legislative power to the President to exercise an unfettered discretion to make whatever laws he thinks may be needed or advisable," stressed Hughes. "We think that code-making authority thus conferred is an unconstitutional delegation of legislative power," Hughes concluded.

The law, as applied to the Schechter companies, fared no better under the Commerce Clause. The government argued that the Schechters affected interstate commerce because the chickens they acquired included those bred and raised outside of New York. But the functions that comprised the Schechters' actual trade did not directly affect interstate commerce, they were wholly performed in Brooklyn, the Court explained. "Neither the slaughtering nor the sales by defendants were transactions in interstate commerce," Hughes wrote. Consequently, the Court "was of the opinion that the attempt through the provisions of the code to fix the hours and wages of employees of defendants in their intrastate business was not a valid exercise of federal power." Having invalidated the NIRA under the non-delegation doctrine and the Commerce Clause, the Court saw no need to address the Fifth Amendment due process argument.

The Supreme Court issued three momentous decisions on May 27, 1935 (what the media called "Black Monday") with the author of each decision reading it, saving the biggest bombshell, *Schechter*, for last. As the justices read the decisions from the bench, it became apparent that the Court was intent on clawing back Roosevelt's executive overreach across the board. Marian C. Mckenna writes: "There had been doubts as to the advisability of dealing such 'jolts' to FDR all at once, but Justice Brandeis, considered by some to be an unofficial representative of the New Deal on the Court, said he saw no reason to postpone any decisions 'on that account.'"

The first decision to issue that day was *Humphrey's Executor v. U.S.* read by Justice Sutherland. In the Federal Trade Commission Act, the law prohibited removal of an FTC commissioner except for "inefficiency, neglect of duty or malfeasance in office." When Roosevelt entered office, he asked Commissioner William E. Humphrey to resign so he could replace him with a person committed to New Deal policies. As the decision records, "on August 31, 1933, [President Roosevelt] wrote the commissioner expressing the hope that the resignation would be forthcoming and saying: 'You will, I know, realize that I do not feel that your mind and my mind go along together on either the policies or the administering of the Federal Trade Commission, and, frankly, I think it is best for the people of this country that I should have a full confidence.'" Following a consult with allies, Humphrey refused to go. On October 7, 1933, the President wrote to him again: "Effective as of this date you are hereby removed from the office of Commissioner of the Federal Trade Commission."

Humphrey then filed suit. In an opinion written by Justice Sutherland, the Court distinguished executive departments from independent regulatory agencies, recognizing that while the President had plenary power to fire subordinates in the executive department, he did not have that same power vis-à-vis an independent regulatory agency, like the FTC. Justice Sutherland wrote: "The authority of Congress, in creating quasi-legislative or quasi-judicial agencies, to require them to act in discharge of their duties independently of executive control cannot well be doubted; and that authority includes, as an appropriate incident, power to fix the period during which they shall continue in office, and to forbid their removal except for cause in the meantime. For it is quite evident that one who holds his office only during the pleasure of another, cannot be depended upon to maintain an attitude of independence against the latter's will." Yet again, Roosevelt was humbled; his power was circumscribed.

The second decision to issue that day was *Louisville Joint Stock Land Bank v. Radford* read by Justice Brandeis. The case assessed the constitutionality of the Frazier-Lemke Farm Mortgage Act of 1934. Under the Act, farms foreclosed upon could be reacquired by the farmers who formerly owned them and farms in foreclosure could be forced out of foreclosure by an automatic suspension of the proceedings. The federal government financed the acquisition of the farm mortgages and farmers were permitted to rent their old farms from the federal government under lenient terms. Writing for the Court, Justice Brandeis held the law to violate the Takings Clause of the Fifth Amendment because the mortgages had been taken from the foreclosing parties without according them just compensation from the federal government. Brandeis concluded: "[T]he Fifth Amendment commands that, however great the Nation's need, private property shall not be thus taken even for a wholly public use without just compensation. If the public interest requires, and permits, the taking of property of individual mortgagees in order to relieve the necessities of individual mortgagors, resort must be had to proceedings by eminent domain; so that, through taxation, the burden of the relief afforded in the public interest may be borne by the public."

The third decision read that day was *Schechter*. Following it, the one member of the liberal wing of the Court, whom Roosevelt referred to affectionately as "Old Isaiah," made clear his dissatisfaction with the authoritarian direction of the New Deal. He met administration attorneys Thomas Corcoran and Benjamin Cohen in the robing room following the reading of *Schechter*. Marian C. McKenna records what transpired:

> [T]he seventy-eight-year-old Brandeis, visibly agitated, sent this oral message: "This is the end of this business

of centralization, and I want you to go back and tell the President that we're not going to let this government centralize everything. It's come to an end." Gasping for breath, he said: "The President has been living in a fool's paradise." The three decisions handed down by a unanimous Court, he added, meant that everything the administration had been doing must be changed. Redrafting of existing and pending legislation would be necessary. Brandeis wanted the message relayed to New Deal lawyers: "As for your young men, you call them together and tell them to get out of Washington—tell them to go home, back to the states. That is where they must do their work."[263]

Although a result that did not surprise Frankfurter, Corcoran, or Reed, *Schechter* did send shock waves through General Johnson and the attorneys in the NRA legal office. At once it became apparent that the holding against legislative delegation compelled either a major rewrite of the NIRA or its demise. If any code continued to be enforced, suits would fill the judiciary to invalidate them. The National Recovery Administration's days were not numbered, they were over, unless Congress acted to create a new NIRA; but the revisions would have to reduce substantially the power and control of the NRA.

Although furious at the Court's actions, which he took as a personal affront, Roosevelt reconciled himself to the eventual demise of the NRA. It failed to achieve its purpose of revitalizing the economy and returning the unemployed to gainful employment. Although Congress redrafted the law and extended it for six months, the NIRA as amended expired on April 1, 1936, and neither the President nor a majority in Congress attempted to extend it. The centerpiece of Roosevelt's first one hundred days in office, professed to represent a permanent change in the relationship between the government and the private sector and to enable government to control every aspect of American enterprise, was no more.

The Agricultural Adjustment Administration (AAA) was the second great New Deal behemoth of economic planning. Like the NRA, the AAA became a place of employment for those who believed fundamentally in government control of the private sector, including communists. "[T]he AAA did hire a number of true leftists," writes Amity Shlaes, "including people who later turned out to be Communists, or spies, such as Alger Hiss."[264]

The Agricultural Adjustment Act bill was produced in haste, the product of rancorous disagreements between the authors, a divisive group that included Secretary of Agriculture Henry A. Wallace (who favored federal purchase and storage of agricultural produce in years of agricultural abundance and federal sales of the stored surpluses in years of agricultural scarcity, what he termed the "ever normal granary" plan); Assistant Secretary of Agriculture Rexford Guy Tugwell (a lover of planned economies favored his "domestic allotment plan" with direct government control of agricultural production, land use, and prices along with human resettlements); the prospective Administrator of the Agricultural Adjustment Administration, George Peek (who opposed Tugwell's planned economies, preferring the dumping of crop surpluses on foreign markets and subsidies to farmers); Peek's personal attorney Frederick Lee; agricultural economist Mordecai Ezekial; NRA Administrator Hugh Johnson; and General Counsel of the Department of Agriculture Jerome Frank.

The overall aim of the bill was to raise farm prices but the bill's provisions were schizophrenic with certain ones inviting the Secretary to dole out enormous subsidies, which would encourage production, while others invited the Secretary to limit production. The Peek and Tugwell proposals conflicted and were hotly debated by their respective factions within the Department of Agriculture. Under Peek's "two-price" approach, crop surpluses would be "dumped" on foreign markets at below-market rates with the government paying farmers the difference between the sale price and the market price from a tax levied on agricultural processors.[265] Under Tugwell's "domestic allotment plan," farmers would be limited to strict quotas that would force a reduction in their output to trigger a general rise in prices. The government would subsidize or give benefits to farmers for taking land out of production or reducing their food animal populations, which subsidies or benefits would be paid from a tax levied on agricultural processors.[266]

A very persistent lobbyist, Peek succeeded in getting the ear of President Roosevelt before Tugwell. Tugwell assumed Roosevelt would perceive the merits of his plan over Peek's. Irons writes: "To his dismay, the politically naïve Tugwell soon learned an unpleasant political lesson. . . . Tugwell discovered that George Peek had reached Roosevelt's ear. . . . Peek's plan to allow processors freedom to fix prices and escape the antitrust laws . . . 'made a good deal of sense,'" Roosevelt told Tugwell.[267] The final bill did not include a selection of the Peek over the Tugwell plan but authorized either or both in the discretion of the Secretary of Agriculture.[268] Roosevelt was confident that Secretary Wallace would choose the best plan in each particular instance.

Inside the Department of Agriculture, the bill's hastily written and conflicting provisions gave legal counsel grave concerns. Department of Agriculture General Counsel Jerome Frank found the rushed law to contain language so ambiguous in parts as to provide no clear direction. As McKenna records, when a perplexed Frank questioned his sixty-member AAA legal staff to help him understand what the sections of the AAA meant, "he found that 'nobody could make head or tail of it. It was just absurdly incomprehensible.'"[269]

The bill included a provision giving the Secretary of Agriculture virtually unlimited power to "provide for reduction in the acreage or reduction in the production for market, or both, of any basic agricultural commodity, through agreements with producers . . . and to provide for rental or benefit payments" that were "fair and reasonable." The bill gave the Secretary taxing power to draw from processors fees equal to the difference between market prices and sale prices of agricultural products. The bill forced the federal licensure of all farmers and those in the agricultural trade on penalty of a $1,000 fine for any in business that operated without a license.[270]

The AAA gave the government discretionary power over the disposition of agricultural land and products in place of farmers' free choice. The AAA placed under federal control such basic decisions as those affecting the leasing and cultivation of farmlands and the harvesting, storage, disposition, and price of crops and feed animals. In other words, under the AAA farming in America became a business totally dominated by the federal government, largely at the unfettered discretion of Secretary of Agriculture Henry Wallace.

Jim Powell explains that the AAA "disbursed the proceeds [of the tax on processors] to farmers who followed government 'guidelines' to reduce their cultivated acreage of wheat, cotton, corn, hogs, rice, tobacco, and milk. The agriculture secretary was authorized to make 'marketing agreements' restricting the output of food processors."[271] In addition, federal banks were authorized 'to issue bonds that would help refinance farm mortgages.'"[272] The bill was signed by the President on May 12, 1933, one day before a nationwide farm general strike was scheduled to take place.

The bill arrived too late to stem the overproduction crisis driving down farm prices in 1933, so Secretary of Agriculture Henry Wallace took matters into his own hands, acting before the effective date of the bill's provisions. He ordered an army of county agents throughout the South to contact cotton farmers and direct them to plow under their fields.[273] Powell writes: "Agriculture Department officials signed up about a million cotton farmers, and they were paid $100 million to plow under some 10 million acres of farmland."[274] That move drove cotton prices higher and immediately led to a rash of substitutes as consumers opted for less expensive alternatives, predictably causing long-term damage to cotton markets, thus backfiring. Another unilateral move by Secretary Wallace to stem supply triggered outrage and even horror.[275] Wallace had government agents pay hog farmers "to slaughter some 6 million baby pigs." Wallace also had his agents pay tobacco farmers to plow under "12,000 acres of tobacco;" owners of California orchards were paid not to harvest their peaches but to let them rot in the fields.[276]

John T. Flynn reported on the flurry of bureaucratic activity set in motion by Wallace's rapid moves to reduce agricultural products in what was a uniformly unsuccessful attempt to rescue farmers in need:

> In the Agricultural Department a vast bureau was set up with a wilderness of check-writing machines and, amidst thundering mechanical noises, was pouring out a flood of checks to farmers in return for killing their stock, plowing

back crops and burning grain in their fields. The hotels and boarding houses of Washington were crowded with the delegations from the farms, from villages and cities, from counties and chambers of commerce and boards of trade and colleges and trade organizations, all standing in long lines with their hats in their hands for the easy money that gushed from the Federal Treasury at the touch of the President.[277]

The forced removal of lands and livestock from production together with the payment of federal funds for those actions benefited a minority of large-scale farming operations but harmed the majority of poor farmers and sharecroppers, whose poverty defined the agricultural problem. "Reduced farm acreage devastated the poorest farmers, who were sharecroppers," writes Powell. "The 1930 census reported there were about a million and a half sharecroppers—671 blacks and 937,000 whites. Their estimated annual cash income fell from $735 in 1929 to $216 in 1933." Moreover, the processing tax Wallace levied to obtain revenue for subsidies also harmed those with the least resources, as Secretary Wallace conceded: "[T]he most serious objection to the processing tax," he said, was "that the greatest burden falls on the poorer people."[278]

Once implemented in full, the AAA's effect was catastrophic, variously making a minority of large farming concerns extremely wealthy while driving all others into even greater poverty and bankruptcy. John T. Flynn writes: "The AAA produced all sorts of dislocations in our economic system. For instance, we had men burning oats when we were importing oats from abroad on a huge scale, killing pigs while increasing our imports of lard, cutting corn production and importing 30 million bushels of corn from abroad."[279] The amount of money pumped out through subsidies was astronomical in 1930's dollars, some $700,000,000, yet poverty remained rampant in farming communities nationwide.[280] While poor farmers became even more impoverished, large producers fared well; for example, "one big sugar corporation" received "over $1,000,000 not to produce sugar."[281]

When the AAA reached the Court in the case of *United States v. Butler*[282], *Schechter Poultry Corp.* had already been decided. Unlike *Schechter*, the 6–3

Butler majority did not invalidate the act as an unconstitutional delegation of legislative power to the executive but as an unconstitutional exercise of Congress's taxing power in Article I, Section 8 of the Constitution, focusing on the agricultural processors' tax.

Justice Owen Roberts wrote the majority opinion, which was delivered on January 6, 1936. He explained that the regulation and control of agricultural production was beyond the delegated powers of the federal government and invaded the reserved power of the states. Moreover, he reasoned that the AAA used economic coercion against farmers: "[I]t is a scheme for purchasing with federal funds submission to federal legislation of a subject reserved to the states," he wrote. He explained that a national emergency did not relieve the federal government of its obligations to abide by the Constitution.

The government defended the AAA by arguing, in part, that the Section 8 taxing provision of Article I should be read broadly such that any form of taxation in furtherance of the "general welfare" would be allowed. Justice Roberts rejected the argument. He explained that an expansive reading of general welfare would defeat the limited government intended by the framers and would cause the United States to move from a dual federalist system into one amalgamated central government, exercising police power superseding all local control over local concerns.

In *Butler*, the Hoosac Mills Corporation had been presented with a claim for processing and flour taxes that it refused to pay, arguing the tax was unconstitutional. While the United States District Court upheld the tax, the United States Court of Appeals reversed. The Supreme Court agreed with the Circuit Court. Justice Roberts explained that the Article I, Section 8 taxing provision was meant to raise revenue for the general government, not to redistribute resources in the market by taking from, here, processors and redistributing those funds to farmers. "It is inaccurate and misleading to speak of the exaction from processors prescribed by the challenged act as a tax," he wrote. "A tax as used in the Constitution signifies an exaction for the support of the government. The word has never been thought to connote the expropriation of money from one group for the benefit of another."

Congress based the Act not on the commerce clause but on the taxing power, yet the Court reasoned that regardless it exceeded congressional power because it invaded the province of the states, intrastate agriculture. "The act invades the reserved rights of the states," wrote Roberts. "It is a statutory plan to regulate and control agricultural production, a matter beyond the powers delegated to the federal government. The tax, the appropriation of the funds raised, and the direction for their disbursement, are but parts of the plan. They are but means to an unconstitutional end," he wrote. The Constitution prescribes a government of limited powers with all others reserved to the states and people by the Tenth Amendment. There was no constitutional power granted to the federal government for regulation of agricultural production and, so, "legislation by Congress for that purpose is forbidden." While Congress was free to impose taxes to "carry into operation another power also expressly granted" the federal government, Congress could not tax to raise revenue to carry into operation a power not granted by the Constitution. In short, the AAA created "a scheme for purchasing with federal funds submission to federal regulation of a subject reserved to the states," thus rendering the Act unconstitutional.

In the aftermath of *Schechter*, the Supreme Court continued to invalidate various pieces of New Deal legislation. In the case of *Carter v. Carter Coal Company*[283], a bare majority of the Court held the Bituminous Coal Conservation Act (which replaced the unconstitutional NRA coal codes) unconstitutional under the commerce clause. Like the NIRA, the Bituminous Coal Conservation Act established comprehensive federal government control over the wages and hours of coal miners, the price of coal, the quantity of coal produced, and the distribution of coal and used taxation to coerce compliance through "voluntary agreements."

The first named plaintiff in the case before the Supreme Court was a shareholder in Carter Coal Company who sued the company seeking to obtain an injunction blocking Carter Coal from complying with the Act. Carter filed suit in the Superior Court of the District of Columbia on August 31, 1935, one day after the Bituminous Coal Conservation Act took effect. The Superior Court held the labor provisions of the Act and the coal code itself unconstitutional but upheld the price-fixing and taxing provisions of the Act. Carter appealed to the United States Court of Appeals for the DC Circuit but sought issuance of a writ of certiorari from the Supreme Court before the Circuit Court hearing, which writ was granted.

Justice George Sutherland delivered the opinion for the Court, which addressed four coal case appeals of which the Carter case was one. The primary constitutional challenge hinged on the Commerce Clause, which was the stated constitutional basis for the Act. Although the Act, including its taxing provisions, were represented by the government to be constitutional only under the Commerce Clause, Justice Sutherland nevertheless explained that the so-called tax was not one cognizable under the Constitution. He wrote: "It is very clear that the 'excise tax' is not imposed for revenue but exacted as a penalty to compel compliance with the regulatory provisions of the act. The whole purpose of the exaction is to coerce what is called an agreement—which, of course, it is not, for it lacks the essential element of consent. One who does a thing in order to avoid a monetary penalty does not agree; he yields to compulsion precisely the same as though to avoid a term in jail."

Turning to the Commerce Clause argument, the Court deemed coal production "a purely local activity." It also viewed many other activities regulated by the Act "essential antecedents of production," thus also falling outside the realm of interstate commerce. The Court found the remaining provisions of the Act, germane to price-fixing and labor, inseparable from the unconstitutional provisions, thus dooming the entire act.

Roosevelt was not chastened by the Court's multiple decisions against the New Deal. He was embittered and remained defiant. In the advent of a massive landside victory in his re-election campaign in 1936, where he promised a Second New Deal, Roosevelt now had the political mandate he needed to do battle with the Court, and the justices were already mindful of that political reality. The victory was heady medicine for Roosevelt, but he could only apply strict federal controls over the nation's economy if the Court, and indeed the Constitution, was removed as an obstacle.

Roosevelt's Attorney General Homer Cummings and, separately, Felix Frankfurter considered the options and presented them to Roosevelt. Cummings at first considered but then dismissed the idea of amending the Constitution in favor of a more direct approach, one he developed in absolute secrecy. Frankfurter preferred an amendment to the Constitution that would expand the commerce clause to permit federal regulation of the most intimate local affairs and an amendment to reduce the scope and redefine the meaning of the Due Process clause, effectively neutering it so that regulations could deprive individuals of liberty and property without running afoul of the Constitution.

Before the election, Roosevelt conferred with Cummings on how best to curb the Court's power so the New Deal could be revived. The administration's devastating loss in *Butler* stirred Cummings to action. "I tell you, Mr. President, they mean to destroy us," he said in reference to the Court. "We will have to find a way to get rid of the present membership of the Supreme Court," he said. Cummings began his research on ways to undermine the Court's independent decision-making power.[284] The project proceeded in secrecy with only two hard-core New Deal lawyers intimately involved: Solicitor General Stanley Forman Reed and Cummings' personal assistant, attorney Alexander Holtzoff. Others were consulted and sworn to secrecy, including presidential aide Thomas Corcoran, White House Counsel Samuel Rosenman, and presidential advisor Donald Richberg (who helped draft the NIRA and served as NRA General Counsel). Cummings received advice on a way to change the composition of the court based on requiring by statute the addition of one member for every member then sitting of a certain senior age, thus diluting the anti-New Deal faction. That advice came in a December 16, 1936 letter from Princeton Professor of Political Science Edwin Corwin who, in turn, had acquired the idea from Harvard Professor of Government Arthur Holcombe.[285] A few days after the election, Cummings met with Roosevelt to discuss his progress "on the secret drafting" of a bill to reconstitute the Court.[286]

The idea of amending the Constitution, favored by Frankfurter, did not win over the President who worried about the state-by-state consideration of the amendments, the amount of time it would take, and the high-profile contest it would engender. Presidential aide Thomas Corcoran told Secretary of the Interior Harold Ickes, state opposition to amending the Constitution might be formidable and made the option impractical.[287]

Instead, Cummings and Roosevelt banked on Democratic control of Congress in the aftermath of Roosevelt's 1936 landslide re-election to serve the President well by implementing the legislative plan Cummings devised in secret. That same essential idea came to light from another source, a history of the Justice Department that Cummings and his assistant Carl McFarland were developing. They discovered that then sitting Justice James Clark McReynolds had recommended the following in 1914 while he served as Attorney General in the Wilson Administration:

> I suggest an act providing that when any judge of a federal court below the Supreme Court fails to avail himself of the privilege of retiring [at age 70] now granted by law, that the President be required, with the advice and consent of the Senate, to appoint another judge, who would preside over the affairs of the court and have precedence over the older one. This will insure at all times the presence of a judge sufficiently active to discharge promptly and adequately the duties of the court.[288]

The delicious irony of implementing just such a bill while McReynolds (then seventy-five years old) remained on the Court was too great for Roosevelt to resist.[289]

Roosevelt could not abide by the Supreme Court's decisions prohibiting delegation of legislative power to the executive; federal regulation of wholly intrastate transactions; and use of the federal taxing power for other than the raising of revenues for the general welfare. He would instead remake the Court and rely on executive intimidation to bend decisions in favor of New Deal constitutionality, along the lines articulated by Cummings. Cummings then drafted the Judicial Procedures Reform Bill of 1937. Among its other provisions, the bill would add one justice for each one then sitting who had attained the age of seventy, capped at a maximum of six.

President Roosevelt submitted the bill to Congress on February 5, 1937. He could not wait longer to introduce the bill because he wanted it passed by Congress before the Supreme Court ruled on several key pieces of legislation then before it, which helped define his Second New Deal: The Social Security Act and the National Labor Relations Act, among others.[290]

The bill encountered prompt and stiff opposition from the media, the public, and members of Congress: "[T]he plan's announcement prompted an immediate and intense firestorm of criticism . . ."[291] The President was transparently lacking candor when he explained his justification for the bill. He gave judicial inefficiency as the reason for the bill, denying any intent to stack the Court with New Deal justices. He said that the Court suffered from a backlog of cases. That was not true, as Chief Justice Charles Evans Hughes made clear in congressional testimony: There was no congestion in the Court's docket. Roosevelt's false justification together with the apparent real reason provoked a backlash with the popular media portraying Roosevelt as attempting to bully the Justices of the Court to change their votes. Having lost the media battle on the new bill, Roosevelt shifted to explain his real justification in a radio fireside chat on March 9. He admitted that the Court's conservative members were making it impossible for him to implement his New Deal.[292] Still, neither the public, the media, nor Congress would be moved. The bill languished in Committee for the better part of six months.

In the critical decision month for the Court of March 1937, it was anything but clear that the bill would go down to defeat. Indeed, "one month after its introduction, the proposal seemed likely to prevail" in the overwhelmingly Democratic Congress.[293] The Supreme Court was now embroiled in a major political controversy. The Second New Deal upon which the President had been re-elected with a landslide would entail a series of legislative measures, each one likely to challenge the Court's constitutional sensibilities. A series of decisions striking down the Second New Deal, including among them the Social Security Act and the National Labor Relations Act, might well provoke even greater action by the President or Congress against the Court, perhaps resulting in passage of the court-packing bill or curtailing the Court's jurisdiction. Although a degree of controversy surrounds what the swing voter, Justice Owen Roberts, held as his reason for changing his position to side with the New Deal, it appears likely that he did so mindful of the political consequences associated with not doing so. In his autobiographical notes from 1936, Chief Justice Hughes indicated that the President's landslide compelled the Court to abandon its "fortress in public opinion." In retirement, Justice Roberts explained: "Looking back, it is difficult to see how the Court could have resisted the popular urge for uniform standards throughout the country—for what in effect was a unified economy."[294]

Like the Chief Justice, Justice Roberts appears to have taken stock of public opinion as a bellwether against further efforts to strike down the New Deal. Despite that perception of potential public opinion, Gallup Polls from the time revealed a majority of voters "opposed restrictions on the Court, supported Court decisions striking down the National Recovery Act and the Agricultural Adjustment Act, and hoped that Roosevelt's second term could be more conservative than his first."[295] Still, a failure by the Court to relent would intensify the conflict between the President and the Court and, in that contest, the President's communication skill and popularity would weigh heavily against the largely cloistered members of the Supreme Court. The political branches had the upper hand and, at least in the first month following introduction of the court-packing plan, tilted the balance in favor of executive power. That proved all important, causing a judicial revolution that sent into exile key constitutional doctrines that had restrained federal government power. United States Court of Appeals Judge Douglas H. Ginsburg famously refers to the period from then until now as one in which those key power limiting doctrines have formed a "constitution-in-exile."[296]

Although his court-packing plan failed to become law, even being opposed by his own Vice President, Roosevelt's objective was in fact achieved. On "White Monday," March 29, 1937, the Supreme Court backed down in what New Deal historian William E. Leuchtenburg described as "the greatest constitutional somersault in history."[297] On that day, the Court published three decisions upholding the President's preferred position: *West Coast Hotel Co. v. Parrish*[298]; *Wright v. Vinton Branch*[299]; and *Virginia Railway Co. v. System Federation No. 40*[300]. The decisions telegraphed the administration and Congress that the court-packing plan was no longer needed; the Court had flipped.

In *Parrish*, the Court performed a *volte face* on interpretation of the Due Process clause, signaling an end to substantive due process. By a 5–4 majority (with Roberts in the majority), the Court severely restricted the meaning of the term "liberty" in the Fourteenth Amendment Due Process clause, overruling its earlier decision in *Adkins v. Children's Hospital*[301], where it had held liberty under the Fifth Amendment Due Process clause violated by a Washington, D.C. minimum wage law for women and children. The Court distinguished its decision of just ten months before in *Morehead v. New York ex. rel. Tipaldo*[302], where it had in reliance on *Adkins* declared a New York law unconstitutional that granted a state commission the power to second guess an employer's wage rate if it deemed that rate not "fair" and to compel whatever rate it deemed fair. Examining another minimum wage law in *Parrish*, the Court suddenly shifted from a focus on individual rights to one on collective rights, signaling a Hegelian change in constitutional interpretation: "[T]he liberty safeguarded [by the Fourteenth and Fifth Amendments] is liberty in a social organization," wrote Chief Justice Hughes for the majority, "which requires the protection of law against the evils which menace the health, safety, morals, and welfare of the people. Liberty under the Constitution is thus necessarily subject to the restraints of due process, and regulation which is reasonable in relation to its subject . . . " Suddenly an individual right to be free of government constraints on freedom of contract, i.e., with economic liberty, had been transformed into a community right to wages deemed commensurate with the health, safety, morals, and welfare of the people at large. Now, due process would be satisfied if the law was "reasonably" "adopted in the interest of the community."

In *Wright v. Vinton Branch*[303], the Court accepted as constitutional revisions Congress made to the Frazier-Lemke Act, the original version of which the Court held unconstitutional in *Louisville Joint Stock Land Bank v. Radford*[304] as a deprivation of property in violation of the Fifth Amendment. Now, because the deprivation of property was qualified on a court's ability to alter stays of foreclosure and protect rights of the mortgagees, it was accepted as consistent with Fifth Amendment due process.

In *Virginia Railway Co. v. System Federation No. 40*[305], the Court performed a *volte face* on the Commerce Clause, expanding the reach of Congress by expanding the scope of transactions now regulable by federal power. In *Virginia Railway*, the Court considered the constitutionality of the Railway Labor Act, which mandated collective bargaining and defined the constitutional basis of the act as the Constitution's commerce clause. The railroad "back shop" repair workers at issue functioned wholly intrastate but worked on equipment that, like Schechter's chickens, came from out of state, but unlike Schechter's chickens, that equipment would now justify federal regulation under the Commerce Clause. The Court reasoned, as it had not in *Schechter*, that the back shop repair work occurred "upon the equipment used by petitioner in its transportation service, 87 percent of which is interstate commerce . . . The activities in which these employees are engaged have such a relation to the other confessedly interstate activities of the petitioner that they are to be regarded as part of them. All taken together [they] fall within the power of Congress over interstate commerce."

These dramatic shifts by the Court in deference to Congress and the President presaged the veritable end to Court invalidation of New Deal economic regulation, an end signaled in *National Labor Relations Board v. Jones & Laughlin Steel Corp.*[306] Handed down just two weeks after *Parrish*, the *NLRB* decision blew apart the Court's prior constrained view of "commerce," making it clear that so long as there was some tangible link to interstate commerce from an otherwise wholly intrastate economic activity, Congress could reach it with federal regulations. Writing for a 5-4 majority, Chief Justice Hughes reasoned that Congress could regulate activities that were "intrastate in character" if they had "such a close and substantial relation to interstate commerce that their control is essential or appropriate to protect that commerce from burdens and obstructions." *NLRB* distinguished several other recent decisions of the Court where Roberts had been in the majority and had applied the Commerce Clause to strike down New Deal legislation.

On Wednesday, April 14, 1937, just two days after the *NLRB* decision was handed down, a young reporter who wrote for *The New York Post* unwittingly coined a phrase that would perfectly describe the reverse in course engineered by a majority of the Justices. Cal Tinney placed in his small boxed column on the bottom of page 21 of the paper the following line: "I've been thinking for an explanation of why Justice Roberts switched from the conservatives to the liberals. Is it this?—Maybe he figured that a switch in time'll save nine." From that point forward, "the switch in time that saved nine" became a shorthand reference for the Court's dramatic reversal from striking down the New Deal to ushering it in through a revolutionary reinterpretation of the Constitution to negate its limits on power.

In *Helvering v. Davis*[307], decided May 24, 1937, the Supreme Court in a 7–2 decision written by Justice Cardozo upheld a major centerpiece of the Second New Deal, the Social Security Act. The Court held that Social Security Act taxes levied on employers and employees were constitutional, and not beyond the delegated powers of Congress, reasoning that the Social Security Act fell within Article I, Section 8 as facilitating expenditures in aid of the "general welfare." The general welfare provision was thus uncoupled from its prior requirement that it not embrace a function beyond the powers expressly delegated in the Constitution.

With *NLRB* and *Helvering*, the Supreme Court made clear that it would no longer stand as an obstacle to New Deal regulation of the economy, ushering in a new era of virtually limitless federal government. Roosevelt had achieved the substantive victory over court resistance he had sought in his court-packing bill without need for the bill's passage. A week before *Helvering* was decided, on May 18, 1937, one of the "Four Horseman" retired, Justice Willis Van Devanter. He was replaced by New Deal advocate, a self-professed "believer in expanding governmental power," Hugo Black, securing support for New Deal legislation and for an end to constitutional protection for economic liberty. "From 1937 to 1947, the New Deal Court overturned thirty pre-1937 decisions."[308]

Roosevelt achieved essentially unlimited government, in hundreds of instances of government intervention in the market that replaced freedom of choice with government controls (involving the government in nearly every aspect of American economic life). He not only greatly burdened enterprise with regulatory entanglements, but he also added substantial taxes to employers and employees. He did so in the worst depression in American history, exacerbating it such that America could not climb out of the economic doldrums for over nine years while several other nations did.

America's Great Depression did not end until the entire nation was put on a war footing, factories employed tens of thousands to make war munitions, and generations of males eighteen to forty-five were sent overseas to fight. Jim Powell summarizes:

FDR tripled taxes during the Great Depression, from $1.6 billion in 1933 to $5.3 billion in 1940. Federal taxes as a percentage of the gross national product jumped from 3.5 percent in 1933 to 6.9 percent in 1940, and taxes skyrocketed during World War II. FDR increased the tax burden with higher personal income taxes, higher corporate income taxes, higher excise taxes [indeed, the highest and largest number of them in American history], higher estate taxes, and higher gift taxes. He introduced the undistributed profits tax. Ordinary people were hit with higher liquor taxes and Social Security payroll taxes. All these taxes meant there was less capital for businesses to create jobs, and people had less money in their pockets.[309]

Roosevelt applied "excise taxes" (taxes on specific goods and services) to more products and at higher rates than ever before in American history. In the 1930s, excise taxes were applied to alcohol, tobacco, soft drinks, movie tickets, phone calls, bank checks, telegrams, gasoline, cars, and car tires, among other products. Burton Folsom, Jr. explains that Roosevelt effectively shifted the principal burden of federal taxation from the wealthiest to middle and lower income earners through his heavy reliance on excise taxes, considered one of the most regressive forms of taxation.[310] Illustrating the impact, Folsom, Jr. explains:

> In other words, the "forgotten man" [i.e., "the forgotten man at the bottom of the economic pyramid" that Franklin Roosevelt referenced in his April 7, 1932, Albany New York radio address[311]], who pumped gas into his car and drove it to a theater to smoke a cigarette and watch a movie paid four new taxes (and one old one) to pay the WPA worker in Chicago to build a bridge and the wheat farmer in Kansas to take his land out of circulation (so that the farmer could then receive a higher price for wheat, which translated into more expensive bread for the "forgotten man").[312]

The Revenue Act of 1934 included higher tax rates for those earning taxable income over $9,000 per year, a new tax on undistributed net income of personal holding companies, and a higher estate tax of 60%. That Act also expanded federal tariffs to include coconut and other imported oils. The Revenue Act of 1935 raised the top income tax rate on taxable earnings above $100,000 to 75% from 63% and increased estate and gift taxes. The Revenue Act of 1937 increased taxes on personal holding companies and limited corporate and certain other deductions, including those for nonresident taxpayers. The government also began collecting payroll taxes for Social Security in 1937.

In reviewing the economic impact of the New Deal tax policies, Price Fishback explains that "[i]ncreases in income tax rates . . . likely contributed to tax avoidance and inhibited economic activities at the top of the income distribution. A series of taxes on capital, dividends, and undistributed profits led to relatively small amounts of revenue at the cost of chilling some forms of investment activity. New excise taxes . . . slowed growth in the leading technological growth sectors in the economy."[313] As Jim Powell notes, Roosevelt's own tax adviser Randolph F. Paul confessed that the addition of so many taxes on corporate and private income earners, not to mention the excise taxes on middle and lower income earners, "intensified the depression they were working to correct."[314]

Moreover, Roosevelt left in place the Smoot-Hawley tariff, merely tinkering with it by adding more tariffs on oils from the Philippines rather than repealing them. Roosevelt "raised some tariffs, while Secretary of State Cordell Hull negotiated reciprocal trade agreements which cut tariffs only about 4 percent." The dumping of agricultural products overseas at the direction of Secretary of Agriculture Wallace aggravated international trade tensions at precisely the time when lessened tariff rates would have helped spur trade.[315]

The combined effect of regulations that drove out of existence small firms in favor of large ones, thus creating industry cartelization under the NRA; agricultural subsidies paid principally to large agricultural concerns at the expense of small ones and of taxes levied on processors; tariffs which choked off trade; and major new income, excise, estate, and gift taxes was devastating, maintaining the depression and even trigger an economic downturn from 1937 to 1938. Indeed, unemployment levels remained in double digits until World War II, revealing the New Deal and the Second New Deal to be catastrophic failures: 1933 (24.75% unemployment, 12,830,000 unemployed); 1934 (21.60% unemployment, 11,340,000 unemployed); 1935 (19.97% unemployment, 10,610,000 unemployed); 1936 (16.80% unemployment, 9,030,000 unemployed); 1937 (14.18% unemployment, 7,700,000 unemployed); 1938 (18.91% unemployment, 10,390,000 unemployed); 1939 (17.05% unemployment, 9,480,000 unemployed); and 1940 (14.45% unemployment, 8,120,000 unemployed).

One of the President's most intimate friends, advisors and confidants, Secretary of the Treasury Henry Morgenthau, Jr. would confess that the massive sums spent to supplant the market with federal work programs, federal farm labor programs, federal codes governing wages, prices, production, labor and services, and federal reforms of Wall Street, financial markets, and banking had utterly failed.

On May 9, 1939, into the second term of the Roosevelt "recovery," Secretary Morganthau made the following unsettling confession to the House Ways and Means Committee:

> We have tried spending money. We are spending more than we have ever spent before and it does not work. And I have just one interest, and if I am wrong . . . somebody else can have my job. I want to see this country prosperous. I want to see people get a job. I want to see people get enough to eat. We have never made good on our promises . . . I say after eight years of this Administration we have just as much unemployment as when we started . . . And an enormous debt to boot![316]

As Burton Folsom, Jr. explains, "[n]o depression, or recession, had ever lasted even half this long."[317] The New Deal was prolonging the Depression, not ending it. Consistent with the philosophy of Marx, Progressives viewed the collapse of the markets as an inevitable byproduct of an advanced stage of capitalism with the struggle between capital and labor yielding labor unrest and market failure that could only be remedied through vigorous government intervention and redistributionist tax policies. Government would tip the scale in favor of labor, take profits and redistribute them to those deemed in need to further social welfare goals, and establish government-planned economies to employ and build a new, post-capitalist society. It is a solution tried many times by governments intent on varying forms of socialism, and it has failed every time, exacerbating recession and depression, not alleviating human misery but compounding it. It failed again with Roosevelt.

Common Progressive perceptions in the Roosevelt Administration of the Great Depression's root causes we now know to be false. The Great Depression likely arose not from failings of capitalism but from actions by governments domestic and foreign, policies that ultimately caused credit to evaporate, export and import markets to collapse, and banks to close in the face of sudden and substantial withdrawal demands. One factor was European governments' refusal to repay over $10 billion in war loans given them by the United States to help finance World War I.[318] A second was the Smoot-Hawley Tariff Act, the highest tariff in American history, ultimately covering some 3,218 categories of imported goods. The Smoot-Hawley Tariff triggered European retaliatory tariffs, leading to a spiral that deprived both sides of the Atlantic of needed goods. American exports to Europe fell from $7 billion in 1929 to $2.5 billion in 1932. The American-European tariff wars drove the cost of products used in the manufacture of all manner of consumer goods beyond affordability, bringing production to unsustainably low levels or to a halt. For example, American car sales declined from in excess of 5.3 million in 1929 to 1.8 million in 1932. A third factor was the lending policies of the Federal Reserve, created during the Wilson Administration in 1913. The aforementioned rise in interest rates from 3.5% to 6% between 1928 and 1929 had the effect of sucking out of the market money needed for business loans.

Neither Hoover nor Roosevelt ever embarked on a program to liberate the besieged market from regulatory constraints and to lower tariffs and taxes. Both were intent on addressing the Great Depression by replacing the private sector with government control. The untried alternative was free market capitalism. Instead of maintaining the highest and most extensive regime of tariffs in American history, they could have repealed the Smoot-Hawley tariffs and negotiated reciprocal repeals of foreign tariffs. Instead of raising corporate and individual taxes, they could have slashed them. Instead of endeavoring to pick winners and losers in the market through policies that cartelized favored enterprises while diminishing and destroying all others, they could have allowed the market to operate unimpeded. Had they done so, the enormous loss of individual liberty and sovereignty attendant to the unlimited growth of the federal government and the "switch in time that saved nine" may have been avoided and a return to better economic times could have been hastened.

Instead, the New Deal banished from jurisprudence doctrines that limited the power of the federal government; established a large, extra-constitutional and permanent bureaucratic oligarchy in the form of an authoritarian administrative state unaccountable to the people, the Congress and the Courts; obliterated all barriers to central government planning over the intimate details of even purely local enterprise; and ended protection for economic liberty. At once, the sovereignty of the people had been drawn away to the state, and the bureaucratic enslavement of individuals and businesses became the order of the day. Hegel and collectivism had won. Locke and liberty had lost.

CHAPTER 3

THE DENIAL OF GOD-GIVEN RIGHTS

mpatient for expeditious economic and social change, leading Progressives of the late nineteenth and early twentieth centuries harbored disdain for constitutional limits on government power, protection for individual rights, the slow pace of legislation, and the slow issuance of decisions by Article III courts. Influenced by the German administrative model, which they applauded for efficiency in pursuit of what they deemed a "common good," the Progressives created an administrative state in the United States beyond constitutional limits. They created, in effect, a government external to, and largely independent of, the Constitution's three branches of government, a new centralized government vested with authoritarian powers. The American administrative state was the very antithesis of the limited government model the Founders created; it was far more akin to European absolute monarchies than to America's limited federal republic.

In the Founders' construct, rights are derived from God, not the state. The Declaration of Independence reflects this in the first sentences of its second paragraph: "We hold these truths to be self-evident, that all men are created equal, that they are endowed by their Creator with certain unalienable Rights, that among these are Life, Liberty and the pursuit of

Happiness—That to secure these rights, Governments are instituted among Men, deriving their just powers from the consent of the governed." That rights-centric view arose from the fundamental truth held by the Founders that rights do not come from the state but are pre-political and come from the "Creator." That view demands in matters of rights, the individual, not the collective, be accepted as sovereign; indeed, the very reason the state exists is to "secure" the rights of individuals. Consistent with the Founders' individual rights-centric view is a government of limited powers, one forbidden to act in ways that deprive life, liberty, and property without due process of law, by which the Founders meant without at least a jury trial before an impartial and independent court where the burden would remain on the state to prove criminal wrong-doing by no less a standard than beyond a reasonable doubt.

There are profound consequences that flow from acceptance that rights are unalienable bequests to each person from God. In the first instance, because God is a higher power than any single person, group of persons, or the state, no state actor may presume a power to deny a right that God has granted, there being no human authority to undo that which God has done. God having given each person rights at birth, no political power may justly take those rights away. Rights thus precede the state, are independent of the state, and are superior to it because the source of the authority is superior to the state. Further, the rights endowed are extraordinarily broad in scope, enveloping "Life, Liberty, and the pursuit of Happiness." In short, they guarantee the full spectrum of individual freedom to the maximum extent, limited only by the equal rights of others. This then creates an expansive private sphere of individual action into which the state may not trespass if by so doing it takes away rights, because no just state can presume to act in place of God or to usurp the authority of God.

Because rights are bestowed by God on each individual, that logically compels the conclusion that minority rights, even down to a minority of one, must be respected and protected by the state. Contrary to the collectivist model, no single individual's unalienable rights may be violated to achieve a "common good," because rights, even those of just one person, may not be deprived. In this way, the Bill of Rights becomes a bulwark of individual liberty. Were it not for the investment of rights to each individual by the Creator, then government could presume a role to protect "collective rights" against the assertion of "individual rights," which, of course, is precisely what the Progressive state demands in contravention of the Declaration's promise and the Constitution's defense of individual liberty in the Bill of Rights.

The Founders' premise that individuals are endowed by God with rights is the opposite of the Hegelian concept of the state being legitimate only when it acts in defense and furtherance of collective rights, a notion at the heart of the German model for the administrative state. Individual rights and state defined collective rights cannot coexist without predictable conflict. Under Hegel's construct, individual rights have no serious recognition unless they further collective rights because the import of the individual lies entirely in his or her utility to the state. By contrast, under Locke's construct, individual rights are paramount because the import of the state lies entirely in its protection of the rights of the governed, who are sovereign.

Under the Hegelian state, the "common good" is defined by state experts. The administrative state follows the lead of experts to redirect human action away from privately chosen endeavors and toward state preferred endeavors that advance the "common good." In this way, the state through its experts exercises authoritarian control over the individual to ensure that the individual unwaveringly serves the state. Individual dissent from state demands is forbidden by law. In other words, the Hegelian conception embraced by Progressive scholars called for state sovereignty exercised through control over individual choice and it rejected the individual sovereignty demanded by the Founders in the Declaration of Independence and rejected the Constitution's limits on state powers.

Under the Lockean state, the exercise of rights is entirely a matter of individual self-determination, limited only by the equal rights of others. The Lockean state operates in a limited sphere defined by the Constitution, which sphere is constrained by the foundational premise that the state may not deprive the individual of rights, that the individual is sovereign, and that the state's primary purpose is to defend rights from threats domestic and foreign. Individual dissent from the state is expected, as the Bill of

Rights directs its defense of liberty expressly against state action. Moreover, reliance on a written Constitution of enumerated powers and a system of jealous competing legislative, executive, and judicial powers and checks and balances proceeds from the notion that government must be disabled by impediments to absolute power because absolute power is understood to be tyranny.

The movement to shift rights from the classical American foundation, vested in the individual, to the Progressive ideal, vested in the state, required a profound change in American education. So long as God remained the recognized source of rights, as it is in the classical model of the Founders, the notion that the collective had rights superior to the individual lacked an essential precondition and was thus a *non sequitur*. The only sure way to destroy the notion of individual rights in favor of collective rights and to substitute the state for God as the source of rights was to challenge the existence of God, and Darwin's theory of evolution offered Progressives that opportunity. The challenge was impossible so long as man remained humble in his acceptance of the Divine and in his inability to know all things, but science, particularly that of evolution, gave rise among Progressives to the haughty notion that man could know all or virtually all things through exploration, hypothesis, and testing. Among some Progressives science in general, and Darwinian evolution in particular, enabled a new rejection of religion, not an agnosticism but an atheism.

A number of Progressive educators moved from acceptance of God as the author of rights to belief in the state and, indeed, to a new secular dogma, social Darwinism. That change, at first academic led principally by the socialist John Dewey who was originally a Fabian Socialist, and the strong proponent of social Darwinism Herbert Spencer, erupted into a public fissure between Progressive Christians and Progressive atheists, the Scopes trial. In that show trial biblical Creationism and Darwinian evolution were artificially pitted against one another, on the premise that the two could not co-exist. Although there is no reason to believe that the two could not co-exist (for example, God could be the ultimate creator of all things and evolution could be one of God's means to develop life on earth), to view it that way disserved the interests of both competing factions among

Progressives, the Progressive Christians who believed in Creationism, like William Jennings Bryan, and the Progressive atheists who believed in social Darwinism, like Clarence Darrow. Consequently, as depicted in the Scopes trial, either the story of Creation in the Bible was true, and thus religion was true, or it was false and religion was false.

By the time of that contest (the orchestrated case of *State of Tennessee v. John Thomas Scopes*, the so-called "Scopes Monkey Trial"), the shift away from the classical Founding Era model of rights derived from God was well underway across the United States in universities and, to an increasing degree, in public primary and secondary education, prodded along by Progressive educators.

The participants in the Scopes trial (Progressive Christians and Progressive atheists) depicted social Darwinism and Creationism as diametrical. So-called Modernist Christians viewed the two as not necessarily in conflict, but they were pushed aside by the predominant Christian and atheist Progressives. Although the Christian Progressives prevailed in the court contest because John T. Scopes was found guilty by the trial court, the ultimate triumph was that of the Progressive educators. In state after state, they eventually succeeded in rooting out Creationism in favor of secular humanism. In so doing, the proponents of Progressive education implicitly altered the perception of generations concerning the source of rights. When reference to God is increasingly forbidden in the classroom, the Founders' basic construct of rights in the Declaration of Independence loses its comprehensibility. It is not enough under that construct that rights exist, they are pre-political and from God, thus making an act by the state to deprive individuals of them an act against God. Instead, increasingly, the Hegelian notion (that rights are political grants from the state and have utility only when exercised to serve the common good) gained sway.

The American Fabian socialist John Dewey became the most notable proponent of what came to be known as Progressive education. Dewey opposed *laissez-faire* capitalism and individualism; he argued against competition among students in the classroom, favoring cooperative approaches to learning. Dewey sought to expand public education "using the state's control of schooling to reconstruct society through educational reform."[319] Education was no longer to build knowledge for independent individual action; it was to build model citizens to serve the state. Borrowing from social Darwinism, he and, more directly, social Darwinist Herbert Spencer rejected the notion of individual rote memorization in favor of group role playing and lessons derived from projects said to depict community life in the industrial age. The aim was not simply to educate but to turn out model citizens inculcated with collectivist "virtues," rendering them supporters not of individual excellence but of the "common good." In that respect, Dewey drew from the French political philosopher Jean Jacques Rousseau, who wrote: "[E]very man is virtuous when his particular will is conformable to the general will of the community . . ."

Underlying this conception is an elitist sense that those taught to favor the "common good" would accept indoctrination and follow expected behaviors supportive of the state in adulthood. To John Dewey's great dismay, he found that the generation which served in World War I largely rejected the Progressive educators' indoctrination. They did not build a socialist state but remained dedicated to individualism, individual liberty, and free enterprise.

Professor at the University of Chicago, founder of the University of Chicago Laboratory School, President of the American Psychological Association, President of the American Philosophical Association, member of the socialist Fabian Society, and Chairman of the American Committee for the Defense of Leon Trotsky, John Dewey, the scion of Progressive education in America, was perhaps more of a communist sympathizer than simply a socialist in his later years. He took a trip to the Soviet Union and fell in love with Stalinist Russia and the propagandistic education of youth in Stalin's Union of Soviet Socialist Republics. Writing in 1928, Dewey gushed in his *Impressions of Soviet Russia and the Revolutionary World*[320] about all aspects of communism he witnessed on his journey. These tours were heavily controlled by the communist party to depict communism in an artificially positive light for Western guests. Making no serious mention of Stalin's campaigns of genocide (his purges), Stalin's deportations and forced relocations, his labor and prison camps (gulags), and political and religious persecutions and executions, which cost the lives of millions, Dewey was, as he said, "impressed" by Soviet Moscow "more so than my own country."[321]

Deluded by his visit, Dewey believed there to be "no country in Europe in which the external routine of life is more settled and secure."[322]

Dewey celebrated Stalin's often ruthless demand for conformity in all things, viewing it not as slavery, but as a "release of human powers on such an unprecedented scale that it is of incalculable significance . . . for the world."[323] Rather than experience revulsion at the teaching of Marxist-Leninist ideology to orphaned youth along with demand for their absolute allegiance to the Soviet state, Dewey praised the indoctrination as ideal, writing: "I have never seen anywhere in the world such a large proportion of intelligent, happy, and intelligently occupied children."[324] By forcing children to conform to and accept Marxism, the Soviet Union, according to Dewey, created an excellent way for educators to mold children into model citizens. He lavished effusive praise on the communists, writing, "The animating purpose and life of [Soviet Russia is] reflected in its educational leaders and the work they are attempting."[325] It was that unity of progressive purpose achieved by a propagandized state education that became the beau ideal of Dewey's quest for educational reform in America. He was not unaware of how the Soviet state bent the truth to promote total subservience to its wishes in its youth. Rather, he embraced the notion of using propaganda as an educational tool to cause children to become zealots for the collectivist ideals of the state. "Propaganda is education and education is propaganda," he wrote.[326]

Following the Civil War and continuing to 1870, suburban towns and cities across America replaced private schooling at home or in small, parent supported, one-teacher schoolhouses with taxpayer-funded, public elementary schools. Those public schools increasingly reflected a predisposition toward molding young minds to serve the "common good," as advocated by Progressive educators.

The conception of model citizenship was not new to the Progressive era, but it gained new meaning, reflecting not individual excellence in service to the ideals of the American Revolution but collectivist service to the state. Conceptions of model citizenship had roots in early American education but to a different end. Immediately after the American Revolution, Lydia Maria Child, Catherine Maria Sedgwick, and Lydia Sigourney were among those who advocated what has become known as "republican motherhood," whereby children were taught by their mothers the history of the American Revolution and the struggle for, and importance of, individual rights; the denial of those rights by a tyrannical king and parliament; the need for eternal vigilance in defense of individual rights against rapacious government; the creation of a limited government under a written Constitution, and Christian virtues, including respect for individual freedom of choice and for rights to life, liberty and property.[327] Progressive education abandoned republican motherhood and rejected rote memorization in favor of collectivist values and project based learning, emphasizing the new social sciences, and evolution, even eugenics. Although Dewey originally insisted on the importance of Protestant theology to direct student behavior to serve state interests, increasingly after 1900, he advocated a secular education that, in certain respects, was consistent with the views of one of the foremost polymaths of the age, the agnostic Herbert Spencer.[328]

Unlike the socialist Dewey, Spencer abhorred public education and believed in capitalism from a social Darwinist perspective, subscribing to the view that, over time, laissez-faire would produce a master race that would govern. He coined the term "survival of the fittest." Spencer shared much of Dewey's abhorrence for classical education, including its preference for rote memorization. Spencer advocated education geared to the relative perceived mental stage of development of the child and education that was derived from experiential learning rather than lecture, repetition, and memorization. In line with his belief that children's brains accommodated varying kinds of information dependent on their age, he preferred to teach concepts in age-dependent sequences from simple to complex and in classrooms limited to those of specific ages. His sociological and secular humanist approach to education became popular and was adopted by Progressive educators, including Dewey.[329] Although his approach held sway among Progressive educators, it often evoked opposition from local political leaders who oversaw public education.

The Scopes trial of 1925 drew the keen attention of Americans nationwide and, most notably, those who taught in public schools, who held jobs in public school administration, and who served on elected school boards. The trial epitomized a struggle underway in different jurisdictions across the country. As Progressive educators adopted curricula emphasizing secular humanism in elementary school, lay members of school boards and local governments, backed by anti-evolution fundamentalist Christians, used their political power to block the moves, insisting that teachers include theologically based conceptions, such as creationism, in classroom instruction. Former member of Congress, former Secretary of State under President Woodrow Wilson, and three-time unsuccessful Democratic candidate for President of the United States (1896, 1900, and 1908), William Jennings Bryan was a Christian Progressive who believed in pure democracy and majoritarian rule with little or no protection for the rights of dissenters.

Preceding the Scopes trial, in which he would be the lead anti-evolutionist witness in favor of Tennessee's 1925 Butler Act (which forbad public school teachers from denying creationism in classroom instruction), Bryan described Dewey's form of Progressive Education as "[a] scientific soviet . . . attempting to dictate what is taught in our schools," characterizing it as "the smallest, the most imprudent, and the most tyrannical oligarchy that ever attempted to exercise arbitrary power."[330] In this sense Bryan clashed strongly with Dewey who, as explained, was wedded to the idea of using education as a means to indoctrinate youth into lifelong fulfillment of state-supportive roles.

The Scopes trial was contrived, a show trial designed to "prove" in a dramatic, public way, either that Creationism and, more broadly, theology, was bunk or that Darwinian evolution was. The hype concerning the trial led the public to believe that either religion or science would prevail and determine the course of education thereafter. If a dagger of evolutionary science could be driven into the heart of creationist teachings, then secular education might wholly replace education reflective of Christian mores (or, so thought Progressive education advocates, including Clarence Darrow, the agnostic attorney for the defendant John T. Scopes)."

Progressives split along religious versus secular lines, with disbelief in God common among the academic Progressives. More fundamentally, by either placing theology on a par with science or replacing theology altogether with science, Progressive educators endeavored to advance secular humanism.

The logical consequence of this shift would inevitably align public education with the German model for the administrative state. With God and Creationism removed from the classroom or, if mentioned, equated with unproven theories questioned by modern science, then the concept in the Declaration of Independence which undergirds rights theory (that people are endowed by God with unalienable rights) would lose its sure footing. If Progressive educators could plant seeds of doubt as to the existence of God, or do more and cause the scriptures to be regarded as but theory disputed by science, then it could be said that rights may not appropriately be viewed as a product of divinely bestowed free agency but as instead a product of state benevolence. If not that, at least the way would be paved to the conclusion that rights came from the state, not from God, if theological teachings could be driven from the schools. Once accepted as a product of state benevolence, the state, and not a power superior to the state, God, could be recognized as the source of rights, and it would logically follow thereafter that the state could take away rights in its discretion to pursue its "public interest" objectives.

The Scopes trial revealed a divide among Progressives over the question of government control over curriculum. Could the state forbid the teaching of evolution, or did that violate academic freedom? The state's chief prosecutor, Thomas Stewart, the Attorney General for the 18th District in Tennessee, tried to frame the issue to avoid any discussion of the conflict between Creationism and evolution, to no avail. As he put it, the trial concerned simply whether a high school science teacher, John T. Scopes, who admitted he taught the subject of evolution in the classroom, violated Tennessee's Butler Act (Tenn. H.B. 185, 1925) which, in pertinent part, made it "unlawful for any teacher in any of the Universities, Normals and other public schools of the State . . . to teach any theory that denies the Story of the Divine Creation of man as taught in the Bible, and to teach instead that man descended from a lower order of animals." A teacher who violated the law was guilty of a misdemeanor and subject to between a $100 and $500 fine for each offense. Scopes, who agreed to his arrest to test the legality of the measure, taught a high school science class on biology that relied on Progressive educator George W. Hunter's then popular textbook *A Civic Biology* (1914). On page

194 of that book, Hunter described the theory of evolution: "We have now learned that animal forms may be arranged so as to begin with very simple one-celled forms and culminate with a group which contains man himself . . . The great English scientist, Charles Darwin . . . explained the theory of evolution. This is the belief that simple forms of life on the earth slowly and gradually gave rise to more complex and that thus ultimately the most complex forms came into existence." The book also endorsed eugenics based on social Darwinism, concluding as to individuals the eugenicists deemed unfit: "If such people were lower animals, we would probably kill them off to prevent them from spreading. Humanity will not allow this, but we do have the remedy of separating the sexes in asylums or other places and in various ways preventing intermarriage and the possibilities of perpetuating such a low and degenerate race. Remedies of this sort have been tried successfully in Europe and are now meeting with some success in this country."[331]

Neither the prominent fundamentalist co-counsel in the case, the non-lawyer William Jennings Bryan, nor Scopes' lead defense counsel, the renowned criminal defense attorney and agnostic Clarence Darrow, had any interest in derailing "the show trial of the century" by avoiding a contest over Creationism versus evolution. Indeed, while it was possible, as the Modernist theologians argued, to interpret the scriptures and evolution theory as in harmony, the two Progressives Bryan and Darrow cast the battle as an irreconcilable conflict: the factual validity of scripture versus the scientific integrity of evolution. Although prosecutor Stewart succeeded in cabining much of the live testimony to avoid a long list of experts Darrow planned to call (resulting in that testimony coming in as a proffer in the form of affidavits), Stewart could not defeat a clever late trial move by Darrow to call opposing counsel Bryan as a witness, and Bryan was all too willing to be called to defend scripture, stating: "They came here to try revealed religion. I am here to defend it, and they can ask me any questions they please."[332] Darrow's cross-examination of Bryan, carried by the press to a nation riveted by the events, put theology itself on trial with questions that demanded demonstrable evidence of the miraculous biblical accounts of, for example, Jonah and the whale; Noah and the flood; the creation of Eve from Adam's rib, and the story of the earth's creation in Genesis.[333] Bryan explained that belief in each event depended on faith, and for the faithless, there would never be enough proof.

Although Darrow's client lost, was convicted of the misdemeanor and fined $100, Darrow's examination of Bryan gave impetus both to the cause of Progressive educators in their quest to rid the classroom of theology and to the cause of fundamentalist Christians in their efforts to criminalize the teaching of evolution. On John Scopes' appeal from the trial court's judgment, the Supreme Court of Tennessee deftly sidestepped the controversy by reversing the trial court on a technicality, deleting Scopes' conviction on the basis that the court below erred in assessing the fine, a function the Supreme Court held exclusively the province of the jury. The Supreme Court thus voided the substantive dispute but left the Butler Act in place. The Butler Act remained the law of Tennessee until 1967 when it was repealed.

The Scopes' trial revealed how far the nation had come from its limited government roots under the direction of Progressives. The once predominant home schooling of America until the late nineteenth century had been largely replaced with public education, causing the once predominant teachings in favor of classical liberalism, God-given rights, and limited government and against absolutism to give way to the Progressive educators' emphasis on new model citizenship, evolution and eugenics, collectivist rights, and government intervention to correct perceived private evils. Progressive educators thus did their part in laying a foundation for the new administrative state. They shook the foundations of belief that rights were unalienable bequests from God to man in favor of the Progressive educators' belief that rights were alienable and came not from God but from the state.

CHAPTER 4

THE FATHER OF THE ADMINISTRATIVE STATE

From the 1860s to the present, Progressive reformers have chiseled away at American constitutional government. They have condemned the Constitution as inefficient and archaic. They have embraced Hegelian collectivism underlying Marxism and have rejected Lockean individualism underlying constitutional government. At times, they have welcomed socialists and communists within their ranks; have sometimes adopted and advanced socialist and communist proposals; have helped socialists and communists obtain federal employment, sometimes in key positions; have even joined Fabian socialist and communist organizations; and have occasionally come to the aid of socialists and communists prosecuted for espionage. They have called for a "living" Constitution, by which they mean one unconstrained by the power limiting doctrines of the Constitution. They have called for regulations to promote the "common interest," which they have insisted is superior to "private interests," and they have rejected legal protection for individual rights that have stood in their way. They have embraced social reforms, such as immigration restrictions based on race and ethnicity, and have imposed mandatory collective bargaining, speech suppression, and even eugenics to remove from society those they have deemed immoral, unfit, or of a disfavored race or ethnicity. They have promulgated regulations over the market to cartelize enterprises they favor and destroy enterprises they oppose. They have levied high tariffs and taxes to bolster government wealth and power, finance government-planned economies, and redistribute income, all at the expense of private wealth and power. They have effectively replaced individual sovereignty with government sovereignty, denying individual freedom of choice with legal proscriptions that have outlawed conduct, which not only involves no injury to others but also involves enterprise on which others depend for their livelihoods.

They have moved ever more government power to rule from the constitutional branches of government to the regulatory branches, promising to implement entire agendas for governance through the unelected heads of federal agencies rather than through the constitutional branches of the government.

Through it all, Progressives have succeeded in depriving Americans of political and economic freedom in favor of virtually unlimited government control. The costs have been enormous. Since the end of the Civil War, Progressive policies have caused recessions, prolonged depressions, retarded innovation and human progress, and sacrificed the health and lives of millions.

By the time of the New Deal, Progressives had long abandoned the Constitution's essential power limiting provisions and doctrines, such as the legislative and judicial vesting clauses, the separation of powers doctrine, and the non-delegation doctrine, which--since the founding of the republic--had protected a vast private sphere of individual freedom of choice into which government could not tread save to arrest transgressions against others' lives, liberty, and property. They defeated those barriers and in their place erected a new a government of unlimited power, an administrative state nowhere mentioned in the Constitution and unconstrained by it. That administrative state was granted combined legislative, executive, and judicial powers, what the founding fathers described as the very definition (or essence) of tyranny. That state could act against private companies and individuals in ways the original constitutional branches could not, violating rights to life, liberty, and property with virtually unbridled discretion in service to a politically defined "common good." Dissenters' rights were left unprotected. Gone were individual rights to an independent court of law, to a presumption of innocence, to a trial by jury, to confront one's accusers, and to clear and fixed notice of the charges alleged. The bureaucrats were both prosecutors and judges, an inherent conflict of interest, that makes a sham of administrative adjudication by ensuring that the government invariably prevails.

The "common good," oftentimes referred to as the "public interest," was, in truth, the agency head's own self-interest operating underneath a superficial "public interest" cover. From the start agency heads achieved through regulation the ends desired by the dominant regulated industry, effectively ensuring that when the bureaucrats left government service they enjoyed lucrative employment as a payback from those regulated parties. Corruption thus became commonplace in the administrative state.

A government of, by, and for the people became one of, by, and for the unelected heads of the bureaucracy and their chosen private sector corporate beneficiaries. America's new bureaucratic ruling class governed in a manner indistinguishable from absolute monarchs, thus replicating the very institutions of oppression against which America's founding fathers revolted. This new ruling elite came from the nation's best schools taught by professors who drank heavily from the well of Hegelian doctrine, having been educated in the Germany of the Chancellor Bismarck by those who condemned the Lockean principles underlying the Constitution as anachronistic and ill-suited for the industrial era; defined majoritarian values and "common interest" as superior to individual rights; celebrated the efficiency and correctness of authoritarian governance through the administrative state; and bred in the minds of their American students a desire to recreate in America the aspirational authoritarian utopia the German professors depicted.

More so than any other institution, the enormous federal administrative state, comprised of hundreds of regulatory agencies and bureaus, became a means to supplant private choice in business with regulations to which the people's representatives never consented, the very offense that served as a primary impetus for the American Revolution ("No taxation without representation").

Truth be told, the administrative state is our first experiment in socialism and, like all socialist experiments, it has failed miserably if our metric is one of human freedom and prosperity. The unparalleled success of American capitalism has occurred despite government, not because of it. Progressive law and regulation has produced cartelization, reduction in competition, loss of innovation, loss of consumer choice, loss of jobs, and loss of freedom. As in the case of the New Deal, the more government has lorded over the private sector and replaced the free choice of individuals and entrepreneurs with that of bureaucrats, the more the nation has suffered from a winnowing away of freedom and prosperity. The New Deal which was promised to America as the way to lift Americans out of poverty and restore economic growth became instead a regulatory albatross, one that heavily burdened, even destroyed, small businesses, maintained double digit unemployment, and prolonged the misery of the Great Depression.

We have seen that several Presidents of the United States helped create the administrative state, but who behind the scenes was its chief architect? We have seen that Hegelian collectivism took root in American universities and colleges in the mid-nineteenth century, but who from academia is most responsible for transforming collectivist theories into the unrepresentative federal bureaucracy that exists today?

If there is a founding father of the administrative state in America, that father is Felix Frankfurter. More than any single other, Frankfurter is responsible for moving the locus of governance from the founding fathers' three branches to the over two hundred federal agencies and bureaus generated during the Roosevelt administration. The NRA's General Hugh Johnson said Frankfurter was "the most influential single individual in the United States."[334] While that is an overstatement, he surely was the most influential single individual in the administrative state.

Louis Brandeis served as Frankfurter's mentor and benefactor, and Frankfurter was Brandeis's agent within the Roosevelt administration and in supporting legal advocacy, especially while Brandeis served on the Supreme Court. Brandeis despised large enterprise and market concentration. He advocated anti-trust law enforcement, law he helped create, to break apart the "trusts" or "monopolies." He supported a constant government presence in the market to arrest acts by large businesses that caused what he perceived to be consumer harms. He despised advertising, which he thought manipulated people into making purchases not in their best interests, a sentiment shared by many who work at the Federal Trade Commission to this day. He was the one who, with the help of Frankfurter's Harvard Law School graduate James Landis, devised a market-policing role for the FTC.

Frankfurter shared Brandeis's aversion for big business, but Frankfurter's dislike extended beyond that, to capitalism itself. Frankfurter admired the socialist labor movement in Great Britain that arose during and after the First World War. Indeed, he joined and supported Fabian socialist institutions and causes. In the 1920s, the socialists became a major part of the Progressive Party in the United States under Robert La Follette, who served as Wisconsin's Governor and a member of Congress from that state. Frankfurter was an active member of the Progressive Party and endorsed its socialist platforms. Like Brandeis, Frankfurter wanted government to break apart the "trusts" and maintain a constant presence in the market but he wanted more, he wanted to tax the rich heavily and redistribute the proceeds to constituencies he preferred, and he wanted to compel collective bargaining and place the thumb of government on the labor side of the labor-management scale. Frankfurter believed strongly in government regulation of labor relations, to force all businesses to permit unionization of their work forces and to compel businesses to bargain with labor. He believed in a broad welfare state dependent on heavy taxation.

In 1935, the President soured on the idea of reinvigorating Rexford Tugwell's planned economy under the NRA and AAA, which had been struck down by the Supreme Court. Instead, Roosevelt turned increasingly to Frankfurter for an approach that attacked individual and corporate wealth concentration and relied on redistributionist policies to fund welfare and social engineering projects. Indeed, Roosevelt invited Frankfurter to live in the White House at that time, and he welcomed Frankfurter (and his Harvard "boys") to draft progressive tax bills that "soaked the rich," substantially increasing tax rates despite an unending depression.

Within the ranks of Progressives influencing Roosevelt, there were essentially two major camps. Rexford Guy Tugwell represented one faction that held sway during the first year of the Roosevelt administration. Louis Brandeis represented another faction, which increasingly held sway through

Brandeis's proxy, Frankfurter, during the remainder of the first term and the rest of the Roosevelt administration. Tugwell believed business concentration inevitable in the industrial age. Rather than break big business apart, he wanted government to capitalize on that bigness in line with the national socialist model of one of his idols, Benito Mussolini. As Shlaes explains: "Tugwell . . . liked the idea of big companies and thought that, as he would later write, 'modern concentrations' could be taken advantage of, that government could become a 'senior partner in industry-wide councils.'"[335] Tugwell wanted the government to impose through regulation of the largest firms a government-planned economy.[336]

Industry leaders would agree to this, as they did in the case of the NRA and AAA codes and controls, in no small measure because fixed prices would permit those leaders to cartelize their industries (driving out small firms that depended on price cutting to compete). In other words, government would enable large firms to enjoy fixed, above market prices, so long as government could prescribe all manner of market conditions, governing everything from production, product price, labor wage rates, and labor conditions. This monopoly rent/market regulation *quid pro quo* underlay the regulatory apparatus of the NRA and the AAA.

In the first months of the Roosevelt administration, Tugwell's essential position held sway, at least until the Supreme Court struck down the NRA and AAA. Indeed, Roosevelt echoed the Tugwell line when he "declared his support for 'economic planning, not for this period alone but for our needs for a long time to come.'"[337] Frankfurter never liked Tugwell's approach, finding little in the first hundred days of the Roosevelt administration he strongly supported with the exception of the Securities Act and the Tennessee Valley Authority.[338] Brandeis did not like Tugwell's approach either. He viewed the large enterprises allied with government as evil despite the association and favored eliminating the government entities responsible for protecting the big firms. He instead preferred a return to the old trust-busting model that he helped create.

In the resulting ideological contest, Frankfurter largely prevailed, steering Roosevelt to expand the regulatory state. Rather than depend on the NRA and AAA corporatist model, which had failed to lift America out of the Great

Depression, as even Roosevelt could see, Frankfurter argued that government should instead tax concentrations of wealth and large enterprise, redistribute the wealth to the unemployed through sundry welfare initiatives, and rely on a heavy regulatory presence in the market through the administrative state to check perceived market excesses, most notably through the Securities and Exchange Commission and the Federal Trade Commission. Frankfurter thus defined the modern Democratic Party's essential political objectives. Michael E. Parrish records: "Frankfurter's antidepression program drew heavily upon the prescriptions of Brandeis and [British economist (and Fabian Society socialist member) John Maynard] Keynes. It emphasized a drastic attack upon financial and corporate bigness through progressive taxation and a huge expenditure of public funds to employ idle workers and resources, especially for conservation."[339] This approach was in line with Brandeis's thinking. As Jim Powell puts it, "FDR advisers Brandeis, Frankfurter, [and Frankfurter Harvard Law students] Corcoran and Cohen cherished . . . taxes and regulations."[340] Parrish adds, "[t]hese ideas all echoed Brandeis, who had urged Frankfurter to support a public works program of 'great magnitude' financed at first through government deficits, but later with 'high estate and income taxes.'"[341] As had Tugwell's planned economy approach, Frankfurter's redistributionist and constant regulatory intervention approach failed miserably. It did not lift America out of depression (indeed, it helped trigger a market contraction in 1937), leaving America to be saved by the Allies' demands for war munitions during World War II, the financing of America's intervention into the war, and the post-war reconstruction that fueled an American market comeback.

In 1935, following the defeat of the NRA and the AAA in federal court and no evidence that the New Deal had any real impact on the economic downturn, Tugwell urged the President "to jettison the pretense of cooperation with big business and opt for a program of full-scale nationalization."[342] Tugwell essentially favored the Soviet model. Sympathetic to the urgings of his advisers not to recoil from government intervention in the aftermath of the Supreme Court's rebuke but to have government assume an even greater role, Roosevelt looked to Frankfurter for options. Frankfurter seized the opportunity to define a radical agenda that would achieve the essential aims of direct nationalization but through a combination of taxation and redistributionist policies and regulatory coercing and cajolery of the market. Roosevelt embraced Frankfurter's position, and Frankfurter then took up residence in the White House, becoming a near and constant adviser to Roosevelt.[343] This then led to a series of new laws manufactured by Frankfurter and his Harvard "boys," as Michael E. Parrish summarizes:

> [Spring and Summer 1935] saw the adoption of a $4.8 billion work relief program, the single largest peacetime appropriation in the nation's history. The National Labor Relations Act guaranteed industrial workers the right to form unions and to bargain collectively. The Social Security Act provided old age pensions, unemployment compensation, and federal money for the care of dependent mothers, the blind, and the disabled. The Bankruptcy Act concentrated greater regulatory authority over the commercial banks in the Federal Reserve Board to be appointed by the president. The Reserve Act raised the maximum surtax on personal incomes to 75 percent, hiked estate taxes upon the very rich, and levied a graduated tax on corporations.[344]

These new laws, along with passage of the Guffey-Snyder Bituminous Coal Act and the Public Utility Holding Company Act and other legislation (creating the Resettlement Administration and the Rural Electrification Administration), led to massive industry reforms but little in the way of economic uplift from the depression economy. Bill after bill from the White House to Congress came from the work of Felix Frankfurter, Thomas Corcoran and Benjamin Cohen. Parrish writes that Frankfurter "placed his personal mark upon more pieces of legislation in 1935 than any other adviser."[345]

FRANKFURTER'S RADICALISM

Frankfurter met Roosevelt in 1917 when Roosevelt was the Navy Department representative on Woodrow Wilson's War Labor Policies Board; Frankfurter chaired the board on leave from Harvard.[346] He impressed

Roosevelt who offered him the position of Solicitor General of the United States just four days after the inauguration. Frankfurter turned the position down in favor of retaining his Harvard faculty job, writing Roosevelt, "I can do much more to be of use to you in Cambridge than by becoming Solicitor General."[347] His words were prophetic.

One of Frankfurter's biographers described Frankfurter this way: "[H]e placed his faith in the good sense, the educability, and the benevolence of the country's old elite, represented by Holmes, Henry Stimson, and Franklin D. Roosevelt. The gentry and the new intellectuals, he believed, would moderate the excesses of American capitalism, discipline the vulgar business classes, uplift the poor, and usher in the benign future of expanded social welfare and security. He believed, finally, in the desirability of democratic change tempered by an elite; in this respect he remained throughout his life a typical turn-of-the-century progressive."[348] In other words, Frankfurter was a paternalist.

At root, he clung to the belief that elites in government could best restructure business and order people's lives because their superior education enabled them to know better than the typical American what was in that American's best interest. He believed government a force for good that could direct people and business away from vice, avarice, and self-interest. His most essential creed was Hegelian and collectivist, contrary to the core principles underlying the Declaration of Independence and the Constitution. That creed became the *raison d'être* of the administrative state Frankfurter helped construct, a *raison d'être* that persists to this day. The administrative state is inherently paternalist and antagonistic to individual freedom of choice, precisely because Frankfurter and his loyal Harvard Law School graduates who populated the New Deal government made it so.

Frankfurter was born in poverty, living his childhood years in the Leopoldstadt ghetto. In 1894, when Frankfurter was twelve, his family emigrated from Vienna to the Lower East Side of Manhattan. He spent his teen years in a community comprised of poor immigrants. Frankfurter's teachers steered him to avoid a life of labor and poverty through academic advancement. As a young man, he often attended The Cooper Union for the Advancement of Science and Art in Manhattan, doing so free of charge, listening to lectures on union issues, socialism, and communism. He distrusted riches derived from the rough and tumble of commerce, preferring the pristine environment of academia. Frankfurter was precocious, indeed brilliant. He graduated at the top of his class from the City College of New York. He was first in his class each year at Harvard Law School. His legal and political mentor was Louis Brandeis, also a remarkable scholar, who helped him financially and guided him in distrust of private wealth and large corporations.

At twenty-two, Harvard Law School student Frankfurter listened to a lecture by Brandeis (then a famous Harvard Law alum who had graduated in 1877 from the law school at 20 with the highest grade average ever attained in the school's history). Known as the "people's attorney," Brandeis despised big business, viewing it as avaricious, corrupt, and an enemy of labor, consumers, and competition. Frankfurter greatly admired Brandeis, shared many of his views, and communicated with him regularly thereafter, building a close, personal, and even financial, relationship. Following Frankfurter's graduation and a brief stint in a private law firm, Brandeis recommended him to Harvard's law faculty, where he would remain until Senate confirmation of his nomination by Roosevelt to the Supreme Court on January 17, 1939.[349]

Socially astute and loquacious, Frankfurter made it a point to meet, impress, and assist prominent academics and political figures. He worked in public and private capacities where his intellect and achievements were always of note. He came to exercise considerable influence in Washington in no small measure due to the strong favorable introductions and endorsements he received from Associate Supreme Court Justice Louis Brandeis. Part of Frankfurter's success arose from his direct association with Presidents Theodore Roosevelt, Woodrow Wilson, and Franklin Delano Roosevelt, and part was due to his placement of hundreds of his Harvard law students in key positions in the White House, in federal departments, in regulatory agencies, and in Supreme Court clerkships.[350]

Frankfurter taught administrative law, constitutional law, jurisdiction and procedure in federal courts, and public utilities law at Harvard. In his classes, which some students found droll and others found lacking in sufficient emphasis on the law, he praised public service. He encouraged a favorable view of the administrative lawyers' role in crafting regulation to constrain and tame the market. He associated government with the common good and its power as a foil for private excesses. ""What [Harvard] provided, through Felix Frankfurter and his colleagues James Landis and Calvert Magruder (both former students of Frankfurter), was an emphasis on lawyers as members of the emerging mandarinate of the regulatory state," Peter H. Irons explains.[351] Frankfurter "preached the ideals of administrative expertise and 'disinterested public service.'"[352] Frankfurter encouraged his students to learn the ropes through a short stint in private Wall Street firms and then forego hefty private firm salaries to become career civil servants instead.[353] He consistently directed his students "toward reform and regulation."[354]

Amity Shlaes explains that at Harvard "a few star professors encouraged students to push for radical change—both in law, and in government."[355] "The brightest star was Felix Frankfurter," she writes. "With the exception perhaps of the aging Clarence Darrow," writes Irons, "no other lawyer of his time shared Frankfurter's deserved reputation as a dangerous radical."[356] Frankfurter had "a European model—Britain, where labor reforms were taking place. And when thinking politically, or as an advocate, Frankfurter viewed American law as a vehicle for European-scale reform."[357]

Indeed, in 1924, Frankfurter, a supporter of the Progressive Party's candidate for president, Robert La Follette, attended the Progressive Party nominating convention, endorsing a platform that called for government ownership and control of a large part of the American economy, heavy taxation of individual and corporate wealth, and politicization of the judiciary. The 1924 Progressive Party Platform included planks that urged the federal government "to crush private monopoly;" take "ownership of the nation's water power" and "create a public super-power system;" own and control "all natural resources, including coal, iron, and other ores, oil, and timber lands in the interest of the people;" "promote public works in times of business depression;" impose a "surtax on swollen incomes;" tax "excess profits," "stock dividends," and "profits undistributed to evade taxes;" impose "progressive taxes on large estates and inheritances;" "provide for direct public control of the nation's money and credit to make it available on fair terms to all;" "guarantee . . . industrial workers the right to organize and bargain collectively through representatives of their own choosing for the maintenance or improvement of their standard of life;" "assure farmers fair prices for their products, and protect consumers from the profiteers in foodstuffs;" establish "cooperative enterprises by national and state legislation;" take "ownership of railroads, with democratic operation;" abolish "the tyranny and usurpation of the courts, including the practice of nullifying legislation in conflict with the political, social or economic theories of the judges;" and abolish "injunctions in labor disputes."[358]

The Progressive Party Convention of 1924 brought together those who represented the far left of the political spectrum, including such fans of the Soviet system and strong advocates of government-planned economies as Rexford Guy Tugwell. In the *New Republic*, Frankfurter wrote of his disgust with the two main political parties and of his support for the Progressive Party, explaining that the main parties had "an identical record of economic imperialism" and endorsed instead the British labour model, a model of socialism.[359] Daniel T. Rodgers explains: "The socialists, depleted by the fissures of 1917, enlisted [in the Progressive Party of 1924] with enthusiasm. So, with explicit reference to the British example, did the *New Republic* and the *Nation.* Jane Addams, Paul Kellogg, W.E.B. Du Bois, John Dewey, John R. Commons, Rexford Tugwell, Felix Frankfurter, and Paul Douglas, among others, all lent their support."[360]

The core beliefs that caused Frankfurter to join the Progressive Party and break bread with socialists, even adopt socialist labor proposals, never left him. Indeed, many of the 1924 Progressive Party planks Frankfurter would help turn into law during the administration of Franklin Roosevelt.

Frankfurter's pupils formed an army of dedicated public servants who populated the federal agencies, bureaus, departments, and White House from 1933 to 1945. Frankfurter sent scores of law graduates and law students to Washington, several of the latter as clerks to the Justices. William E. Leuchtenburg quotes a Washington bureaucrat as saying that a "plague of young lawyers" descended on the capitol to populate the New Deal departments, agencies, and bureaus; "[t]hey all claimed to be friends of somebody or other and mostly of Felix Frankfurter and Jerome Frank,"[361]and Frank himself acquired his position in Washington at Frankfurter's recommendation. "Critics of the administration," writes

Leuchtenburg, "learned to single out Frankfurter, who sent a great number of his most promising students at Harvard Law School to Washington . . ."[362] New Deal economist Raymond Moley (later a staunch critic of the New Deal) referred to Frankfurter as the "patriarchal sorcerer who cast dark spells of magic over the administration's young lawyers."[363] Michael E. Parrish writes: "Frankfurter ranked high on everyone's list of those who influenced Roosevelt, shaped policies, and pulled bureaucratic wires."[364] Frankfurter recommended his student Tommy Corcoran for a position as a clerk to Justice Oliver Wendell Holmes, Jr.[365], and then relied in part on Corcoran to place many more students in key administration posts.[366]

Within the agencies, some took umbrage at the socialist and communist tendencies of the young lawyers filling the bureaucracy, called Frankfurter's "Happy Hot Dogs." AAA's first Administrator George Peek did not like them at all. He called them "boys with their hair ablaze" and condemned their efforts as a "'socialist' plot to collectivize agriculture."[367] General Hugh Johnson, no enemy to national socialism (having expressed his deep admiration for the Italian dictator Benito Mussolini and Mussolini's corporatist state), nevertheless did not like the fact that Frankfurter's "boys" had "insinuated" themselves into "obscure but key positions in every department" of the New Deal government.[368] Johnson ordered the FBI to investigate certain of the Happy Hot Dogs, causing one to be fired who was found to possess "subversive" literature.[369]

Several academics came to find prominent posts in the New Deal agencies, bureaus, and departments due to Frankfurter's recommendations and influence. Among them was the author of *Law and the Modern Mind*, Jerome Frank, who Frankfurter recommended for the position of General Counsel at the Department of Agriculture, finding Frank's predisposition in favor of government-planned economy a complement to Under Secretary of Agriculture Rexford Guy Tugwell's like views.[370] Frank would later become the Chairman of the Securities and Exchange Commission and a judge on the United States Court of Appeals for the Second Circuit.

Frankfurter was a supporter of many liberal causes and organizations. He and the communist Roger Baldwin were among those who helped create the American Civil Liberties Union in 1920. Frankfurter was also a member of the socialist Fabian Society's affiliate at Harvard Law School.

Founded in London in 1884, the Fabian Society (sporting a coat of arms which depicts a wolf in sheep's cloth) favored attaining socialism through incremental changes labeled for the common good but without public mention of the title "socialism," instituting socialist reforms within the existing political system rather than through violent revolution. Its name came from the Roman General Fabius Cunctator who employed stealthy tactical maneuvers to overcome larger opposing armies, defeating them piecemeal with a much smaller force.[371] The Fabian Society was founded by Thomas Davidson, a Scotsman, and its founding members included George Bernard Shaw, Sidney Webb, Annie Besant, Edward R. Pease, and Graham Wallas. The society succeeded in influencing political opinions in England in support of socialist labor policies by the end of World War I. Its members also had international ambitions.[372]

The Fabians helped organize the Labour Representation Committee in England, which became the Labour Party. Fabians Sidney Webb and Edward R. Pease came to New York in 1888 and established (with the active assistance of socialist Upton Sinclair) a Fabian affiliated organization, the Intercollegiate Socialist Society (ISS), in 1905. The ISS opened chapters at several prominent colleges and universities in the United States, including at Wesleyan University, Columbia University, Princeton, Barnard College, New York University Law School, the University of Pennsylvania, and Harvard. The ISS endeavored to encourage college students to become socialists by teaching them that *laissez-faire* economics was exploitative of labor and inherently evil, that capitalism was on the verge of total collapse, and that the American government needed to be transformed into a socialist state. The chapter at Harvard was formed in 1908.[373]

In 1912, Frankfurter was all in for Teddy Roosevelt and was delighted when Roosevelt left the Republican Party and formed the Progressive "Bull Moose" Party. Frankfurter wrote approvingly to his Harvard Law School roommate: "We are in for government as the biggest responsible agency for organized social reform."[374]

The American economist and communist Stuart Chase became a member of the ISS. Chase graduated from Harvard in accounting in 1910. During World War I, he was employed by the Federal Trade Commission to investigate the meatpacking industry (the "Beef Trust"). Chase met then New York Governor Franklin Roosevelt in 1931 and became an informal adviser to President Roosevelt, serving in Roosevelt's "kitchen cabinet." In 1932, Chase published a book entitled *A New Deal*, which declared American capitalism dead, a government takeover of industry imminent, firing squads to be appropriate for America's wealthiest, and communism the ultimate solution. The last sentence of his book reads: "Why should the Soviets have all the fun remaking the world?"[375] Chase and Florence Kelley, also a member of the Intercollegiate Socialist Society, recommended that Roosevelt adopt the book title, "New Deal," as the slogan for his presidential campaign. Roosevelt did just that, in appreciation for the book's anti-capitalist bias.

By 1914, Harvard had over sixty ISS members, including Walter Lippmann, Roger Baldwin, Harry F. Ward, Stuart Chase, and Felix Frankfurter. Following American abhorrence at the bloodshed and tyranny associated with the Bolshevik Revolution, ISS's officers felt the need to change the organization's name to something more obscure, choosing the "League for Industrial Democracy." Stuart Chase, George Soule, Norman Thomas, Alvin Johnson, Harry A. Overstreet, Thorstein Veblen, Scott Nearing, and Felix Frankfurter were all members of the League. In 1960, Students for a Democratic Society became an affiliate of the League.

In the late 1880s, Frances Perkins (who would become Franklin Roosevelt's Secretary of Labor) was "a committed socialist" and member of the Socialist Party.[376] Like Frankfurter, she was deeply impressed by the British Labour movement, which coalesced rapidly during and after World War I, driven by socialist ideology. Frances Perkins headed the New York office of the National Consumers League. She was hired for that position by the organization's Executive Secretary Florence Kelley, and it was Kelley who introduced Perkins to socialism.[377] Louis Brandeis represented the National Consumers League until he became a Supreme Court Justice. In his place, in 1917, Frankfurter became the League's counsel and worked with Perkins, defending the labor positions of the League.[378] Perkins would later deny that she had ever been a socialist. As Kirstin Downey explains, in the period before she became Secretary of Labor, she "eras[ed] her tracks," "insisting that she had been apolitical and didn't even know what party she belonged to until she joined the Democrats several years later."[379] Although no longer admitting her ties to socialism, she remained strongly supportive of British socialist labor policies, which caused Frankfurter to lobby Roosevelt to offer her the position of Secretary of Labor.[380]

The Marxist Harold Laski was a lecturer in history at Harvard in 1916 and close friends with *The New Republic* editor Herbert Croly, Walter Lippmann, Edmund Wilson, Charles A. Beard, and Felix Frankfurter.

Frankfurter's recommendations for government service in the Roosevelt administration included lawyers who were socialists and communists. The Harvard Law faculty, and especially Frankfurter, cultivated an environment that welcomed views in support of government intervention into the economy, government support of unions, and government prosecution of monopolies. By failing to temper the enthusiasm for ideas championed by socialists, and indeed by catering to them, Frankfurter must not have been surprised to learn that several of the students he helped land jobs in the Roosevelt administration betrayed their country by becoming spies for that bastion of communism, the Soviet Union.

SPIES IN THE ROOSEVELT ADMINISTRATION

Lee Pressman and Alger Hiss were Harvard Law School classmates and worked together on the Harvard Law Review in 1928 and 1929. They "both became protégés of Felix Frankfurter, from whom they absorbed the ideal of the lawyer as the indispensable civil servant . . ."[381] Frankfurter recommended Hiss to work as a law clerk for Oliver Wendell Holmes, Jr. After Hiss clerked for Holmes, Frankfurter recommended Hiss to Jerome Frank for work in the legal office at the AAA.[382] Frankfurter had recommended Frank to Tugwell, and Tugwell saw to it that Frank was hired as the General Counsel at AAA.[383] Hiss, in turn, recommended Lee Pressman to the office. Frank accepted Pressman for the job, ultimately elevating Pressman to Assistant General Counsel, having worked well with him when the two were in private practice at the New York firm of Chadbourne, Stanchfield & Levy.[384]

Pressman would become the General Counsel of the Works Progress Administration in April 1935. He would also become the General Counsel of the Resettlement Administration in June 1935. In addition to Hiss and Pressman, Frank added a total of "some sixty lawyers" to the AAA, each "[i]mbued with . . . Frankfurter's civil service ideals."[385] Among the sixty, Frank employed Harvard Law School graduate John Abt (ultimately employed as AAA Director of Litigation) who had been a junior lawyer in one of Frank's firms and Harvard Law graduate Nathan Witt, on Frankfurter's recommendation.[386] Both Abt and Witt had been Frankfurter's students.

By 1933, the Harvard men Hiss, Pressman, Abt, and Witt, while deeply involved in one of the two largest New Deal regulatory efforts, the AAA, became active members of a secret communist cell established by the communist agriculturalist and AAA employee Harold Ware in service to Soviet military intelligence.[387] The so-called Ware Group operated under the direction of Boris Bykov, a Russian military intelligence officer. The Soviets were interested in American agriculture, believing "that the American 'peasants' would be a revolutionary force along with the American factory workers."[388]

In his testimony before Congress, and in his book, *Witness*, Whitaker Chambers (also a member of the Ware Group but who, in 1939, renounced communism) testified that a Russian spy, Josef Peters, interacted with members of the group to obtain government documents and information that would be passed along to the Kremlin. Peters was succeeded by other Russian spies who performed the same role. Chambers stated that between 1933 and 1938, the Soviet spy operation in Washington, proceeding through federal government employees in different cells like the Ware Group, infiltrated the Department of Agriculture, the Department of Justice, the Department of Interior, the National Labor Relations Board, the Agricultural Adjustment Administration, the Railroad Retirement Board, the National Research Project, the State Department, the U.S. Treasury Department, the Bureau of Standards, and the Aberdeen Proving Ground. At each of those locations individuals holding federal government positions, including some in positions with proximity to Department heads and the President, supplied their Soviet handlers with secret or confidential information. Although uncertain of the full extent of the spy operations, Chambers believed there may have been sixty or seventy members in different cells feeding information to the Soviets.[389]

Based on previously classified intelligence, Herbert Romerstein and Eric Breindel explain that the Ware Group formed the center of what became an extensive network of cells within the Roosevelt administration that fed all manner of government secrets to the Soviets:

> When Chambers met Ware in 1934, the underground group Ward led consisted mainly of employees of the Agricultural Adjustment Administration (AAA). Chambers called it "Apparatus A." Among the members were Lee Pressman, Alger Hiss, Donald Hiss, Henry Hill Collins, Jr., Victor Perlo, John Abt, Nathan Witt, and Charles Krivitsky, who later called himself Charles Kramer. Chambers told the FBI, "Ware then quickly realized that the possibilities for the Communist Party exceeded this little group in AAA."

The Party members fanned out into other agencies, and each set up additional cells, first organized as study groups, which evolved into Community Party intelligence gathering units. Leaders of the units identified those members who would be willing to collect information from their agencies for the Communist Party national leadership. They were soon collecting information for Soviet military intelligence.[390]

In September of 1939, Chambers became disillusioned with communism following Stalin's purges (which eliminated an entire generation of Bolshevisks and, ultimately, Lenin protégé Leon Trotsky, who was assassinated by one of Stalin's henchmen in Mexico), the Hitler-Stalin pact (whereby the two dictators agreed not to attack each other's countries, which Hitler betrayed in 1941), and the disappearance of his spy compatriot Juliet Stuart Poyntz (who vanished after she expressed disillusionment with communism).[391] He also for a time feared that he himself was suspected of disloyalty by Soviet military intelligence and might be marked for execution by the Soviet secret police, the GPU.[392]

Chambers agreed to meet with Assistant Secretary of State Adolf A. Berle and inform him about the Ware Group on the condition that he be granted immunity from prosecution.[393] Berle notified the FBI, but the FBI took no significant action and may have doubted Chambers' story until after communist spy Elizabeth Bentley independently repudiated her membership in the communist party and divulged her own espionage details to the FBI, which confirmed much of what Chambers said.[394] Even then, the FBI and the Department of Justice did not act against the spies in the government.

Chambers implicated Hiss as a Ware Group spy. Hiss sued Chambers in an unsuccessful suit for libel, alleging the accusation to be false and defamatory. During discovery, Chambers produced evidence in the form of an envelope containing four notes allegedly written by Hiss along with sixty-five copies of State Department documents and five rolls of 35 mm film allegedly supplied by Hiss to Chambers for submission to the Soviets. Certain of the documents were classified and coded diplomatic correspondence. Out of fear for his safety, Chambers hid the documents in a pumpkin, causing the press to refer to them as the "pumpkin papers."[395]

After the statute of limitations had run on espionage counts, Hiss was prosecuted for two counts of perjury, convicted, and sentenced to five years in prison based in part on the pumpkin papers. In Hiss's trial, Justices Felix Frankfurter and Stanley Reed appeared as character witnesses on Hiss's behalf.[396]

Chambers also implicated several other Roosevelt administration officials as spies for the Soviets: Lee Pressman (AAA, later the Congress of Industrial Organizations); Nathan Witt (NLRB); Harold Ware (AAA and Department of Agriculture); John Abt (Department of Agriculture; Works Progress Administration; Senate Committee on Education and Labor; Department of Justice); Charles Kramer (National Labor Relations Board; Office of Price Administration; Senate Subcommittee on War Mobilization); Vincent Reno (Aberdeen Proving Grounds); Philip Reno (Social Security Administration); Elinor Nelson (Federal Employees Union); Richard Post (Department of State); Laurence Duggan (Department of State); Julian Wadleigh (Department of State); Leander Lovell (Department of State); Noel Field (Department of State); Lauchlin Currie (White House); Solomon Adler (Department of the Treasury); Frank Coe (Department of the Treasury); Donald Hiss (Department of State; Department of Labor); Harry Dexter White (Department of the Treasury); George Silverman (Railway Retirement Board); and Henry Collins (Department of Agriculture; Department of State).[397]

In 1945, information courier for the communists, Elizabeth Bentley, who had served her Soviet handlers for almost a decade, identified over one hundred American operatives working in the federal government.[398] Stan Evans and Herbert Romerstein write, "The largest single group that she identified was at the Treasury, which on her evidence had been well infiltrated by the middle 1930s, with a steady influx of new recruits thereafter. Her main Treasury contact was Nathan G. Silvermaster, who earlier served at other federal agencies and had drawn the notice of security forces . . . without effective action. The most important Treasury suspect was Assistant Secretary Henry White (named as well by Chambers), who by common consent exerted enormous influence with Treasury Secretary Henry Morganthau, Jr." Bentley also named from Treasury: Harold Glasser, V. Frank Coe, Solomon Adler, and Victor Perlo, among others.[399]

In 1995, "half a century after they were first recorded," U.S. Army intercepts of Soviet intelligence communicated from Soviet agents in the United States to those in Moscow corroborated much of Chambers and Bentley's representations concerning the identities of, and nature and extent of, espionage by American communists who worked for the federal government during the New Deal years.[400] The intercepts, referred to as the Venona decrypts (so code-named by the U.S. Army Signal Corps which intercepted them during the 1940s) confirmed extensive communist infiltration of New Deal agencies, bureaus, departments and even the White House. Additional confirmatory information came to light in the 1990s from the archives of the Soviet Union in the form of the Vassiliev papers, named after a former Soviet KGB officer (Alexander Vassiliev) who made copies of the records for authorities in the West when he emigrated to Great Britain in 1996.[401]

Moreover, certain of those identified by Chambers and Bentley later admitted that they had indeed served as Russian assets, including Lee Pressman[402] and Nathaniel Weyl, who confirmed all names with the exception of Donald Hiss.[403] In addition, following the outing of

Chambers and Bentley, the Soviets experienced intelligence failures that caused the KGB officer operating at the Soviet embassy in Washington, Anatoly Gorsky, to report back to his superiors in Moscow those American communist assets who had been compromised. That information came to light from documents supplied by Vassiliev.[404] The following were among those Gorsky listed: Alger Hiss (Department of State); Donald Hiss (Department of the Interior); Henry A. Wadleigh [Julian] (Department of State); F. V. Reno (Aberdeen Proving Grounds); Henry Collins (Department of Agriculture); William W. Pigman (Bureau of Standards); Lee Pressman (CIO; Department of Agriculture); Noel Field (Department of State); V. V. Sveshnikov (Department of War); Harry White (Department of the Treasury); G. Silverman (Air Force); Harold Glasser (Department of the Treasury); Laurence Duggan (Department of State); Franz Neumann (OSS/Department of State); Harry Magdoff (Department of Commerce); Edward Fitzgerald (Department of Commerce); Charles Kramer (Senate Subcommittee on War Mobilization); Donald Wheeler (OSS/Department of State); Allan Rosenberg (Foreign Economic Administration); Stanley Graze (OSS/Department of State); Gerald Graze (Department of War); Charles Flato (Farm Security Administration); Gregory Silvermaster (Department of the Treasury); Lauchlin Currie (White House); Frank Coe (Department of the Treasury); Bela Gold (Department of Commerce); Sonia Gold (Department of the Treasury); Irving Kaplan (Department of the Treasury); Solomon Adler (Department of the Treasury); Ludwig Ullman (Department of War); David Weintraub (United Nations Relief and Rehabilitation Administration); Maurice Halperin (OSS/Department of State); Duncan Lee (OSS); Helen Tenney (OSS); Ruth Rivkin (United Nations Relief and Rehabilitation Administration); Bernard Redmont (Department of State); Robert Miller (Department of State); Joseph Gregg (Department of State); William Remington (Department of Commerce); William Remington (Department of Commerce); Julius Joseph (OSS); and Willard Park (Department of State).[405]

Many of the Soviet assets who supplied their Russian counterparts with United States government information, including classified information, also recruited other American communists to positions in their agencies, bureaus and departments, and they endeavored to influence policies in directions preferred by Soviet military intelligence (ultimately, by Stalin himself). Very few were ever prosecuted for espionage. Hiss and Remington were sent to prison for perjury. Coe and Adler defected to communist China.[406]

From the late 1930s until the 1970s, the FBI, legislative committees, and the House Committee on Un-American Activities and the Senate Subcommittee on Internal Security uncovered evidence of extensive espionage throughout the Roosevelt administration. The evidence leads to the following conclusions reached by Romerstein and Breindel:

> There existed in important agencies of the U.S. government networks of American spies under the control of Soviet military intelligence and NKVD officers. These included individuals whose disloyalty has been acknowledged for years by almost all serious students of the subject. Alger Hiss, Harry Dexter White, and the Rosenbergs through the years have had a shrinking pool of defenders. Others, until the *Venona* documents were aired, were considered heroes of American liberalism.

> *Venona* has shown conclusively that the highest-level American government official working for Soviet intelligence was Harry Hopkins, the close friend and advisor of President Roosevelt. His clandestine contact with "illegal" Soviet intelligence officer Iskhak Akhmerov, to whom he provided secret government information, alone makes the case against Hopkins.[407]

The rise of Soviet spies throughout the Roosevelt administration was a logical outgrowth of the enthusiastic support key figures like Felix Frankfurter and his student Jerome Frank gave to a strong interventionist and paternalist government agenda and to young professionals who endorsed that agenda. Young lawyers and economists who favored an interventionist and paternalist government predicated on a rejection of individual liberty and *laissez-faire* naturally had ideological sympathies with socialists and communists who sought much the same thing. Those who viewed themselves as progressives, socialists, and communists all shared a desire to overcome the Constitution, its limits on government power, its creation of a protected private sphere of freedom and free enterprise, and its defense of individual rights. They all wanted to upend the Constitution in favor of an authoritarian government implemented through an extensive extra-constitutional administrative state. It was therefore entirely logical that they would co-exist peaceably in Frankfurter's Harvard Law School classes, in the Progressive Party of the 1920s, in the Democratic Party of the 1930s, and in the Roosevelt administration. So long as Frankfurter's "Happy Hot Dogs" pursued the same political ends, it appears to have mattered little that certain of them who were communists not only advanced that agenda in America but also advanced it by betraying their country through the provision of classified information to America's enemy, the Soviet Union. Disloyal to their own country, they believed they were true to their authoritarian principles. They thought by furthering the Soviet goal of a communist uprising in America to overthrow the government and replace it with one under Soviet control, they were hastening achievement of the essential ends of the New Deal. The New Deal government too would be one that sought to upend the Constitution and eliminate individual liberty and free enterprise in favor of government control.

FRANKFURTER'S VISION OF THE ADMINISTRATIVE STATE

Frankfurter made clear his opposition to "state's rights, separation of powers, [and] strict construction" of the Constitution, which document he deemed "not a fit instrument for working out the social and economic problems of the day."[408] He believed fundamentally in "government by experts."[409] He found the independence of the judiciary and procedural protections for the accused in Article III courts impediments to achieving social experimentation and thus inappropriate for modern society. He called for a "permanent administrative tribunal" in place of Article III courts.[410]

Frankfurter cultivated a close relationship with fellow progressive Oliver Wendell Holmes, Jr. Holmes believed in rule of a dominant majority and was largely predisposed against protecting individual rights when those rights conflicted with majority rule as embodied in statutory law. Holmes wrote to Frankfurter: "A law should be called good if it reflects the will of the dominant forces of the community even if it will take us to hell."[411] Frankfurter agreed, thinking that the judiciary ought to be replaced by "the judgment of experts, vindicated by legislative majorities."[412] Frankfurter, as a Justice, repeatedly favored dominant majority rule as embodied by enforcement of law against minorities. Frankfurter wrote to Learned Hand on how the Court could best retreat from *Lochner v. New York's* protection of the right to contract and to individual liberty under the Fourteenth Amendment: "A very wide conception of the police power and a restrictive meaning of 'liberty' and 'due process' will allow practically every piece of legislation, at all defensible, . . . to pass [constitutional] muster."[413]

Writing in the *Yale Law Journal* in May of 1925, Frankfurter along with his former student James Landis explained that Article III courts were too inflexible to accommodate needed social experiments implemented by modern legislatures. Rather, such matters needed to be in the hands of administrative tribunals. "The judicial instrument is too static and too sporadic for adjusting a social-economic issue continuously alive in an area embracing more than a half a dozen states," they state. Rather, "continuous and creative administration is needed; not litigation, necessarily a sporadic process, securing at best merely episodic and mutilated settlements."[414]

FRANKFURTER'S SECRET ROLE AS BRANDEIS' FRONT MAN

Between 1916 and 1939, Justice Louis D. Brandeis sent Felix Frankfurter over $50,000 to finance Frankfurter support for liberal public policies, some of which resulted in legal contests that rose to the Supreme Court itself and came before the Court while Brandeis was sitting. Brandeis set up a "joint endeavors for the public good" fund for Frankfurter that Brandeis financed with as much as $3,500 per year. Professor Bruce A. Murphy discovered the letters confirming the payments. He explained that they were "designed to free Brandeis from the shackles of remaining nonpolitical on the bench and to permit him to engage freely in political affairs."[415] *New York Times'* reporter David M. Margolick explains:

. . . Frankfurter undertook many chores for his political patron [Justice Brandeis]. In some instances, Brandeis asked him either to draft legislation designed to remedy what he considered incorrect rulings by his Supreme Court colleagues or to criticize them in the pages of the Harvard Law Review. On another occasion, he asked Frankfurter to research a constitutional question being considered by the Court. . . . Frankfurter devised intricate mechanisms to disseminate Brandeis's ideas in suitably camouflaged fashion, largely through the Harvard Law Review.[416]

In addition, during the Roosevelt administration, Justice Brandeis, through Frankfurter, played an undisclosed role in crafting legislation designed to restrict business activity and stock offerings:

Letters in the Brandeis-Frankfurter correspondence show, moreover, how the two collaborated with Benjamin V. Cohen and Thomas G. Corcoran [Frankfurter's Harvard Law students who were placed at his recommendation in key administration positions] to draft such key legislation as the Securities Act of 1933. . . . [Cohen and Corcoran] visited Brandeis . . . as often as twice monthly. Afterward, Brandeis would forward specific legislative proposals on the matters they had discussed to Frankfurter, who would gather support materials and forward them to Roosevelt. The information would then be returned to [Cohen and Corcoran] who would draft the legislation and shepherd it through Congress.[417]

By actively supporting litigation and legislative reform, Justice Brandeis became a biased partisan, defeating the independence that the judiciary is ethically obliged to maintain. Frankfurter aided him in those pursuits and, thus, likewise compromised the Supreme Court and himself.

FRANKFURTER'S ADMINISTRATIVE STATE LEGACY

While a paternalist, a student of socialism, and a member of ISS with close ties to socialists and communists, Frankfurter never overtly declared himself to be a socialist[418], albeit his unwavering support for the socialist British labor movement and the administrative state suggests that he had no real quarrel with socialist economic policies. Indeed, Frankfurter's aversion for the power limiting doctrines of the Constitution gave birth to an extra-constitutional government outside the three branches in the form of an all-powerful administrative state comprised of over 200 federal agencies. As founding father of the administrative state in America, Frankfurter more than any other single person is responsible for an authoritarian revolution that supplanted the constitutional branches of government with an all-powerful bureaucratic oligarchy.

The administrative state that is Frankfurter's legacy arose out of a commitment to exert substantial and pervasive government control over the private sector in a manner indistinguishable from socialism. To this day, a marked suspicion of, and animus against, free enterprise defines the prime motivations of career regulators. They share much of the same hatred for bigness and for concentrations of capital that defined the core philosophies of Louis Brandeis and Felix Frankfurter and that led several of Frankfurter's students to favor a socialist agenda for America.

More fundamentally, the agencies Frankfurter helped create exist outside the defined parameters of the Constitution, receive extraordinary deference from the courts for their construction of facts and law, and operate with tyrannical powers (combined legislative, executive, and judicial powers). No greater threat exists to the survival of constitutional government in America than from the administrative state and from federal courts that defer to the tyranny of that state.

CHAPTER 5

THE DISMANTLEMENT OF CONSTITUTIONAL BARRIERS

Since Congress created the Interstate Commerce Commission in 1887, the administrative state has operated outside of the Constitution, not subject to its limits on government power. It is, in this sense, extra-constitutional. Because it is now responsible for almost all federal law, it is in substance the principal government of the United States. That comes as a surprise to most Americans who have long believed that those they elect are responsible for the laws that govern them, but, although that is the plain meaning of the legislative vesting clause in Article I, Section 1 of the Constitution, that is not the reality. The administrative state is the primary law-making and law-enforcing body of the United States. That bureaucratic oligarchy, not the Congress, not the President, and not the Courts, governs all enterprise in America and, increasingly, affects or governs all-important individual and business decisions.

The Founders' notion that just governments were instituted for the very purpose of securing the rights of the governed explains why they adopted a Constitution of limited and expressly enumerated powers. The Constitution gave the federal government only those powers conveyed by the language of the instrument, leaving to the states and the people all powers not expressly delegated. Indeed, to ensure that the federal government was one of specifically enumerated powers, the founding fathers insisted on a written Constitution (the "Constitution" of Britain was unwritten). The Tenth Amendment makes the point manifest: "The powers not delegated to the United States by the Constitution, nor prohibited by it to the States, are reserved to the States respectively, or to the people." The Bill of Rights served as an added safeguard, confirming that the people's liberties could not be abridged by the federal government (which the Federalists had at first argued could not occur because the enumerated powers did not permit federal action in violation of individual rights, making a Bill of Rights unnecessary). The Bill of Rights adopted by the first Congress, i.e., the first ten amendments to the Constitution, was not an exclusive listing. Rather, as the Ninth Amendment makes clear, "[t]he enumeration in the Constitution, of certain rights, shall not be construed to deny or disparage others retained by the people."

The Progressives envisioned and then created an administrative state outside of the Constitution and unresponsive to it. Nearly all Progressives decried the Constitution as a relic of a bygone era. Consistent with Progressive leaders' disdain for the Constitution and desire for direct and immediate government intervention to transform the economy and society into the ones they desired, they refused to wait for the passage of constitutional amendments to bring about the monumental shift in government power they desired. They did not propose any amendment to the Constitution to authorize the administrative state, ignoring the dictates of Article V and the Lockean requirement for just governments that they be based on the consent of the governed.

Instead, they favored legislation signed into law by Presidents Grover Cleveland, Theodore Roosevelt, Woodrow Wilson, Herbert Hoover, and Franklin Delano Roosevelt, that blithely violated the Constitution's vesting clauses in Articles I, II, and III, granting administrative agencies and departments supreme and combined legislative, executive, and judicial powers.

In the first round of major federal agency creation, the Progressives created the Interstate Commerce Commission (1887); the Federal Trade Commission (1914); the National Park Service (1916); and the Federal Radio Commission (1927) with sweeping investigatory and, in some instances, licensing and rate-setting powers. Since the founding of the republic, specific administrative bodies did come into existence on an *ad hoc* basis to interpret and enforce the laws. With rare exceptions, none created new laws by administrative fiat alone until the Progressive and New Deal eras. Those that did, acted in the same way as the Progressives' preferred agencies; they proceeded without constitutional amendment yet performed law-making functions that the Constitution grants exclusively to Congress.

In 1933, in President Roosevelt's first one hundred days, dozens of new agencies with combined legislative, executive, and judicial powers were created. All powerful, agency after agency came into existence without amendment to the Constitution. Among them were the following created in 1933 alone: Agricultural Adjustment Administration; Civilian Conservation Corps; Civil Works Administration; Subsistence Homesteads Division; Emergency Banking Act; Federal Aviation Administration; Farm Credit Administration; Federal Deposit Insurance Corporation; Federal Emergency Relief Administration; Federal Surplus Relief Corporation; Home Owners' Loan Corporation; National Recovery Administration; Puerto Rico Reconstruction Administration; Public Works Administration; and Tennessee Valley Authority.

Between the first one hundred days and the end of the Second New Deal, several additional federal agencies were created, including the Federal Communications Commission (1934); Federal Housing Administration (1934); National Labor Relations Board (1934); Securities and Exchange Commission (1934); Drought Relief Service (1935); Federal Art Project (1935); Federal Music Project (1935); Farm Security Administration (1935); Federal Theatre Project (1935); National Labor Relations Act (1935); National Youth Administration (1935); Resettlement Administration (1935); Rural Electrification Administration (1935); Social Security Administration (1935); Social Security Board (1935); Works Progress Administration (1935); United States Maritime Commission (1936); United States Housing Authority (1937); Fair Labor Standards/U.S. Department of Labor (1938); and Federal Works Agency (1939).

At first, the agencies relied principally on investigative powers; meetings with the heads of regulated entities; strong-arm tactics; and disclosure laws that revealed to the public alleged corporate wrong-doing. But soon thereafter Congress acquiesced to their expansion of powers, enabling them to restrict all manner of business relationships and market entry. Progressives Theodore Roosevelt, Woodrow Wilson, Felix Frankfurter, and Franklin Delano Roosevelt provided a superficial constitutional justification for the changes wrought but gave whole-hearted support to the construction of the administrative state.

Wilson, like all Progressives thereafter, held fast to the view that the Constitution could not survive the exigencies of modernity unless it was viewed as a "living" document, by which he meant one interpreted elastically, and against its power limiting provisions, to embrace substantial delegations of power from the three constitutional branches of government to the new administrative state.

To appreciate just how far the governing power has departed from its constitutional moorings, it is important to examine those moorings in some detail, at each point of departure. The powers assumed by the administrative state are vast and, indeed, violate the plain and intended meaning of the Constitution. These are among the powers employed by the administrative state that violate the Constitution:

1. **Regulations are laws enacted without the consent of the governed.** Regulatory agencies and bureaus are ruled by individual commissioners (e.g., FDA and EPA) or a slate of commissioners (e.g., FTC and FCC) who are appointed by the President and usually approved by Congress. The agency and bureau heads are not elected, and the regulations which have the full force of law that they create are not the product of elected representatives.

By contrast, the Constitution requires that all laws be created by Congress, which is, of course, elected by the people. Consequently, no law is enacted by Congress which is not the subject of a vote by the elected representatives of the people. This notion of consent of the governed is foundational to constitutional government. Indeed, the founding fathers believed, as did

John Locke, that no just government could exist unless it was based, in the first instance, on the consent of the governed. That is why the Constitution was not simply adopted by the constitutional convention but was proposed to conventions in the states, where state legislatures, representatives of the people, voted on whether to ratify the Constitution.

The essential principle is that no one has a right to govern another without that other's consent. The principle defines the difference between freedom and slavery. A free people consent to limitations on their freedom, slaves do not. In this sense, administrative law is retrograde. It is a form of enslavement because it is imposed on the governed without their consent either directly (by their individual consent) or indirectly (by their elected representatives' consent).

The founding fathers understood this principle of consent to be Lockean, derived from John Locke's Second Treatise on Government (1689), Sections 119–122. In Federalist No. 22, Hamilton put it this way: "The fabric of American empire ought to rest on the solid basis of THE CONSENT OF THE PEOPLE. The streams of national power ought to flow immediately from that pure, original fountain of all legitimate authority."[419] In Federalist No. 37, James Madison explained: "The genius of republican liberty seems to demand on one side not only that all power should be derived from the people, but that those [e]ntrusted with it should be kept in dependence on the people by a short duration of their appointments."[420] In Federalist No. 39, Madison related that a republican form of government would devolve into tyranny if powers originally derived from the consent of the governed were delegated to "a favored class" unaccountable to the people, constituting a body of "tyrannical nobles" who could oppress the people.[421] He there spoke prophetically because the administrative state is that very thing, a favored class of people touted to be experts, and that class does indeed govern like "tyrannical nobles."

The adoption of laws by those who are unelected destroys the principle of accountability to which Madison referred in Federalist No. 37. Those who govern justly are fiduciaries of the people; they are trustees who must account to the people for their official actions. Laws made by the elected representatives of the people are made by those who must stand for election and defend their enactments. If they favor laws that deviate from the majority will, they may lose elections and those who replace them may well alter or abolish the disfavored laws.

In the administrative state, no such accountability exists. The unelected who create administrative regulations do not stand for election and, so, if they enact a regulation that is contrary to the will of the people or in deprivation of individual right, they suffer no consequence. They do not stand in a fiduciary relationship with the people. Moreover, unlike elected representatives, if they govern corruptly, they cannot be removed from office by vote of the people and, while they may suffer prosecution for their offenses, that is itself an action initiated not by the elected representatives of the people but, instead, by an unelected administration, e.g., the United States Attorneys or the Attorney General (themselves, appointed, not elected).

This feature of no accountability provides decision-makers in the agencies tremendous power to enforce their will in ways that would be roundly rejected by the public. As we shall see in the chapter on administrative tyranny, regulatory agencies have taken draconian actions that result in the taking of private property, the destruction of entire businesses, the destruction of innovation by business, and the stifling of vital health information, all without ever having to account for those actions to the American people. Undoubtedly, legislators often favor delegating broad powers to agencies precisely because those legislators do not want to be held accountable by their constituents for actions they desire but that have draconian consequences (such as the closing of plants, costly compliance in satisfaction of compulsory environmental regulations, or the censorship of information affecting freedom of choice, health, and life).

The administrative state thus suffers from a foundational illegitimacy problem. By the constitutional measure of the founding fathers, the administrative state is not a "just government" because it is not based on the consent of the governed.

2. **The administrative state exists in breach of the non-delegation doctrine.** The powers wielded by administrative agencies are derived initially from their enabling statutes.

> Those delegations include not only congressional power to make law but also, in an act of usurpation by Congress, the powers of the executive and the judiciary. Congress most frequently delegates to the agencies not only the power to make law (i.e., regulations) but also the power to enforce those regulations and to adjudicate alleged regulatory transgressions.

The Constitution vests legislative, executive, and judicial powers exclusively in the respective branches of the federal government, and only in those. It does not authorize a re-delegation of the powers to entities outside the branches. This concept of reserved powers within the constitutional branches is called the non-delegation doctrine and was explained by John Locke in his Second Treatise on Government and thereafter adopted by the founding fathers. At root, it defends the sovereignty of the people and is a derivative of the concept that just laws depend on the consent of the governed. The people have not consented to invest constitutional powers of governance in any entities other than the three constitutional branches of government, to which they have consented. Thus, delegation to agencies and bureaus of those powers creates a fundamental illegitimacy problem. John Locke explains, "[t]he legislative cannot transfer the power of making laws to any other hands. For it being but a delegated power from the people, they, who have it, cannot pass it over to others." That is because "[t]he people alone can appoint the form of the commonwealth . . . And when the people have said, We will submit to rules, and be governed by laws made by such men . . . no body else can say other men shall make laws for them; nor can the people be bound by any laws, but such as are enacted by those, whom they have chosen."[422] Recognizing the direct line of authority comes from the people by their consent to the specific repositories of power in the Constitution, it is thus literally unconstitutional for those who control those repositories to transfer any part of that power to others, to which the people have not given their consent.

3. **The administrative state is comprised of agencies and bureaus having legislative, executive, and judicial powers combined, what the founding fathers understood to be the very definition of tyranny.** The administrative state usurps the individually separated and vested powers of the Congress, the President, and the Courts and, indeed, consolidates those formerly separate powers into single, absolute power centers, the individual agencies and bureaus of the federal government.

By contrast, the Constitution exclusively vests the legislative power in Congress; the executive power in the President; and the judicial power in the federal courts. Why did the founding fathers separate those powers, and what harms did they foresee stemming from a consolidation of them in single power centers (like the administrative agencies)? The answer is given by James Madison in Federalist Nos. 47 and 51. Drawing from Montesquieu's *Spirit of the Laws,* Madison presents an accepted "political maxim that the legislative, executive, and judiciary departments ought to be separate and distinct." When one or a few individuals rule with absolute power independent of any other check on that power, they are by definition tyrants indistinguishable from absolute monarchs. That was Madison's understanding: "The accumulation of all powers, legislative, executive, and judiciary, in the same hands, whether of one, a few, or many, and whether hereditary, self-appointed, or elective, may justly be pronounced the very definition of tyranny."[423] The hereditary example mentioned by Madison would be that of an absolute monarch. The self-appointed example would be that of a recipient of delegated power, e.g., the heads of the administrative state. The elective example would be, for example, if executive and judicial powers were usurped by the legislative branch. Relying on Montesquieu, "[t]he oracle who is always consulted and cited on this subject," Madison explained, quoting him, "'[t]here can be no liberty where the legislative and executive powers are united in the same person, or body of magistrates,' or, 'if the power of judging be not separated from the legislative and executive powers . . .'"[424]

Admitting that there would, of necessity, be some degree of overlap in powers among the three constitutional branches, Madison insisted that never could "the *whole* power of one department [be] exercised by the same hands which possess the *whole* power of another department."[425] To do so would cause "the fundamental principles of a free constitution [to be] subverted."[426]

There is more to the separation of powers than denying one branch authority to absorb the power of another. Madison explained that each political power center could be expected to guard its separate reserve of authority jealously and thereby to form a check on the excesses of the others. He described that feature as a "great security against a gradual concentration of the several powers in the same department."[427] The separation of powers thus gives each department "means and personal motives to resist encroachments of the others."[428] In this way, ambition "counteract[s] ambition."[429] Madison believed human nature invariably leads to efforts born of selfishness or avarice to accumulate more political power and that the separation, combined with allowance for competing ambitions, stands in the way of those motives. "If men were angels, no government would be necessary," wrote Madison, and "[i]f angels were to govern men, neither external nor internal controls on government would be necessary."[430] Because men are neither angels who reliably follow the Golden Rule (Matthew 7:12; Luke 6:31), nor are reliably willing to be governed by angels, the separation of powers was necessary, so that each department "may be a check on the other—that the private interest of every individual may be a sentinel over the public rights."[431]

The great fault of the administrative state, indeed the superficial position that gave rise to the doctrine of separate functions in the administrative context as a substitute for separation of powers, is the presumption that employees of an agency can function independently of agency political heads in their prosecution of the accused such that they may serve the ends of justice rather than the dictates of those who created agency rules and ordered prosecutions. For those who practice law before the administrative agencies, that assertion is laughable. There has never in fact been a true separation of functions in the administrative state. Agency employees, including agency prosecutors, depend on the favorable opinions of agency heads for advancement. To achieve advancement, agency prosecutors must pursue cases relentlessly without an independent scruple (even when the facts adduced do not reasonably support the charge alleged). Likewise, administrative law judges; they too are dependent on the favorable opinion of the agency heads for their continued employment within the agency and, so, ordinarily dare not go too far astray from the desires of those heads. Indeed, unlike Article III judges in their relationship with lawyers in the federal courts, administrative law judges lack the authority to impose sanctions for prosecutorial misconduct by agency litigators and lack independent employment and life tenure sufficient to remove themselves from the political influence of the agency heads.

There is, in short, no substitute for Article III independence. In the agencies, invariably the prosecutors do the bidding of the agency heads, the administrative law judges shy away from decisions that conflict with what they perceive to be the agency heads' desires, and then, ultimately, because the agency heads who initiated the prosecutions are also the final judges, they almost always find fault with the party they have accused.

4. **The administrative state violates the guarantee of independent judicial review.** Administrative "trials" are hearings before agency-employed administrative law judges in response to agency demands for prosecution for an alleged violation of agency rules or the agency's enabling statute, or both. Unlike judges in Article III courts, administrative law judges are neither appointed for life nor independent of the agency bringing charges. They are beholden to the agency for their continued employment and bound by agency precedent. Indeed, administrative law judges are duty-bound to apply the agency's interpretation of its regulations (they may not overrule the regulations or declare them unconstitutional). When they do issue decisions or recommendations of decision, those rulings are then reviewed by the agency heads themselves who can easily overrule the administrative law judge, rendering his

or her opinion of no force or effect, and impose an entirely different decision. In this way, the party that writes the legislative rules and orders the administrative prosecution ultimately judges the party accused. There is, in this, no justice. An inherent conflict of interest exists. Agencies are not known for calling into question the wisdom and legality of their own rules and decisions to prosecute. They must report to Congress their expenditure of agency resources, and they are loathe to report that they expended hundreds of thousands of dollars on prosecutions that were ill-advised or did not result in adverse determinations against those they have accused. While a political directive from the executive branch can reduce the incidence of agency prosecutions, neither the President nor Congress may intrude into an ongoing prosecution, no matter how ill-advised it may be.

Administrative law judges are thus biased in favor of the agencies that employ them. Philip Hamburger contrasts the role of independent Article III judges with that of administrative law judges:

The office of a judge has traditionally been a duty of independent judgment in accord with the law of the land. A judge, in other words, has a duty to exercise his judgment independently . . . In contrast, administrative decisionmakers hold offices that require both more and less of them. Administrative decisionmakers must do more than follow the law, because they must follow administrative rules and interpretations—indeed, they often must exercise judgment about the implementation of administrative policy. They also must do less than exercise independent judgment, for they are precommitted to carrying out the government's policy in its regulations, and they must submit to having their decisions reconsidered by executive officers—neither of which is compatible with judicial independence.[432]

The effect of the administrative law "courts" is to diminish the authority of Article III courts. There arose in the law a deferential doctrine of considerable consequence whereby those accused of violating agency regulations are ordinarily foreclosed from challenging the agency in federal court until the agency has finally disposed of the party's case. That doctrine requires exhaustion of administrative remedies before an Article III court may hear an administrative case. It is often the case that those prosecuted by administrative agencies suffer significant financial burdens in their defense during the agency prosecution. Indeed, it is common for administrative agency attorneys to use the subpoena power liberally to, in part, financially cripple the accused, forcing the accused to give up its defense and comply with agency demands or suffer an adverse agency ruling yet lack the resources necessary to pursue an appeal. Agency lawyers achieve that corrupt end by sending burdensome subpoenas to all business contacts and financial institutions with which the party accused operates.

The subpoena to a non-party alerts the non-party to the fact that a powerful federal agency or bureau is prosecuting one with whom the non-party conducts business. That connection, for all the non-party knows, may force it into the proceeding or even open the subpoena recipient to agency prosecution. Consequently, many with whom the accused do business will find it prudent to halt or discontinue business with the accused, so as not to become embroiled in the matter. The consequential loss of business can deplete resources and deny the accused sufficient wherewithal to proceed in the action or appeal an agency judgment to a court, making the agency's will a *fait accompli* through emasculation of the accused's procedural rights.

As explained in Chapter 7, the courts' standard of review is so highly deferential to agencies as to make appeals oftentimes worthless. That factor exacerbates the denial of justice attendant to administrative rulings because more times than not those rulings are final adjudications from which no meaningful appeal is possible.

5. **The administrative state violates the constitutional guarantee of due process of law.** The agencies and their administrative law judges rely on an inquisitorial process whereby the accused is legally obliged to supply whatever evidence is demanded in aid of prosecution (regardless of relevance) and is effectively presumed guilty until he, she, or it marshals exculpatory evidence and, even then, is oftentimes still prosecuted. This stands in stark contrast with the independent Article III courts where innocence is presumed, the prosecutorial party bears the burden of proof and persuasion, both parties engage in an adversarial process of discovery under the Federal Rules of Civil or Criminal Procedure and must conform their discovery to that which is calculated to lead to relevant evidence, and a failure to adduce evidence supportive of a case ordinarily results in dismissal or a summary judgment against the prosecutorial party.

The historic irony is that the due process clauses of the Constitution (the Fifth Amendment as to actions by the federal government, the Fourteenth Amendment as to actions by the states) are a direct response to (and meant to guard against recreation of) the prerogative courts of England, such as the Courts of Star Chamber. As Philip Hamburger explains, while the federal courts have liberally allowed inquisitions in administrative bodies, they have forbidden them in Article III courts. The Courts of Star Chamber in fifteenth- to seventeenth-century England were often political bodies that secretly prosecuted enemies of the state, including religious dissenters such as John Lilburne (who coined the term "freeborn rights" as God-given and distinct from rights said to be granted by the state); William Prynne; and Alexander Leighton -- all for the publication of unlicensed religious tracts. The Courts of Star Chamber were abolished by order of Parliament in the Habeas Corpus Act of 1640 and were condemned by the United States Supreme Court in, *inter alia*, *Faretta v. California* (1975)[433].

Effectively, administrative proceedings are inquisitions that mirror in many respects the political prosecutions of the Courts of Star Chamber. Philip Hamburger well explains the deviations from due process common in administrative proceedings:

> [T]he [constitutional principle] requires that all judicial power be exercised with the "due process of law," which was that done through the law and its courts. . . . Nonetheless . . . administrative agencies have returned to the inquisitorial process of the prerogative courts. . . . [L]ike the prerogative courts, administrative agencies often begin their proceedings not with indictments, but on the accusations of anonymous or secret informers, or merely on the suspicions or policy decisions of executive officers. Indeed, agencies impose ex officio demands for information about compliance, thus coercively fishing for violations before formal charges are brought. The agencies thereby combine functions that the due process of law separates. For example, the agencies serve as initial investigators and interrogators, then as prosecutors, then as grand juries, and then as judges and juries; in other words, they coercively collect information, formulate charges, determine their sufficiency, and finally try them. Last, but not least, the agencies impose self-incriminating questions and even require persons to self-report their departures from regulations before they are questioned—thus reviving the confessional character of inquisitorial process.[434]

There is an inherent, ongoing conflict of interest never addressed by the agencies because it calls into question their existence. The agency is, after all, a party, not an impartial judge. As a party, it cannot be an impartial judge. It creates the rule, prosecutes the accused rule violator, and judges the rule violation.

Moreover, the Progressive creators of the administrative state never intended administrative "trials" to be impartial. They sought, above all else, prompt results in support of their political agendas (they meant to have the ends dictate the means). Agency rules are political. They aim to alter market behavior in ways politically preferred by agency heads. In the vernacular of the Progressive era, agency heads were in the business of creating a utopian society. The entire process is not one of independent adjudication of charges with independence that affords the administrative law judge the power to declare the regulations themselves illegal or unconstitutional or to declare the prosecution unlawful. Instead, administrative law begins with fixed rules stacked against the accused. The administrative law judge's interpretations of agency rules must reflect the ends desired by the agency, i.e., the accusing party, even if those ends violate statutory law or are unconstitutional. The administrative law judge has no power to grant an accused relief based on the illegality of a regulation or statute giving rise to it; his or her grant of authority to decide agency cases presumes the legality of the agency's rules and of its enabling statute. Administrative law judges are disarmed of any power to declare agency law unlawful or impose sanctions on or exclude agency counsel, no matter how errant they may be.

6. **The administrative state permits charges at variance with administrative complaints, without restriction.** As in courts of law, in administrative cases, the accused receives notice of the charges against the accused in the form of a complaint. Unlike in courts of law, the accused in administrative cases may not demand a bill of particulars to obtain further detail, even when the charges are inexact, confusing, or bereft of essential facts. Moreover, in administrative cases, the agencies' counsel frequently modify the charges as the case proceeds, hopping from ones that fail for want of facts to new ones that may be stronger, doing so without amending the complaint or otherwise serving notice to the accused, doing so even after administrative hearings are over and all witnesses have testified (and even up to and in final proposed findings of fact and conclusions of law), effectively denying the

accused any, let alone meaningful, notice of the operative charges. The accused thus faces a moving target and perpetual uncertainty. The changing charges also deny the accused a meaningful opportunity to obtain germane discovery and argue against the ultimate charge. This act of legerdemain is, of course, unfair, but it is more than that: It deprives the accused of essential due process needed to ensure a just result. Indeed, in administrative "trials," a fair trial is rarely, if ever, possible, and, so, injustice is the norm, not the exception.

In the federal courts, by contrast, complaints are required to include a plain statement of the charges against the accused and cannot be changed except by amendment. Bills of particulars are commonly granted in the face of ambiguous charges. Moreover, amendments are disallowed after deadlines set by the court, so as not to prejudice any party by denying it a full and fair opportunity for discovery under the charges. Moreover, the fluidity of charges in administrative "trials" violates the Sixth Amendment when fines, forfeitures, or corrective action are sought by the government. That is because the Sixth Amendment guarantees in criminal prosecutions the right of the accused "to be informed of the nature and cause of the accusation."

7. **The administrative state violates the right to confront one's accusers and against self-incrimination.** In an administrative case, the accused does not have a right to know who alleged wrongdoing to the agency or to see what was submitted to the agency by the accuser. The accused is not even allowed to know if the agency itself originated the charges. Also, because the burdens of proof and persuasion are effectively on the accused in administrative proceedings, the accused is forced to admit or deny specific acts that may be inculpatory under the agency's regulations. The agency thus does not recognize a meaningful right against self-incrimination.

In the criminal context (such as where the accused may be subjected to fines, forfeitures, or corrective action), the Sixth Amendment guarantees the accused the right to confront opposing witnesses and to have compulsory process for obtaining witnesses in the accused's favor. Also in the criminal context, the Fifth Amendment guarantees the accused the right against self-incrimination. Those rights are violated routinely in administrative hearings where fines, forfeitures, or corrective action remedies are available to the agency. Although such remedies are ordinarily deemed criminal because they force the divestiture of property or constrict liberty, in the administrative context they are presumed to be civil. Based on that presumption alone, Fifth and Sixth Amendment rights are declared inapplicable.

8. **The administrative state uses constitutionally prohibited general warrants.** In England, during the 1763 prosecution of John Wilkes for seditious libel (his publication of a seditious libel in *The North Briton* (No. 45), a case followed closely in the American colonies where sympathies lay for Wilkes, Wilkes argued the warrants were illegal. Chief Justice Charles Pratt agreed, declaring the general warrant used to arrest Wilkes "unconstitutional, illegal, and absolutely void."[435] In *Wilkes v. Wood* (1763)[436] and *Entick v. Carrington* (1765)[437], Pratt declared general warrants unlawful without equivocation.

James Otis earlier challenged writs of assistance used by the Crown in the colonies in *Paxton's Case* (1755)[438], which case (along with *Wilkes* and *Entick*) contributed mightily to the adoption of a prohibition on general warrants in state constitutions and in the Fourth Amendment. General warrants (called "writs of assistance" or "general writs of assistance" and also known as "administrative warrants") were issued to administrators not by a judge but at the behest of the Crown or colonial governors. They "did not specify the person to be seized or place to be searched," leaving that to the enforcing officer, thus enabling unbridled discretion in the making of arrests and the seizing of documents. General warrants were issued on mere suspicion alone and were not supported by declarations under oath. Many in England and the colonies joined Wilkes in condemning general warrants as tyrannical.

Although prohibited by the Fourth Amendment, general warrants have come back to life in the form of administrative subpoenas and administrative inspection orders. As with general warrants, administrative subpoenas and inspection orders are often issued based on nothing more than mere suspicion, are often done on an *ex parte* basis (i.e., without notice to the parties affected), and are issued by the administrators themselves, not by judges in Article III courts. Consequently, they suffer from the same defects of unbridled official discretion and unrestricted license that gave rise to the bar against them in the Fourth Amendment. The Supreme Court has upheld use of these sweeping warrants in the administrative context. As Philip Hamburger explains: "Although [the Supreme Court] generally has balked at allowing intrusions into homes, it has allowed agencies, when acting under open-ended inspection statutes, to exercise their own discretion in invading private property—at least when an agency sanitizes its discretion by specifying it in an inspection plan . . . Agencies thus often make their own decisions to send their officers onto private premises, and because these decisions are treated as legally binding, they amount to administrative warrants."[439]

9. **The administrative state does not follow the Federal Rules of Civil Procedure and Evidence and allows into the record for decision irrelevant and unreliable evidence.** In administrative proceedings, the general rules of civil procedure and of evidence routinely followed in the federal courts are not required to be followed. Virtually anything an agency's attorneys wish to put in the record is allowed, even if highly prejudicial or tangentially relevant or irrelevant and even if comprised of unverifiable hearsay (out of court statements offered for the truth of the matter asserted), thus inviting irrelevance and prejudice to triumph over probative value. In addition, allegedly expert reports are admitted along with allegedly expert testimony without proof that those who have drafted the reports and

testimony are truly expert. In federal court under *Daubert v. Merrell Dow Pharmaceuticals, Inc.* (1993)[440] and its progeny, the judge serves as a gate-keeper blocking testimony that is not qualified as expert under Federal Rule of Evidence 702. The court examines the expert's background carefully and determines if the expert has requisite "knowledge, skill, experience, training, and education" and whether the opinion expressed is based on generally accepted scientific principles and methods, rejecting junk science. Administrative law judges are not required to perform any of that screening and, so, unscientific and unreliable materials routinely pepper administrative records, create bias, and feed into decisions. The bias is rendered more profound because efforts to challenge the credentials of government experts in administrative hearings are oftentimes disallowed.

10. **The administrative state authorizes biased discovery.** Although the administrative agencies give themselves sweeping discovery powers, they deny the accused discovery against the government and oftentimes interfere with subpoenas issued to non-parties possessed of evidence germane to government investigations. The effect is to skew evidence in favor of the government and hide corrupt activities of agency officials and litigators that may involve collusion in the creation of evidence. There is, thus, no ability to use discovery to check agency actions, reveal true motives for the prosecution, and uncover instances of corruption and abuse of power.

11. **The administrative state denies the accused trial by jury as required by the Sixth and Seventh Amendments.** There are no jury trials in administrative proceedings. The administrative law judge is the trier of fact and law. That

is said to be in aid of efficiency and to be of no concern because administrative proceedings are deemed "civil."

Under the Sixth Amendment to the Constitution, "[i]n all criminal prosecutions, the accused shall enjoy the right to a speedy and public trial, by an impartial jury of the State and district wherein the crime shall have been committed." Under the Seventh Amendment, "[i]n suits at common law [civil suits], where the value in controversy shall exceed twenty dollars, the right of trial by jury shall be preserved . . ." Although the Constitution guarantees a right to trial by jury in both civil and criminal proceedings, the administrative state does not afford those it accuses a jury trial.

The argument that elimination of a jury is efficient comes at the expense of what would otherwise be the only independent check on the factual integrity of the government's case. An impartial jury would not harbor a bias in favor of facts selectively gleaned in support of the government's case, a common complaint about administrative proceedings and administrative law judges. Instead, it would be independent and neutral, capable of giving credence or not to any fact alleged in the case. It would also by its factual determinations temper administrative law judge conclusions of law because if a jury were to find no facts sufficient to support a charge, the administrative law judge would be hard-pressed to conclude in favor of the government on that charge.

Philip Hamburger has challenged the argument that administrative proceedings are exclusively civil. He explains that government proceedings that culminate in fines are criminal, regardless of whether those fines are imposed in a judicial or administrative proceeding. "Indeed, all government proceedings brought on behalf of the government for penalties or correction," he writes, "have long been considered criminal in nature." Most administrative proceedings against a party involve either a command for corrective action or an imposition of fines, forfeitures, or restitution. They are thus indistinguishable in that regard from criminal prosecutions that impose fines and restrict liberty. The only kind of order beyond the reach of administrative agencies is one imposing a jail sentence or capital punishment.[441]

12. **The administrative state's decisions are exempt from meaningful judicial review.** Administrative agency decisions are ordinarily accorded broad deference by the courts, enabling them to escape any searching, *de novo* review of their determinations of which facts are material and their construction of the law. The deference accorded extends not only to the agency's rendition of the facts but also to the agency's construction of its own regulations, its enabling statute, and even the Constitution. Beginning in the 1932 case of *Crowell v. Benson*[442], where Chief Justice Charles Evans Hughes endeavored to accommodate Progressive demands for greater allowance of the administrative state, the law began to cede substantive elements of judicial review back to the agencies. By 1984, that movement had reached a high point, with Justice John Paul Stevens ruling in *Chevron USA, Inc. v. Natural Resources Defense Council, Inc.*[443] that except in instances where a statute at issue is clear in addressing agency power, administrative agencies would be given deference in their interpretation of enabling statutes, which interpretations would be upheld so long as they were reasonable, meaning so long as they were not arbitrary and capricious. Under *Chevron*, the deferential standard has led to common judicial affirmation without probing review of agency determinations that violate rights to property and liberty, effectively denying the accused meaningful redress through appeal. That problem has rendered the law schizophrenic. In instances where the government sues in federal courts, the appeals are fulsome with the record and law reviewed *de novo*. By contrast, in instances where an agency sues before its own administrative court, the appeals are deferential with the agency's findings of fact and conclusions of law ordinarily upheld if even a scintilla of evidence supports them. Agency decisions are most often rubber-stamped unless they are patently

unreasonable, arbitrary, and capricious. Chief Justice John Roberts, Justice Clarence Thomas, Justice Anthony Kennedy, and Justice Neil Gorsuch have each expressed reservations about *Chevron*. Justices Brett Kavanaugh and Amy Coney Barrett are believed likely predisposed against *Chevron* deference as well.

Justice Anthony Kennedy expressed his misgivings with *Chevron* in a concurrence in *Pereira v. Sessions*[444], where he disapproved of the "reflexive deference" given by federal courts to agency actions. He called for reconsideration of the decision, concluding that, "[t]he proper rules for interpreting statutes and determining agency jurisdiction and substantive agency powers should accord with constitutional separation of powers and the function and province of the judiciary." The import of the last phrase is clear, recalling Chief Justice John Marshall's famous statement in *Marbury v. Madison* (1803)[445]: "It is emphatically the province and duty of the judicial department to say what the law is." *Chevron's* days may be numbered.

In Adrian Vermeule's *Law's Abnegation*, he faults Philip Hamburger (author of *Is Administrative Law Unlawful?*) for arguing that administrative law violates the non-delegation doctrine because it is a "subdelegation," or "re-delegation," of legislative power from Congress to the agencies. In reliance on *Loving v. United States*[446] and *City of Arlington v. FCC*[447], Vermeule argues that "administrative law denies that there *is* any delegation of legislative power at all, so long as the legislature has supplied an 'intelligible principle' to guide the exercise of delegated discretion."[448]

Vermeule trivializes Hamburger's position. Whether the legislature supplies an agency it creates with an "intelligible principle" to guide its delegation of legislative power, or not, the delegation itself remains unconstitutional under original principles. The vesting clause of the Constitution emphatically limits the power to make law to the Congress. The power to make law may not be sub-delegated. More fundamentally, and the point that escapes Vermeule, is that the constitutional power to make law is based on the principle of consent of the governed. While the people have consented to the Constitution and its vestiture of power in the constitutional branches, they have not consented to the transfer of any one of those powers, e.g., law making, to an entity outside of the branches.

Just governments depend on the consent of the governed under the Lockean principles undergirding our republic. This notion is embodied in the legal maxim first cited by the Supreme Court in *United States v. Savings Bank* (1881)[449]: *delegata potestas non potest delegari* (no delegated powers can be further delegated) or *delegatus non potest delegare* (one to whom power is delegated cannot himself further delegate that power). The notion is reinforced by statements made in Locke's *Second Treatise on Government* and by Montesquieu in *The Spirit of the Laws*. It is fundamental that the entities into which the public has consented that powers be placed have no authority to transfer those powers to others for execution. When those powers are transferred to an unelected agency, the consent necessary for the legitimacy of government action is removed. The problem in this instance arises not because Congress has authorized an entity *to execute* the law but because Congress has authorized an entity *to make* the law. All agencies of the federal government are empowered to create regulations, which in the exercise of that function are quintessentially usurping the law-making power exclusively vested in Congress. Under original principles, it is not within Congress's constitutional authority to delegate to any entity its law-making function, just as it is not within Congress's constitutional authority to delegate to any entity the executive's law-enforcement power or the judiciary's adjudicatory power. That the Supreme Court in deference to the administrative state has embraced the "intelligible principle" rationale as an excuse for delegation is indeed the case, but that does not make the rationale consistent with the Constitution's foundational principles. Hamburger's argument proceeds from first principles and concludes the delegation is one contrary to the plain and intended meaning of the Constitution. Vermeule fails to engage Hamburger on that level.

As we have seen, the administrative state is an extra-constitutional government freed from the power limiting doctrines of the Constitution. Its existence stands as a violation of the Constitution's vesting clauses, the separation of powers doctrine, and the non-delegation doctrine. Set adrift from the Constitution, the agencies operate the modern equivalent of Star

Chamber Courts where the bias in favor of the government is profound and the rights of the accused are left unprotected.

The administrative state has dispensed with traditional Due Process protections for those accused of violating regulations and has denied the accused the protections of the federal rules of civil and criminal procedure. The administrative state has denied the accused the power to perform discovery against government accusers or even to confront those whose complaints to administrative agencies have led to actions against the accused, thus negating the Sixth Amendment. The administrative state knows no limits to its discovery powers, enabling it to obtain as a matter of course information beyond that allowable as relevant in civil and criminal courts of law. It denies the accused static charges, preventing the accused from knowing with certainty the nature of the charges brought, with administrative complaints morphing without formal amendment to include charges not presented in the written complaint. It robs the accused of a trial in an independent Article III court. It denies the accused a trial by jury before impositions of restrictions on liberty and deprivations of property, thus negating the Sixth and Seventh Amendments. It denies the accused the right against self-incrimination guaranteed by the Fifth Amendment. It denies the accused a presumption of innocence and refuses to impose the burden of proof and persuasion on the government accuser, effectively placing those burdens on the accused, instead.

The Progressives have thus through the administrative state dismantled the Constitution's barriers against government power and in defense of individual rights. In so doing, they largely abandoned the ideological and functional foundations of America's limited federal republic and replaced it with virtually unlimited authoritarian powers in the administrative bureaus, departments, and agencies. The primary bases for limits on power and protection of individual rights in the Constitution have been eliminated for the sake of efficient achievement of Progressive goals. In the world of the authoritarians who created the administrative state, the ends forever justify the means and justice is perpetually denied.

CHAPTER 6

THE CARTELIZATION OF FAVORED ENTERPRISE

The irony of the anti-trust era is that monopolization did not arise in the market, as has so often been contended, but from government intervention on behalf of industry. At first railroad regulation at the state, and then federal, levels imposed price controls and service restrictions that gave the large railroads a decisive edge, and then this practice of government regulatory favoritism continued in all other major industries throughout the twentieth century, culminating in the National Recovery Administration and Agricultural Adjustment Administration's wage, price, production, and distribution controls that assured market consolidation and control beneficial to the largest firms at the expense of smaller competitors who went out of business in droves.

The history of the late nineteenth century is one of cartelization, i.e., monopoly, but not due to supposed failings of capitalism, but, instead, due to government intervention that skewed markets in favor of the largest firms. Attaining monopoly proved to be an elusive goal for large firms in the market, but when government intervened to fix prices and to limit areas of service, the large firms gained market share and became larger than ever before, enabling them to achieve market consolidation, which, without government, was impossible. Gabriel Kolko observes: "It is business control over politics (and by 'business' I mean the major economic interests) rather than political regulation of the economy that is the significant phenomenon of the Progressive Era."[450]

The history of government-induced cartelization of markets is one well documented in the economic and historical literature of the last several decades. Rothbard writes: "[T]he essence of Progressivism was that certain elements of big business, having sought monopoly through cartels and mergers on the free market without success, turned to government—federal, state, and local—to achieve that monopoly through government-sponsored and enforced cartelization . . ."[451] Economic regulation is driven by politicians who determine its direction, ordinarily against market segments they disfavor, thus benefiting those that are politically favored with monopoly or oligopoly. All government departments and agencies are headed by political appointees of the party controlling the executive branch. It is they who authorize specific enforcement actions, thus inevitably causing those actions to reflect political preferences. Such was the case with the anti-trust laws from the start. According to Rothbard:

> . . . [T]he Morgans were dominant interest behind the Democratic Party, and the Rockefellers behind the Republican Party. While the last Cleveland administration (1893-1897) was Morgan dominated, the subsequent McKinley administrations (1897-1901) were Rockefeller dominated, with the Morgans as junior partners since they supported McKinley over Bryan. Matters quickly changed when McKinley was assassinated in 1901 and his vice president, the Morgan affiliated Theodore Roosevelt, took office, and the Morgans were to remain the dominant financial group for the next decade. Ultimately, the Roosevelt administrations (1901-1909) were dominated by the Morgan interests, who were largely able to shield their larger corporations from antitrust and divert Roosevelt's "trustbusting" to non-Morgan companies, in particular

Standard Oil in 1906. This led to a Rockefeller counterattack, mainly through the more Rockefeller-affiliated William Howard Taft, whose administration (1909-1913) launched anti-trust suits against the Morgan-dominated companies U.S. Steel and International Harvester. Infuriated at Taft, the Morgans deliberately sabotaged his reelection by encouraging Roosevelt to come out of retirement and run on the Progressive Party ticket in 1912, which split the Republican vote and allowed the Democrat Woodrow Wilson, with Morgan and other financial affiliations, to squeak by and capture the presidency—the only Democrat to do so in the fourth party era.[452]

Over the last several decades, economists and historians have carefully reviewed the evidence demonstrating the politically biased enforcement Rothbard summarizes. Those include Gabriel Kolko, James Weinstein, James Gilbert, Samuel P. Hays, and Louis Galambos, among others.

The charge that the railroads in the nineteenth century were monopoly controlled is belied by the facts. "The idea that rates were in some sense 'too high,' or that railroads were monopolies, ran against the hard fact that railroads were tremendously and even fiercely competitive, and that the consuming public was being served, not only by land-based transportation across the Continent, but also by continued, competitive, and substantial lowering of freight rates. Railroads competed between the same cities and towns, they also competed with each other between regions, and they competed with canals and coastal shipping."[453] The argument for regulation arose from two sectors that one would think at odds: the Grangers and the leading rail companies.

The Granger Movement advocated government controls to reduce the costs their farmer members were experiencing in shipping agricultural goods by rail. As Richard Hofstadter explains, relying on the historic view of farmers that "any government was a failure that did not foster the interests of the agricultural class," the Grangers succeeded in liberating "farm leaders from allegiance to the prevailing notions of *laissez faire* and left them without inhibitions about advocating whatever federal measure seemed likely to aid the farmers, whether it was government ownership of transportation or government warehousing."[454]

By 1884, the railroad managers (who had tried unsuccessfully for years to monopolize rail service) seized upon the Granger movement as an ally in justifying federal fixed rates and terms of service, which they heavily influenced, they being the owners of the principal rail concerns. As railroad civil engineer Alfred Fink explained in 1876, "Whether this cooperation [i.e., industry cartels to fix prices and terms of service] can be secured by voluntary action of the transportation companies is doubtful. Governmental supervision and authority may be required to some extent to accomplish the object in view."[455] By 1879, a consensus emerged among railroad executives that voluntary cartelization to achieve monopoly pricing was not feasible and that "the federal government would have to step in to cartelize railroad freight."[456]

As the Interstate Commerce Commission bill written by state regulator Charles Francis Adams proceeded through Congress it received the strong backing of railroad interests. Their representatives testified, almost without exception, in support of the creation of legalized cartels (government fixed prices and terms of service) and the outlawing of railroad rebates, which had been the principal means of achieving competitive pricing. Without rebates, smaller rail concerns would find it very difficult to remain in business. "J. P. Morgan had become the foremost sponsor of railroad pools, and his as well as other railroads had now endorsed the ICC as an instrument of imposed cartelization."[457] The bill favored by the railroad industry "passed both houses overwhelmingly in January 1887 by a vote of 36 to 12 in the Senate, and 219 to 41 in the House."[458]

The Grangers soon learned that they had been had. Their desired reduction in rail rates never materialized. Rather, the new Interstate Commerce Commission facilitated monopoly pricing and the creation of state-sponsored cartels that had eluded industry leaders when they tried to achieve monopolies on their own. As Murray Rothbard explains:

The ICC was . . . in keeping with the law when, to the delight of the railroads, it decided to give its sanction and imprimatur to the freight rates worked out by the railroad rate associations—in short, to use the federal government to ratify rates decided upon by private railroad cartels. Despite the official outlawry of pools, therefore, the ICC was to serve as a powerful instrument of railroad cartels. It is no wonder that, very soon after its inception, the Interstate Commerce Act and the ICC were lauded by the railway men, while the merchants' and farmers' groups who had high hopes for the ICC quickly came to call for its repeal.[459]

As in the railroad industry, so too in the petroleum industry, fervent private efforts to cartelize that industry failed in the market, even as one of the largest concerns, Standard Oil, succeeded in achieving an oligopoly in refining. Rothbard explains that as Standard Oil began to obtain higher profits in specific areas where it was able to achieve market concentration, those gains soon evaporated as competitors arose and cut into Standard Oil's returns across the board. "Standard was clearly never able to use its position to restrict production and raise prices," explains Rothbard. He writes:

Independent pipelines began to grow to challenge Standard's dominance in this area. [A]fter 1900, and log before the anti-trust dissolution of 1911 and unrelated to it, Standard's dominance of petroleum refining began increasingly to fade. Whereas in 1899 Standard Oil had 90% of the petroleum refining in the country, this share had slipped to 84% during 1904-07, to 80% in 1911, and then to 50% (including together all the separate Standard Oil companies) in 1921. . . . [N]ew independent refiners were attracted to the petroleum industry by Standard's high profit margins. Whereas there was a total of 67 refiners in 1899, they had more than doubled to 147 by 1911. The independents, furthermore, led Standard in various innovations in petroleum: in the concept of retail gas stations; in the discovery and production of petrochemicals; in tank cars and tank trucks for conveying oil.[460]

Just as competition sank industry plans to monopolize rail and monopolize oil, so too it sank efforts to monopolize steel, to the chagrin of J.P. Morgan. In a 1900 trade publication, *Iron Age*, the editor lamented that industry efforts at consolidation had failed because competition continued to manifest itself, writing: "Experience has shown that very few of the promises of the promoters of consolidation have materialized. That some of them are satisfactorily profitable is undoubtedly true. . . . Others are less so; some are conspicuously unprofitable; some have dissolved; and more will have to dissolve within the next two or three years. Before another wave of the consolidation movement overtakes us, if it ever does, the experiment will have proved itself by the test of time."[461] As Rothbard records:

[T]here were 719 companies either in the blast furnace, steel work, or rolling mill industry in 1889. Throughout the 1880s and 1890s, there were repeated attempts at pools and cartels to reduce production and raise prices. Pools in pig iron, steel, steel billet, wire, and wire-nails all failed, breaking down from failure of one or more firms to abide by the agreement. Finally, a series of extensive mergers and trusts, incorporation of 138 companies consolidated into six trusts, merged in turn to form a new mammoth trust-like holding company, the $1.4 billion United States Steel Corporation, in 1901. . . . Even so, since there were still 223 firms with blast furnaces and 445 steel work and rolling mill companies by the turn of the century, U.S. Steel only controlled 62% of the market.

* * * *

U.S. Steel shares, priced at $55 in 1901, fell precipitately to $9 by 1904. Steel's profits also dropped sharply, yielding 16% in 1902 and falling to less than 8% two years later. Steel prices fell steadily, and U.S. Steel did not dare raise prices for fear of attracting new and active competitors. Finally in late 1907, Judge Elbert H. Gary, chairman of the board of U.S. Steel and another Morgan man at the company, inaugurated a series of "Gary dinners" among steel leaders, to form "gentlemen's agreements" to keep steel prices elevated. But by as early as mid-1908, smaller independents began cutting their prices secretly, and this broke the agreements and forced U.S. Steel and the other majors to follow suit. By early 1910, even the formal structure of the Gary dinners had completely collapsed.[462]

Repeatedly, the frantic efforts at mergers to consolidate industries under one major player fell apart as new competitors seized the opportunity to enter markets, cut prices, and compete. "The new mergers, with their size, efficiency, and capitalization, were unable to stem the tide of competitive growth," writes Kolko. "Quite the contrary! They were more likely than not unable to compete successfully and hold on to their share of the market, and this fact became one of utmost political importance."[463] Having failed miserably to cartelize on their own, invariably industry leaders looked to the government to cartelize industry for them, and all too often the regulatory state obliged.

This same pattern is replicated in the context of the agricultural machinery, iron, copper, automobile, sugar, meatpacking, biscuit, and other major industries.[464] All private attempts at cartelization failed, and the frustrated industry leaders then looked to government to cartelize the industries for them through regulatory commissions that were dominated by the leading industry players.[465] In this way, repeatedly, agencies tasked with regulating industry became captives of those industries.

Gabriel Kolko explains that it was an "illusion that American industry was centralized and monopolized to such an extent that it could rationalize the activity in its various branches voluntarily. Quite the opposite was true."[466] Rather, "[d]espite the large number of mergers, and the growth in the absolute size of many corporations, the dominant tendency in the American economy at the beginning of [the twentieth century] was toward growing competition."[467] That reality caused industry leaders to favor regulation as the means to cartelize, riding on the backs of disgruntled groups, like the Grangers, who sought to reduce costs. As Kolko explains, "It was not the existence of monopoly that caused the federal government to intervene in the economy, but the lack of it."[468]

The rise of government commissions to regulate pricing and terms of service continued through the Progressive era past the New Deal era and remains to this day a common means by which the federal government and industry leaders cooperate to drive out competition. For example, with nascent radio regulation, the government aided the major broadcasters and networks by culling hundreds of competing licensees, shutting them down, while retaining all licenses associated with the major networks.[469] One may ask what incentive government regulators would have to aid in the elimination of competition, aside from the obvious fact that doing so might enable them to attain lucrative post-government employment in the leading firms benefited? That potential is indeed a major incentive, but there is more for politicians to gain. They gain a degree of control over the direction of the industry. So, for example, government may compel certain changes in manufacturing, distribution, and employment practices that advance the interests of favored political constituencies (e.g., labor, racial minorities, environmentalists, or other advocates of special interests). By licensing the right to market, government may set the terms for market entry and service, as it did through the NRA and AAA codes, creating a skewed market. Industry leaders ordinarily embrace that arrangement if assured above market rates of return through the elimination of competition. In this way, government can collude with industry, pander to special interests, and advance the personal interests of the regulators themselves (e.g., the prospect of post-government employment for themselves or for family members).

The parties harmed by these industry-government deals are small businessmen, people in need of employment, and consumers, yet the causal link to those effects is oftentimes hidden, not apparent to the public. Indeed, cloaked beneath a public interest veneer that appeals to the public, the bills cartelizing industry proceed and, most often, harm the very interests they are said to advance (as happened in the case of the Grangers). Small businesses squeezed out by the licensing regimes either limp along or die. Because small business is the primary engine of employment in America, the inhibition of and closure of small businesses increases unemployment and human misery. The reduction in competitors tends to maintain or increase prices above competitive levels, which harms consumers. The winners in these arrangements are almost always industry leaders and politicians, and almost never small businesses and consumers.

It is thus the case that when Progressive and Democratic Socialist politicians regulate, they do so in ways that invariably cartelize industry. The political deal reached with industry leaders translates into greater government intrusion and control of the market but also into above market rates of return for the industry leaders. This unseemly compact harms consumers and employees but most have a very difficult time perceiving the harm as causally linked to the laws and regulations. The politicians thus escape accountability for their actions. Even when elected representatives are asked to account, they have a ready answer: that it was not they who caused the harm but, rather, the regulators (ignoring the common fact that they have supported the agency's existence). Because the regulators are unelected and unaccountable to the people, they have little difficulty deflecting criticism for their actions harmful to consumers and employees. In every instance, they raise the flag of the public interest as their justification and count on the fragmented and unorganized public to lack the political cohesiveness needed to upset agency market interventions.

CHAPTER 7

THE ABANDONMENT OF MEANINGFUL JUDICIAL REVIEW

Progressives of the late nineteenth and early twentieth centuries created an extra-constitutional government, the administrative state. Although the administrative state is nowhere mentioned in the Constitution, the Progressives created it without resort to a constitutional amendment, required by Article V. The choice not to proceed by constitutional amendment as the nation's charter commands is indicative of the Progressives' contempt for constitutional governance. Indeed, the Progressives who drafted the legislation enacting the administrative state, who voted for it, and who signed it into law were disdainful of individual rights, limited government and democracy; sought to circumvent constitutional limits; and believed fundamentally that "experts" could better discern what was in the best interests of the American people than the American people themselves.

Congress created the administrative state with the full support of the executive branch (Presidents Grover Cleveland, Theodore Roosevelt, Woodrow Wilson, Herbert Hoover, and Franklin Delano Roosevelt). Progressives were well aware that the administrative state violated the bedrock principles of the original Constitution: the consent of the governed (by which no individual or entity is possessed of a legitimate power to make law other than those duly elected by American citizens); limited government (by which the Constitution reserves all powers not expressly delegated to the federal government to the states and the people, respectively); the non-delegation doctrine (by which powers delegated to the three constitutional branches may not be re-delegated); the separation of powers doctrine (by which legislative, executive, and judicial powers are separated into three competing branches to avoid tyranny from the consolidation of those powers in single entities), and an independent judiciary (by which the law-giver would not also be the accuser and judge). Those Presidents, along with Progressive leaders, viewed the Constitution's bedrock principles as obstacles to the creation of a new utopia, a utopia they intended to be created by all-powerful experts who would rule as oligarchs. They valued expert administration and efficiency in government far more than the protections of rights in the Constitution, and they were distrustful of the public, so much so that they would not submit their extra-constitutional plans to constitutional amendment under Article V.

In short, the Progressives achieved a revolution that up-ended the Constitution without firing a single shot, doing so through legislation and, then, intimidation of, and eventually the complicity of, the federal courts. The Progressives' revolution began, as most revolutions do, with discontent over social and economic changes, discontent particularly among elites who benefited from society in the antebellum North and South, a society transformed and upset by the industrial revolution.

In *Law's Abnegation*, Adrian Vermeule tracks the history of judicial deference to the administrative state. As Vermeule explains:

> In area after area, lawyers and judges, working out the logical implications of their principles with a view to rational consistency, have come to the view that administrators should have broad leeway to set policy, to determine facts, to interpret ambiguous statutes, and even—in an intolerable affront to the traditional legal mind—to determine the boundaries of the administrators' own jurisdiction, acting as "judges in their own cause."[470]

An advocate of the administrative state, Vermeule explains that his history reveals, "that legal controls crafted by actors who sought to constrain the gradual advance of administration have given way,"[471] and, indeed, he is right. As Vermeule sees it, administrative law predominates and pushes aside the Article III courts:

> [T]he administrative state threatens law's imperial sway. It threatens to relegate courts and judges to a lower status, as marginal officials who are stationed in the outlying provinces and are charged with patrolling the very outermost boundaries of executive authority, but who are no longer central actors—no longer guardians of principle.[472]

Vermeule assumes, as is fashionable among many who work in civil service positions, that recent Supreme Court moves in the direction of dismantling doctrines favoring deference to administrative agencies will not work, even if those moves fully repudiate that deference. He writes:

> [The] roots [of deference] run far deeper than this or that recent opinion [of the Supreme Court]. Rather deference arises from the long-term working out of legal principles by judges who, over time, become aware of the limits of their own knowledge and who build deference into law itself— the essence of abnegation.[473]

The problem with Vermeule's analysis is that it gives far too much weight to one of the rationales principally relied upon to justify judicial deference: the idea that agencies are uniquely expert in their areas of regulation and that this expertise justifies the failure of an Article III court to perform an in-depth, independent review of the facts and law. Indeed so convinced is Vermeule that Article III courts are ill-suited to deal with complex matters of science and economics that he believes if doctrines of deference were done away with, courts would still look to agencies as the experts and defer to them, whether or not admittedly. Vermeule's assumptions are doubly ill-informed by fact. Agencies are frequently inexpert, and Article III courts routinely evaluate complex issues of science and economics.

The assumption that agencies are uniquely expert is dubious at best. In all areas of law, lawyers and judges in Article III courts become "expert" through receipt of testimony and evidence from those who, based on education, training, experience, and publication are authoritative. Those experts are most often from academia, not from government. Article III courts routinely evaluate expert opinion and depend on it, when duly qualified, to support decisions.

By contrast, administrative agencies are, at root, political beasts. Their heads are politically chosen and are often inexpert, having little technical knowledge in the areas in which they themselves will serve as ultimate judges. The Federal Trade Commission is an excellent example of this phenomenon. Although credited by federal courts with a superhuman ability to perceive what the public understands words in advertising to mean,[474] the Commissioners of the FCC are the equivalent of modern day soothsayers and all too often proclaim strangely illogical definitions for key terms used in advertising even when those definitions conflict with reliable survey evidence to the contrary.

Moreover, when expertise exists in an agency, it is frequently colored by political selection. Consequently, it is common in agencies for department heads, who are politically chosen, to cherry pick among expert opinions those most supportive of a pre-determined, politically desired outcome (a common Food and Drug Administration occurrence), regardless of the extent to which the opinions chosen are reflective of a consensus in the scientific community. Consequently, it is a myth to presume, as Vermeule does, that administrative agencies are filled with unbiased experts whose opinions when melded into rules or agency adjudications are somehow deserving of deference due to unique and unalloyed expert merit.

Consider the case of *Pearson v. Shalala*[475] and its progeny, cases that I argued before the United States Court of Appeals for the DC Circuit and the United States District Court for the District of Columbia. As those cases make clear, the Food and Drug Administration (assuredly one that Vermeule would consider "expert") repeatedly censored health claims supported by a wealth of competent evidence. That censorship sacrificed lives. For example, FDA censored claims associating folic acid supplements with a reduction in the risk of neural tube defect births; omega-3 fatty acids with a reduction in the risk of coronary heart disease; and antioxidant vitamins with a reduction in the risk of certain kinds of cancers. The evidence favoring the claims was overwhelming. In the case of the folic acid supplement/neural tube defect claim, an estimated 2,500 preventable neural tube defect births and countless neural tube defect abortions occurred each year for decades because women of childbearing age were unaware that taking an 800 microgram containing folic acid supplement daily would reduce the risk of a neural tube defect birth by as much as 80%. In the case of the omega-3 fatty acid/coronary heart disease risk reduction claim, an estimated 100,000 sudden death heart attacks could have been averted each year if all adults consumed between 250 to 500 milligrams of omega-3 fatty acids every day. In the case of the antioxidant vitamin/cancer risk reduction claim, countless lives could have been spared cancer or experienced it later in life had antioxidants been consumed daily by the entire population. As the Court of Appeals found, the evidence supporting the claims was credible, yet the FDA kept the information from the market, doing so even after the Office of Management and Budget sent a "prompt letter" to the FDA Commissioner urging immediate approval of the omega-3 claim to help reduce the incidence of heart attacks and even after the Centers for Disease Control and Prevention urged physicians to recommend folic acid supplements to women in family planning.

As Dr. David Graham, the former Associate Director of the FDA Office of Drug Safety, explained in congressional testimony and in his interview in the September/October 2005 edition of *Fraud Magazine*, the "expert" FDA is hopelessly corrupt, controlled by political appointees who favor protection of pharmaceutical company interests over public health. The real story underlying the many cases I provide as examples in Chapter 8 is one of political managers controlling career bureaucrats (the so-called "experts"). It is a story of those political managers favoring certain industry players because it is in those managers' self-interest to do so. Whether motivated by ideology or the prospect of lucrative post-government employment, the political managers inside the agencies call the shots, and they frequently make outrageously unscientific and inexpert decisions that cause significant harm to lives, properties, and liberty. If compelled to undergo *de novo* review in Article III courts and carry the burdens of proof and persuasion for their decisions, agencies would often not survive a true test of their vaunted "expertise."

The *Pearson v. Shalala* case is an illustrative example.[476] Through FDA's acts of censorship, based on politically driven and unscientific motivations, that agency kept from the market vital health information that could have saved countless lives. If, rather than suppress the folic acid supplement/ neural tube defect claim for decades against the weight of the evidence, the FDA had allowed that information to enter the market and reach consumers at the point of sale, tens of thousands of women and their children would have been spared the horror and life-debilitating effects of neural tube defect births and related abortions. If, rather than suppress the omega-3 fatty acid/ coronary heart disease claim for decades against the weight of the evidence (confirming the nutrient to be anti-thrombotic, anti-coagulant, and anti-arrhythmic), the FDA had allowed that information to enter the market and reach consumers at the point of sale, hundreds of thousands of Americans who died from preventable sudden death heart attacks might instead have lived a full lifespan. If, rather than suppress the antioxidant vitamins/cancer risk reduction claim for decades against the weight of the evidence, the FDA had allowed that information to enter the market and reach consumers at the point of sale, countless individuals would have experienced a cancer risk reduction perhaps sufficient to prevent cancer altogether or fend off the disease until later in life.

Had the DC Circuit not risen to the occasion and reversed the common order of review in *Pearson v. Shalala* to consider the pressing First Amendment claims first, had it instead deferred as did the United States District Court, all of those horrors would have continued, possibly in perpetuity. But, fortunately for the world, Circuit Judges Laurence Silberman, Patricia Wald, and Merrick Garland did rise to the occasion and in a landmark decision struck down FDA's acts of censorship as a violation of the First Amendment.[477] The government's petition for rehearing en banc was likewise denied by the full circuit without a single vote in dissent.[478] Had the DC Circuit followed Vermeule's lead, they presumably would have affirmed deferentially despite the harms to the public.

Why, you ask, did FDA countenance such horrors? The answer is simple. In its regulatory history, FDA has done everything in its power to make its health claims regime unusable, such that few, if any, scientifically supported nutrient-disease risk reduction claims ever reach the public. It has done so to protect the drug industry from competition and to maintain its control over the market. For almost a century, FDA has jealously guarded a pharmaceutical industry monopoly over disease treatment and prevention claims. The prospect of competition to that old regime has frequently been intolerable for FDA, even in the face of legislative changes in the Nutrition Labeling and Education Act and the Dietary Supplement Health and Education Act mandating greater allowance of claims. FDA thus protects its principal regulatee, the pharmaceutical industry, from new sources of competition arising from public awareness that elements in foods may be therapeutic. It has favored suppression over disclosure of nutrient-disease information as a matter of course, despite the *Pearson* Court's constitutional command to the contrary.

The essential problem with Vermeule's analysis is that he is either ignorant of, or dismissive of, the realpolitik of administrative law. In the agencies, it is not expert opinion, but political judgment, that determines outcomes. Political appointees rule the agencies and pursue political agendas or, more crassly, their own economic self-interest. Science in conflict with those agendas is ordinarily discounted or rejected out of hand.

Moreover, deferring to agencies on the notion that they are more expert than Article III courts is deference predicated on a myth. Even were an agency's decisions not ones politically preferred by agency leaders, it would still be a myth that Article III courts lack the wherewithal to evaluate the science and make independent judgments. Lawyers argue complex matters of science before Article III courts every day of the week, and Article III judges pass upon those matters based on the testimony and evidence of experts. Moreover, there is a natural limit to the degree of scientific complexity at issue because regulation, dependent upon industry wide compliance, also depends on a translation of scientific foundations for action into more or less comprehensible rules. That translation is written by and decodable by lawyers, Courts, and industry. The notion that there is some sort of alchemic science that only regulatory wizards can understand, although proclaimed in defense of agency authority, has never been true, and it is certainly false today when scientific acumen sufficient to interpret regulation is common in industry, law, and the courts.

Another common argument raised in favor of deference is that industrial age complexity demands rapid regulatory responses which, if bogged down in judicial process and second-guessing of agency action, will leave those problems unaddressed for lengthy periods, inviting social and economic chaos. That argument is nothing more than a truism about all deliberative processes whether in agencies or in courts. It is not an argument to justify a denial of meaningful protection for individual rights. Moreover, as the founding fathers well understood corruption is rife in government when combinations of legislative, judicial, and executive powers are allowed, making the necessity for meaningful judicial review even more pronounced.

In Federalist No. 10, James Madison wrote: "No man is allowed to be a judge in his own cause, because his interest would certainly bias his judgment, and, not improbably, corrupt his integrity. With equal, nay with greater reason, a body of men are unfit to be both judges and parties at the same time."[479] In Federalist No. 78, Alexander Hamilton added: It is the duty of the federal judiciary "to declare all acts contrary to the manifest tenor of the Constitution void" and "without this, all reservations of particular rights or privileges would amount to nothing."[480]

Vermeule also operates on the assumption that the pervasiveness of the administrative state (and the long history of precedent deferring to agency judgments) establishes an effective barrier to elimination of administrative adjudication or revocation of the doctrines of deference. That argument is specious, at best. The Congress of the United States possesses the inherent power to eliminate the regulatory agencies and administrative adjudication. Given the political will, it could achieve that end in one bill. Congress wisely eliminated the Interstate Commerce Commission in December of

1995. While the mission of ending administrative agencies is politically formidable, it is far from impossible.

Moreover, it is unwise to prejudge the predilections of the Justices of the Supreme Court who now, by a majority, may be poised to reign in the doctrines of deference. They may do so based on realities not apparent before, such as the extent to which individual rights have been violated by the administrative state in case after case since the 1930s. In short, the record now amply supports the conclusion that the administrative state, when given broad deference, has experienced an enormous degree of unchecked corruption, abuse of power, and violation of individual rights, which can only be stopped if agency decisions are subjected to meaningful *de novo* review as to the law and the facts. Vermeule's assumption that change will not be forthcoming because the federal courts will simply not abide by the change is against the weight of modern realities and the reality of Supreme Court power. Those realities not only disprove that administrative agencies are uniquely expert but also reveal that the trust given them has been greatly abused.

Vermeule dates the doctrine of deference to Charles Evans Hughes' 1932 decision in *Crowell v. Benson,* where he explained that Article III courts would defer to agency decisions on questions of fact involving "public rights" (contests between government and citizens) and would defer less so, subject to agency proof of "substantial evidence," to agency decisions on questions of fact involving "private rights" (contests between private citizens). On questions of law, and on evaluations of "jurisdictional facts" and "constitutional facts," Article III courts would decide *de novo*, meaning that no particular deference would be accorded.[481]

The Hughes' doctrine of deference did not stand the test of time and, in fits and starts, emerging in earnest in 1937 and beyond, federal court precedent began to move in the direction of ever greater deference to administrative agency decisions. Without belaboring each fit and start, suffice it to say that the role of the Courts in deciding jurisdictional facts *de novo* "has more or less vanished altogether" and the role of the Courts in deciding constitutional facts *de novo* has largely been limited to "free speech cases and scattered areas of criminal procedure and individual rights."[482]

The pinnacle of judicial deference to agency decision-making and adjudication came in the Supreme Court's 1984 decision in *Chevron v. Natural Resources Defense Council.*[483] There, the Supreme Court held challenges to an agency's interpretation of its enabling statute would be rebuffed by the federal courts, dependent on a two-step evaluation. In the first step, the Court asks "whether Congress has directly spoken to the precise question at issue. If the intent of Congress is clear, that is the end of the matter; for the court, as well as the agency must give effect to the unambiguously expressed intent of Congress."[484] It is a rare instance in which Congress speaks directly to a precise regulatory question and, so, decisions based on the first step are comparatively rare. Under the second step, if the statutory language is "silent or ambiguous," then the Court determines "whether the agency's answer is based on a permissible construction of the statute."[485] So long as the agency's answer is not "arbitrary, capricious, or manifestly contrary to statute," "is supported by a reasoned explanation," and is "a reasonable policy choice for the agency to make," the Court will uphold it.[486]

In practice, *Chevron* has covered all manner of administrative sins. By not affording each administrative challenge *de novo* review and, instead, deferring broadly to agency fact and law determinations, the federal courts have avoided meaningful federal judicial review. The effect is to leave unchecked gross abuses of power. Because in the agency the prosecutor is also the ultimate judge, that conflict of interest leads invariably to injustice, as the ultimate judge will almost never second-guess the prudence of initiating and maintaining litigation against the accused. The agency's fact-findings are ordinarily skewed, such that facts harmful to the agency are frequently omitted or glossed over to suggest a stronger case. Agency procedural rules are biased in favor of the agency, so that evidence harmful to the agency is often not admitted into agency proceedings. Agency determinations of law invariably contort the law, bending it to favor the agency, there being no reliable and independent review of agency action. The essential character of judicial review, its independence, is thus defeated by broad deference to agency decision-making.

In the ordinary case, if the agency can articulate some logical rationale for its action, the Court will rubber-stamp the agency decision, never subjecting it to meaningful review, never compelling the agency to defend its factual determinations or its legal interpretations. In every case, the decision of an oxymoronic agency (it being both prosecutor and ultimate judge) is presumed just, despite the conflict of interest. As Chapter 8 reveals, that presumption often conflicts with reality.

The doctrine of deference has expanded beyond instances in which an agency interprets ambiguous language in its enabling statute. The Supreme Court applies deference to an agency's interpretation of ambiguous language in its own regulations, having created that deference in the 1997 case of *Auer v. Robbins.*[487] In those instances where an agency issues a non-binding opinion, an intermediate form of deference has been applied since the 1944 case of *Skidmore v. Swift & Co.*[488] In *Skidmore* deference, an agency's non-binding opinion is accorded weight "depending upon the thoroughness evident in its consideration, the validity of its reasoning, its consistency with earlier and later pronouncements, and all those factors which give it power to persuade."[489]

The deferential regime has served as an effective roadblock in front of the federal courthouse. The intended departure of the administrative agencies from the rule of law, intended by the Progressives of the nineteenth and early twentieth centuries, has been achieved in no small measure because the federal courts have abdicated their essential role of providing meaningful federal judicial review. While decisions of the district courts (which operate under the justice protective strictures of the federal rules of civil and criminal procedure and the federal rules of evidence) are subjected to *de novo* review in the appellate federal courts, decisions of the administrative agencies in adjudicatory cases (which do not operate under the protective strictures of the federal rules and include overt bias in favor of the agencies) are the subject of broad deference. That is true although both forums involve matters that result in the deprivation of liberty and property.

If the aim is to achieve justice, there is no substitute for the independent Article III courts. The substitute, which now predominates in federal law, is the administrative agency. To be just, the agency cannot be its own judge when it is in truth a litigant. To serve the ends of justice, to avoid the tyranny typical of administrative courts (the High Commission Courts and the Courts of Star Chamber in England), a tyranny rejected by the founding fathers, and to provide full due process to the accused before suffering a loss of liberty or property, there is no substitute for trial by jury before an Article III court. The law must also be changed to eliminate deference to agency decision-making to ensure that full safeguards against statutory and constitutional abuses are arrested. Ultimately, the law must be changed to end administrative adjudication in favor of a return to the independent Article III Courts. From a wink and a nod at agency decisions, the federal courts need to return to a penetrating stare that pierces beneath the superficial justifications offered for agency action. Only in that way will the Article III courts serve their proper role as guardians of the law and, especially, the Constitution.

CHAPTER 8
ADMINISTRATIVE TYRANNY

W hen administrative adjudication is substituted for litigation in an independent Article III court, the prosecutor is the ultimate judge, and unbiased justice is impossible. Administrative adjudication is today pervasive on the federal level but it operates in a manner not much different from the Courts of High Commission and of Star Chamber of the fifteenth to the seventeenth centuries. Those courts were condemned by the founding generation as an archetypical example of tyranny.

In his publication of *Blackstone's Commentaries* (1803), lawyer and law professor St. George Tucker described those courts as "two of the most infamous engines of oppression and tyranny that were ever erected in any country."[490] Those inquisitorial courts of royal prerogative deprived the accused of, among other fundamental rights, the presumption of innocence, the fundamental right against self-incrimination, the right of trial by jury, the right to an independent court, and the right to due process. Like today's administrative agency "courts," the Courts of High Commission and of Star Chamber conjoined the prosecutorial and judicial functions, destroying independent review. As Philip Hamburger explains in detail, the same features which created such profound injustice, hardship and tyranny in the high commission and star chamber courts have been replicated in the modern administrative courts.[491] Hamburger concludes that "[a]dministrative legislation and adjudication . . . restore[s] a prerogative regime—a system of governance outside the lawful channels of legislation and judicial power," creating a system that is "not merely contrary to law, but outside and above the law" and, thus, "returns to the preeminent danger that constitutional law was understood to have defeated."[492]

Born of a denial of rights and an inherent conflict of interest, administrative adjudication creates a mockery of justice that has nevertheless been left largely unchecked by the only independent courts of law, the Article III courts. Since the 1932 decision in *Crowell v. Benson*, federal courts have increasingly deferred to agency findings of fact and conclusions of law, refusing to subject agency judgments to more than a cursory judicial review. Frequently the only requirement a federal court imposes on an agency is in fact no serious requirement at all: the ridiculously low demand that the agency articulate some rational explanation for its actions which, so easily offered, yields a rubber stamp decision from the court, regardless of the underlying merits.

Moreover, the exhaustion doctrine, whereby the Courts refuse to hear a case unless all avenues of administrative appeal have been completed, ensures that the injustices imposed on the party accused by the agency remain in place for years, during which time the accused must finance enormous litigation costs, resulting in a severe winnowing of those who can afford an appeal from an adverse agency decision. The Courts' broad deference to agency decisions thus negates meaningful judicial review and shields from correction a myriad of agency sins, abuses, and corrupt acts, leaving a long train of abused, financially destitute, and condemned victims.

Because agencies have gotten away with abuses of power for nearly a century, they and the attorneys within them have become more and more emboldened in their excesses. Having experienced no rebuke for all manner of investigational, discovery, and trial malfeasance, unethical conduct, and deprivation of the rights of the accused, they proceed with whatever tyranny *du jour* suits their wishes to achieve a foreordained political and adjudicatory end.

For thirty-five years I have litigated against the administrative state. Within the agencies, the proceedings have been heavily biased in favor of the government. The accused has ordinarily been inundated with extensive production demands before an administrative complaint is served. Those demands have reached all manner of corporate and personal financial data of the owners, officers, directors, and shareholders; the identities of all sources of financing, borrowing, lending, supply, production, and distribution; and all proof, not just that germane to the basis for the agency's action, of any matter affecting regulatory compliance over long periods (including satisfaction of other federal and state agencies' requirements). Agency attorneys routinely use the trove of information obtained not only to draft their complaints but also to determine the relative financial wherewithal of the accused and what sources might be affected by receiving subpoenas from the agency. Those attorneys fully appreciate that any subpoena sent to a business contact might well cause that contact to cease doing business with the accused and might cripple or shutter the accused's business long before any formal determination of liability is made, forcing the accused to settle on the government's often exorbitant financial terms. Those attorneys may encourage state attorneys general and state regulatory agencies to proceed against the accused simultaneous with the federal agency action, compounding costs and increasing the *in terrorem* effect. They may also encourage other federal and state agencies and departments to conduct investigations and bring charges of their own.

Discovery is disallowed against the government in all but a relatively few instances. That legal bar hides all manner of agency abuses and gives confidence to those within agencies intent on malfeasance that their bad acts will go undiscovered. Moreover, when the accused relies on non-party subpoenas to reach documents possessed by potential sources used by the government, the government may intervene and instruct those sources not to respond to the subpoenas, thus denying the accused what may be critical information supporting its defense and what may be proof of government motives. While such interference is strictly prohibited in federal courts, administrative agencies liberally permit it, for themselves alone. While the government may block a response to the accused's subpoena; the accused may not block a response to the government's subpoena. If the accused in any way interferes with response to a government subpoena, he or she may be criminally prosecuted for obstructing justice. The government reserves to itself this abusive power to block the search for truth.

When the government relies on experts, those experts are presumed by administrative law judges to be qualified without performance of the kind of gate-keeping ascertainment of knowledge, education, training, experience, and publication required in the federal courts. The federal courts assess the extent to which the so-called experts are qualified by those criteria and prohibit them from testifying if not so qualified. That is not the case in the administrative courts.

Moreover, oftentimes the agencies refuse to produce any empirical evidence on which government experts rely. Having access to that empirical evidence is critical to challenge an expert opinion because examination of it may reveal interpretations of the evidence at odds with the facts or dependent on a methodology not generally accepted in the scientific community to yield accurate and reliable results. The empirical support for government experts' opinions as well as correspondence between the government and those experts are kept from the accused, disabling an attack upon the validity of the government experts' opinions. Conversely, the government entitles itself to all the sources of empirical support for the accused's experts and all of the correspondence between the accused, its attorneys and the experts. One can readily see that the deck is stacked against the accused and in favor of the government.

Federal courts require all such evidence to be produced by both parties to an action. The one-sided non-disclosure in the agency setting invites and condones abuses, such as when agency attorneys are undisclosed authors of part or all of the reports said to be from the "experts" on which the government relies.[493]

The following are, except for the EPA and FDA examples, administrative cases in which I have served as counsel for the accused. The proceedings are offered as representative of administrative abuses. In four of the cases, the party accused by the agency was punished unreasonably, without having caused any proven injury to anyone; to the contrary, their businesses helped many people. In the fifth, the FDA took unilateral action to help a drug company now notorious, Purdue Pharma, liberalize its directions for use labeling on opioid drugs, encouraging greatly expanded use, thus facilitating the opioid epidemic in America. Few know of FDA's role in triggering that epidemic, yet the agency is the prime mover behind it.

Each case is illustrative of the kind of bias that pervades the administrative law substitute for Article III courts. Moreover, in two, the administrative law judges themselves, on a record overwhelmingly favoring the accused, decided in favor of the accused (a rare event and a courageous move for those administrative judges), only to have their recommended decisions summarily reversed by the agency heads who brought the original charges. It is a very rare day indeed (completely unheard of at the FTC and DEA) for the agency that authorizes the prosecution of the accused to find that its authorized prosecution was mistaken. Both maintain a 100% track record. Everyone accused is found liable.

In the administrative state when mistakes happen, even egregious ones, they ordinarily are covered up or glossed over in the ultimate opinions issued by agency heads. Those opinions selectively cull from the factual records isolated tidbits which, out of context, favor the government; arbitrarily discount relevant evidence; and invariably conclude that the accused, no matter how honest and true, is a villain who threatens the "public interest," deserving the punishment sought by the agency when it initiated the prosecution.

The appalling lack of due process becomes apparent when we superimpose the administrative model on an Article III court. Imagine in an Article III court that the judge is duty bound to uphold even an unconstitutional law. Imagine that only one party, the plaintiff or prosecutor, was possessed with unlimited discovery and subpoena power. Imagine that the defendant would be presumed liable or guilty of any offense alleged unless he or she proved to a near conclusive degree otherwise. Imagine that the plaintiff or prosecutor could at whim and without leave of court amend the charges brought at any point during the trial, making the charges a moving target. Imagine that no motions for a more particular statement would be entertained from the defense. Imagine that the court could declare any action other than one to imprison or execute the defendant to be a civil proceeding in which there was no right to confront witnesses against the accused and no right against self-incrimination. Imagine no right to a jury trial. Imagine at the end of the case, the Article III Judge's decision was but a recommendation to the ultimate judge, who happened also to be the plaintiff or prosecutor him or herself, and that this ultimate judge could then reject the recommended decision in whole or part and adopt instead whatever decision he or she wanted. Does anyone seriously doubt that the plaintiff/prosecutor/judge will decide every case in his or her own favor? Does anyone seriously doubt that justice in the presence of such blatant bias and conflict of interest is impossible? Does anyone seriously believe that such a system is fundamentally different from the tyrannical inquisitorial Courts of High Commission and of Star Chamber that the founding fathers intended to eliminate in the Constitution?

When the agency decides against a party, it usually publicizes the decision, alerting the world to its findings of fact and conclusions of law, to what is in fact a foregone conclusion from the start, and assigning fault to the accused. This effectively places the full weight of the federal government behind a public pronouncement covered by local, state, and national media that resonates with those similarly situated in business and those who have done, or who otherwise would do, business with the accused. Markets respond, and the accused is punished in an endless series of deleterious events from loss of business contacts, loss of sales, loss of stock value, and loss of good will and reputation. That is the very point of these press releases. They aim to make the accused a pariah, and they aim to terrorize others to cease any business activity similar to that which landed the accused on the agency's hit list. It is not enough for the agencies to rely on their biased and inherent conflicts of interest to bring about predictably adverse decisions; they go beyond and endeavor to vilify the accused in the court of public opinion. They thus condemn the accused to the world before an appeal on the merits to an Article III Court has even begun. These agency press releases isolate the accused, reduce its business prospects, and cause those who had been willing to engage in business transactions with the accused to look elsewhere (fearing possible agency prosecution themselves).

While most decision-makers at the agencies are loathe to admit agency bias and conflict of interest, that is not so for former FTC Commissioner Joshua D. Wright. Wright admits that at FTC there is no true separation of functions within the agency. The Commissioners "act[] as both prosecutor and judge," he concedes.[494] Wright explains that over at least a two-decade period he could find not a single case in which the Commissioners of the FTC held their prosecution of a single defendant for deceptive advertising to have been in error. Wright found that in 100% of the cases when an Administrative Law Judge recommended a ruling in favor of the FTC, the FTC affirmed, and in 100% of the cases when the ALJ recommended a ruling against the FTC, the FTC reversed.[495] He concludes: "This is a strong sign of an unhealthy and biased institutional process."[496] Indeed.

In short, the FTC Commissioners are remarkably "perfect" by their own measure. They have determined that they, political appointees all, are incapable of mistakenly charging anyone with deceptive advertising. Viewed from the other side of the barrel, that means statistically everyone charged with deceptive advertising is guilty of the offense, even before the matter is tried and regardless of the prosecutorial theory asserted and the defenses raised. The implausibility of that perfection is underscored by a painful reality: FTC frequently initiates its complaints without any proof whatsoever that the party accused lacks adequate substantiation for its advertising, based on nothing more than a hunch, bias or whim.

The matter is rendered more sinister by the ease with which highly subjective regulatory standards can be interpreted to condemn just about anyone engaged in business. Using the FTC example, that agency can pursue actions against a party for both the claims it actually makes (express claims) and those that FTC deems to be implied. Some may recall the popular Coca-Cola advertising campaign, "Coke adds life." Likely, most consumers would not understand that claim to be literal, i.e., that drinking Coca-Cola would extend the human lifespan. Nonetheless, it is possible to give a literal interpretation to the words. If FTC wanted, it could take that latter interpretive position and charge Coca-Cola Enterprises with deceptive advertising. It could demand that Coca-Cola Enterprises supply the FTC with all studies, including human clinical trials, documenting that consumption of Coca-Cola increases human longevity by a statistically significant extent or be deemed to have engaged in unlawful deceptive advertising practices. Coca-Cola Enterprises could be forced to divulge its secret formula to the FTC, provide all of its finances and officers, directors, and dominant shareholders financial information, provide all of its business contacts, and suffer subpoenas to those contacts, etc. In short, Coca-Cola could be made to pay a heavy price for what is in context a flippant and whimsical phrase. Indeed, even if Coca-Cola were to conduct a national survey and prove that literally no one in the country believed "Coke adds life" to mean that Coca-Cola extended the human lifespan, the Commissioners, under precedent that has declared them unquestionable experts on the meaning of words in commerce, could reject the survey and declare their interpretation the only one that counts. Indeed, under the agency's precedent, the FTC could declare that any minority of opinion suspected or found that "Coke adds life" is literal could carry the day and force Coca-Cola Enterprises to change its advertising to mirror the FTC's desires. Such is the tyranny of the Federal Trade Commission.

To make matters worse, administrative agencies, including the FTC, are fond of altering the charges brought in the agency complaint as the litigation proceeds, and without notice to the accused (by contrast, amendments to complaints are forbidden in court without formal amendment or, when occurring after an answer or responsive pleading is filed, without leave of court). Agencies change the grounds for proceeding when initial grounds prove difficult to maintain or are untenable, often with no notice to the accused and after the period for discovery has closed. They thereby deny the accused basic due process: notice of the true charges and an adequate opportunity to defend against them. Again, former Commissioner Wright distinguishes himself from his colleagues by being forthright, explaining: "[F]irms typically prefer to settle Section 5 [i.e., deceptive advertising] claims rather than go through the lengthy and costly administrative litigation in which they are both shooting at a moving target and may have the chips stacked against them."[497]

I have selected five cases each in a different federal agency to illustrate that federal agencies are in the business of denying the rights of the accused, depriving the accused of due process, and remaining unaccountable for their abuses. In each instance, the agency concerned caused considerable harm, not only to the accused but also to those dependent on what the accused had to offer, which universe of dependents may include thousands or tens of thousands of people. The history and views I express concerning each case are decidedly my own. They are not those of my former clients.

THE FEDERAL TRADE COMMISSION

In the world of biodegradable additives for plastics, there are several competing groups. One group consists of additive makers, one of bioplastics makers, and one of oxo-degradable plastic makers. Plastics that must be durable (such as those used in automobiles, grocery bags, and plastic pillows) are ordinarily not composed of bioplastics and oxo-degradable plastics, which tend to break apart when stressed.

An Ohio company, ECM BioFilms, Inc., obtained the rights from inventor Patrick Riley to a proprietary technology he invented in 1988 that enabled a bioactive component to be heat melded into rugged conventional plastics like a colorant. That process caused those conventional plastics to become biodegradable. That is a significant breakthrough because conventional plastics are ordinarily very slow to biodegrade, potentially lasting thousands of years in the environment.

ECM sold its additive, "Master Batch Pellets," to plastics manufacturers, not consumers. To give prospective corporate purchasers the confidence of knowing that the additive actually worked, ECM would supply them with sufficient free quantities of the additive to test. The state-of-the art test, generally accepted in the scientific and manufacturing communities, was an accelerated gas evolution test in a glass chamber. Over the years, dozens of companies performed accelerated gas evolution tests on the ECM product before making a purchasing decision. Those independent tests redundantly proved that conventional plastics containing the ECM additive biodegraded faster than conventional plastic controls in accelerated gas evolution tests, tests which replicated the environment in landfills.

Due in no small measure to the success of ECM BioFilms, Inc. and other additive companies in the market for biodegradable plastics, its competitors wanted to find a way to get a leg up on the competition. When direct competition failed, they went to the FTC to see if that agency could help. They lobbied the FTC, urging the Commissioners to come up with a definition of "biodegradable" that would benefit them and harm the plastic additive companies. In response to that lobbying, in 2012, the FTC modified an industry guidance (which, in reality, was treated as a legislative rule) to specify restrictions on the marketing use of the term "biodegradable" to mean something that competent scientists who studied biodegradation and manufacturers in the field did not understand the term to mean at all. Indeed, consumers did not understand the term to mean what FTC decreed it meant.

Commonsensically, consumers understand that if something is biodegradable it breaks down in nature. Neither consumers nor scientists, however, comprehend the arbitrary and unscientific position that the break down will occur within a set time, certainly not within a set twelve months. Undeterred, the FTC Commissioners decided to defy science and logic with law, ruling that "[i]t is deceptive to make an unqualified degradable claim for items entering the solid waste stream if the items do not completely decompose within one year after customary disposal." That rule appeared in 16 CFR § 260.8(c). Hence, the FTC took the position from that point forward, and in the ECM case, that the term biodegradable could be used only for products that caused plastics, in the words of FTC's complaint counsel, "to break down into elements in nature" and only for products that caused that complete break down "within one year after customary disposal."

The definition was wrong-headed on a number of levels, apparent to anyone familiar with the science. First, biodegradation is a process that occurs in nature when there are active biota present. Active biota differ in their relative rates of consumption of biological materials, dependent upon ambient environmental conditions, such as the relative temperature and humidity. Consequently, biodegradation would ordinarily be expected to occur at a slower rate in Barrow, Alaska than in Miami, Florida. Despite that, scientists who have determined that a substance, like a banana, is biodegradable, deem it intrinsically so regardless of the speed with which it biodegrades. The selection of one year was profoundly ignorant because it is an arbitrary cut-off having no tether to logic or science; indeed it is anti-scientific.

Moreover, the Commissioners revealed ignorance in another way. Through their complaint counsel they demanded that the substance at issue break down "into elements in nature." But biodegradable substances do not break down into elements (e.g., elemental carbon, oxygen, or hydrogen). Rather, they break down into compounds, most notably for the purposes of the present discussion, into carbon dioxide (CO_2) and water, dihydrogen monoxide (H_2O). Thus, from the start, the FTC's foray into environmental science was inexpert. Before FTC would allow the term "biodegradable" to be used in commerce, it demanded that the substance break down into elements in nature (an impossibility) within one year of customary disposal (an absurd time limit on nature).

With the competitors urging action against ECM and the additive makers, and the FTC and its staff anxious to expand its "green" deceptive advertising cases, the FTC, comprised of five commissioners (including 3 in the majority who were liberal Democrats appointed by President Obama) took aim at ECM BioFilms, Inc. After months of gathering all manner of financial and business data from the company, FTC issued an administrative complaint against the company on October 13, 2013.

The Administrative trial took place from August 5, 2014 through August 29, 2014 at the FTC's headquarters in Washington, before Chief Administrative Law Judge D. Michael Chappell. Over that time, a large amount of evidence was admitted into the record and numerous fact and expert witnesses testified. The discovery phase of the proceeding was marked by all too common irregularities in which FTC attorneys engaged in abusive practices designed to disable the accused and make it impecunious. They initiated typically broad discovery, sending subpoenas to all entities that had business relations with the company, thereby intimidating them into diminishing or halting their business dealings with the accused for fear of further involvement in the FTC's enforcement action. In at least one case, they, without notice to the accused, contacted a party that had received a subpoena from the accused and instructed the recipient that it need not answer, thus interfering with adduction of evidence damaging to the FTC's case. That practice, while ordinarily permitted by administrative agencies, is considered a severe abuse in Article III courts, ordinarily resulting in significant sanctions against a party that in any way interferes with a federal subpoena.

In one of the more remarkable instances of agency abuse, the FTC attorneys contacted a private scientist and, with the help of an ECM competitor, had the ECM product manufactured and tested. The circumstances surrounding the test are highly questionable. Ordinarily, competent scientists when engaged in testing a product ensure the integrity of the test by maintaining a meticulous chain of custody and control over the test article from acquisition to manufacture to ultimate testing. In this case, no competent chain of custody was maintained. Moreover, the agency condoned the use of an ECM competitor to prepare the test article. There is no evidence concerning how the test article was prepared. That is a critical omission because the ECM Additive had to be heat melded into conventional plastic in accordance with a precise protocol, involving carefully regulated temperatures and duration of melding. The Additive includes a food source for biota. The food source cannot be scorched through excessive heat melding or it is rendered inert, thus insuring a negative test result. Consequently, if an ECM competitor wanted to cause a negative test result, it could do so simply by overheating the additive during melding.

The FTC expert had no knowledge of how the ECM Additive was prepared or even of the preparation requirements, yet used it nonetheless in a gas evolution test. He then performed the test without requisite controls in place. The test yielded a negative result. Touting that result as proof positive that the additive did not work, the FTC then aided the expert in getting the study published in a peer-reviewed journal, albeit the expert did not provide the journal with any information concerning potential conflicts of interest (such as, the very fact that he was employed by the FTC to do the test and that he had the test article prepared by a competitor to ECM). In the end, ALJ Chappell saw through the agency's machinations and did not credit the study, finding the test not credible.

Having aided the scientist in getting the test result published, all without any notice to the accused despite discovery requests that would have required that disclosure, the FTC then received a copy of the published article and presented it for the first time days later at a deposition of ECM's CEO. At the time of that deposition, the background history of FTC interaction with the scientist was not known to the accused, yet it clearly established that FTC had known for a very long time before the deposition of ECM's CEO that a study had been prepared, completed and submitted for publication to a journal. FTC had been involved with the expert for months preceding the date of the deposition. Under the FTC's rules, a party is required to amend its disclosures of documents responsive to discovery to permit adequate preparation and avoid unfair surprise.

Apparently believing themselves either unaffected by that rule or unlikely to be caught in violating it, the FTC attorneys did not at any time reveal the existence of the study, supplied no drafts of it to the accused, gave the accused no correspondence between the agency and the scientist, and provided no pre-publication copy of the study to the accused. Instead, the FTC attorneys hid the information and endeavored to surprise ECM's CEO in the middle of his deposition.

When the FTC attorney presented the study at the deposition, I objected. The interchange with FTC counsel is captured in a subsequent decision by ALJ Chappell:

> MR. EMORD: . . . You gave us no advanced notice of this document. None. You had it on Friday, you knew you were going to use it in a deposition –
>
> MS. JOHNSON: I did not know I was going to use it.
>
> MR. EMORD: When did you decide you were going to use it?
>
> MS. JOHNSON: We packed up our stuff on Saturday afternoon.

MR. EMORD: This is highlighted. Who did the highlighting on the document?

MS. JOHNSON: I'm not going to reveal that.

MR. EMORD: . . . In any event, you did not turn this document over to us when you had the opportunity to do it and—

MS. JOHNSON: This is your opportunity . . .

When the matter was presented to ALJ Chappell, he agreed that FTC counsel had engaged in improper withholding. In a March 21, 2014 Order, he reasoned:

> Complaint Counsel does not dispute that it was under an obligation to supplement its previous document production by providing the Ohio State Article to Respondent. The disputed issue is whether, under the circumstances presented, complaint counsel's conduct in delaying production of the [article] until five days after its receipt, during the middle of the second day of a previously scheduled deposition, violated Complaint Counsel's obligation to supplement "in a timely manner."

> * * * *

> Complaint Counsel clearly recognized the relevance of the [article], if not immediately upon receipt, then certainly no later than Saturday afternoon, February 15, 2014, when Complaint Counsel packed the document in order to use it at ECM's deposition . . . Yet Complaint Counsel declined numerous opportunities to provide the [article] to Respondent and thereby fulfill its duty to supplement . . .

The ALJ ordered the deposition testimony concerning the article excluded from use at trial and for any other purpose.

A short time thereafter, the saga of abuses took another peculiar turn, this time with an improper demand by FTC counsel. At a break in the deposition of FTC's survey expert, the FTC attorney defending the deposition pulled me aside for a private, off-the-record discussion. He warned that unless ECM filed a motion to withdraw ECM's earlier motion for sanctions and seek deletion of the ALJ's order on the wrongful withholding of the article at the deposition of ECM's CEO, there would be no chance that the FTC would enter a settlement agreement with ECM. That was an unethical, even extortionate demand.

As the history of FTC litigation reveals, in every case where the FTC charges a party with deceptive advertising, it holds them to have so engaged even when agency Administrative Law Judges recommend against finding deceptive advertising. It being an unethical demand, I rejected it promptly, but the fact that it was made boldly and directly to an opponent reveals much about the dire state of legal ethics in administrative litigation. Conduct of a comparable sort, were it to have taken place under the jurisdiction of an Article III Court, would have almost certainly resulted in significant sanctions. Given the bias in favor of FTC in every FTC proceeding, and the distinct possibility that the attorney involved would deny that he ever made the demand, pursuit of sanctions would have entailed significant costs with little likelihood of success. Moreover, ALJs lack authority to impose meaningful sanctions against FTC counsel. Justice does not exist in the FTC adjudicatory environment.

In yet another example of weird behavior by government counsel, at the very first appearance of all counsel before ALJ Chappell, preceding the hearing and in initial trial appearances thereafter, FTC counsel pressed ECM's counsel to agree in advance not to raise any objections to the introduction of any evidence or witness testimony in the proceeding. In effect, FTC counsel wanted the accused to disarm itself and take no action during the administrative trial that would defend the accused's rights.

The mere fact that this demand was made at all is astounding proof that the agency lacks any sincere commitment to due process. FTC counsel represented that the ALJ would not deny the government every opportunity to present evidence, so objection would be futile. That was demonstrably false as anyone familiar with ALJ Chappell could attest. Although administrative trials relax procedural and evidentiary rules and do not require adherence to the federal rules of evidence and civil procedure applicable in Article III courts, they still permit objections concerning evidence, such as those concerning relevance, lack of foundation, hearsay, improper impeachment, prejudice exceeding the weight of probative value, etc. An agreement with opposing counsel not to make such objections would be malpractice. Nevertheless, the FTC counsel had the hubris to press for the relinquishment of all rights to object, doing so repeatedly. Each attempt was rebuffed. Such efforts by attorneys for the government raise serious ethical concerns. Were they engaged by prosecutors in an Article III court, the actions would likely be considered prosecutorial misconduct. As it happens, ALJ Chappell sustained dozens of objections against FTC Counsel during the administrative trial.

In the case FTC brought against ECM, FTC alleged more than one basis for deceptive advertising, but its principal argument centered on the claim that ECM engaged in deceptive advertising when it claimed that its additive caused conventional plastics to be rendered "biodegradable." Indeed, without any peer-reviewed scientific support for the proposition, FTC and its biodegradation expert, Dr. Stephen McCarthy, took the position that conventional plastics were intrinsically non-biodegrade. After a thorough review of all of the evidence, including testimony from leading experts in the field (among them world renowned biodegradation expert Morton Barlaz who testified for ECM), ALJ Chappell determined that the FTC's prosecutors, called "Complaint Counsel," had failed to make their primary case. They failed to prove by clear and convincing evidence that the "biodegradable claim" was deceptive, and they failed to prove by clear and convincing evidence that consumers understood "biodegradable" to mean that plastics infused with the additive would break down into elements in nature within one year of customary disposal.

In his Initial Decision, which is a recommendation on how to decide the case to the Commissioners of the FTC, ALJ Chappell concluded, "Complaint Counsel has failed to prove that the ECM Additive does not render plastics biodegradable." He explained: "Complaint Counsel has failed to prove that the many scientific tests presented by [ECM] at trial [of which there were over two dozen independent tests] showing that the ECM Additive renders conventional plastics biodegradable, including in a landfill environment, are inadequate to substantiate [ECM's] biodegradability claims. Rather, the evidence shows that [ECM's] testing constitutes competent and reliable scientific evidence demonstrating that ECM plastics are biodegradable, including in a landfill."

Although the claim that consumers comprehend the term "biodegradable" to mean that a substance will break down into elements found in nature within one year of customary disposal had no competent support, FTC counsel tried to bolster the point with inherently unreliable Google survey evidence. Its expert employed inexpensive Google ad surveys that included no screening methods to guard against false answers. The survey appeared as a pop-up on randomly selected content pages. A person interested in accessing the content would not be able to do so without giving an answer to the survey question. Thus, individuals who may have no interest whatsoever in the subject of the survey and no basis for an opinion one way or the other were forced to respond to get at the content they desired. No screening was used to determine relative understanding or interest in the subject matter by the survey takers. No effort was made to distinguish those who answered randomly just to get to the content they desired from those who answered earnestly.

The only expert with substantial qualifications in surveys and statistics, Dr. David Stewart, was an expert for ECM. He identified numerous essential faults in the FTC evidence, and the ALJ concurred, finding it not credible. Even so, the FTC manipulated the Google survey ad responses to suggest at least some consumer belief that biodegradation was linked to a set time less than a year within which to achieve complete disintegration. ALJ Chappell found that manipulation, too, unscientific and unreliable. In his Initial Decision, he wrote:

> Weighing the qualifications of Dr. Stewart and of Dr. Frederick [the FTC expert], Dr. Stewart is much more

qualified in the field of designing, implementing, reviewing, and evaluating consumer surveys than Dr. Frederick, and Dr. Stewart's opinions are entitled to greater weight.

* * * *

Having reviewed, evaluated, and weighed the opinions of both Dr. Stewart and Dr. Frederick, and the bases therefore, Dr. Stewart's opinions are well supported and are more well-reasoned, credible, and persuasive than the opposing opinions of Dr. Frederick.

* * * *

Dr. Frederick's Google survey is not reliable and is not valid, and the results cannot be relied upon to draw any conclusions, including about consumer interpretation of "biodegradable" claims, the validity of other surveys, or for any other purpose.

While the FTC expert relied on unverifiable Google ad surveys, Dr. Stewart performed a nation-wide telephone consumer opinion survey through an independent phone survey organization well respected for its work and in strict accordance with generally accepted survey practices to achieve competent and reliable survey results, including vetted survey questions to ensure lack of bias, blinded randomized calling, and screens to ensure unbiased response. ALJ Chappell concluded: "Dr. Stewart's survey was designed in a fashion that is very consistent with accepted standards and best practices in the design of survey research."

Not a single telephone survey respondent asked to explain what he or she understood the term "biodegradable" to mean stated that it involved a break-down of the substance into elements in nature within any set time frame, such as a year or less. ALJ Chappell concluded: "Not one respondent to Dr. Stewart's survey understood biodegradation to mean the complete breakdown of the substance into elements in nature within one year after customary disposal."

The instances of abusive FTC attorney conduct continued in the trial itself. During cross-examination of the FTC's biodegradation expert, it became apparent that his own publications defined the term differently than he did in footnote 1 of his expert report. In that footnote, he defined the term precisely as the government defined it (replete with the arbitrary one year limit and the complete break down into elements language). When pressed on cross-examination, Dr. Stephen McCarthy revealed that his report was, in fact, not exclusively his, at least not with regard to the all-critical definition of "biodegradation." It was, rather, a "collaborative effort," he said, with FTC counsel drafting it along with him. That admission, combined with the fact that the position taken in the report on the central question of the scientific meaning of "biodegradable" conflicted with McCarthy's own published writings, led the ALJ to reject McCarthy's opinion. ALJ Chappell explained: "Complaint Counsel's degradable polymer expert, Dr. McCarthy, used in his expert report a definition for biodegradable provided to him by Complaint Counsel." ALJ Chappell continued, "In the words of Dr. McCarthy, his expert report was the result of a 'collaborative effort' between Dr. McCarthy and Complaint Counsel." Moreover, ALJ Chappell found that "[n]o peer-reviewed literature defines 'biodegradation' to be limited to a 'complete breakdown of plastic into elements found in nature within one year after customary disposal.'" He concluded that Dr. McCarthy's "opinion is unsupported, unpersuasive, and rejected."

On appeal, the Democratic majority of three Commissioners who brought the prosecution in the first place unremarkably decided (with the exception of the lone Republican appointee, Maureen Olhaussen, who dissented) that they were right all along and that the ALJ was wrong, reversing his decision by a vote of three to one (Commissioner Wright, also a Republican appointee, having resigned a short time before the decision).

The fact that the overwhelming weight of the evidence proved that, indeed, the ECM additive worked was of no consequence. Likewise of no consequence was the fact that the only competent survey evidence (from an expert the FTC itself had credited in case after case) proved that consumers did not understand the term "biodegradable" to mean that a substance completely broke down into elements in nature (a scientific impossibility) within one year. Rather, assuming its role as an ultimate arbiter of the meaning of words and of consumer understanding (a degree of understanding only the Creator possesses), the FTC without a shred of competent supportive evidence declared its Green Guides' definition of biodegradable to be a definition that at least a significant minority of consumers understood the term to mean.

Thus, because any biodegradation achieved by the ECM product occurred in periods greater than a year, labeling the product "biodegradable" deceived consumers. They reversed the ALJ's meticulous and well-reasoned Initial Decision without the slightest concern for the fact that their action harmed a business that employed honest, hard-working people, forcing several to lose their jobs. Indeed, they reversed the ALJ's Initial Decision although doing so would disable industry efforts to promote sale and use of conventional plastics that were biodegradable, thus encouraging reliance on cheaper conventional plastics without established biodegradability, exacerbating the harm to the environment worldwide. They thus reinforced Commissioner Wright's point that the Commission in 100% of the cases rules in its own favor and against the accused, regardless of the recommendation of the Administrative Law Judge, regardless of the evidence, and regardless of the impact on the accused and the world.

The tyranny of the FTC is an administrative tyranny that dates back centuries in England. Comparable victims of the Courts of High Commission and Star Chamber may be heard groaning from their graves. Yet again a victim had been unjustly abused by yet another haughty, authoritarian magistracy. A short poem written by Samuel Butler in the mid-seventeenth century comes to mind:

Authority intoxicates,
And makes mere sots of Magistrates;
The fumes of it invade the brain,
And make men giddy, proud, and vain:
By this the fool commands the wise,

The noble with the base complies,
The sot assumes the rule of wit,
And cowards make the base submit. [498]

THE DRUG ENFORCEMENT ADMINISTRATION

On January 17, 2008, the DEA suspended its List I chemical registration for a company in Greenfield, Indiana called Novelty, Inc. Todd Green created the company as a teen in 1984, starting it in his parents' garage. Through diligence and intelligence, Green transformed his company into Greenfield's largest employer. As it expanded, Novelty added to its inventory of products certain cough and cold remedies, some containing List I chemicals, ephedrine and pseudo-ephedrine.

With the rise in methamphetamine use in the United States, and the diversion of ephedrine and pseudoephedrine for use in making meth through domestic meth labs, Congress demanded that DEA act to limit the supply of ephedrine and pseudoephedrine to legitimate medical uses and to increase DEA interdictions of meth from across the border.

Meth is highly addictive and terribly debilitating and injurious. Addicts are physically and mentally devastated, turning themselves into shells with erratic and unpredictable behavior. Many meth addicts, incapable of holding down a job, became petty criminals to feed their habits, breaking into pharmacies, stealing ephedrine and pseudoephedrine containing products, and robbing people for cash and other things of value that may be pawned for cash. DEA required all who sold ephedrine and pseudo-ephedrine containing products to obtain DEA registrations and to submit to extensive regulations governing, and investigations of, their holding, distribution, and sale of the products. Novelty obtained a DEA registration in 1998, going above and beyond DEA regulatory requirements, even developing a comprehensive proprietary system that tracked every ephedrine and pseudoephedrine product and ensured that those products remained in Novelty control, locked and encased, from within a fenced cage in its warehouse to the point of sale. While unfounded allegations were made by the government of risk of diversion, that were ultimately deemed credible by the DEA Deputy Administrator despite their unreliability, there was never any credible evidence that any Novelty List I chemical product had ever been diverted to the illicit meth amphetamine trade and the DEA Administrative Law Judge so held. That is remarkable given the fact that over the years millions of units of product were sold from the thousands of convenience stores Novelty served across the United States.

Between 2002 and 2004, the DEA Administrator Michele Leonhart came under increasing pressure from Congress to interdict the meth trade and stem the incidence of diversion of Schedule I ephedrine and pseudoephedrine used in the meth labs. The overwhelming majority of meth came from Mexico. DEA had very limited success at stanching the flow from across the border. Its difficulty in stopping that primary traffic (accounting for over 80% of the meth on the streets) caused it to increase its efforts domestically to show Congress at least some effort and "success."

In 2004, Leonhart announced her intention to remove all ephedrine from the domestic retail market.[499] After that announcement, she met with lobbyists for Pfizer and Wyeth, the makers of Sudafed and Primatene.[500] Following that meeting, she reversed course, dropped her intended move against all ephedrine at retail, and commenced instead a one-sided campaign of enforcement against the so-called "independents" (i.e., the non-pharmacy sellers of ephedrine and pseudo-ephedrine containing products). Pharmacies were the principal points of sale for the Pfizer and Wyeth products; thus, by blocking independent sales Leonhart would increase demand for pharmacy sales and, thus, benefit Pfizer and Wyeth. In other words, Leonhart became an effective agent of Pfizer and Wyeth cartelization of the ephedrine and pseudoephedrine over-the-counter drug market.

Leonhart waged a relentless, multi-year campaign against the independents, not only the few for which there was circumstantial evidence that their product had been diverted to the illicit meth trade but also the many for which there was no such evidence. Remarkably, she did not prosecute a single distributor of Sudafed and Primatene.

From the 2004 lobbying visits to DEA by representatives of Wyeth and Pfizer until the Novelty case, Leonhart revoked the registrations of fifty-four independents and not a single non-independent. That represents an adjudication success rate of 100% (of fifty-four cases brought she achieved fifty-four revocations). An economic analysis of Leonhart's campaign undertaken by Novelty's retained expert Emory University Professor of Law and Economics Joanna Shepherd, Ph.D. revealed biased enforcement to the economic benefit of the non-independents supplied by Wyeth and Pfizer. The facts of the cases DEA waged against the independents vary, but the outcome was always the same. She revoked with and without evidence of diversion (only three of the fifty-four cases involved actual evidence of diversion), and she revoked even when the Administrative Law Judge recommended continued registration.[501] Not one of the cases involved a Wyeth or Pfizer distributor to big box stores, pharmacy chains, or grocery chains, despite the fact that retail outlets in each of those categories had experienced diversion.

The biased enforcement became glaringly apparent as retail sellers of Sudafed and Primatene, who had been convicted in the states on evidence of diversion, nevertheless did not have their DEA registrations revoked. While Leonhart gave a pass to Sudafed and Primatene distributors, she prosecuted to revocation the independents one after another, whether she had evidence of diversion or not.[502]

On January 17, 2008, Leonhart issued an order to Novelty, Inc., demanding that it bear the burden of proof to justify why it ought not have its DEA registration revoked. On February 26, Novelty requested an expedited hearing on that order to show cause. The hearing took place between March 24, 2008 and April 1, 2008 before Administrative Law Judge Gail A. Randall. As virtually all federal administrative hearings do, the hearing involved lax rules of evidence and admissibility, allowing the DEA to fill the record with all manner of irrelevant and prejudicial documents and hearsay, suggestive of illicit marketing arising from the operation of the independents in general. None of those records provided any credible evidence that Novelty products had been diverted to the illicit meth trade, despite millions of transactions.

While troubled by certain minor record keeping errors, the ALJ found the most significant issues, concerning actual evidence of diversion, adequacy of security measures to guard against diversion, and credibility of witnesses, to bode in favor of Novelty. In particular, she agreed with Novelty's expert that the DEA expert's report lacked a credible foundation that sale of ephedrine and pseudoephedrine-containing products in excess of $14.39 per month was *per se* evidence of "excessive selling" indicative of diversion to the illicit meth trade. She wrote; "Dr. Shepherd, an expert witness in the areas of statistics and applied statistics, found major flaws in Mr. [Jonathan A.] Robbin's statistical methodology . . . These flaws resulted in raising fundamental concerns about the reliability of Mr. Robbin's analytical process, and, thus, his ultimate opinion." She found no credible basis for the DEA's assertion that diversion accompanied sales beyond $14.39 per month, writing, "based on this record, I do not infer that any convenience store that sells more than $14.39 worth of . . . product per month is selling such product to individuals who will divert it to the illicit manufacture of methamphetamine."

Weighing all relevant factors and evidence, ALJ Randall concluded it inappropriate for the DEA Deputy Administrator to take the draconian step of revoking Novelty's registration, stating instead, "this is a case where teamwork between the DEA and this major distributor would further facilitate the public interest." She therefore recommended that the Deputy Administrator "not revoke this registrant's registration."

On appeal to the ultimate prosecutor who was also the ultimate judge, the person who ordered the campaign to revoke the registrations of the independents in the first place, Deputy Administrator Leonhart, the ALJ's recommendation was, predictably, rejected. Leonhart thereby preserved her 100% record of finding herself right in every prosecution. While ignoring the critical issue of the competence of her primary expert's analysis and the ALJ's findings and conclusions concerning that analysis, she nevertheless revoked the registration. She did so in reliance, *inter alia*, on a new interpretation of law that held Novelty improperly used unregistered storage units for its products, on her conclusion that Novelty's records had in certain respects been deficient, and on allegations, unproven, of product diversion which had been given no credence by the ALJ. Once again, the inherent conflict of interest in the combination of prosecutor and judge proved itself dispositive in denying justice, with the wise recommendation of the ALJ rejected without reasoned justification.

THE ALCOHOL AND TOBACCO TAX AND TRADE BUREAU

In early 2014, Harsha Chigurupati and his company Chigurupati Technologies completed development of a proprietary blend of three Generally Recognized as Safe (GRAS) ingredients (glycyrrhizin, potassium sorbate, and mannitol) that when diffused in alcohol through a proprietary process reduced the adverse effects of alcohol on DNA. Through a number of well-known mechanisms, alcohol damages DNA. The additive developed by Chigurupati Technologies significantly reduces the incidence of that damage as confirmed by in vitro, animal, and human clinical trials. The studies revealed that the additive reduced damage to DNA caused by alcohol by a statistically significant 83%. No scientific evidence to the contrary exists. Leading authorities who reviewed the evidence, including the renowned Tufts Research Professor Jeffrey B. Blumberg, confirmed that the testing was credible and reliable and that the DNA damage reduction effects were supported by that testing.

Were this health claim to enter the market, consumers would be able to distinguish from among alcohol products those with less deleterious effects to DNA. That would create a new market and new competitive pressure, upsetting the staid, centuries old distillery business by forcing major companies in the industry to consider alterations to historic formulas capable of reducing harms caused by alcohol. TTB stands foursquare against that competition, operating like a guild in defense of the old guard interests. The Alcohol and Tobacco Tax and Trade Bureau (TTB), formerly Alcohol Tobacco and Firearms (ATF), has a long history of protectionism, using its regulatory discretion to blunt or fend off competitive change that would upset industry incumbents.

For years, ATF forbad companies selling beer from placing on their labels the quantity of alcohol in the products. Coors Brewing Company challenged that ban on truthful speech and won a landmark ruling from the Supreme Court condemning the agency for acting on suspicion rather than proof of harm. When called to defend the ban, ATF claimed it was necessary to prevent strength wars from happening in the alcohol market. There was no evidence of the strength wars, only speculation, and the Supreme Court made clear that speculation was not enough to satisfy ATF's burden under the First Amendment. [503]

On July 30, 2014 and September 3, 2014, representatives of Chigurupati Technologies along with members of their science staff visited the Alcohol and Tobacco Tax and Trade Bureau (TTB), a division of the United States Treasury, in Washington, D.C. At that meeting, they presented the scientific evidence supporting their discovery and explained that they and their TTB registered distiller would soon seek TTB authority to place specific health claims on the label and in the advertising of a vodka product. The TTB attorneys and officials at the meeting explained that the TTB would not grant any such allowance and strongly discouraged Chigurupati Technologies from pursuing a health claim. Further, the TTB attorneys and officials at the meeting explained that TTB did not have competent staff to evaluate scientific evidence concerning the health effects of an alcohol additive. TTB had adopted regulations authorizing the filing of health claim petitions, following earlier disputes with industry over whether industry would be allowed to explain certain positive health effects of red wine to consumers (TTB rejected the idea but agreed to develop rules for the filing of a health claim petition). Revealing the rules to be superficial with no real intent of effectuation, TTB never hired any competent staff to evaluate health claims under the rules. Rather, as was done with Chigurupati Technologies, it chose instead to pressure regulated entities against pursuing any health claims.

Undaunted by TTB's attempt to dissuade a filing, Chigurupati Technologies and its distiller filed, respectively, a citizen's petition with TTB seeking allowance of label claims and advertising and a request for certificates of label authorization (COLAs) to place the claims on the label of their vodka product. Professing an inability to evaluate the science, TTB referred the petition to FDA for evaluation. At first, TTB asked FDA to determine whether Chigurupati proposed a "drug claim," unlawful under both agencies' regulations. Presumably because the claims had nothing to do with drugs, TTB then withdrew that request and asked FDA to evaluate whether the claims were supported by the evidence. TTB gave FDA no criteria to apply under TTB's own statutory regime. Under that regime, TTB was supposed to allow claims to be made that were "adequately substantiated" (an inherently ambiguous term). Rather than give meaning to the term, TTB deferred to FDA's evaluation of the science under FDA's inapplicable regulatory rubric "significant scientific agreement" (used for food and dietary supplement claims).

Concerning the DNA claims ("helps protect DNA from alcohol-induced damage" and "reduces alcohol-induced DNA damage"), FDA determined that while the clinical trial evidence "show[ed] a significant reduction in certain measures of DNA damage at some but not all time points after administration of NTX," it could not be sure what dose of additive was used. FDA also admitted that the science supportive of the claim showed "reduced ROS, dROM, GSSG, MDA, PC and 8OH-DG levels [which] were significantly reduced for one or more time point." Although it played down the significance of these findings, it placed principal reliance on the fact that it said it did not know what dose of the additive was used. In fact, the dose level had been revealed repeatedly to TTB. Rather than subject FDA's analysis to its own evaluation, TTB presumed FDA's assessment (under a standard of review inapplicable to alcohol) was fully accurate, even to the point of accepting, against its own knowledge to the contrary, the false assertion that the dose amount of the additive used was unknown. Repeatedly, Chigurupati Technologies had supplied TTB with information concerning the dosing of the additive used in the trials, which was the same dosing it used in its commercial product.

The TTB issued a decision denying the claims on the basis that they were not backed by credible science and, in the case of the DNA claims, that the dosing was not known. It thus adopted without any material change, the FDA's analysis. Aside from its superficiality, the FDA analysis was performed by agency staff who, in correspondence with TTB, admitted that they were unfamiliar with DNA testing, the very testing at issue. TTB also refused to define its own "adequately substantiated" scientific standard while stating that its own standard was different from that of FDA, thus obfuscating but also denying Bellion and any future applicant the benefit of knowing what level, degree, quantity, and quality of scientific evidence TTB expected to support a health claim petition.

Fundamentally, the TTB regime, like FDA's health claim regime, violates the First Amendment because it imposes a prior restraint on all health claims and unconstitutionally shifts the burden of proof to the party wishing to speak to prove its speech true to the regulators' subjective satisfaction before speech may occur. This is thus a regime of unbridled official discretion to which the First Amendment has historically been held anathema. Under the First Amendment, as it was intended, the burden of proof is on the government to establish that a statement is false before it may be suppressed. Contrary to that requirement, the TTB and the FDA have in place a licensing regime forbidding the communication of any health claim unless the party wishing to speak first proves to the agency's satisfaction that the statement is true. That is directly contrary to the plain and intended meaning of the First Amendment. It was supposed to disarm government of censorship power. FDA and TTB suppress an enormous quantity of truthful health information that would otherwise enable consumers to make informed choices in their own health interest. They operate on the paternalist assumption that they know better than the American people what is in the people's self-interest, and they presume it appropriate to deny people access to information on the assumption that if given it they may use it in ways the government thinks unwise.

THE FOOD AND DRUG ADMINISTRATION

While the incidence of death associated with opioids appears at last to be coming down, the United States has experienced an opioid epidemic from the mid-1990s to the present. The evidence gathered by the Centers for Disease Control and Prevention and by the National Institute on Drug Abuse of the National Institutes of Health is startling. According to those agencies, opioids such as fentanyl, oxycodone, hydrocodone, codeine, and morphine, kill an estimated 128 people in the United States every day. An estimated 1.7 million Americans suffer from opioid addiction. In 2017 alone, 47,600 people died from opioid overdoses (compared to 4,030 in 1999). Twenty-one to 29% of patients prescribed opioids for chronic pain eventually abuse the drugs. Eight to 12% develop an opioid use disorder. Four to 6% who misuse prescription opioids graduate to heroin. Eighty percent of those who use heroine began with misuse of prescription opioids.[504]

What triggered the massive opioid crisis, estimated to cost some $78.5 billion in costs to the health care system, not to mention the cost to businesses and families? The little known fact is that the Food and Drug Administration is to blame for unleashing this plague.

The opioid crisis began in earnest in the mid-1990s when Purdue Pharma, with the backing of FDA through a decision by then FDA Commissioner David Aaron Kessler (at the behest of FDA Team Medical Reviewer Dr. Curtis Wright) approved to market OxyContin as a largely non-addictive drug appropriate for use in treating "moderate to severe pain" on a long-term basis. Prior to Commissioner Kessler's approval of the labeling change, the FDA only approved opioids for "acute" pain (largely cancer related) and for short-term use. Commissioner Kessler's approval expanded the indicated use of the drug, officially permitting use in "moderate" pain cases and for long periods of time.

Instrumental in securing Kessler's approval to the expanded use, Dr. Wright left FDA two years after the expanded use approval and went to work for Purdue Pharma, the maker of OxyContin and the company that reaped huge profits off the expanded use labeling authorized by Kessler.

To permit expanded labeling and use of OxyContin, Commissioner Kessler had to turn a blind eye to both internal FDA and external medical science concerning the risks of, and the dangers inherent in, opioid addiction in favor of the drug maker, Purdue Pharma. Kessler was recently quoted by reporter Jerry Mitchell of the *Clarion Ledger* as admitting his error: "No doubt it was a mistake. It was certainly one of the worst medical mistakes, a major mistake," he said.[505]

FDA reviewed no long-term safety and efficacy data on OxyContin before it approved the drug for moderate pain and long-term use. Also, without adequate scientific proof, it accepted the marketing message of Purdue Pharma to allow for greater physician prescription, putting in the FDA approved label for the drug that OxyContin had "delayed absorption" which was "believed to reduce" the risk of opioid abuse. That was entirely false. The FDA approved label also included the false representation, unproven at the time FDA authorized it for use on the OxyContin label, that "'addiction' to opioids legitimately used in the management of pain is very rare." Moreover, while FDA approved a single tablet dose of 160 mg of OxyContin, Kessler now admits, as Jerry Mitchell quotes, "[t]here is very little pharmaceutical use for an 800 mg OxyContin. There's way too much drug in that tablet." [506]

In its OxyContin promotional campaign, Purdue Pharma told physicians that opioids were not being prescribed enough for pain. A Purdue Pharma promotional video entitled "I Got My Life Back," sent to 15,000 physicians made the claim that OxyContin was "less than 1 percent addictive," which was false. In his revelatory article in *The Ledger*, Jerry Mitchell quotes the Co-Director of the Opioid Policy Research Collaborative at Brandeis University, Dr. Andrew Kolodny, as stating: "I believe we wouldn't have an opioid epidemic if the FDA had done its job properly."[507]

Purdue Pharma and Johnson and Johnson played a major role in promoting broad prescription of opioids for all manner of moderate to severe pain from the mid-1990s forward, falsely touting opioids as non-addictive and faulting physicians who under-prescribed them, goading them to experience guilt for not prescribing them enough to those in pain. Although in 1997, there were 670,000 individual prescriptions for OxyContin, that figure exploded to 6.2 million by 2002. By 1997, Johnson and Johnson as well as other top U.S. drug companies redesigned their marketing strategies (after the incredibly profitable Purdue Pharma model used by the Sackler-family owned enterprise) to cash in on a market growing annually by several hundred percent. Drug companies selling opioids joined in the call for physicians to increase their opioid prescriptions, explaining that those in pain were "undertreated" and describing the risk of abuse as low. Many physicians obliged, and the incidence of opioid abuse and addiction skyrocketed.

In *The Rise of Tyranny*, I explain the industry capture regulatory phenomenon at work at FDA. As the former FDA Associate Director of the Office of Drug Safety, Dr. David Graham, testified before Congress and explained in an interview in the September/October 2005 edition of *Fraud Magazine* (the publication of the Association of Certified Fraud Examiners):

"FDA is inherently biased in favor of the pharmaceutical industry. . . . The pro-industry bias leads to an environment where FDA tends to see things from industry's perspective. Many are the advisory committee meetings where the drug company presentation and the FDA presentation are virtually super-imposable. It makes you wonder who wrote the presentations." Graham further explains, "When FDA reviews a new drug, it assumes that the drug is safe, and it facetiously asks the company [sponsor] to prove that it's not safe. Of course, there is no incentive for a company to prove that their drug is not safe because then FDA might not approve it. So, with a nod and a wink, drug companies jump through the very low hoops that FDA sets up for safety, and the public pays in two ways—with its money and its lives."[508]

THE ENVIRONMENTAL PROTECTION AGENCY

Chantell and Michael Sackett own a two-thirds-acre residential lot in Bonner County, Idaho. They bought it in 2005 for $23,000. It is just north of Priest Lake, separated from the lake by lots containing permanent structures. The lot is in a partially built residential neighborhood. Other houses and a road separate the lot from Priest Lake, which is about 500 feet away.[509] After they received permits from the County, the Sacketts began construction on a three-bedroom home, covering a half-acre portion of their lot. In aid of construction, the Sacketts filled a part of their lot with dirt and rock. A few months after that preliminary construction work was completed, the EPA sent the Sacketts a cease and desist compliance order. The order stated that the Sacketts' property lay in what EPA referred to as "jurisdictional wetlands." That meant that while the property itself was not regulated as a "navigable water" under the Clean Water Act, it was near enough to one, Priest Lake, that EPA in its regulatory discretion would assume jurisdiction over the property. EPA explained that by filling approximately one-half acre of their land with "discharged fill material" without EPA permission, the Sacketts disturbed the regulatory wetland. The EPA ordered the Sacketts to cease construction and "immediately [to] undertake activities to restore the Site in accordance with [the EPA's] Restoration Work Plan" and to give EPA agents "access to all records and documentation related to the conditions at the Site."[510]

The Sacketts were ordered to remove the gravel dumped on the lot, restore the vegetation, which existed before they began construction, fence off the property, and file reports with the EPA documenting their compliance activity. If they refused to do as the EPA demanded, the agency threatened them with fines of up to $32,500 per day and, if they persisted in their violations, and EPA prevailed in legal action against them, the amount that would be due was $75,000 for each day of violation.

The Sacketts chose not to follow the EPA Order and asked the agency for a hearing, but EPA refused. It did not have a regulatory pathway for the Sacketts to appeal the agency's cease and desist order. So, the Sacketts sued EPA in federal court. In litigation, the EPA insisted that its cease and desist letter was not a ripe or final agency action because the agency had not instituted suit against the Sacketts. The EPA argued that the Sacketts' suit was an attempt to obtain a "pre-enforcement judicial review of compliance orders," which was forbidden under the Administrative Procedure Act. The EPA admitted, however, that it had no regulatory appellate process available, thus leaving the Sacketts in an indefinite regulatory loop, a procedural no man's land. They would thus be potentially fined astronomical sums and unable to construct their home until EPA got around to suing them for non-compliance, at which point the fines could be impossible for even Bill Gates to pay. The U.S. District Court and the Ninth Circuit each held that the Sacketts had to await EPA action in federal court to enforce the order before they would have standing to be heard in Court. The Sacketts appealed to the Supreme Court, and the Supreme Court reversed.

The Supreme Court determined that the cease and desist order was a final agency action, that there was no adequate remedy at law for the Sacketts, and that the Clean Water Act did not bar the Sacketts' suit. The decision did not resolve the underlying issue of whether, indeed, the EPA could constitutionally compel the Sacketts to abandon construction and pay enormous fines on the assertion of EPA jurisdiction over "jurisdictional wetlands." The EPA actions reveal just how powerful and life-altering federal regulations can be, bringing the unreasonable weight of the entire federal government down on a humble property owner without any regard for the property rights of that owner.

The five examples given here of agency abuse of power are typical. Every day across America owners of companies and of property struggle to cope with the cost and burdens of regulations enforced by the federal government. Created in the Progressive and New Deal eras as means to overcome constitutional barriers to government action, over 200 federal regulatory agencies deprive Americans of their rights to life, liberty and property without due process of law and without accounting for their actions to the courts, the Congress, and the American people.

CHAPTER 9

THE MISERY OF SOCIALISM

S ocialism may be defined as the transfer of sovereign control over property and life-affecting decisions from the individual to the state. There are varying kinds of socialism on a transfer of power continuum. Some involve state regulation of enterprise without total ownership of all property along the Fabian socialist model; some involve a combination of state cartelization of select enterprise and regulation akin to Mussolini's corporatist state; and some involve total state ownership of all property along the Marxist model. Each involves a loss of individual freedom and self-determination. We may refer to socialism as collectivism and to capitalism as individualism. In his foreword to Igor Shafarevich's *The Socialist Phenomenon*, Alexander I. Solzhenitsyn writes: "It could probably be said that the majority of states in the history of mankind have been 'socialist.' But it is also true that these were in no sense periods or places of human happiness or creativity."[511]

In *The Road to Serfdom*, F. A. Hayek defined socialism as "the abolition of private enterprise, of private ownership of the means of production, and the creation of a system of 'planned economy' in which the entrepreneur working for profit is replaced by a central planning body."[512] In *Socialism*, Ludwig Von Mises defined the term this way: "All the means of production are in the exclusive control of the organized community."[513] While modern socialist variants sometimes coopt and direct private enterprise rather than abolish it or take ownership of it, centralized government economic planning in place of private economic choice is the aspect that has survived the ages, regardless of socialist form.

Socialism tears down what is above, favors mediocrity, and demands uniform compliance with state demands. Individualism, creativity, and innovation are discouraged; indeed, the characteristics that define the uniqueness of each person, and joy in life, pose a direct threat to the monopoly of power reserved by the socialist state. Socialism thus begets and maintains human misery. Yet if socialism begets misery, why do half of all Millennials and Generation Zs prefer it?[514] Why do half of all women eighteen to fifty-four prefer it?[515] Why do 64% of Democrats say they have a favorable view of socialism?[516] Why has the Democratic Party allowed itself to be dominated by socialists? The answer lies in its false allure: Its promise of something of value for free (of free health care, free college tuition, or free money (a living wage)), but nothing of value is free, and sooner or later, the cost must be paid. What government gives, government demands in return either through taxation or, if deficit spending is the preferred method, a general rise in the costs of all goods and services, or both taxation and inflation.

Despite its many different forms in different ages and its ability to mutate and resurrect itself, "there is one single, unifying feature shared by every version of socialism: the subjugation of the individual to the collective"[517] And therein lies its tie to authoritarianism and its assurance of misery: what you want you cannot acquire and cannot be given unless it is approved by the collective, which is embodied in the state.

Equality is said to be a fundamental tenet of socialism: equality of class; equality of the races; equality of the sexes and genders; and equality of outcomes. But this equality is not equal justice under law, it is instead a leveling equality, whereby the state promises to take from a rich Peter to pay a poor Paul; eliminates luxury goods and services in favor of those deemed more common, rationing the common to all; and disallows the assertion of individual rights against what the state declares the common interest.

In *The Socialist Temptation*, Iain Murray describes six of the many variants of socialism in the modern world, each sharing in common a commitment to collectivism and a rejection of individual rights. There is *Marxism*, based on "a class struggle between the capitalist bourgeoisie and the proletariat working class" yielding a workers' revolution that overthrows the capitalists, giving control of "means of production, distribution, and exchange" to a worker-controlled state which evolves from socialism to communism, i.e., from state regulation of all enterprise to state ownership of all enterprise.[518]

There is *Communism* whereby the state owns, controls, and directs all enterprise, obtains all revenue from enterprise, and redistributes all revenue, presumably equitably, to all. The entire economy is thus directed "through a system of command and control by public officials, who are members of the Communist Party."[519]

There is *Democratic Socialism* whereby democracy is used as a Trojan horse to enable socialists to infiltrate and take over the government peaceably and, once in power, to then enable labor reforms that place workers in control of business or to seize specific industries for operation directly by the government. All facets of the market (wages, prices, production, and distribution) are controlled through government regulation. The needs of politically favored constituencies are supplied by the state in the form of, e.g., a guaranteed living wage, "free" education, and "free" medical care. "This was historically the approach of Western European socialist parties such as Britain's Labour Party, which after winning the election of 1948 proceeded to nationalize vast areas of British industry."[520]

There is *Social Democracy* whereby the state maintains high taxes and high regulation of enterprise along with a massive welfare state.[521] This is typical of Western Europe. Unlike communist regimes, social democracies allow varying degrees of freedom, such as the right to protest, write or communicate sentiments critical of the government, albeit the degree of communicative freedom lawfully allowed is less than that permitted in the United States.

There is *Market Socialism* whereby states like Yugoslavia, Cuba, Belarus, and Ethiopia in apparent recognition of the economic failures of socialism or communism endeavor to reinsert a degree of market capitalism by transferring specific enterprises from public ownership to worker cooperatives, allowing a degree of worker retention of profits to incentivize the workforce to better and higher levels of production.[522]

There is *State Capitalism* in communist China[523] whereby the government through local party officials authorizes private enterprise by individuals and entities owned, operated, and controlled by individuals who are either members of the communist party or have established loyalties to the communist party. Businesses loyal to the party must then provide aid and support to the party in addition to taxes to the government. In turn, the government provides financial assistance and protective tariffs to hamper or eliminate external competitive pressures that might otherwise reduce the likelihood of survival or success of the business.

There is *Fascism* in, e.g., Mussolini's Italy (his "Third Way"), whereby no enterprise is permitted unless licensed by the state and operated under strict government direction and controls. In fascist states, "[c]ompetition [is] replaced by state-organized cartels, small companies [are] dissolved, and corporations [are] instructed to act in the national interest—as defined by the ruling fascists."[524]

There is *Green Socialism* whereby for the sake of the environment government prohibits all manner of enterprise and then authorizes and provides grants to induce the creation of enterprises and business practices and services deemed environmentally friendly by state regulators. This kind of socialism has been proposed in the Green New Deal (introduced as a resolution in the House by Alexandria Ocasio-Cortez and in the Senate by Edward Markey, cosponsored by 103 members of Congress) and adopted to a considerable degree by Joe Biden.[525] The proposal involves bans on carbon emissions that will end the use of fossil fuels, the principal energy source in America. The proposal also involves substantial new taxes, including carbon taxes, along with tax incentives to channel private behavior away from products and services deemed deleterious to the environment in favor of others deemed helpful to the environment. As Jeremy Rifkin explains, "[w]e will have to decommission and disassemble the entire . . . fossil fuel and nuclear energy infrastructure" and replace that with "solar, wind, and other renewable energies."[526] In addition to ending reliance on gas fed automobiles and airplanes, Green Socialism requires that "buildings . . . be retrofitted to increase their energy efficiency and be equipped with renewable-energy-harvesting installations and converted into micro power-generating plants."[527] The "Green New Deal" calls for an enormous expansion of government regulation through the administrative state, essentially Franklin D. Roosevelt's New Deal many times over.[528]

Green New Deal advocates envision the largest government-planned economy in world history, regulation that forces an end to carbon-based enterprise, the construction of green alternatives, and major taxation and redistribution initiatives to direct the nation to a new green paradise. The Ocasio-Cortez/Markey proposal would end fossil fuel use in the United States by 2029; create a massive new social welfare state that includes a large federal jobs and socialized medicine program; and would establish new statutory rights and benefits to create "social, economic, racial, regional and gender-based justice and equality and cooperative and public ownership."[529] The Green New Deal is in fact Green Socialism, as Ocasio-Cortez's chief of staff admitted in a conversation with Sam Ricketts, climate director for Washington Governor Jay Inslee. Ocasio-Cortez's then chief of staff, Saikat Chakraborti, stated: "The interesting thing about the Green New Deal is it wasn't originally a climate thing at all . . . Do you guys think of it as a climate thing? Because we really think of it as a how-do-you-change-the-entire-economy thing."[530]

All forms of socialism depend on actions that deny self-determination, invite tyranny, and reduce productivity, innovation, and quality. They, therefore, lead to mass poverty, hopelessness, and enslavement.

All forms of socialism empower the collective and disempower the individual. None protects individual rights against the common interest. Socialist regimes depend on a government-directed economy, which means on government direction of private pursuits. Inherent in this model is a degradation, or elimination, of protections for individual rights. It is impossible meaningfully to advance a "common interest" of the collective without abridging private interests. For example, if the government determines that a minimum wage should be prescribed to advance the "common interest," necessarily employees who would work for under that wage, or employers who cannot afford to pay all of their employees that wage, suffer, as do consumers who will be charged more for goods and services supplied at a higher cost. The employee who would work for less than the minimum wage may fall into a category of people unable to find work, and the employer who cannot afford to pay all of his employees the minimum wage must let the ones he cannot afford go.

Every intervention into the market to benefit one select group comes at the expense of others and distorts the direction of the market. In the aggregate, when the economy is directed by government planners, it follows a path that fails to take into account innovation, momentary changes in demand, and a whole host of other minute-by-minute changes which would otherwise affect the nature, quantity, quality, and availability of particular goods and services.

So, for example, if the government determines that a particular commodity, like a college education, ought to be available to everyone for free because that commodity in an open market carries with it a cost subject to supply and demand, the effect is to increase dramatically the demand for college education, resulting in shortages, forcing some to wait for years to get into college. Some will have to forego college education altogether unless a black market arises in for-pay college outside of the government system. The same is true for "free" health care, as governments in Canada and Britain can well attest in light of severe shortages in available medical services, including the availability of certain life-saving examinations and operations. Socialism thus empowers the collective and disempowers the individual by denying the individual choice and opportunities that would otherwise arise in a free market.

All forms of socialism compel equality of outcome despite inequality of talents, thus eliminating incentives necessary for economic progress. Socialism operates on the false Marxian premise that all people are of equal talent. While classical liberalism operates on the premise that God creates all equal in their rights (but not in their talents), socialism presumes no person has rights except by grant from the state and that all are literally equal in their talents. The problem with that supposition of perfect equality of talent is that it defies nature and is demonstrably false. Each person is possessed of unique talents. The effort to compel equality, to pay all in an occupation the same wage regardless of merit, and to discourage exceptionalism depresses innovation and retards progress. Civilization depends on exceptionalism to advance. Were Einstein discouraged from developing his exceptional theories we may never have had the benefits of his special and general theories of relativity; his quantum theory of light; and his link between mass and energy, among others. In September of 1933, he fled Nazi Germany to the West in no small measure because only in the West (and ultimately in the United States) could he enjoy the freedom necessary to develop his talents in full.[531] When inequality of talent is celebrated, and merit is compensated, innovation results, the benefits of which enable progress. When inequality of talent is shunned and discouraged, and merit is left uncompensated, innovation suffers, the consequences of which disable progress.

All forms of socialism destroy the rule of law in favor of the arbitrary will of the state bureaucrat. The rule of law ensures equal justice under law for all regardless of station in life, race, creed, or religion. In socialist countries, there is no permanent or fixed rule of law but, rather, the arbitrary will of the administrative magistrate (mutable in each circumstance and based on political directives of the state). That arbitrary will determines the fate of individuals. Private property has little legal protection and may be disposed of as directed by the state without an avenue for legal redress.

F. A. Hayek explained that government planning in a socialist state depends on a substitution of state judgments for a myriad of private ones made by businesses, which makes arbitrary decision-making inevitable, contrary to the demands of legal certainty and predictability, which are requisite for the protection of liberty, the rule of law. Hayek writes: "Stripped of all technicalities, [the Rule of Law] means that government in all its actions is bound by rules fixed and announced beforehand—rule which makes it possible to foresee with fair certainty how the authority will use its coercive powers in given circumstances to plan one's individual affairs on the basis of this knowledge." The problem with socialist economic planning is that it "necessarily involves the very opposite of this," writes Hayek.[532] Rather, socialist governments are governments of unlimited power in which "the most arbitrary rule can be made legal; and in this way a democracy may set up the most complete despotism imaginable."[533]

All forms of socialism ensure the lowest common denominator in production and quality because from each according to his ability, to each according to his need (Marx) translates into: from each as little productive work as possible to each in equal measure. The fundamental problem in a socialist economy is that "need" is a political determination and "equal pay" creates a disincentive for anyone to do more than the lowest common denominator.

Since everyone has needs, the determination of whose needs are greatest in an economy where a distant state, not a market conscious entrepreneur, divvies up the economic pie results invariably in flat pay schedules tied to occupations, regardless of individual merit. Indeed, it is a fundamental tenet of socialism that pay not be based on merit, but on need. Need equates with inability, not ability. Merit garners no profit beyond common pay. Thus, the most productive are to be paid equally with the least productive. Thus, if factory work is assigned a set sum for weekly pay, those who produce beyond a prescribed minimum receive nothing more for their effort. Lacking any incentive to produce more, laborers avoid the effort. Indeed, leisure time then becomes of pronounced benefit. There is in the emphasis on the collective a natural hiding place for he who avoids distinction and work. This then leads invariably to production quotas in response, but quotas set above what the typical worker produces are unrealistic and may well result in a worker response that yields production below prior minimums, as workers become even more discouraged.

In addition to a lower level of production, socialist economies also produce a lower quality of product. In the first instance, the product is ordinarily one that has been bureaucratically selected. Consequently, unaware of market demands, incapable of accurately or timely predicting market trends, and required to take into account political considerations affecting what goods may be used in production and the nature of those goods and that production, government bureaucrats often approve inefficient, ineffective, or substandard goods and services. In this way, Russian submarines, nuclear power plants, and battleships in the Soviet era were notoriously hazardous and inefficient. Likewise, commercial goods like automobiles, refrigerators, and televisions in the former Soviet Union and Eastern Bloc were notoriously dysfunctional and inefficient. Consistently, goods and services made in socialist countries commonly suffer from defects in quality and utility when compared to comparable goods and services in capitalist countries.

All forms of socialism promise free goods and services that have intrinsic value, such as free food; free education; free healthcare; and free daycare but result in shortages and rationing. When something of value is given away for free, all those who want it (rather than just those who can afford it) demand that something. That creates shortages. Short supplies of goods and services (or the inputs necessary for them) increases the cost of the goods and services. This leads to an upward spiral of cost and a failure to satisfy demand. The hunger thus perpetually outstrips the feed. Moreover, because area demand is impossible to predict without a free market, bureaucratic allocation of goods and services results in some areas having a surplus and others having a shortage or all areas having a shortage.

When the free good or service is a thing of precious value, e.g., food, education, healthcare, daycare, etc., the consequence is that some who could afford to purchase it will be denied it along with those who cannot afford it but are last in line. Moreover, as demand exceeds supply and as rationing proves insufficient to stem the backlogs, governments incapable of affording the higher cost of the scarce goods and services invariably reduce quality to expand supply. The net effect is to aggravate human misery. Whether it is for rationed food, education, healthcare, or daycare, people must enter a cue and must hope that their number is called, knowing full well that they may be at a point beyond available supply and always mindful that what is supplied may be of substandard quality.

The effect is catastrophic. "As any freshman economics student should know," writes Thomas J. DiLorenzo, "declaring *anything* to be a 'free' good or service will cause an explosion of demand, which in turn will ratchet up the costs of providing the good or service."[534] Healthcare rationing provides a good window into the problem.

In Britain more than one million people are waiting to be admitted to hospitals at any one time; in Canada, one study found that 876,000 people were waiting for treatments; in Norway, more than 270,000 people are daily waiting for hospital admissions and other medical treatment; and in New Zealand, some 90,000 people wait for medical care on any given day.[535] The story of socialized medicine is one of delay and ultimate receipt of inadequate care.

As a consequence of delays in receiving care, some 20% of colon and lung cancer patients in Britain were declared incurable by the time they reached the hospital for diagnosis, and some 25% of cardiac patients died while waiting to see a doctor.[536] Consequently, those who can afford to fly to the United States for diagnosis and treatment from Canada, Britain, Norway, France, New Zealand, and elsewhere do, while the others must languish in agony and uncertainty until they reach the head of the cue. That exodus to the United States will continue to be a salvation for those in socialist countries unless the United States adopts Medicare for all, the Democratic Party version of socialized medicine.

All forms of socialism destroy market specialization needed to satisfy consumer demand, thus diminishing the quality of life and the progress of society. Socialism eradicates dissent and inequality among the public (although not the unequal lifestyles of socialist leaders, for while the socialist public is impoverished, socialist leaders live lavishly). Socialism encourages one size fits all production and discourages specialization. In a free-market economy, specialization is a common and desired feature. Enter any store in a capitalist country and a plethora of goods greet the eye. There is not one kind of pasta but dozens of kinds. There is not one kind of grape but many kinds. There is not one kind of cucumber, but many. There is not one kind of bicycle for sale but dozens of kinds. There is not one kind of analgesic but many and varied combinations. The list is endless. In a socialist economy, there are far fewer options because there is no economic incentive to engage in specialization and, indeed, collectivism dissuades reliance on the kind of individualism needed for specialization. Moreover, government-planned economies aim at rationing to meet expected demand for single, politically chosen goods in a category, without provision for uniqueness. Indeed, there is no financial reward associated with the investment of more time, effort, and expense in specialization, so it disappears.

But specialization is a form of fine tailoring to meet individual demand, a form of market experimentation to test receptivity to innovation, and one means by which market economies advance the welfare and standard of living of all by creating far more options. So, for example, while a standard hypodermic needle is certainly capable of drawing blood from patients, the specialization which results in butterfly needles instantaneously creates an advance such that the pain associated with blood withdrawals, particularly for those with small veins, is lessened. The quality of life is improved. Yet, that innovation occurred when an American, Kenneth C. Raines, undertook the expense and experimentation necessary to come up with the butterfly needle, patent it, and acquire approval for it, cognizant that it might be valued in the medical community. Such innovation is not possible in a highly regulated socialist state, and, even were it possible, the disincentives associated with not being able to profit from the innovation substantially reduce the incentive for creating the breakthrough.

All forms of socialism ignore the inherent risks of unbridled government power and lack of bureaucratic accountability. Socialism depends on the incompetent notion that a myriad of independent individuals pursuing their own self-interest is less able to enhance the standard of living and the welfare of a nation than a small group of government bureaucrats empowered by law to replace private choice with public demands. Socialism creates a false, even counter-intuitive, dichotomy: the assumption that people subject to economic pressures who operate in the market are reliably evil and disserve the public, while those subject to political pressures who operate in government are reliably beneficent. While some in the private sector commit crimes to benefit themselves, they are accountable to consumers and under the civil and criminal laws. That reality creates a powerful incentive in favor of lawful enterprise and a solution for unlawful enterprise. The same cannot be said for bureaucrats. They ordinarily enjoy sovereign immunity, preventing them from being held accountable for misconduct. They are thus unaccountable to the public for their actions. They are not elected and cannot be removed by the electorate, and they are thus largely free from political consequence for their actions, making them far more dangerous to the public than private enterprise which depends on the public for the sale of goods and services and suffers a direct and palpable loss in stock values, loss of consumer purchases, and loss of profits from civil and criminal liability risks whenever they are inattentive to or disregard consumer wants and needs.

Moreover, private actors ordinarily affect a subset of the population rather than the whole of it, while those in government affect the entire population because their actions take on whole industries (and thus, goods, services, employment, and wealth generation). Thus, malfeasance by a single enterprise may harm some consumers but malfeasance by government bureaucrats harms everyone. Corrupt acts in the government bureaucracy are well documented, including in this book's Chapter 8, yet they escape justice and proceed without accountability. That reality emboldens bureaucrats, giving them a sense of invincibility, which leads to the common supposition that it is a blessing that bureaucrats are inefficient because, were they not, they would establish a more comprehensive tyranny, magnifying the misery of everyone.

Indeed, as control over property and life-affecting decisions is transferred to the state, thus diminishing private power while increasing public power, the risks of, and consequences that flow from, abuse of government power are magnified. The simple fact that greater power is given and centralized in the state, which has a monopoly over use of the police, creates a clear danger to the public. As Thomas J. DiLorenzo explains in *The Problem with Socialism*, quoting F. A. Hayek, "To a socialist, said Hayek, there is nothing 'which the consistent collectivist must not be prepared to do if it serves 'the good of the whole,' This socialist mindset accepts if not celebrates 'intolerance and brutal suppression of dissent,' and 'the complete disregard of the life and happiness of the individual,' because the 'selfish' individual does not matter; the socialist will argue that what he does is 'for the good of the whole.'"[537]

All forms of socialism destroy economic incentives for productivity, innovation, and quality. Socialism depends on heavy taxation of the rich. The rich include those who have distinguished themselves in competitive markets by attracting the most consumers. That is either due to their creation of an innovation needed by the public, efficiencies or economies of scope and scale that have lowered the cost per unit of a product, or modifications in methods of production or in the characteristics of a product that make it of greater availability and/or utility to consumers. Thus, ordinarily, those who make the most money in a free market are those who benefit consumers the most.

The rich are universally made targets in socialist states. Indeed, ordinarily, they are villainized, presented as enemies of the people, and falsely accused of profiting through exploitation of labor. In truth, the profits derived are due to market preferences of consumers, having no redistributive relationship with labor beyond the fact that if more labor is needed to satisfy demand, that could well increase the market price the employer must pay to attract labor. Moreover, while the Marxist claims labor is at odds with the capitalist, which is sometimes true, the more common or usual circumstance is that labor is aligned with the capitalist, in that both seek to profit from the same enterprise. The employee only has a job because the employer provides it, and the employer can provide it only because he has amassed sufficient wealth to pay for the entire concern, which, indeed, depends on the continuing success of that employer in satisfying the demands of consumers, which success depends on the employee. The entire metric, then, works steadily and regularly to make with as much efficiency and quality as can be afforded goods and services at the price consumers are willing to pay. The engine of progress thus benefits everyone under capitalism.

Something awful happens when socialists "soak the rich." They do so with considerable popular support, but the aftermath of their efforts redounds to the public's extreme detriment. When taxes imposed on the rich become confiscatory and when regulations imposed on profitable enterprise direct that enterprise away from what the public demands to what the government demands, dislocations occur that harm consumers and employees. First, because the wealthy entrepreneur is denied wealth, he or she loses the incentive to engage in enterprise or to be as productive and innovative. Moreover, the cost of the taxes ordinarily is passed on to consumers and affects the costs of the goods or services supplied. The second dislocation is that government taxation and regulation hampers the ability or, at least, the efficiency of the wealthy entrepreneur or company in satisfying consumer demand. So, any alterations of the market structure will beget changes that might deny consumers ready access to the goods or services by altering availability or the quality of the goods or services. The third dislocation is that government taxation and regulation reduces the funds necessary and the flexibility required to employ others, resulting in an increase in unemployment.

The overall effect is to reduce the productivity, innovation, and quality of all goods and services affected by the socialist state, redounding to the detriment of consumers. Consumers unable to obtain as good or better products and services, as are available in a free market, suffer. That suffering hurts those on the lowest end of the income ladder the most because wealthier consumers can more readily afford cost increases or costly substitutes. Nevertheless, all suffer from a lessening in innovation and quality, which ultimately lowers the standard of living across the board: the poor become poorer along with everyone else.

In other words, socialists always fall behind; they never advance ahead. They are always limiting, modifying, and redistributing the known economy (which is backward-looking). They are incapable of accurately predicting the myriad of consumer demand changes and market innovations that define the economy of tomorrow. They, thus, lock the market into an archaic structure, ever dwindling down to the lowest common denominator. Moreover, if successful in plundering all pockets of wealth to fuel government planning, the socialists ultimately invite the destruction of their own redistributionist endeavor. The common plight of the parasite; if it achieves its ultimate goal of sapping every usable thing from its host, the parasite kills its host and, thereby, itself. This was aptly observed by Prime Minister Margaret Thatcher when she said of socialists that they "always run out of other people's money."[538] While in the first years of plunder, socialist governments may obtain large sums, in the years following as wealthy entrepreneurs and companies operate with less available capital, the entrepreneurs and companies function at lower levels of productivity and efficiency, thus yielding lower income and profits. The socialist state thus plunders from an ever-dwindling pool of national resources to finance the grand plans of bureaucrats who neither comprehend in real time the full extent of damage done to the productive elements of society by their planning nor possess the clairvoyance sufficient to anticipate the adverse impacts of their planning in future years. The problem becomes catastrophic with time as the needed rise in gross domestic product becomes impossible to achieve, there being no incentive, and as government scrambles to find and tax all remaining pockets of wealth, leaving nothing behind with which to rebuild the economy.

All forms of socialism stigmatize wealth and create class division, inviting social and political unrest, class-based violence and revolution. Socialism depends on class conflict. Workers are invariably pitted against capitalists. That is a battle everyone loses. When those who perform the labor necessary to sustain enterprise attack those who create and maintain the enterprise, the result is a loss of capital accumulation and a loss of jobs. In short, everyone loses, including the hapless consumer who depends on the goods produced. Marxism in its variant socialist forms operates on a fiction—that there will be wealth remaining equal to the wealth stolen after labor destroys capital. The reality of the situation is to the contrary. When labor attacks capital, capital disappears and labor is unemployed.

Moreover, when the monopoly of police power, the state, condemns a class of people, e.g., capitalists and all those with wealth, as is the typical rant of the socialist and socialist state, the effect is to encourage capitalists and all those with wealth to flee to avoid persecution and not lose their riches. Class division in which the state puts its thumb on the scale in favor of labor and against capital creates social instability, thus encouraging labor strikes, labor rioting, violence and ultimately revolution. The resulting destruction redounds to the detriment of consumers, indeed of everyone. When the capitalists have fled the country, been plundered, been imprisoned, or been murdered, the nation is suddenly left with very few haves and very many have-nots. The infrastructure needed to support the distribution of needed goods and services usually falters or disappears, leaving all needy and in a far worse condition than before and leaving the government with far fewer resources than necessary to support the socialist planned economy. In other words, socialism is inherently dysfunctional and not self-sustaining.

All forms of socialism transfer economic power from the most efficient or best and highest uses to inefficient systems of government bureaucracy

that pursue political ends in the face of countervailing economic realities.
The market is a tremendous sieve that winnows out from the universe of all
offerings those that are most needed by consumers. He who invents that
product which is of greatest need and utility to consumers wins the capitalist
race. He is paid by consumers, which is their vote reflective of the degree
of need and satisfaction associated with the product. If the product is in
greater demand because it well satisfies a need, the producer can expect
to profit. The greater efficiency, quality, and availability of the product to
the needy consumer, the greater the profit. Thus, the market force works
magnificently in channeling to consumers what they need and presenting
them with innovations that improve their lot and raise their standard of
living.

By contrast, government planners can never get it right. Not privy
to the minute by minute changes in demand that arise from the market
(and directly subject to political demands for market changes), the socialist
bureaucrat is forever playing catch-up in a losing game. The bureaucrat
relies on economic data defining how the market was, not how it is. All
data is by definition dated, reflecting yesterday (or at best today but not the
present). On that data, he or she operates but within a universe defined by
political demands, e.g., the demand that all fossil fuels disappear and that
wind and solar energy arrive. The effect is to create a government plan for
the economy that can never match the genius of the market in satisfying
real consumer demand. The problem is compounded by the fact that the
government bureaucrat is so separated from the market and the interests
of the entrepreneur and consumer that he or she has no way of reasonably
anticipating future demand or adjusting the plan sufficiently to address
consumer need.

The effect is a downward spiral resulting from constant misapprehension
of consumer demand and misallocation of resources. Moreover, because
the government plan presumes consumer demand in advance, it invariably
fails to match actual consumer demand. Consider some Green New Deal
scenarios. The Green New Deal calls for the elimination of all fossil fuels by
2029. What happens if consumers do not want to buy electric cars either
because they prefer fossil fuel vehicles or cannot afford the cost of the cars?

What happens if consumers do not want to live in homes heated by solar panels either because they do not think solar panels reliable or cannot afford the installation costs? What happens if windmills populating the farmlands take out of production lands indispensable to farm profitability? Unintended consequences are commonplace. The effect is either massive non-compliance or enforced compliance through fines and imprisonment for those individuals who dissent from the government mandates.

All forms of socialism cheapen the value of life, deny self-determination, and forbid dissent. Socialist governments override the minority and the individual, in favor of the collective. The collective will is a fiction, but those who govern in socialist governments presume to know what it is and order the administrative state to implement regulations over enterprise and life that compel those interests to be served. When private interests conflict with collective interests, the private interests are prohibited without any opportunity for meaningful redress. The effect is to punish individualism and dissent and to deny individual rights to self-determination. Anything done to advance the politically preferred interest is a protected form of activity. Anything done to oppose that interest or to block its progress is a prohibited form of activity. The effect is to cheapen the value of life, subsuming the individual beneath the collective will, eradicating individualism, individual merit, and credit for uniqueness in favor of a coerced common that affects everything from what is allowed in art, fashion, academic curricula, and business. Rather than being driven by consumer demand, aesthetics increasingly reflect the dominant socialist culture, which condemns wealth, celebrates commonality, and dictates what is socially acceptable behavior. The drab architecture, boring statist art, and state sanctioned media of the former Soviet Union are but classic examples of the dumbing down of culture, art, and life that is the hallmark of socialist societies.

The principal method of coercion to force individuals into uniform patterns of commerce and conduct is economic. As Hilaire Belloc observed, "[t]he control of the production of wealth is the control of human life itself."[539] By confiscatory taxation, redistribution of wealth, and control over production, prices, wages, and distribution, the state achieves in a very real sense domination over every life, denying self-determination and compelling compliance. Whereas in a capitalist economic system, the individual's choice governs outcomes and options and diversity abound, in a socialist economic system, the state's choice controls, thus revealing a transfer of sovereignty over all basic life-affecting decisions that spells the end of freedom, options and diversity.

All forms of socialism impoverish socialist nations and peoples. The economist Thomas J. DiLorenzo well describes the shattered and bankrupt societies around the world left in the wake of socialism:

> In the early twentieth century it turned Ukraine from "the breadbasket of Europe" to a desolate, barren land where the people could hardly feed themselves let alone export food to anyone else . . . When the Chilean government adopted socialism in the early 1970s and nationalized industries and farms, the economy ground to a halt and the government did what all socialist governments eventually do to bail themselves out: it printed massive amounts of money . . . The result was that the cost of living rose by 746 percent . . . unemployment was sky high . . . The Soviet economy was so dysfunctional, thanks to seventy years of socialism, that by the time the entire system collapsed in the late 1980s it was probably only about 5 percent of the size of the U.S. economy . . . Soviet socialism never produced a single product that succeeded in international competition, with the possible exception of Russian caviar which comes from a fish (the sturgeon), not a factory. All of the socialist "satellite" countries . . . suffered a similar economic fate . . . [T]he common people were equal in their poverty while the political elite lived privileged lives . . . Britain had been the wealthiest country in the world up to the beginning of World War I . . . But within twenty years the entire world was talking about "the British disease," a phrase that was used to describe the gross inefficiency of all those socialist, government-run monopolies in the British steel, automobile, telephone, electric, and other industries

. . . [Argentina under Juan Perón's socialism experienced] economic ruination and hyperinflation that led to Perón's ouster in 1955 by military coup. Argentina, however, remained socialist. Its economy continued to stagnate and, several coups later, by the late 1980s, it was suffering from 12,000 percent inflation from years of trying to cover up the failures of socialism by printing money to pay for all the socialist programs . . . Argentina was once the world's tenth-largest economy, but by 2016 it was barely ahead of Kazakhstan and Equatorial Guinea.[540]

The irony of socialism is that it promises paradise following a revolution that destroys the perpetual wealth generation necessary to finance paradise. The logical consequence of every socialist revolution is universal poverty and mediocrity with the burden landing hardest on those who were said to be in the vanguard of the revolution: the poor, the disenfranchised, and the agricultural and industrial worker. The only people who escape that fate are those who govern. In every socialist country those who govern enjoy riches, vastly beyond what they could have obtained otherwise, while the governed experience drudgery, including those of talent who would prosper in a market economy. Indeed, as socialism inevitably falters, governments compel workers to work and rely on deficit spending to finance worker salaries because all incentives to produce high quality goods disappear. As meager stocks and rationing come to predominate and inflation places out of public reach basic goods and services, misery takes hold and does not let go. That is socialism.

As James Madison well understood in his essay "On Property," freedom and property are inextricably intertwined. Consequently, when the state presumes to control property by regulation or to own it outright, the individual is denied a most basic freedom, not only from ownership of the property but from use of it as an expression of individual will, shaping it into invention, using it as a platform to project a preferred message, or making it into a refuge to withdraw from the world. The individual chooses to dispose of it, that person is its master and, thus, derives freedom from that mastery.

When the state takes it over either through regulation or ownership, the state supplants the individual and robs the individual of his property and his liberty. F. A. Hayek explains: "What our generation has forgotten is that the system of private property is the most important guaranty of freedom, not only for those who own property, but scarcely less for those who do not. It is only because the control of the means of production is divided among many people acting independently that nobody has complete power over us, that we as individuals can decide what to do with ourselves. If all the means of production were vested in a single hand, whether it be nominally that of 'society' as a whole or that of a dictator, whoever exercises this control has complete power over us."[541]

Eighty-four years ago, Walter Lippmann observed a truism of socialism, applicable fully now as it was then: "[T]he generation to which we belong is now learning from experience what happens when men retreat from freedom to a coercive organization of their affairs. Though they promise themselves a more abundant life, they must in practice renounce it; as the organized direction increases, the variety of ends must give way to uniformity. That is the nemesis of the planned society and the authoritarian principle in human affairs."[542] Socialism always tears down what is above, never lifts up what is below. The only riches in a socialist state are those rapaciously stolen by its leaders from the people. The people promised all get nothing.

CHAPTER 10

THE BLESSINGS OF LIBERTY

Liberty may be defined as "unobstructed action according to our will" and "rightful liberty" as "unobstructed action according to our will within limits drawn around us by the equal rights of others." Those are Thomas Jefferson's words, and they define liberty better than any definition offered before or since. Liberty embraces the entire universe of natural rights to which each of us is a recipient at birth, from God. There is much power in the fact that our rights are pre-political; great protection in the fact that they are unalienable (having come from God and not the state); and great justice in the fact that no one may rightfully deprive us of them without our consent. The object of a just government is to protect those rights, and, as history confirms, the greater the protection given, the greater the degree of happiness the people enjoy.

This is the recipe for prosperity given to us by the founding generation, first proclaimed in the Declaration of Independence and then secured in the Constitution. That recipe yields tremendous blessings. No other nation on earth has achieved the heights of invention, the standards of living, the extent of opportunity and upward mobility, or the degree of diversity in opportunities, products, and opinions as the United States when following this recipe.

People derive happiness from freedom, and they are precisely unhappy to the extent that their freedom of choice is taken from them. No people in the world denied the freedom to choose are happy; rather, they consider their plight to be that of a slave, a slave to the state. Indeed, slavery may be defined as the deprivation of individual liberty, regardless of the source. Under that definition, just as one person may deprive another of liberty by force, undue influence, or artifice, so too may government. We broadly refer to that state deprivation of liberty as totalitarianism of which socialism and communism are species.

When regulations deny us a liberty or property right, we are diminished and those who could benefit from our exercise of the right are also diminished. All invention and attendant experimentation associated with the denied right that would otherwise occur is blocked. The regulator's assumption is that constricting freedom advances a political goal that is for the common good, but neither the individuals affected nor the public at large have any power to prevent the regulation from being adopted and implemented if they think otherwise. The process is one of centralized control and authoritarianism; it enslaves.

Regulators are unelected, and unaccountable for the regulations (the laws) they enact. They have perverse incentives to regulate in ways that favor certain industry players over others because in the long run, their post-government employment prospects and opportunities are shaped by the regulatory choices they make.

I recall well that Mark Fowler, the libertarian chairman of the Federal Communications Commission under President Reagan, was threatened again and again by, among others, then Congressman Edward Markey: that his deregulatory course would be used to blacklist him, to prevent him from obtaining lucrative post-government employment. Markey, in particular, despised Fowler's moves to eliminate content regulations on broadcasting (censorship) because he did not want to lose, in the end, the rules compelling broadcast stations to subsidize candidates for federal elective office by charging them the lowest rates for prime ad spots during election season. To his great credit, Fowler ignored the threats and pursued the deregulatory course. He behaved honorably and atypically, because ordinarily a threat like

Markey's would tame the regulator. To his great credit, Fowler remained a stalwart in defense of the First Amendment and free enterprise throughout.

Rarely do regulations constraining human behavior on the argument that doing so will bring about specific benefits result in those benefits. Commonly agency restrictions on freedoms if never adopted, could bring about innovation, employment, and improvements in living standards. Regulations ordinarily produce anti-competitive effects; indeed, that is why an army of lobbyists inhabit Washington, D.C. and pursue adoption of them on behalf of industry giants. Regulations typically harm not only those whose freedoms are directly impacted but also consumers at large who must then buy from a smaller universe of goods and services and pay higher prices for the ones the regulators will allow. Innovation and quality also suffer. While thousands of such regulations slice and dice markets and distort supply and demand to the detriment of consumers, the regulators responsible ordinarily avoid public notice and escape unscathed. Indeed, they ordinarily benefit by securing lucrative private sector positions from grateful industry leaders who have benefited from their actions.

As I explain in *The Rise of Tyranny*, that is what happened to FDA Commissioner Lester A. Crawford. FDA approved the non-steroidal anti-inflammatory drug Vioxx despite a Merck study revealing a seven-fold increase in the risk of heart attack from low doses of the drug.[543] In 2004, several years after the FDA's 1999 authorization for Merck to market the drug, FDA's then Associate Director of the Office of Drug Safety, David Graham, told his supervisors, including the FDA Commissioner, that research revealed high-dose prescriptions of the drug tripled the risk of heart attack. Numerous additional sources of reputable evidence came to light revealing the drug to be heart toxic, along with FDA receipt of adverse event reports about the drug's heart toxicity. Crawford, however, defended the drug resolutely. He sought to prevent FDA scientists critical of the drug from having their views made public. He tried to dissuade Graham from testifying about the evidence of harm, even offering him a position in the Commissioner's office if he would do as Crawford desired. Crawford rejected FDA medical reviewers' urgings that he order restrictions on the marketing of the drug. Indeed, in the face of those urgings and the overwhelming evidence of heart toxicity, he defiantly approved the drug for use in pediatric rheumatoid arthritis patients (in children), just weeks before Merck under tremendous public, medical community, and scientific community pressure (not to mention an avalanche of product liability suits) volitionally withdrew the drug from the market. Where did Crawford go when he resigned from the FDA? He went to work for a lobbying firm called Policy Directions, Inc. And what company was among the prominent clients of Policy Directions, Inc.? Merck.[544]

It was the intellectual foundation of the Declaration of Independence and the purpose of the Constitution to ensure, to the maximum extent possible, freedom for all, as is consistent with Jefferson's definition of liberty. Thus, if we are true to those founding principles and purposes, we must limit the power of government to avoid deprivation of liberty, as Jefferson defined it. Only then will we be assured of having that freedom necessary to attain self-fulfillment, and thus ensure the highest degree of happiness attainable. Only then will we protect the full dignity of the individual, respect the individual's physical, mental, and spiritual integrity and uniqueness to the fullest, and witness the flourishing of every human contribution in all arts and sciences.

It is inherent in our very nature that we seek self-fulfillment (what Jefferson termed "the pursuit of happiness"). Humans pursue their own self-interest constantly. They pick not any fruit but the best fruit they can find. They read not just any book but what they consider to be the best book on a topic. They listen not to just any music but to the music most pleasing to their ears. They view not just any video but the video that contains content of most interest to them. This process of free selection on the unending road to self-fulfillment cannot proceed reliably and in earnest without staid protection for individual liberty. The innovators, manufacturers, distributors, and consumers whose interchange produces prosperity must all proceed without serious impediment, or the pursuit of happiness is stymied, the condition of humanity is reduced, and misery ensues.

Our quest for self-fulfillment involves transforming our talents into achievements through action, and we achieve our desired ends, our dreams, only if we are protected in our free pursuits of those ends. We learn of our talents as we grow in age, knowledge, and experience. We discover areas in which we excel, and we recoil from efforts to prevent the use of our talents, or to deprive us of the benefits of using them. We are therefore quite naturally an enemy of slavery and of every slave state.

It is the cruel trick of socialism to induce people to believe that if they part with their freedom, they may be given something of value for nothing in return. When the value they expect is not delivered by the state, they realize the trick too late to spare themselves from the consequences of parting with their freedom.

We naturally aim to capitalize on our talents, which is to say that we aim to make a contribution to others by putting our talents to use in helpful ways. As we strive to make a contribution to others, we are often rewarded financially and spiritually in proportion to how successfully we satisfy others' wants and needs. In this way, a truly free society is one of an endless competition among people to satisfy each other's wants and needs, yielding progress (change) as a byproduct. That redounds to the benefit of all.

Through diligent effort, we may succeed to a greater or lesser extent in supplying others' wants and needs. As we do, we are rewarded variously with recompense, opportunity, position, and notoriety. Our individual standards of living rise in proportion to our success in satisfying others' wants and needs, as do theirs from our efforts. The artisan who creates a rich, unique, and useful piece of furniture may enjoy the compliment of a market demand for his or her wares beyond a first sale. The engineer who discovers a simple and inexpensive means to render an internal combustion engine more fuel efficient; the host who is so attentive that no need of a customer is left unsatisfied; the computer programmer who develops an app that enables a patient with chronic illness to self-diagnose his or her status and report that status in real time to attending physicians; the driver whose deft handling of the wheel ensures delivery of her passenger to the desired location in a manner more expeditious than any other competitor; and the physician whose grasp of the most up-to-date medical science enables him or her to diagnose with near perfect accuracy ailments from symptoms that have caused others in the profession to misdiagnose the disease—are all examples of the manner in which a society built on liberty leads to a myriad of enhancements to life impossible in societies that sacrifice liberty for state control.

Notice that none of this broad expanse of exploration, application of talents, and creative invention reliably proceeds unless government avoids actions that inhibit or forbid the liberties on which we depend. If government dedicates itself to the end prescribed for it in the Declaration of Independence, it necessarily takes no action that would deprive us of our lives, liberties, and pursuits of happiness. By so dedicating and rededicating itself, and so acting, government gives us confidence we will remain free; if that confidence is shaken, perverse effects occur, as individuals withhold invention, avoid expenditure, and withdraw from public pursuits. We must have that assurance if we are to enjoy the full extent of exploration, application of talent, and creative invention we must have to progress, to benefit others, and to attain happiness.

The freedom to exploit our unique talents entails the freedom to direct our own course of industry and improvement, such that we may invent and offer the products of our free minds transformed into things we suspect are of value. When we present these things to the world, we test a hypothesis of their relative worth with the ultimate determinant being the free will of others. Through billions of such interactions each day, a free people populate a free country with ideas and inventions that invariably advance civilization at a rate far faster than any country entangled with the state planning of socialism or communism.

Of those billions of daily interactions, a subset satisfies popular demand in countless, often remarkable ways that transform the nature and quality of life (e.g., holography enhanced virtual reality hastening and perfecting complex architectural design or medical procedures; advances in microchip technology improving the processing power and speed attainable; and 3D-printing in its myriad applications, such as creating artificial human organs). The overall effect is to advance society in ways that lift us, perpetually. Protected liberty in those few countries which have avoided the plagues of socialism and communism has enabled humankind in two centuries to advance apace, to reduce poverty dramatically, and to extend the dignity, quality, and term of human life to a far greater extent than ever before.

In a country where the individual is free, each person strives to make the best and highest use of his or her talents, to supply the world around with what it demands, needs, or may need. In that way, we achieve the highest degree of satisfaction, for we offer what is the product of our unique genius to others, and others in return respond by purchasing that creation, benefiting everyone. As Adam Smith observed in *The Wealth of Nations:* "It is not from the benevolence of the butcher, the brewer, or the baker, that we expect our dinner, but from their regard to their own interest."

Regulation is the use of government coercion to prevent through prior restraint kinds of actions disfavored by political leaders. Regulations differ from criminal laws, which ordinarily depend on evidence of intent, proof of injury, a presumption of innocence, a trial in an Article III court, and a conviction before deprivation of liberty may follow. Regulations are "thou shalt not" edicts, prior restraints, which prohibit actions in advance of their occurrence ordinarily without regard to the intentions of the actor or the effect on anyone.

So it is that the Federal Communications Commission regulated broadcast speech by prohibiting the airing of any opinion on a controversial issue of public importance unless opposing opinions were also aired (the so-called "Fairness Doctrine"). That had the effect of suppressing the airing of all opinions about controversial issues to avoid potential FCC scrutiny and liability, which could involve loss of a broadcast license. That regulation was revoked during the Reagan administration and gave birth to a vast multiplicity of views over the broadcast media.

The Federal Trade Commission prohibits the labeling of a product as "biodegradable" unless it completely breaks down into elements in nature within one year after customary disposal. That regulation is scientifically nonsensical because substances are compounds, not elements, and do not break down into elements (rather, common byproducts of biodegradation are carbon dioxide (CO_2) and water (H_2O), which are obviously compounds, not elements). Nothing in nature breaks down into elements. The selection of a year as a cut-off is likewise wholly arbitrary. That absurd regulation creates a market advantage for businesses that sell less durable, rapidly degrading products (e.g., plastic bags that break when a gallon of milk is put into them or disintegrate in sunlight) and a market disadvantage for businesses that sell more durable degradable plastics that degrade over time.

The Food and Drug Administration prohibits the sale of any food or dietary supplement that is labeled to cure, treat, prevent or mitigate a disease, even when that statement is not one the government can prove false. So, for example, if a company that sells prune juice puts on the label of its product that the juice treats chronic constipation (which everyone knows is true), its products can be confiscated by the federal government and prohibited from being sold and its officers can be prosecuted, even incarcerated.

There are thousands of such regulations, prior restraints, that prohibit actions by enterprising people without proof that those actions cause injury to anyone, and never do the regulators focus on the harm caused by the regulations (the loss of property, employment, and innovation caused). The effect of them individually is to deny freedom of choice, and the effect of them in the aggregate is to take away liberty without any proof that the specific party denied rights has caused a single injury to anyone. This denies due process in the individual case but it also devalues humanity, robbing us of precious freedoms that enable progress.

Regulation operates on the assumption that restrictions on liberty are consonant with just government without need for actual proof of injury to others adjudicated in an independent Article III Court. That assumption violates Jefferson's definition of liberty and conflicts with the basic premise of the Constitution, which is to forbid government from acting against individuals' lives, liberties, and property in the absence of proof established in an Article III court beyond a reasonable doubt consistent with all of the guarantees of the Fifth, Sixth, Seventh, and Eighth Amendments.

Regulation disrupts the fulfillment of individual wants and needs, reducing prosperity and self-fulfillment to those increasingly rare areas of commerce in which the regulator has not yet acquired control. The administrative state interposes a relentless uncertainty destructive of liberty, making investment in property and use of rights a risky proposition. Just from these few examples above, we may see effects that reduce our freedom of choice and our standard of living.

As Bernard Siegan explains in his *Economic Liberties and the Constitution*: "A foremost principle for a society which has limited its government in order to maximize freedom is that no one should be needlessly deprived of liberty. Thus, a law that has no benefit for society yet restrains human action has no legitimate purpose or utility. The same holds true for a law that impedes individual choice much more than necessary . . ."[545]

We are today inundated with federal regulations that impose restraints without any evidence whatsoever that the party restrained has caused or will cause any injury to anyone. Such laws are arbitrary and enslaving. Siegan draws to our attention a lesson known before the American Revolution by the author of *Commentaries on the Laws of England*, Sir William Blackstone: "[T]he law that restrains a man from doing mischief to his fellow citizens though it diminishes the natural, increases the civil liberty of mankind: but every wanton and causeless restraint of the will of the subject, whether practiced by a monarch, a nobility, or a popular assembly, is a degree of tyranny. Nay, that even laws themselves whether made with or without our consent, if they regulate and constrain our conduct in matters of mere indifference, without any good end in view, are laws destructive of liberty . . . [T]hat constitution or frame of government, that system of laws, is alone calculated to maintain civil liberty, which leaves the subject entire master of his own conduct, except in those points wherein the public good requires some direction or restraint."[546]

The argument is made that the public good is anything experts in government conclude will advance the public interest. Recall that the slave owners defended slavery on the same essential proposition, substituting the word "slaveowners" for the words "experts in government" in the preceding sentence. That is unbridled discretion, which enables the deprivation of individual liberty at the whim of government officials. The assumption proceeds, as it did in the oral argument of the Department of Justice in one of my cases, *Pearson v. Shalala*[547], that regulators are not constrained by, in that case, the First Amendment. Yet, it follows ineluctably that elimination of constitutional constraints on power leads to unbridled discretion, and unbridled discretion leads to deprivation of individual rights without due process of law, which is tyranny.

The Due Process clauses of the Fifth and Fourteenth Amendments provide explicit defense against precisely the kind of abuses ordinarily visited upon

Americans by the administrative state. Were those clauses honored, the balance would tip back to its original setting in favor of individual liberty, compelling the government to meet its burdens of proof and persuasion in independent Article III courts before depriving Americans of their liberties and properties, but substantive due process in all areas of economic liberty was effectively eliminated in *Nebbia v. New York* in 1934.[548] Richard Epstein explains:

> The Due Process Clause of the Fifth Amendment, binding against the federal government, provides that "no person shall be deprived of life, liberty, or property, without due process of law." Even in its most modest form, this sweeping provision guarantees that all persons shall have individualized adjudication before they can be subject to any penalties that result in the loss of any of the three entitlements (life, liberty, or property) . . .[549]

The liberty so greatly protected by the plain and intended meaning of the Constitution, inclusive of the Bill of Rights, is diminished in each instance where the federal government acts through power not granted in the instrument or, worse, forbidden by it. The administrative state, itself extra-constitutional, acts in every instance with power beyond the Constitution, including combined legislative, executive and judicial powers.

The administrative state thus is not an occasional violator of individual rights to life, liberty, and property, but is a constant violator of those rights. It arbitrarily constricts liberty in ways that prevent individuals from attaining self-fulfillment and from enabling progress.

There can be no blessings of liberty in full without defense of rightful liberty in full. With liberty limited and the fruits of liberty taxed, the value of every human life is diminished. Only if the courts, the Congress, and the executive rededicate themselves to the plain and intended meaning of the Constitution, and to the Lockean principles defined in the Declaration of Independence, can we restore that degree of liberty necessary to self-fulfillment, advancement, and happiness. If that rededication does take place, we can expect tremendous blessings.

The following are principles to govern action in government, which, if honored, would restore constitutional protections for individual liberty. Today, each is violated by bureaucrats with impunity every day of the week and in countless ways.

Government should pursue no action unless authorized by a specifically enumerated power in the Constitution. The protection for individual liberty is meaningless unless constitutional restraints on government power are honored such that arbitrary discretion by government officials does not replace the rule of law of the Constitution.

Government should take no action that transforms the United States from its republican form to another form. The Constitution prescribes for both the federal and state governments a republican form (i.e., a mixed constitution of enumerated powers and protections for individual liberty in which legislative, executive, and judicial powers are separated, checked and balanced). No action should therefore be taken to violate the republican form by transforming the government into, for example, a socialist or communist state.

Government should take no action pursuant to the Commerce Clause of the Constitution unless that action promotes rather than retards interstate commerce. Although the founding fathers intended the commerce clause to enable Congress to eliminate barriers to interstate transactions, laws and regulations have repeatedly been adopted since the New Deal era that impede commerce or coerce the purchase of certain goods over others (e.g., health insurance under the Obamacare individual mandate).

Government should take no action contrary to individual rights to life, liberty, and property unless to prevent harm. There is never an instance in which government should act to restrain individual liberty unless to prevent harm. Deprivation of rights to life, liberty and property to advance a utopian government goal can never be accepted as lawful and constitutional without unjustly enslaving the individual.

Government should take no action unless authorized by a law adopted by Congress, not by a regulation adopted by an administrative agency. The vesting clause in Article I, Section 1, makes law-making the exclusive province of the Congress of the United States. Today the administrative state makes the overwhelming majority of all laws that govern Americans. That violates a fundamental principle underlying the Constitution: that governments derive their just powers from the consent of the governed. In ratifying the Constitution, the people through their elected representatives agreed to the delegation of legislative power to Congress, exclusively. Because those who rule in administrative agencies are unelected, the regulations they promulgate are not derived from the consent of the governed and are thus illegitimate. To avoid this most basic offense, which poses an ever-present threat to the liberties of the people, government should take no action unless authorized by a law adopted by Congress, rather than a regulation adopted by an agency.

Government should take no action to deprive an individual of life, liberty, or property unless upon criminal conviction following a trial on the merits before an independent Article III court. There is no justice when the prosecutor is also the judge. That is the condition under which we live when administrative agencies pass upon violations of their own regulations. That system not only codifies an inherent conflict of interest, it also, historically, has led to processes and results that are heavily biased against the accused, denying him or her justice. The deprivation of life, liberty or property is a criminal offense. Despite that fact, administrative agencies deprive individuals of liberty and property in the ordinary course but do not afford the accused the rights to due process and to confront accusers, to a jury trial, and to avoid self-incrimination guaranteed by the Fifth, Sixth, and Seventh Amendments.

Government should pay market value for any action that causes a person innocent of criminal wrong doing to be deprived of property or the value of property. If a government action results in the devaluation of property owned by an individual who has not committed a crime involving the property, the government should pay the party so deprived the full market value of the property.

Government should protect property and liberty rights equally. The founding fathers intended the Constitution to prohibit government from depriving individuals of their rights to life, liberty, and property. They intended that prohibition to apply equally to liberty and property such that property rights would not be given less protection than liberty rights. Since *Nebbia v. New York* (1934)[550], the Supreme Court has afforded property rights only rational basis protection, but has afforded non-economic rights strict scrutiny protection, resulting in virtually any action by government restrictive of economic liberty being upheld and virtually any action by government restrictive of non-economic liberty being struck down. For example, in the area of commercial speech, the Court arbitrarily accords truthful speech in commerce intermediate scrutiny but virtually all other truthful speech strict scrutiny. If anything, the need for protection of economic rights is equal to or greater than that for non-economic rights because of the close link between economic liberty and livelihoods. In any event, as I have explained elsewhere, the commercial/noncommercial distinction is contrived and alien to the plain and intended meaning of the Constitution.[551]

Government should prohibit administrative agencies from adjudicating any case and should instead require that all agency actions be tried in independent Article III courts. The federal courts currently defer to the findings of fact and the conclusions of law of federal administrative agencies following adjudications in administrative courts. The effect is to enable the agency, having a conflict of interest (serving as prosecutor and judge), to have the last word on whether its own regulations are lawful; which facts will be of record and which will be deemed material; and whether the agency's own prosecution complies with the Constitution. Because the agency is inherently biased because it is a party to the action, it cannot serve as an impartial judge. Agency adjudication is inherently unjust. Those victimized by it deserve an independent adjudication in an Article III court from the start of the action, so as not to impose on every party accused the effective penalty of legal fees, loss of business, and public excoriation that accompanies agency prosecutions.

In the Constitution, the founding fathers endeavored to guard against encroachments on liberty. They understood encroachments to be inevitable occurrences that would arise despite their best efforts. They depended on a people who would jealously protect their own liberties to guard against government excesses. The British Whig clergyman, popular in the revolutionary colonies, James Burgh explained in his *Political Disquisitions* (1774): "No single man, or set of men, ought to be trusted with power without account to the people, the original proprietors of power . . . This evil [unlimited government power] has its root in human nature; men will never think they have enough, whilst they can take more; nor be content with a part, when they can seize the whole."[552] Burgh also explained, "power is of an elastic nature, ever extending itself and encroaching on the liberties of the subjects."[553]

In his May 27, 1788 letter to Edward Carrington, Thomas Jefferson warned: "The natural progress of things is for liberty to yield and government to gain ground."[554] Jefferson understood, "[e]xperience hath shown that even under the best forms of government those entrusted with power have, in time, by slow operations, perverted it into tyranny."[555] George Washington agreed, writing: "Arbitrary power is most easily established on the ruins of liberty abused to licentiousness."[556] He feared "the spirit of encroachment," which "consolidate[s] the powers of all departments in one, and thus create[s] . . . a real despotism."[557] James Madison too understood that the Constitution would be meaningless if those in government chose not to abide by it, writing:

> Will it be sufficient to mark, with precision, the boundaries of [government] departments, in the constitution of the government, and to trust to these parchment barriers against the encroaching spirit of power? This is the security, which appears to have been principally relied on by the compilers of most of the American constitutions. But experience assures us, that the efficacy of the provision has been greatly overrated; and that some more adequate defense is indisputably necessary for the more feeble, against the more powerful member of the government. The legislative department is everywhere extending the sphere of its activity, and drawing all power into its impetuous vortex.[558]

While there are limitless ways in which those in government can abuse their powers to violate individual rights, there are few avenues available for individuals whose rights have been violated to end the abuses and obtain redress for their grievances. One method is to vote the rascals out, but that does not affect bureaucratic offenders because they are appointed, not elected, and does not end the rights violations stemming from administrative action. The other method is to sue the government for redress, but that method is currently severely disabled because suits oftentimes must begin with exhaustion of administrative remedies (meaning within the biased and costly confines of an agency adjudication before court access is possible) and then, when an appeal is made to a federal court, that court ordinarily defers to the agency judgment (making the appeal either worthless or of limited value). There is thus a crying need to elect to office those committed to end the administrative state and rededicate the nation to laws made by Congress alone, within the bounds of constitutionally delegated power.

CHAPTER 11

BEYOND SLAVERY

W e have been led to believe that the institution of slavery in America was exclusively one of white colonizers enslaving blacks and Native Americans. The *New York Times*' 1619 Project (the brainchild of *Times*' reporter Nikole Hannah-Jones) introduced nationally a critical race theory of American history said to be historically based: that white enslavement of blacks defined the period from the early days of the Jamestown Colony in 1619 through the Civil War; that a primary reason why the colonists rebelled against Great Britain was to protect the institution of slavery; and that American capitalism is an extension of plantation economies in the antebellum South. The assertion is made that the United States began not with the Declaration of Independence but with racial division at the crucible of a white foothold on the Indian continent of America. A narrow grouping of scholars writes for the Project, most coming from the "New History of Capitalism" school of thought.[559] The 1619 Project critical race theory suffers from an insurmountable problem, however. It is based on a false representation of the historical record, with avowed ideological ends dictating which facts to select from the record. It is propaganda, not history.

Project authors tie slavery to modern capitalism (based on sociologist Michael Desmond's 1619 Project essay), contending, "American capitalism is infused with the brutality of the slave system."[560] The project admits an ideological bias in its recast of history; in other words, it effectively admits it is a propaganda operation. Its supporters advocate reliance on that revised history to support the payment of reparations to all black Americans and new efforts to advance LGBQT rights and socialism. Equality is the flag raised and socialism appears to be the system advocated.

The project has come under withering attack from the nation's foremost historians: Princeton Professor of History James McPherson, author of, among others, *Battle Cry of Freedom*; Brown University Professor of History Gordon Wood, author of, among others, *The Creation of the American Republic 1776–1787*; City University of New York Professor of History James Oakes, author of, among others, *The Radical and the Republican: Frederick Douglass, Abraham Lincoln, and the Triumph of Antislavery Politics*; and Pro Vice-Chancellor of Oxford University Richard Carawardine, author of, among others, *President Abraham Lincoln*.

Interviewed by the World Socialist Web Site, those historians slammed the 1619 Project as "very unbalanced," as a "one-sided account," as "not only ahistorical [but also] anti-historical," and as a "tendentious and partial reading of American history." An additional twenty-one scholars from the National Association of Scholars took the extraordinary step of calling on the Pulitzer Board to revoke Nicole Hannah-Jones' Pulitzer Prize for Commentary. In their letter to the board, they explain that her lead 1619 Project essay entitled, "Our democracy's founding ideals were false when they were written," for which she received the prize, was "itself" "false when written" "making a large claim that protecting the institution of slavery was a primary motive for the American Revolution, a claim for which there is simply no evidence."

There are many problems with the 1619 Project's recreation of American history through a left eye lens. It rests on false facts. But what is the real history of slavery in America? Does that history of the institution of slavery (which took eighty-nine years to arrest through the December 6, 1865 ratification of the Thirteenth Amendment) define the political ideology animating the founding and giving rise to the American Revolution, or is it a hypocritical departure from the principle of unalienable rights declared to be God-given to humanity in the Declaration of Independence, one that had to be abandoned for the principle to be honored in full?

First, we must understand the actual history of slavery in America. That history is falsely depicted by the 1619 Project.

The very first slaves in America were not black. They were white.[561] Before the first shipment of twenty blacks to the Jamestown colony, one hundred white slaves arrived. The white slaves were English children apprehended as vagrants from the streets of Bridewell by order of the Lord Mayor of London. The Lord Mayor sought to diminish the incidence of pick pocketing and other petty crimes on the streets which arose following a massive rise in the number of displaced, homeless, and destitute people in London. The migration of the poor to London arose because of liberal use of the Writ of Novel Disseisin by the lords, who aimed to dispossess the poor of lands they historically occupied, and of the enclosure laws, which enabled properties to be fenced off, ending squatting by the poor.[562] The solution to the rise in London crime caused by the new city vagrants, a solution endorsed by the Crown, was to ship the city's vagrants to the colonies. Don Jordan and Michael Walsh explain: "In 1618, the authorities in London began to sweep up hundreds of troublesome urchins from the slums and, ignoring protests from the children and their families, shipped them to Virginia."[563] In early 1619, adjudged vagrants, one hundred white youth were ordered "held for Virginia."[564] Jordan and Walsh record: "The first 100 children arrived in America around Easter time 1619, four months before the arrival of a shipment of black slaves that has attracted more attention than any other . . ."[565]

More shipments of white slaves followed ("[s]hipments of children continued from England and then from Ireland for decades"[566]), including not only children but adults ("50,000 to 70,000 convicts (or maybe more) were transported to Virginia, Maryland, Barbados and England's other American possessions before 1776"[567]), establishing a multi-racial slave community in Jamestown, a multi-racial slave population that eventually filled plantations throughout the South in the colonial period. Tens of thousands of white slaves eventually populated the antebellum plantations, most in abject slavery equal to that of black slaves. Whites were variously penal slaves for life or indentured servants who were given equal status with black slaves (also denoted as chattel in legal documents): i.e., slaves promised freedom or land that never materialized or slaves kept in captivity for five, ten, or fifteen years with terms extended at the whim of their masters as recompense for alleged "infractions" (such as work failings, runaway status, or marriage and child bearing without the master's permission).[568]

At the end of August 1619, the English man-of-war *White Lion* under Dutch colors (to avoid charges of piracy) arrived at Jamestown, delivering a cargo of twenty black slaves.[569] They joined the one hundred white slave children already suffering under subjugation. More white slaves soon came thereafter. As Rhetta Akamatsu records: "One hundred children were sent in 1619, one hundred more in 1620, and in 1622, after the Indian Massacre [at Jamestown] of 350 colonists, 100 more were sent with the reinforcements."[570] For decades to come in the Jamestown colony, black and white slaves toiled side by side in an equal state of bondage and deprivation. Social historian Lerone Bennett Jr. explains:

> Not only in Virginia but also in New England and New York, the first Blacks were integrated into a forced labor system that had little or nothing to do with skin color. That came later. But in the interim, a fateful 40-year period of primary importance in the history of America, Black men and women worked side by side with the first generation of Whites, cultivating tobacco, clearing the land, and building roads and houses.[571]

If anything, white masters would have an economic incentive to favor their black slaves over the whites because, of the two, white slaves were cheaper ("a third of the price of black slaves"[572]) and, thus, more expendable. Indeed, the cheapest of all slaves were the Irish, who were given the most arduous tasks and were berated not only by white slave masters but also by blacks. Gary J. Sibio writes: "As badly as [Black slaves] were treated, the Irish were actually treated worse. This was in part due to the British anti-Catholicism but also because the black slaves cost more by a factor of ten.

Blacks were sold for 50 sterling while the Irish seldom went for more than 5 sterling."[573]

The arrival of twenty black slaves turned out to be a singular event in the early Jamestown colony because those who followed were, for decades, white slaves, not black. "It took decades more for the plantation owners of the Chesapeake to begin to buy people in any numbers from the black slave market . . ."[574] Jordan and Walsh explain: "No flood of Africans followed . . . The transaction was a one-off . . . Six years later, in 1625, there were still only twenty-three Africans in the colony. Many decades later, there were still only a few hundred. That would change late in the century; but for the moment, the poor of England remained the colony's main source of chattel labour."[575] Jordan and Walsh conclude: "During the five years to 1624, when the Virginia Company was wound up, 4,500 settlers arrived, which was as many as had been shipped in throughout the previous twelve years. Between a third and a half were [white slaves, called servants]."[576]

Moreover, while certain black slaves were selected to work in the slave master's plantation house, white slaves were often not allowed to do so and remained in the fields. [577] There would be 200 years of white slavery in America.

With Oliver Cromwell's ethnic cleansing of Ireland, tens of thousands of Irish prisoners and those otherwise corralled by the authorities, were shipped to the American colonies[578], leading to a population of tens of thousands of white Irish slaves in the antebellum states. While the number of black slaves was at least four times higher than that of white slaves by the 1860s, it is nevertheless the case that when colonists corresponded about slaves (such as when they offered slaves for sale or sought recapture of runaways), they were not infrequently referring to whites. And when the 13th Amendment was ratified on December 6, 1865, it liberated not only black slaves in America but also the white slaves who toiled with them.

Jordan and Walsh explain, ". . . at the time of the Declaration [1776] nearly 1,000 [white] convicts a year were being dumped in America, mostly in Maryland and Virginia. A convict dealer intimated that in the 1700s more than 30,000 convicts had been sold in Maryland alone."[579] By 1700, "some 200,000 men, women and children from the British Isles" were shipped to America as slaves.[580] While runaway slaves in the nineteenth century were predominantly black, runaways in the eighteenth century were predominantly white.[581]

White slaves came from England and Ireland, some were street urchins, some were petty felons, some were political prisoners, and some were "spirited" away by agents of the slave trade. As Jordan and Walsh explain, "[a]stounding numbers are reported to have been snatched from the streets and countryside [of England] by gangs of kidnappers or 'spirits' working to satisfy the colonial hunger for labour. Based at every sizeable port in the British Isles, spirits conned or coerced the unwary onto ships bound for America."[582] Indeed, the term "kidnapper" arose at this time, as "kid nabber." Michael A. Hoffman writes: "The very word 'kidnapper' was first coined in Britain in the 1600s to describe those who captured and sold White children into slavery ('kid-nabbers')."[583] Moreover, the word "slave" itself originates as a reference to white slaves, to Slavic peoples.[584]

The slave trade was a booming international enterprise from the fifteenth through the nineteenth centuries with enslavement popular in Europe, the Middle East, the Barbary Coast, the Americas, and the Caribbean. As Robert C. Davis explains: "I have been struck that slavery both in the Mediterranean and across the Atlantic arose and flourished – if such a term can be used – at almost exactly the same time . . . [I]t was only at the beginning of the modern age that slavery in each of these regions took a leap in quality and quantity, until both became institutions of large scale and high efficiency. The cause, at least in part, can be traced to the events of 1492. In August of that year Christopher Columbus set sail to find the New World for Europe, and in so doing put in motion all the mechanisms of conquest and extractive exploitation that would eventually give rise to the sprawling system of plantation slavery in both American continents. . . [Two months prior] Ferdinand and Isabella [of Spain] created an implacable enemy for their resurgent kingdom, one that would find a new home very nearby, in Morocco, Algiers, and eventually along the entire Maghreb. The newly reinvigorated Islamic societies . . . soon set out . . . to square accounts with Christendom, building galleys, attacking European merchant shipping, raiding coastal communities, and taking slaves."[585]

It is false to assert that most white indentured servants and white slaves were treated more favorably than black slaves. As Don Jordan and Michael Walsh explain, based on the available evidence, "tens of thousands of whites were held as chattels, marketed like cattle, punished brutally and in some cases liberally worked to death. . . . [T]his underclass was treated just as savagely as black slaves and, indeed, toiled, suffered and rebelled alongside them."[586] The records of white slave transports to the colonies reveal conditions equal to those endured by black slaves. In 1767, George Selwyn, a member of Parliament, recoiled from what he saw on board a slave ship carrying whites bound for the colonies:

> I went on board . . . I saw this poor man chained to a board
> in a hole not above 16 feet long, more than fifty with him, a
> collar and padlock about his neck and chained to five of the
> most dreadful creatures I ever looked on.[587]

The sales of white slaves were indistinguishable from those of blacks, involving the same grotesque dehumanizing and intrusive inspections and the separation of family members. Jordan and Walsh explain: "What happened to white convicts on their entry to the New World was the same as what happened to Africans. Both were advertised for sale, both were inspected and probed and both were taken off in chains by new masters or by an agent who would find them new masters."[588]

Moreover, it is a false narrative that only whites were slave masters in the colonial and new nation periods. To the contrary, there were dozens of freed blacks who then enslaved blacks and whites[589] from New York to Louisiana and from Virginia to Kentucky. Indeed, those seeking enforcement of the fugitive slave laws for the apprehension of runaway slaves included blacks as well as whites.

Larry Koger has documented the extensive presence of black slave owners in the North and South, some of whom held dozens in bondage working large plantations. Koger writes: "[F]ree black slaveowners resided in every Southern state which countenanced slavery and even in Northern states. In Louisiana, Maryland, South Carolina, and Virginia, free blacks

owned more than 10,000 slaves, according to the federal census of 1830."[590]
Koger explains:

> Many of the black masters in the lower South were large
> planters who owned scores of slaves and planted large
> quantities of cotton, rice, and sugar cane. In 1860, for example,
> Auguste Donatto, a free colored planter of St. Landry Parish
> in Louisiana, owned 70 slaves who worked 500 acres of land
> and produced 100 bales of cotton. About 600 miles to the
> east of Louisiana in the county of Sumter, South Carolina,
> William Ellison, a free colored planter, used the labor of 70
> slaves to cultivate 100 bales of cotton in 1861. In South
> Carolina, Robert Michael Collins and Margaret Mitchell
> Harris used their slaves to till the soil of Santee Plantation
> and grew 240,000 pounds of rice in 1849. But the majority
> of the large colored planters lived in Louisiana and planted
> sugar cane. In 1860, Madame Ciprien Ricard and her son
> Pierre Ricard, free mulattoes of Ibeville Parish, owned 168
> slaves. The joint operation of mother and son used the labor
> of slaves to produce 515 hogsheads of sugar in 1859. Yet
> not all of the black masters were planters or from the South.
> In fact, the city of New York had eight black slaveowners
> who owned 17 slaves in 1830. In short, the institution of
> black slaveowning was widespread, stretching as far north as
> New York and as far south as Florida, extending westward to
> Kentucky, Mississippi, Louisiana, and Missouri.[591]

Black slaveowners arose from the ranks of manumitted slaves (often
because of their kinship to whites), emancipated slaves (often for their
meritorious military service, an heroic act, or faithful service to a deceased
white master), and slaves who purchased their freedom. Others were the
children of freed slaves.[592] Black slaveowners appear to have been respected
by white slaveowners through much of the antebellum period, apparently
because the slaveowners of both races shared a mutual economic attachment

to the "peculiar institution." Koger explains: "In 1835, the editor of the *Charleston Courier* defended the right of the free black to own slaves on the grounds that 'his right to hold slaves gives him a stake in the institution of slavery and makes it his interest as well as his duty to uphold it. It identifies his interests and feelings in this particular with those of the white population . . .'"[593]

There were hundreds of black slaveowners in the antebellum United States. Koger records: "In 1790, the community of slaveholding colored persons stood at 59 slave masters who held 457 bondsmen. . . . By 1820, the number of colored slaveholders began to grow significantly. Between 1800 and 1820, the number of black masters increased by 411 percent, or an addition of 186 slaveowners. The growth of the community of black slaveholders continued for the next 20 years. Between 1820 and 1830, the community of Afro-Americans who owned slaves increased by 95.6 percent. According to the census of 1830, there were 450 slave masters of African ancestry. By 1840, the number of colored masters came to 454."[594]

The shift in sentiment among white slaveowners to segregate black slaves, and eventually assign white slaves and overseers control over black slave populations, appears to have first arisen after a notorious slave rebellion, Nathaniel Bacon's Rebellion of 1676. Disgruntled by Virginia Colonial Governor William Berkeley's refusal to authorize the slaughter of local Indian tribes that disputed Bacon and others' land claims and the Governor's refusal to change tax and land policies, Bacon organized some 300 to 500 rebels, including freed blacks, black slave owners, and black and white runaway slaves, to kill Berkeley and take control of the government. The rebellion fizzled after Bacon died suddenly.[595] This notorious event sent shockwaves of fear through the government and white plantation society. Many feared that the common bonds between white and black slaves and white and black slaveowners could give rise to more rebellions, taking the lives of slaveowners and control of the government. As Jordan and Walsh explain, "[t]he task facing Virginia's rulers now was to fashion a class that gave them 'as many Virginians with a stake in suppressing servile insurrection as there were in fomenting it'. They played the race card."[596] The conscious aim, then, became one of segregating the slaves based on race and giving white slaves a higher position in plantation hierarchy. Increasingly, a system of slave segregation was instituted with white slaves being identified as superior to black slaves, inviting a caste system based on race that eventually took hold throughout the South.[597]

From this history, we may readily see that the 1619 Project's assumptions of fact conflict with the actual factual record. Moreover, far from serving as a rallying cry for the revolution, slavery was gaining disfavor until the late 1790s, viewed generally as a barbaric institution that ought to be abolished. The question was how to accomplish that end. Even those who despised the institution were left with the reality that were they, individually, to manumit their slaves, that act alone would not end the institution throughout the country. Moreover, unilateral manumission would not only result in those slaveowners' loss of the economic value of their slaves but also in their obligation to hire replacements from free labor at a great cost. In addition, it would leave competitors who owned slaves at an advantage economically over those who manumitted their slaves. Increasingly, slave owners, like Thomas Jefferson, James Madison, and George Washington, who wanted the institution of slavery to end depended on a political resolution, one that would legally compel all slaveowners to give up the institution simultaneously, avoiding an economic advantage to those who would keep slaves against any amount of social pressure to the contrary. As for the individual founding fathers, both Jefferson and Washington struggled mightily to avoid bankruptcy throughout their adult lives. Were they to have manumitted their slaves during their lifetimes, they would have bankrupted themselves and forced their families into abject poverty. They therefore looked to an ultimate legal resolution of the question for the whole nation.

Remarkably, Thomas Jefferson included in his draft of the Declaration of Independence a 168-word passage that condemned slavery in no uncertain terms, aiming to achieve the political outcome of abolition, which clause was deleted at the request of Continental Congress delegates, among them those from South Carolina and Georgia, who endeavored to avoid insertion of content that might detract from universal commitment to the primary aim of separation from Great Britain. The deleted content Jefferson wanted to include in the Declaration reads:

> He [King George III] has waged cruel war against human nature itself, violating its most sacred rights of life and liberty in the persons of a distant people who never offended him, [capturing] & carrying them into slavery in another hemisphere or to incur miserable death in their transportation thither. This piratical warfare, the opprobrium of infidel powers, is the warfare of the Christian King of Great Britain. Determined to keep open a market where Men should be bought & sold, he has prostituted his negative for suppressing every legislative attempt to prohibit or restrain this execrable commerce. And . . . he is now exciting those very people to rise in arms among us, and to purchase that liberty of which he has deprived them, by murdering the people on whom he has obtruded them: thus paying off former crimes committed against the Liberties of one people, with crimes which he urges them to commit against the lives of another.[598]

The quoted passage reveals beyond doubt that Jefferson understood the "sacred rights of life and liberty" to be those not only of whites but also of blacks, "of a distant people," which at the time included blacks and whites. This makes apparent that when he simultaneously wrote the preamble, wherein he penned "all Men are created equal, that they are endowed by their Creator with certain unalienable Rights, that among these are Life, Liberty, and the Pursuit of Happiness," he had in mind all races, utterly smashing the contrary contention of the 1619 Project's authors.

In his autobiography, Jefferson explained how the 168-word clause came to be deleted:

> The clause...reprobating the enslaving of the inhabitants of Africa, was struck out in compliance to South Carolina and Georgia, who had never attempted to restrain the

importation of slaves, and who on the contrary still wished to continue it. Our Northern brethren also I believe felt a little tender under these censures; for tho' their people have very few slaves themselves, yet they had been pretty considerable carriers of them to others.[599]

James Madison, who also owned slaves, likewise expressed bitter disfavor for the institution in Federalist No. 42 (published publicly in advocacy of the Constitution's ratification), where, in calling for slavery's end, he wrote:

It were doubtless to be wished that the power of prohibiting the importation of slaves had not been postponed until the year 1808, or rather that it had been suffered to have immediate operation. But it is not difficult to account either for this restriction on the general government, or for the manner in which the whole clause is expressed. It ought to be considered as a great point gained in favor of humanity that a period of twenty years may terminate forever, within these States, a traffic which has so long and so loudly upbraided the barbarism of modern policy; that within that period it will receive a considerable discouragement from the federal government, and may be totally abolished, by a concurrence of the few States which continue the unnatural traffic in the prohibitory example which has been given by so great a majority of the Union. Happy would it be for the unfortunate Africans if an equal prospect lay before them of being redeemed from the oppressions of their European brethren![600]

Not a single founding father praised the institution of slavery and the leading ones condemned it, albeit the Virginians kept their slaves, awaiting a political resolution whereby all would be divested of their slaves equally. The hypocrisy existed as a legacy of British rule and a century of British fostering of the slave trade in the Americas. For the freedom-loving advocates, the radical Whigs of colonial America, the hypocrisy grew as the population of slaves grew in the land, and it never could be reconciled with the Lockean philosophical principles Jefferson championed in the Declaration. It was a blot on the Declaration and then on the Constitution, which promised in the Bill of Rights protection of the rights of the people against government. Yet, it, like the hypocrisy of denying women the right to vote, revealed a universal truth about government (an inherent defect in government itself). The art of the politically possible will necessarily constrain the quest toward perfection and the protection of rights. Hamilton admitted, in Federalist No. 85, that the Constitution was not perfect, but it was the best that could be achieved at the time: "[T]hough it may not be perfect in every part, [it] is, upon the whole . . . the best that the present views and circumstances of the country will permit."[601] Man the imperfect proceeds to perfection only through refinement, and for the founding generation that refinement to enable the promise of protection of the rights of all Americans regardless of race took a Civil War and subsequent amendments to achieve. The story is one of ever reaching toward perfection, not one, as the 1619 Project depicts, of a nation inextricably constrained to relive the sin of slavery in perpetuity.

The Historian C. Bradley Thompson explains well the conflict between the founding fathers' aspirations and the realities surrounding them. The British colonial experience had been one in which the Crown and colonial governors had sought to bring slaves to the Americas to feed an insatiable demand for agricultural labor. As the eighteenth century wore on, the institution spread, replete with black and white slaves, who became a mainstay of the agricultural economy. The cost of paid labor to substitute for slave labor became a major impediment to individual volitional manumission of slaves, as margins of profit, if even attainable by plantation owners, were ordinarily quite thin (indeed, President Washington died largely impecunious because his debts associated with his agricultural businesses mounted beyond returns year after year). Thus, while the institution was immoral and violated the most basic human rights, it was maintained because those plantation owners caught up within it could not economically get themselves out of it without financial ruin. C. Bradley Thompson writes:

It is a tragic irony that American revolutionaries—including, if not most especially, those who owned slaves—understood as well as anyone that slavery was an ugly, degrading, and brutal institution wherever it had been practiced. They hated and condemned it as immoral and anathema to the principles and institutions of a free society. Not a single revolutionary leader ever publicly praised slavery as a positive good. Benjamin Franklin, speaking as president of the Pennsylvania Society of Promoting the Abolition of Slavery, described slavery as "an atrocious debasement of human nature." George Washington, a slaveholder, told a friend, "There is not a man living, who wishes more sincerely than I do to see a plan adopted for the abolition of [slavery]." At the Constitutional Convention in 1787, James Madison told his colleagues, "We have seen the mere distinction of color made in the most enlightened period of time, a ground of the most oppressive dominion ever exercised by man over man." And John Adams told a correspondent in 1819 that he had held "the practice of slavery in abhorrence" throughout his entire life.[602]

But, as Madison understood, men are not angels and instruments of government are but parchment barriers to injustice unless given their full meaning. The hypocrisy of slavery in the face of a Declaration of Independence that proclaimed the truth that all men are created equal and endowed by God with unalienable rights crept on until it could be tolerated no more as a nation fell into civil war, in part, to end it.

The Declaration of Independence proclaimed a bold, universal truth, that all are created equal and endowed by their Creator with unalienable rights to life, liberty, and the pursuit of happiness. That truth was aspirational when written, a pure, unalloyed invitation to achievement thereafter, first through independence from Britain and then for achievement in a new union. It could not be imposed then or eleven years later in the Constitution because all across the land, slaves and indentured servants were integrated into an economy the financial supporters of which might reject the Declaration and the Constitution were the stand then made against slavery. The Civil War of 1861 would have been a civil war decades earlier, and Great Britain, stung from its loss of the revolution, may have rejoiced in its opportunity to reassert control over the colonies. The time while morally past due was politically infeasible.

It is a credit, not a vice, of the people of the United States, including those leaders who insisted on the end of slavery, that they would come to grips with the evil and with the contradiction to the Declaration's great promise, even risking loss of the Union and of tens of thousands of lives in a struggle to end the institution of slavery. Rather than decry the nation for ever having embraced slavery, as the backward-looking 1619 Project does, we should celebrate the nation for recognizing the evil inherent in it and fighting successfully to eliminate that evil and fulfill the Declaration's promise. Likewise, we should celebrate, not ignore or condemn, the movements to expand the promise of the Declaration to embrace women in the 19th Amendment. The seed of liberty grew from the Declaration of Independence and enveloped all people, that is the true origin, history, and legacy of America. The 1619 Project's effort to insinuate slavery into all American history and endeavor is belied by the fact that the nation went in the other direction, recognizing the sin of slavery from the start and then working to eliminate it, despite the enormous social and economic consequences of so doing, the Civil War.

At first, legal protection of rights was limited to a sphere that included male landed gentry, and then it extended to all white men, then to all black men, and then to all women. The expansion is one of fulfillment of promise, extending the Declaration's principle to its logical conclusion. That principle is brilliant, pristine. It served as the lodestar for the slaves who yearned to be free, for the leaders of the civil rights movement, and for all who cherish liberty, and it will so serve in perpetuity. To condemn the principle on the grounds that it was not extended by politicians to its logical conclusion at the start of the American experiment under British colonial rule is to argue a *non sequitur*. It does not follow that the principle is illegitimate simply because it legally applied originally to less than the full complement of Americans. The principle is a true one, reflective of the essential rights to which all people have a claim against those who would use the power of government to enslave. The argument of the 1619 Project is further belied by its apparent goal, of replacing a republican form of government protective of the liberty of all with a socialist or communist form that enslaves all. The great irony of the Project is that while condemning slavery as endemic in America, it advocates a replacement, socialism or communism, that would re-establish slavery in America, wherein everyone would be a slave to the state.

There is another upending of logic that arises in this area. Most advocates of the 1619 Project rely on their distorted view of history as a basis to argue that blacks be given reparations by the federal government to compensate them for their ancestors' slavery. When the actual history is revealed, as it has been here, the argument collapses into illogic. To be equitable, those who advocate reparations for slaves should be advocating reparations for the descendants of African, Irish, and English slaves in America. In short, they should be advocating reparations for all whites and blacks who descended from slaves. As Jordan and Walsh explain, "tens of millions of white Americans are descended from [white slaves]."[603] Perhaps a better course would be to cut everyone's taxes.

But, to be sure, the argument for reparations misses that most essential causal link which, if taken into account, logically compels the conclusion that no one should be paid reparations by the federal government as recompense for the institution of slavery. No one alive today is responsible in any way for the institution of slavery abolished by the Thirteenth Amendment in December of 1865. No slave or slaveowner remains alive today. Consequently, any demand that reparations be paid exacts a new innocent victim, all Americans not responsible for the injustice, who must through taxes pay for the distribution. Americans who in no way caused injury through the institution of slavery will nevertheless be compelled to pay the cost of a massive redistribution scheme from those who did not enslave to those who were not slaves but who are black. In other words, reparations are race-based payments that violate the equal protection principle of the Fifth

Amendment just as surely as affirmative action violates that same principle in the Fourteenth Amendment.[604]

Moreover, what about the break in the train of logic created by the hundreds of blacks who were themselves slaveowners and who enslaved whites and blacks? Should the government perform a detailed genealogical search to find those slaveowners and disallow their descendants who are black from receiving reparations? And what of the whites enslaved by black and white slaveowners, are they to be left out? What if we discover that a half of all Americans in the United States descend from either white or black slaves and that a quarter descend from slaveowners, do we make the descendants of slaveowners pay more in taxes to permit compensation to the descendants of slaves? The absurdity of these enterprises expresses itself through their extreme illogic and injustice. The movement for reparations seeks to divide us based on race because that is indeed all it achieves; it does not cause a single slave to be compensated for the cruelty of a single slaveowner. They are all long dead.

Laws enforcing reparations create a false race-based preference. They presume injuries to others justify payments to the uninjured solely predicated on a race-based distinction. On this principle, rather than limit federal payments to the Japanese Americans Franklin Roosevelt wrongfully placed in internment camps during World War II, the federal payments would need to be made in perpetuity to everyone of Japanese descent living in America. The wrongfully interred Japanese were enslaved, held captive against their will with many having their property taken from them. The law ordinarily and correctly recompenses those who have actually suffered an injury, regardless of race. Were blacks and whites who had been enslaved before ratification of the Thirteenth Amendment still alive today, it would be fitting for the government to pay them for the injustice visited upon them by laws that kept them in bondage. But no one who suffered as a slave still lives in America today. The policy of reparations is a race-based redistribution scheme that does not redress a wrong committed but advances the economic standing of Americans based solely on the color of their skin, thus committing a new wrong. It is Jim Crow flipped upside down. It simply adds a new race-based injury to the old, creating yet another divide among the races.

America must get beyond slavery. We should not make every new generation a captive of the sins of prior generations. We must embrace as a fundamental tenet the full promise of the Declaration of Independence. That promise is the antidote to slavery when implemented in full through law. All Americans are created equal. They are all endowed with pre-political rights to life, liberty, and the pursuit of happiness, not by government but by God. Protection of those rights was to be the very purpose of government. In a more nuanced way, reparations are in fact due all of us. The reparations due us, the making of amends due us, is the restoration of constitutional government based securely on the principle of rights protection for all, as promised by the Declaration.

CHAPTER 12

JUST GOVERNMENTS

In the Declaration of Independence, the essential principles underlying constitutional government are explained. To secure individual rights to life, liberty, and the pursuit of happiness, "Governments are instituted among Men, deriving their just Powers from the Consent of the Governed." The founders understood "just governments" to be ones that *secured* rights. That security depended on: (1) limiting government powers through a written constitution that expressly enumerated the powers and separated them into competing departments, subject to checks and balances; (2) depriving government of any power to transgress rights through the Constitution itself with an added safeguard in the Bill of Rights; and (3) depriving government of any power to transgress rights not expressly declared but nevertheless retained by the people and the states, as stated in the Ninth and Tenth Amendments.

In his First Inaugural Address, March 4, 1801, Thomas Jefferson explained succinctly the practical meaning of "just government," stating, "A wise and frugal Government . . . shall restrain men from injuring one another, shall leave them otherwise free to regulate their own pursuits of industry and improvement, and shall not take from the mouth of labor the bread it has earned. This is the sum of good government . . ."[605] In this succinct statement, Jefferson defines the just extent and limits of government. Government is just only if it leaves the people free to regulate their own pursuits of industry and improvement. It is just only if it taxes in a manner that is not confiscatory (in his metaphorical phrase, by not taking "from the mouth of labor the bread it has earned"). It is just only if it avoids taking any action to interfere with the private sphere except when necessary to "restrain men from injuring one another." The narrow scope of permissible interference in the private sphere is made even more manifest in Jefferson's definition of "liberty." In an April 4, 1819 letter to Isaac H. Tiffany, Jefferson explains the meaning of "liberty:"

> [O]f Liberty then I would say that, in the whole plenitude
> of its extent, it is unobstructed action according to our will:
> but rightful liberty is unobstructed action according to our
> will, within the limits drawn around us by the equal rights of
> others. I do not add "within the limits of the law"; because
> law is often but the tyrant's will, and always so when it
> violates the right of an individual.[606]

Importantly, Jefferson did not view "rightful liberty" as that which is channeled by law. The limit of "rightful liberty" was the "equal rights of others." This, then, defines a degree of freedom as wide as can be conceived short of anarchy, whereby nothing, certainly not a collectivist view of what would be in society's best interest, may limit the choice of each person. The only limit is the equal right of others (thus safeguarding others rights to life, liberty, and property); transgress that equal right and you become subject to prosecution, but avoid doing so and government has no just power over you.

Jefferson's definition of liberty is substantively indistinguishable from Madison's definition. Madison, in his March 29, 1792 essay "Property" explains that "property" in "its larger and juster meaning . . . embraces every thing to which a man may attach a value and have a right; and *which leaves to every one else the like advantage*" (emphasis in original).[607] Thus, Madison's "property" is indistinguishable from Jefferson's "liberty." But Madison adds additional definitional content, which also mirrors Jefferson's conception of "just" government (expressed as well in the Declaration); he writes:

> Government is instituted to protect property of every sort
> [i.e., those things over which one exercised ownership and,
> more broadly, one's opinions, religion, and liberty--limited
> only by the equal rights of others]; as well that which lies
> in the various rights of individuals, as that which the term
> particularly expresses. This being the end of government,
> that alone is a *just government, which impartially secures to
> every man, whatever is his own (emphasis in original)*.[608]

Also like Jefferson, Madison understood a just government as one limited
to intervention only in those instances where one deprived another of equal
rights. He also understood that a just government must avoid confiscatory
taxation and, what is more, redistribution of the proceeds from a disfavored
to a favored class. In "Property," Madison wrote:

> A just security to property is not afforded by that government,
> under which unequal taxes oppress one species of property
> and reward another species: where arbitrary taxes invade the
> domestic sanctuaries of the rich, and excessive taxes grind
> the faces of the poor; where the keenness and competitions
> of want are deemed an insufficient spur to labor, and taxes
> are again applied, by an unfeeling policy, as another spur;
> in violation of that sacred property, which Heaven, in
> decreeing man to earn his bread by the sweat of his brow,
> kindly reserved to him, in the small repose that could be
> spared from the supply of his necessities.[609]

It is against this expansive individual liberty that Progressives took aim,
and it is against this liberty that the administrative state regulates. Progressives
invaded the private sphere with a pervasive and constant administrative state
presence, so that individual choices that do not deprive the equal rights of
others (but are nevertheless inconsistent with the desires of governing elites)
could be denied through agency cajolery or prosecution. They sought to
override freedom of choice in all instances where Progressives' authoritarian

predilections for a society they deemed better were offended, and they commanded all to prove their allegiance to the state by avoiding any choice contrary to state commands. In short, the Progressive era severely curbed individual liberty and was dominated by leaders who rejected the rights centric and limited government premise of the Constitution.

One such authoritarian, Oliver Wendell Holmes, Jr., rose to favor dislodging the Constitution from its moorings when confronted with a case that asked whether government could constitutionally violate liberty of contract. In *Lochner v. New York* (1905)[610], a New York law governing bakeries prohibited them from employing workers for more than ten hours a day and sixty hours a week. The Court struck down the law as a violation of liberty of contract, which it held protected from abridgment by the "liberty" component of the Due Process Clause of the Fourteenth Amendment. The Court did so finding that the maximum hours provision was not demonstrably protective of either the health of bakery workers or that of consumers, there being no persuasive evidence in the record to that effect. Justice Rufus W. Peckham explained for the Court that the bread produced was "clean and wholesome" and "does not depend upon whether the baker works but ten hours per day or only sixty hours a week." If the evidence did show that clean and wholesome bread could not reliably be made by bakery workers employed over those hours, the Court indicated it would uphold the law as a valid exercise of the police power. Moreover, there was insufficient record evidence that the hours worked caused injury to bakery workers. If there was sufficient evidence, the Court explained, it would have upheld the law, again as a valid exercise of the police power. As it stood, the Court did not find any injury arising from the privately contracted hours of the bakery workers either to the public or to the workers and, thus, determined the maximum hour provision to be a "mere meddlesome interference with the rights of the individual."

In *Rehabilitating Lochner*, David E. Bernstein explains the history leading to the case. Progressive legal scholars have long condemned Lochner as an example of inhumane capitalism triumphing over laws for the public good, and of a too "robust constitutional protection of individual or minority rights."[611] Bernstein, however, documents that the law may not have been so benign or beneficent as contemporary scholars suggest. Rather, it appears to have been a product of efforts by the bakers' union and large bakeries to force out of existence small, non-union bakeries that employed Italian, French, and Jewish immigrants in favor of the unionized bakeries that employed predominantly German immigrants.[612] The smaller firms depended on longer working hours to compete with the larger firms. Those economic facts were not recited in the decision itself and, indeed, Bernstein suspects that the case brought to the Court was staged[613], an occurrence not at all uncommon at the time, as the previously discussed *Buck v. Bell* case suggests.

In his dissent in *Lochner v. New York*[614], Holmes famously wrote: "[A] constitution is not intended to embody a particular economic theory, whether of paternalism and the organic relation of the citizen to the State or of *laissez faire.*" Rather, Holmes called for the Court to exercise judicial restraint and uphold all state laws regulating business "unless . . . a rational and fair man necessarily would admit that the statute would infringe fundamental principles . . ." Holmes did not explain what principles he had in mind.

The conclusion Holmes reached directly contradicts the plain and intended meaning of the rights protective provisions of the Constitution. As we have seen, the Constitution was the subject of derision by Progressives of the time, who deemed it archaic and inapplicable in the Industrial Age. They aimed to escape the Constitution's strictures on power. They often depicted *Lochner* as typical of constitutional jurisprudence in defense of individual property and liberty rights from 1897 to 1937, but it was in fact atypical because the Court most often deferred to state legislation in reliance on the police power. For example, in *Holden v. Hardy* (1898)[615], the Supreme Court upheld a statute restricting coal miners' hours to eight per day as a permissible use of the police power on a record replete with evidence of the harms associated with long-term exposure to coal dust. Although the Supreme Court frequently upheld Progressive legislation during that period (and ought not rightly be characterized as anti-progressive[616]), the broad charge is so made, erroneously proclaiming this epoch as "conservative" and opposed to the collectivist "public good."

Holmes, like his colleagues Brandeis and Frankfurter, did not believe that individual rights should stand in the way of laws supportive of majoritarian values. Holmes' dissent became accepted juristic dogma following *Nebbia v. New York* (1934)[617], where the Court held "a State is free to adopt whatever economic policy may reasonably be deemed to promote public welfare, and to enforce that policy by legislation adapted to its purpose."

Holmes' view (indeed, the post-*Nebbia* view) that economic liberty need not be given heightened protection against the state (in contrast with political liberty) offends the Constitution for at least two primary reasons. First, by its very design the Constitution creates and guarantees a form of government on the federal level that is a limited federal republic of expressly enumerated powers. As James Madison put it in Federalist No. 45: "The powers delegated by the proposed Constitution to the federal government are few and defined."[618] Second, under Article IV, Section 4 (the Guarantee Clause), the Constitution forbids each state from adopting any form of government other than a republican form and vests in the federal government the power to guarantee that form, including by the Executive power, using military force to end invasion and domestic violence. That section reads: "The United States shall guarantee to every State in this Union a Republican Form of Government, and shall protect each of them against Invasion; and on Application of the Legislature, or of the Executive (when the Legislature cannot be convened) against domestic Violence." The limited republic envisioned and established by the founding fathers does not provide for a pervasive regulatory presence in the market among its enumerated powers, nor could it and still preserve the aim of securing individual rights.

Socialism and communism (that is, persistent state intervention in or control over the market) violates the Constitution because it compels a transmogrification of the republican form of government it prescribes. Socialism and communism transmogrifies the government from one of expressly limited, enumerated powers into one of unlimited powers, transgressing all constitutional limits. Socialism and communism places government in the market as the predominant or exclusive force, necessarily usurping freedom of choice beyond the powers delegated by the Constitution, indeed defeating the very purpose of that limited delegation: protection of individual rights to liberty and property. That reality was not mentioned, let alone analyzed, by

Holmes in his famous *Lochner* dissent. It is a profound material omission, the veritable elephant in the room that escaped Holmes' eye.

Holmes blithely proceeds beyond that rights issue because he favored majority opinions embodied in law over minority rights. Indeed, he was disdainful of minority rights. He wrote: "This case is decided upon an economic theory which a large part of the country does not entertain. If it were a question whether I agreed with that theory, I should desire to study it further and long before making up my mind. But I do not conceive that to be my duty because I strongly believe that my agreement or disagreement has nothing to do with the right of a majority to embody their opinions in law."

The problem with Holmes' open-ended representation that any economic theory favored by a legislative majority would comply with the Constitution is his failure to recognize that every economic theory, other than capitalism, *requires* the federal government to change its essential form. His dissent thus opens Pandora's box to violations of the Constitution's essential republican form and to the Guarantee Clause. If his theory of constitutionality is accepted it not only permits a majority vote to unravel a bakery contract, it permits a majority vote to unravel the social compact underlying the Constitution, enabling the Constitution itself to be discarded and supplanted. It permits the limited federal republic to which the public consented (the founders' contract with America, if you will) to be replaced by a socialist or communist state, to which the public never consented.

Capitalism is plainly contemplated by a Constitution that protects property rights and limits government involvement in the private sphere so as not to deprive people of the power to dispose of their property. Socialism is plainly antithetical to the Constitution because it requires the government itself to be transformed from its republican form into one that controls the exercise of property rights. Communism is plainly antithetical to the Constitution because it requires the state itself to be transformed from its republican form into one that owns all private property and supplants all personal liberty.

Socialism and communism are economic forms that depend on a transformation of the government from one positioned outside the private sphere with limited involvement in that sphere to one with unlimited control over and involvement in the private sphere, second-guessing or replacing every private choice of any consequence. Under socialism and communism, government dictates who may sell, what may be sold, and on what terms, or takes total ownership of the market. Moreover, under socialism and communism, to achieve the end of market control, the government necessarily denies the existence of rights to individual liberty and property, thus violating not only the Constitution's enumerated powers but also the rights against government action protected by the Bill of Rights, and the rights reserved to the states and the people by the Tenth Amendment. Under socialism and communism, the states could not be allowed to function as republics consistent with the Guarantee Clause because any form of government protective of individual liberty and property would frustrate the property and liberty controls required under socialism and communism.

In their ultimate centralization of control, socialist and communist governments establish an elite with one or a few enjoying most, if not all, personal liberties, while everyone else is denied that liberty. In this way, the socialist or communist state recurs to an old model of government, absolute monarchy. Under absolute monarchy, only the King has rights and others may do nothing of consequence (own property, publish opinions, or engage in trade) without leave of the King (i.e., a license). The unelected heads of administrative agencies, the leaders of socialist countries, and the leaders of communist countries are in this respect largely indistinguishable from absolute monarchs.

Transmogrifying the Constitution into a government of socialist or communist form betrays the essential principle of public consent whenever it is achieved without a constitutional amendment. Of course, it destroys liberty in every instance and, so, gives rise to the Declaration's animadvert of revolution until a "just" government, a government instituted to protect the rights of the governed, is restored.

Every Progressive reform has depended on transferring powers vested by the Constitution in the three branches of government to regulatory agencies and bureaus nowhere referenced, mentioned, or authorized so to rule in the founding charter. In this way, regulatory agencies will be the implementers of any socialist or communist revolution. They already have a long track record of acting outside of the Constitution, unconstrained by constitutional limits, so they are the natural repositories of property and liberty confiscatory acts.

The only way such major structural reform could potentially be attainable under the Constitution would be by a constitutional amendment under Article V. Making that change without an Article V amendment violates the essential principle of consent on which the Constitution is based and is, thus, always an unconstitutional power grab that betrays the people of the United States. Fearful of such change, George Washington addressed the dangers attendant to it at length in his September 19, 1796 Farewell Address. He did so as he left office following his second term, itself not a constitutional obligation, but a precedent he intentionally established to discourage future presidents from seeking presidencies for life, a precedent Franklin D. Roosevelt would break.

Washington explained that "[t]he basis of our political systems is the right of the people to make and to alter their constitutions of government,"[619] ours being a government dependent on the consent of the governed. He emphasized that so long as the Constitution remains unamended, the system of government it prescribes "is sacredly obligatory upon all."[620] He warned against what the Progressives would bring to pass a century later: "[I]t is requisite, not only that you steadily discountenance irregular oppositions to [the Constitution's] acknowledged authority, but also that you resist with care the spirit of innovation upon its principles . . ."[621] He explained that "[o]ne method of assault may be to effect, in the forms of the Constitution, alterations which will impair the energy of the system, and thus to undermine what cannot be directly overthrown."[622] He prophetically reasoned that incremental constitutional impairments over the long term would yield destruction of the limits on power, giving rise to dictatorship, writing: "[T]he disorders and miseries which result gradually incline the minds of men to seek security and repose in the absolute power of an individual."[623] Then, in time, a dictator would arise after contenders were vanquished, and that dictator would turn "this disposition to the purposes of his own elevation, on the ruins of public liberty."[624]

Washington held future governors to the Constitution's standard, arguing not that a fundamental change was impossible under the Constitution but that if it was to be made, it had to be made in fidelity to the principle of public consent upon which the legitimacy of government rests. He wrote: "If, in the opinion of the people, the distribution or modification of the constitutional powers be in any particular wrong, let it be corrected by an amendment in the way which the Constitution designates. But let there be no change by usurpation; for though this, in one instance, may be the instrument of good, it is the customary weapon by which free governments are destroyed."[625]

The argument is raised that among the enumerated powers is an Article I, Section 8, Clause 3 grant to Congress of power to regulate commerce with foreign nations and among the states. Surely that grant embraces regulation that controls the market (including when such controls deprive individual property owners of the full bundle of rights over their property) or invites government ownership of all private property (confiscating it for the government's use). That argument, however, conflicts with the plain and intended meaning of the Constitution. The Constitution does not enable the government to take private property without just compensation. The Fifth Amendment reads in pertinent part: "nor shall private property be taken for public use without just compensation." Perhaps more to the point, the Constitution's very purpose, to protect the rights of the governed, its animating purpose in fulfillment of the Declaration of Independence, is entirely inconsistent with government action that controls the use of or confiscates private property, the private right to which the founding fathers regarded as essential, unalienable, pre-political and God-given.

The legislative power in Article I, Section 8, Clause 3, gives Congress the power "to regulate commerce with foreign Nations, and among the several States, and with the Indian tribes." The power to regulate commerce is not the power to deprive individuals of their property and it is not all-encompassing, nor could it be, if a limited republican form of government is to be maintained. Rather, the sweep of the clause is confined by its intended meaning and by the intended meaning of Article I, Section 8, Clause 18 (the Necessary and Proper Clause).

The Commerce Clause was adopted to break down interstate barriers to commerce, such as duties and tariffs, thereby ensuring the free flow of goods through the states. It was not adopted to authorize the erection of barriers to commerce. Thus, it is a clause supportive of capitalism. James Madison made the meaning manifest in Federalist No. 42. There, he explains in confirmation of the import of the Commerce Clause to the free flow of goods: "Were [the states] at liberty to regulate the trade between State and State, it must be foreseen that ways would be found out to load the articles of import and export, during the passage through their jurisdictions, with duties which would fall on the makers of the latter and the consumers of the former."[626]

The argument is raised that the Necessary and Proper Clause of Article I, Section 8, Clause 19, permits an expansive interpretation that would allow the federal government to adopt socialism or communism. That argument conflicts with the language of the clause, which is limited to granting means necessary to effectuate the enumerated powers, not to add powers beyond those enumerated in Article I, Section 8. The clause grants Congress the power "to make all Laws which shall be necessary and proper for carrying into Execution *the foregoing Powers*, and all other Powers *vested by this Constitution* in the Government of the United States, or in any Department or Officer thereof" (emphasis added). That meaning is reinforced by Alexander Hamilton in Federalist No. 33. Using Congress's taxing power as an illustration, Hamilton writes (emphasis in original):

> [A] power to lay and collect taxes must be a power to pass all laws *necessary* and *proper* for the execution of that power; and what does the unfortunate and calumniated provision [i.e., the Necessary and Proper Clause] in question do more than declare the same truth, to wit, that the national legislature to whom the power of laying and collecting taxes had been previously given might, in the execution of that power, pass all laws *necessary* and *proper* to carry it into effect? I have applied these observations thus particularly to the power of taxation, because it is the immediate subject under consideration and because it is the most important of the authorities proposed

to be conferred upon the Union. But the same process will lead to the same result in relation to all other powers declared in the Constitution. And it is *expressly* to execute these powers that the sweeping clause, as it has been affectedly called, authorizes the national legislature to pass all *necessary* and *proper* laws. If there be anything exceptionable, it must be sought for in the specific powers upon which this general declaration is predicated. The declaration itself, though it may be chargeable with tautology or redundancy, is at least perfectly harmless.[627]

If not the Necessary and Proper Clause, it is argued that the General Welfare Clause should suffice to permit the expansive read needed to allow a socialist or communist government to be adopted in the United States. Does the General Welfare Clause, Article I, Section 8, Clause 1, change the analysis, exploding the enumerated powers to reach everything that might be deemed germane to the general welfare of the people (e.g., a power not enumerated to have the federal government provide health coverage for every American at taxpayers' expense or a power not enumerated to have the federal government provide a collegiate education to every American and every illegal alien at taxpayers' expense)? No, no such powers were intended to be conveyed by the Constitution, as James Madison makes clear in Federalist No. 41. Madison vehemently denies any such intention. He explains that because the clause precedes the enumeration of specific powers and is not separated from that enumeration but is conjoined with it by a semicolon, the general welfare clause defines the enumerated powers as the means for securing the general welfare. Madison explains that construing the general welfare clause as a separate grant of power independent of the enumerated powers mocks the Constitution's draftsmanship because it renders superfluous the strong arguments for and justifications of enumeration. Madison writes:

> Some . . . have grounded a very fierce attack against the Constitution, on the language in which it is defined. It has been urged and echoed that the power "to lay and collect

taxes, duties, imposts, and excises, to pay the debts, and provide for the common defense and general welfare of the United States," amounts to an unlimited commission to exercise every power which may be alleged to be necessary for the common defense or general welfare. No stronger proof could be given of the distress under which these writers labor for objections, than their stooping to such a misconstruction.

Had no other enumeration or definition of the powers of the Congress been found in the Constitution than the general expressions just cited, the authors of the objection might have had some color for it; though it would have been difficult to find a reason for so awkward a form of describing an authority to legislate in all possible cases . . .

But what color can the objection have, when a specification of the objects alluded to by these general terms immediately follows and is not even separated by a longer pause than a semicolon? . . . For what purpose could the enumeration of particular powers be inserted, if these and all others were meant to be included in the preceding general power? Nothing is more natural nor common than first to use a general phrase, and then to explain and qualify it by a recital of particulars.[628]

In the end, after the charade of strained arguments that the Constitution's language can be twisted to embrace a meaning inclusive of socialism or communism, the Progressives are left to choose whether a constitutional amendment is needed or a straight power grab will suffice. As explained in the chapter on the Democratic Party's embrace of authoritarianism, the straight power grab is their preference.

Reciting the precedent of piecemeal power grabs condoned by Supreme Court decisions ever since the post-court-packing "switch in time that saved nine," they argue that constitutional law is now elastic enough (having been stretched bit by bit since the 1930s) to permit the full-blown conversion of the United States from its current form into a completely socialist or communist form.

The Progressives' analysis lacks integrity. The Constitution of the United States is a detailed plan for the government of the United States but it rests on the consent of the people. It is a social compact. So long as the government honors the Constitution, we too are bound by it as the rule of law. If the government dishonors it, however, we are no longer bound.

Once the Progressives have so far abandoned the plain and intended meaning of the Constitution as to supplant it with a socialist or communist government, we are left with an original problem anticipated in the Declaration of Independence with a solution given there (emphasis added): "that whenever *any Form of Government* becomes destructive of [unalienable Rights to Life, Liberty, and the Pursuit of Happiness], it is the Right of the People to alter or to abolish it, and to institute new Government, laying its Foundation on such Principles, and organizing its Powers in such Form, as to them shall seem most likely to effect their Safety and Happiness."

The Progressives' demand that the Constitution be abandoned or reinterpreted to permit a socialist or communist form thus collapses government because it destroys the social compact. In a less theoretical sense, it collapses government because people no longer have faith that government is bound by the ultimate rule of law, the Constitution itself.

When government follows the Constitution, its actions are predictable, and the public and the markets are assured that the freedoms Americans enjoy are protected. When government rejects it and institutes a new governmental form without constitutional amendment, the new government unleashed from constitutional strictures is inherently unpredictable, and the public and the markets have no assurance that the freedoms Americans enjoy will continue to be protected. That predictably leads to civil war.

Once the ultimate rule of law of the Constitution is no longer followed, and the actions of government thus become unpredictable, no property or liberty is secure, and free people react to defend their interests individually and with like-minded others. The inchoate status of rights under the new government drives value out of the market, which is ordinarily then taken over to a greater or lesser extent by government with explanations of "market failure," and the market then is compelled to satisfy a political agenda desired by the governing elites (e.g., the Green New Deal).

Without the security of rights protection, people retreat to enclaves where they can themselves guard their property and liberty: to their homes and businesses. They are strongly inclined to preserve their property and liberty against those in government who would take it away, and they therefore defend it, with force if necessary, from those who try to take it. This is a predictable de-evolution of America if governing elites abandon the Constitution and the rule of law and cleave to a new form of government to which the people have not consented, e.g., socialism or communism. The pace and severity of that de-evolution is entirely predicated on the extent and rapidity of the transformation.

The socialist and communists' problem with America is that we are a people born under a Constitution that defines protections for our rights. We have a long history of revering that protection, of even going to war against communist and socialist states that deprive other people of the freedoms we enjoy. We are therefore quite experienced in defending freedom and, while many may take their freedom for granted in times of peace, when it becomes clear that governing elites are intent on taking liberty and property away, we can fully expect Americans to revolt against the take-over, consistent with the prescription for revolution contained in the Declaration of Independence.

This conflict leads to an ultimate philosophical question: Why is it that the limited federal republic defined by the Constitution is superior to government in a socialist or communist form? The simple answer is that it most consists with human nature. As humans we are individuals, not collectives. While we socialize, we live, breathe, and function as individuals, even when we do so in aid of a group. As explained more fully in the chapter on socialism, people do not function well as slaves whether under an individual master or a state master. No matter how benevolent the master, we yearn to choose our own directions in life. We are born free agents, a momentous, hugely consequential gift from God. While we grow with dependence upon our parents, at every turn we exhibit a desire for freedom, for self-direction. When we are newborns without the ability to crawl, we soon want to crawl and in directions we choose. When we take those first few steps, we do so seeking the ability to move to locations that are of our own choosing. When we depart from parental authority during our teen years, we do so because we want to be independent and develop our own identities, our own place in the world. When we proceed along that course, we are happiest when we have chosen to do what we want to do, not what someone else wants us to do. And so on. Humans are inextricably predisposed to freedom. All constraints, all shackles, whether literal or figurative, we naturally rebel against in favor of freedom. Socialism and communism are nothing more than enslavement. The entire nation then fills the role of the "inferior race" that Hegel believe uplifted by association with a "superior race." In socialist and communist societies, that superior race is comprised of governing elites. They enjoy freedom, while everyone else experiences slavery. They lead on the philosophical principle that they are expert and better able to direct our lives than we are ourselves. That is a poison, cynical, and inhumane view of human nature. We rebelled against that paternalist model in the American Revolution, and we undoubtedly will rebel against it again if imposed by a governing elite, just as the Declaration predicts.

So, the lessons learned by the first generation of Americans are repeated now. There is no substitute for individual liberty. Just governments are not those that leave the rights of individuals insecure and that deprive the individual of control over basic, life-affecting decisions. They are, instead, governments that secure the rights of individuals, leaving them free to decide for themselves, to choose for themselves. They are, instead, governments that maintain the integrity of our private sphere of action, intervening only in those instances where individuals violate the equal rights of others. Only in such a state can people predisposed to freedom remain secure in their freedoms. Only in such a state can the outward attributes of individual freedom (market activity, art, innovation, and progress) occur such that the quality and standard of living of the American people may continuously rise.

CHAPTER 13

THE DEMOCRATIC PARTY'S EMBRACE OF AUTHORITARIANISM

O n Tuesday, February 25, 2020, then Senate Minority Leader Charles Schumer (D-NY) stated that he would be comfortable with self-avowed socialist Senator Bernie Sanders (I-VT) becoming the party's nominee for President.[629] On Wednesday, February 26, 2020, House Speaker Nancy Pelosi (D-CA) said that she too would be comfortable with Senator Sanders becoming the party's nominee for President.[630] For the first time in American history the leaders of the Democratic Party publicly expressed their willingness to back a socialist for President. These principal mouthpieces and leaders of the Democratic Party were reflecting a new reality within their ranks. A well-designed Gallup Poll conducted by telephone between January 16 and January 29, 2020, of 1,033 adults aged eighteen and older residing in the United States and the District of Columbia found that 76% of Democrats; 45% of Independents; and 17% of Republicans said they would vote for a socialist for President.[631]

Throughout the 2020 campaign season, Democratic candidates vied for endorsements from the socialist freshmen nicknamed "the Squad," including socialists Alexandria Ocasio-Cortez, Ayanna Pressley, Ilhan Omar, and Rashida Tlaib.[632] Despite initial efforts by Speaker Pelosi to resist support of socialist measures in Congress, she has since largely avoided conflict with the Squad and has supported the causes they embrace, to a greater or lesser degree. Senate Minority Leader Schumer has followed in lock step. Indeed, much of Joe Biden's platform is drawn directly from Senator Bernie Sanders' socialist policy positions.

The favored policies of Senator Sanders include ones that transform the federal government from its limited republican form into a socialist state, thus violating the strictures on federal power in the Constitution and the Guarantee Clause (which guarantees a republican form of government in the states). Sanders advocates abolition of capital punishment; abolition of cash bail; elimination of private prisons; federal construction of low-cost housing and rent control; substantial increases in federal income, corporate and capital gains taxes; creation of new wealth taxes; creation of a new federal tax on all financial trades; a mandatory federal minimum wage of $15 per hour; mandatory paid leave for workers; federal reparations for blacks; prohibitions on charter schools; federally financed college tuition for all; cancelation of all student loan debt; increases in the salaries of teachers; limits on campaign spending; elimination of the electoral college; pre-emption of all state laws that prevent convicted felons from voting; elimination of all nuclear power reactors; elimination of all oil and gas drilling; mandatory ceilings on carbon emissions; anti-trust actions against agribusiness; federally financed school meals; a mandatory purchase (i.e., mandatory buy back) of all assault weapons; elimination of all limits on abortion, including on partial birth abortion; a ban on all private health insurance and a mandatory program of Medicare for all; citizenship for all illegal aliens; repeal of all statutes limiting immigration into the United States; cessation of funding for a border wall; substantial expansion of public works programs; federal legalization of marijuana; and substantial reductions in defense spending.

Alexandria Ocasio-Cortez, member of Congress from New York's 14th congressional district; Ayanna Pressley, member of Congress from Massachusetts' 7th congressional district; Ilhan Omar, member of Congress from Minnesota's 5th congressional district; and Rashida Tlaib, member of

Congress from Michigan's 13th congressional district, are among those who support a non-binding congressional resolution calling for a "Green New Deal." The measure is principally sponsored in the House by self-avowed Democratic Socialist Ocasio-Cortez and in the Senate by Edward Markey of Massachusetts whose positions largely mirror those of the socialist Squad. Twelve United States Senators, among them former Senator Kamala Harris, and ninety members of the House co-sponsored the resolution. The resolution calls for the single greatest imposition of federal regulation and control over all major market aspects of the American economy in United States history, vastly more extensive and intrusive than Franklin D. Roosevelt's New Deal.

Under the proposal, the federal government would mandate, *inter alia*: (1) net zero greenhouse gas emissions within ten years; (2) elimination of all fossil fuels within ten years; (3) elimination of all gasoline-powered vehicles; (4) elimination of all pollution and greenhouse gas emissions from every manufacturer and industry; (5) reliance on solar and wind turbine generation for all utility power needs; (6) retrofitting all 5.6 million commercial buildings in the United States to no longer depend on fossil fuels; (7) eliminate pollution and greenhouse gas emissions in the agricultural sector; (8) impose federal management on all farms and lands in the United States to ensure "sustainable" practices; (9) pay college tuition for all residents (citizens and aliens); (10) guarantee universal access to "healthy food;" and (11) guarantee a federal job "with a family-sustaining wage, adequate family and medical leave, paid vacations, and retirement security" for every American.

To achieve what would be at best a negligible environmental benefit, and, most likely, a net environmental harm (as explained below), the Green New Deal would destroy the entire economy, replacing it with a socialist or communist state that controls or owns every business in the nation. While ruining the economic engine that employs us all, it leaves entirely unaffected the world's greatest polluter, China. Moreover, because nature itself is a formidable source of pollution, the Green New Deal is a frenetic regulatory absurdity. Finally, by forcing the nation to move away from the most efficient and reliable sources of energy production to among the least efficient and reliable sources, it will likely produce the perverse effect of compelling individuals to deforest the nation to obtain primitive sources for heat in the cold winter months, such as wood burning fireplaces, which will increase pollution and harm the environment.

An independent evaluation of the proposal reveals its cost to be about $93 trillion over ten years, approximately $600,000 per household, a sum beyond the financial wherewithal of the entire American economy.[633] It would place the federal government in direct control of the energy, health care, agriculture, education, and employment sectors, constituting the single most intrusive extension of federal power into American lives in history. It would transform the United States from its republican form to a socialist form. It would destroy major sectors of the economy, including the oil, natural gas, and coal industries, resulting in a loss of an estimated 3.4 to 7 million jobs. It would compel Americans to redesign their homes and to purchase electric vehicles, adding thousands of dollars to a list of required expenditures for each home owner. It would likewise compel the retrofitting of every business in the United States to new federally established green standards. It would require that millions of acres of agricultural land be taken out of production and dedicated for wind and solar power generation. The construction of these facilities would substantially increase demand for steel and rare earth minerals, which could not be domestically produced under the pollution controls but would have to be imported at a cost of billions and at a significant increase in carbon and greenhouse gas emissions. If fully implemented, the reduction in polluting emissions worldwide would be negligible in any event because the most prodigious polluter in the world, China, is unaffected by the restraints, as are all other foreign nations that add to pollution. The proposal would shift trillions out of the private sector and into the public sector, vastly expanding the size and scope of the federal government.

In a Policy Brief for the Heartland Institute, Paul Driessen explains the impracticality of the Green New Deal's demands, including its substantial devastation to the environment, reinforcing the statement of Ocasio-Cortez's former Chief of Staff that, indeed, the Green New Deal really isn't about the environment. It's a Trojan Horse for socialism. The solar panels required to replace fossil fuel and nuclear power would blanket the nation and destroy the environment:

Solar panel farms generate only 1.5% of the nation's electricity and would be an inefficient way to generate the more than eight billion Megawatt hours (MWhrs) of power currently provided by fossil fuels and nuclear for industrial, commercial, and residential use, as well as automotive transportation.

* * * *

... [T]o generate the more than eight billion MWhrs each year with solar would require completely blanketing 57,048 square miles of land—an area equivalent to the size of the states of New York and Vermont—with 18.8 billion solar panels. Obviously, this would wreak much havoc on the environment.[634]

In the case of wind power, it is even worse. Driessen explains:

The Fowler Ridge Wind Farm in Indiana covers 68 square miles, an area larger than Washington, D.C. If similar facilities were used to replace all of the country's fossil fuels and nuclear power, it would require 2.12 million turbines on 500,682 square miles of farm, wildlife habitat, and scenic lands. This would require an amount of land as large as the combined total for Arizona, California, Nevada, Oregon, and much of West Virginia.[635]

Driessen further explains that wind turbines are devastating to bird and bat populations, the losses of which dramatically increase insect populations, causing everything from crop devastation to direct harm to humans.[636] Moreover, to produce the massive quantity of solar panels and turbines needed for America's energy needs massive complexes would have to be created for steel and concrete production and to extract and manufacture various rare earth minerals. That all involves significant environmental damage and pollution. It is not a one-time cost, either, because solar panels and turbines are in constant need of replacement. Driessen points to global examples and explains: "Numerous American states and several countries, notably Germany, are experiencing major environmental problems due to the disposal of solar panels, wind turbines, and batteries after they lose their usefulness."[637]

On October 8, 2020, Ocasio-Cortez, Ayanna Pressley, Ilhan Omar, and Rashida Tlaib joined eleven other members of Congress in endorsing a "Working Families Party People's Charter" which called for, *inter alia*: (1) defunding of police, jails, and detention centers; (2) elimination of local zoning laws to promote racial integration; (3) provision of free COVID-19 testing and treatments for all; (4) extending unemployment insurance to illegal aliens; (5) prohibiting evictions, foreclosures, and utility shut-offs; (6) canceling rent, and suspending debt payments during the pandemic and until all are employed; (7) providing all students at home with the devices needed to acquire education and access to nutrition; (8) providing essential services and housing to all "homeless, migrants, people with disabilities, trans people, and survivors of domestic and sexual violence;" (9) providing federal funds to prevent layoffs and cuts to school, hospital, and other public services; (10) creating a federal works program that employs sixteen million people; (11) creating a mandatory federal minimum wage of $15 per hour; (12) providing federally funded health care for all; (13) guaranteeing the right to join a union so that every worker can bargain collectively; (14) creating federally funded child care, paid family and medical leave, and paid sick leave for all Americans and giving income support for parents caring for children full-time; (15) providing federally financed housing for every American; (16) guaranteeing "home and community based services for everyone, including mental health care;" (17) "tax[ing] the giant corporations who don't pay their share, and the wealth of the billionaires, who have gotten richer during the worst economic collapse in 90 years;" (18) creating federal banks to provide funding for all private businesses that fail; (19) taking federal ownership of all corporations receiving financial assistance; and (20) having the federal government "buy out" all oil and gas companies.

The new Democratic Party respects no limits on government power. Echoing all nascent socialist regimes worldwide, it promises free everything. Consistent with authoritarianism, its faith in the collective comes at the expense of individual rights to life, liberty, and property. Having no limits to what government can tax, control, redistribute, own, and condemn, the government replaces what remains of individual sovereignty and self-determination. The new Democratic Party adheres to a platform indistinguishable from socialist platforms in Cuba, Venezuela, and Cambodia, to name just a few. Like those platforms, it is a prescription for ruin.

In his April 6, 1816 letter to Joseph Milligan, Thomas Jefferson warned against the vilification and plundering of wealth, cognizant of the reality that destruction of a society's wealth generators leads rather quickly to destruction of the society itself, as all depend on those centers of wealth to finance employment, investment, and innovation. "To take from one, because it is thought his own industry and that of his fathers has acquired too much," wrote Jefferson, "in order to spare others, who, or whose fathers, have not exercised equal industry and skill, is to violate arbitrarily the first principle of association, the guarantee to everyone the free exercise of his industry and the fruits acquired by it."[638]

At the heart of the socialist lie now adopted by the Democratic Party is the impossible supposition that if government pillages the nation, through an overwhelming tax burden on all depositories of wealth in the private sector, the government—by its very nature a parasite—will be able to continue the pillaging over time to finance an ever greater expansion of government into the private sector and promised welfare programs. But, as Prime Minister Margaret Thatcher so eloquently stated, "the problem with socialism is that you eventually run out of other people's money."[639] And when you do run out, there is left in the wake the opportunity cost of that spending, the lost jobs, the poverty and human misery, and the hopelessness. That is the history of socialism around the world. At the start, as in the magnificent list of promises offered by the socialists dominating the Democratic Party, there are assurances that every human need will be addressed by government largess. Because that requires money, lots and lots of it, the government turns to all sources of capital, to "soak the rich." But after the soaking, then what? And there is never any clear answer. The federal party commences on a high note of promise and massive spending, the confiscatory taxation follows, and then the whole house of cards collapses and buried underneath the greatest weight of the rubble are those most in need. The betrayal of the poor is the cruelest lie of socialism.

Under the system the Democratic Party envisions, every American is forced into a government channeled direction in commerce, education, health care, and residence. The bulk of wealth is taxed in a confiscatory manner to fuel a massive expansion in the role of the administrative state over every aspect of American life and business. The cost of this bureaucratic command and control economy is astronomical, preventing economic recovery and sustained economic growth. Freedom of choice is replaced with government-mandated selections. Government planners become the new slaveowners.

Fundamentally, the government take-over of the private sector is the antithesis of Jeffersonian "liberty." It inverts the promise of the Declaration of Independence. Under it, no one is created equal. Rather we are all categorized and ministered to by government differently predicated on our race, income, and employment. Under it, none of our rights to life, liberty and the pursuit of happiness is unalienable; each may be violated to pursue whatever those in power define as the "public interest." Under it, the government is no longer centrally premised on protection of our individual rights but is instead premised on advancement of a "collective interest" politically chosen by those in power. Under it, government proceeds through an administrative state controlled by the unelected, thus defeating the promise of the Declaration of a "just" government that derives its powers from the consent of the governed.

Those hallmark characteristics of a republican form of government are all destroyed by implementation of the socialist vision of the new Democratic Party. That new party is the face and embodiment of authoritarianism. Its commitment to authoritarianism is no less profound and no less devastating than that of numerous other authoritarian states, such as Venezuela, Cuba, communist China, and Russia. By punishing the most productive parts of society, looting those whose sin it is to have invented means to satisfy to the maximum extent possible the wants and needs of others, the brave new world of the Democratic Party ensures the destruction of the wealth upon which the government depends. The Authoritarians thus ignorantly plant the seeds of their own destruction as in practice they inevitably prove false the promises they have made to the people. More generally, they pillage and destroy all free enterprise and, thereafter, they destroy the United States itself. We can expect great oppression, destitution, and rights violations from the brave new socialist government the Democratic Party has embraced unless the electorate becomes enlightened, rejects the false promises, condemns socialism, and demands protection of individual liberty and the Constitution's grand design.

CHAPTER 14

A WAKE-UP CALL FROM VICTIMS OF SOCIALISM AND COMMUNISM

Those with a positive view of socialism and communism are not those who have lived under it. The near universal sentiment expressed by those who have escaped from those regimes to the United States is that the experience was dehumanizing. The expatriates from socialist states cannot fathom how American youth and leaders of the Democratic Party harbor such romantic views of socialism and communism when the reality in the world surrounding the United States is so grotesque. The lesson of government assumption of absolute power is that it cannot be controlled, the people are its victims, and the government through its agents may do with the people as the government pleases. Consider four examples: the former Soviet Union, Venezuela, Cuba, and nationalist China.

THE UNION OF SOVIET SOCIALIST REPUBLICS

The first story is that of my client Donna Kasseinova. She grew up in the former Soviet Union. This is her recollection:

> Every single immigrant from the Soviet Union I've known
> has experienced a nightmare in which he or she revisits

Russia and is unable to return to the United States. Among friends we jokingly refer to it as "Back in the USSR."

The plot of the nightmare is remarkably similar. You're back in the USSR on what is supposed to be a short emergency visit. The authorities spot a problem with your documents. Perhaps you never properly renounced your citizenship or didn't pay some obscure fee or some other absurd thing. Now you can't leave the country. For the next several years you're trapped in the maze of kleptomaniacal bureaucracy. The dreaded Iron Curtain rises up once again, cutting you off from freedom, from your American life.

I have this nightmare repeatedly, even though I left the USSR three decades ago. My husband, also from Russia, has it too. It may sound crazy, but I actually think that I gain something from this nightmare. It reminds me how fragile my freedom is and what the alternative feels like. Awakening from the socialist nightmare in the free world feels amazing every time.

Young American socialist activists would take offense at my use of the word "nightmare" and would try to argue with me. "But didn't you have free housing in the USSR?" Yes, but it came with the stamp in your internal passport (called *Propiska)*, which didn't allow you to change your dwelling without the permission of the government, which was impossible to obtain. I personally grew up in a 500 square foot apartment. My mom made it cute and cozy, but we were bound to spend the rest of our lives in that apartment. By the 70s and 80s, it was common for families of 3 generations to live in the same apartment. We could not move within the country, and we were definitely not allowed to travel outside of the country.

"But didn't you have free education in the USSR?" Yes, but you had no freedom of choice in your higher education. You could only study predetermined curricula, of which Marxist-Leninist Theory was a key discipline. We were studying foreign languages from professors who had never traveled abroad and never met a foreigner. Most of the thought-provoking books worth reading were forbidden in the USSR and in order to read copies (sometimes hand-written) smuggled in from the West, we had to disguise them by wrapping them in Soviet newspapers. Upon graduation, the government assigned you your job in a random geographical location within the vastness of the USSR. This was a lottery that could wreck your life and countless bribes were paid to avoid unfavorable assignments.

"But didn't you have free medical care in the USSR?" Yes, we were all vaccinated and had access to cold medicine and other basic things, like casts for broken bones. But our dentistry was barbaric (we never heard of anesthesia), and our hospitals were dilapidated, our diagnosis for people over 60 was simply "old age." Anything more complex than appendicitis was a death sentence.

I'm not describing accounts of people who lived a long time ago. I'm describing MY OWN LIFE just 30 years ago. And I'm not an old person. I am 52 years old. And now I'm watching in disbelief how my worst nightmare is creeping back into my life in the United States. My heart breaks for the young people who buy into socialist ideology and in doing so unwittingly devalue the lives of millions who were tortured, exiled, and executed in the name of building a bright socialist future. Someone calculated that if the bodies of people murdered in Russia and China were stacked, they would reach from the Earth to the Moon.

Evidence that socialism and identity politics lead to oppression and mass murder is abundant. Evidence to the contrary is nonexistent. We have already paid a very steep price for this evidence. There isn't a family in the former USSR that did not have at least one family member executed, tortured, or jailed. Oftentimes, all of those. In our family, the socialist terror manifested itself in the tales of two grandmothers: my husband's and mine.

My husband's grandmother, Julietta Oganov, was 12 years old on May 29, 1938 when she was having a dinner with her parents and 5 siblings in their home in Tbilisi, Georgia (which was part of the USSR in 1938). NKVD (interior ministry) agents stormed in that evening, arrested and took away her father, Ervand Oganov. The outcomes of such arrests were predetermined due to the targeted numbers of citizens to be executed or imprisoned in Gulag labor camps as part of Stalin's Great Purge. Two weeks after his arrest, Ervand Oganov was declared an enemy of the people by NKVD Troika, which means "a group of 3." Those groups were used as instruments of extrajudicial punishments—quick and secret executions or imprisonments of "enemies" without trial. The family later learned that someone in the Party wanted to repossess their upright Bluthner piano, which the Party used as evidence that my husband's family was "bourgeois."

Ervand Oganov was never seen or heard from again. His wife lost her mind over the next couple of years and was locked away in a psychiatric ward. My husband's grandmother, then 15 years old, and her younger siblings were evicted. Branded children of an enemy, they had a hard time finding food and a roof over their heads. They survived only due to the incredible strength of my husband's grandmother, who assumed the role of head of household at 15 and carried that role throughout World War II and beyond.

In 1956, eighteen years after Ervand Oganov's arrest and disappearance, his wife received a single paragraph letter stating that her husband was exonerated "due to lack of evidence." There was no apology in the government's letter, but three months later they issued a financial compensation for his life in the amount of a two months salary, computed as of the date of the arrest, adjusted for inflation.

My grandmother, Polina Rogozhnikova, was born in 1923 in the tiny village of Korovino in Kursk, Russia. There were six children in the family and, just like all of their neighbors, this family lead the humble, countryside lifestyle of Russian peasants. From my grandmother's memory, their life was extremely hard – kids of all ages, even toddlers, had to get up at dawn, feed the animals, clean the barn, milk the cow, spin yarn for hours, and work in the field. She recalls that they ate only one big meal a day. Meat and white bread were delicacies she remembered eating only during Easter and Christmas holidays. The most expensive material possessions of the family were a richly bound Bible, several gilded icons, some agricultural tools, and a few items of primitive jewelry, like wedding bands and silver crosses.

You would think that the Bolsheviks' promise of a better life would also mean a better life for this hard-working family. Tragically, it was the opposite. In 1929, the Bolsheviks initiated an unprecedented massive campaign of political repression, including arrests, deportations, and executions of millions of kulaks, or "prosperous peasants," and their families. My family was branded as kulaks and, due to property ownership and the use of hired labor (a couple of paid helpers during the harvest), they were declared class enemies. The true number of those murdered, vanished, and misplaced during the 1929 Bolshevik campaign is unknown, but according to Aleksandr Solzhenitsyn it could be as high as six million. My family of six people is a part of this number.

In early 1933, overnight, their home was raided. They were stripped of their possessions. They were loaded into cattle cars, and they were hauled to Maykuduk, Kazakhstan (which was part of the USSR in 1933). I have always known of this story of Bolshevik dekulakization, but only now, as I write this, did I realize that modern technology (Google maps) could enable me to determine exactly how far away from their home they were taken. It was over 2,000 miles. Imagine, a 2,000-mile journey in cattle cars with small children (my grandmother was the oldest and she was only ten), traveling across the vast steppes of Russia and Kazakhstan in the middle of the winter with no heat. It's hard to imagine how long this trip took, probably a couple of weeks at least, maybe longer. Upon arrival, they were given food enough for a few days and shovels. They had to dig their own dugouts in the frozen tundra and live underground like animals until they could build some barracks using primitive tools and local wood. The degree of suffering these people had to endure was unimaginable. My grandmother lived a long life and to her last breath she never ate a full plate of food at the table. She would always wait for all of us to finish our meals to make sure that there was enough for everyone else and only then would she pick all the scraps from the kids' plates and scrape the plates clean with a crust of bread. Her posttraumatic stress lasted for over 70 years.

Fast forward 85 years from when my and my husband's grandmothers were victimized by socialism. I am sitting on an oceanfront patio at my friends' house in an affluent small town in the South Bay area of Los Angeles. I am listening to their excited conversation about the current political situation in the United States and simply cannot wrap my mind around their passionate support for the Democratic Party, BLM, and other progressive "heroes," destructive events, and Marxist organizations. My friends are typical upper middle class Californians—radical left sympathizers who started from nothing, worked very hard their entire lives to achieve prosperity and social status, dealt with life's hardships, made sacrifices, and are now enjoying the fruits of their labor in their 50s and 60s. You would think that they would have accumulated some wisdom during their life long pursuits of the American dream. Wrong.

Their thinking is an endless oxymoron. They overcame every obstacle in their own lives with ingenuity and perseverance, but believe that it is impossible for some people in our country to obtain a simple government issued ID to cast their vote, so they call it voter suppression. They support defunding the police and ICE, but expand their private security options at the slightest sign of any societal turbulence, and they call 911 to investigate a stolen garden hose. They contribute money to a charity that bails out "peaceful protesters" of the Antifa type, but would not offer a meaningful raise to their own housekeeper or gardener who have worked for them for several years. They are not bad people, but they are blind and deaf, out of touch with reality and absolutely charmed by the socialists' promise of ultimate equality, which they probably envision as a world in which everyone lives in $3 million mansions similar to theirs. To me, these people are not just ignorant and confused – they are dangerous.

When I listen to their conversations, I can't help but remember a book I read years ago which described the horrors of the Russian Revolution of 1917 and the Red Terror, a period of time in Russian history immediately following the revolution. The Red Terror was one of the bloodiest campaigns of political repression and mass murder known to man and was carried out by the Bolsheviks against their political enemies. One chapter of the book described a crowd of drunken sailors ransacking St. Petersburg in the aftermath of the revolution, breaking into the homes of the Russian intelligentsia, raping women, stealing and vandalizing property, and hanging people in their living rooms from their own chandeliers for the "crimes" of being class enemies of the revolution. The imagery of those heinous crimes has stuck with me for life and, unfortunately, I cannot "un-read" the book or "un-imagine" those visuals. The tragic irony: One night the chandelier illuminates a family dinner, at which family members discuss their donations to socialist causes, the next day that same chandelier is used as an execution tool to murder the very people who enabled Marxist ideologues, revolutionary organizers, and those drunken sailors with their own money and support.

How can I explain this to my friends? How can I make it clear to them that this class warfare playbook in 2020 will be the same as it was in 1917? How can I break it to them that the only equality they think they're helping to build will be an equality of poverty, misery, and oppression, a lucky outcome compared to the prospect of being hanged on your own chandelier.

Why are people still duped into accepting socialist ideology? Remember the so-called "shell game?" It has been around since Cleopatra. It has never been anything but a scam. Everyone knows this. But two years ago I saw a tourist pull out a wad of cash from his sock and lose it all to this millennia-old trick on Hollywood Boulevard. To me, socialism is very much like this scam. It promises a lot, but the shell is always empty.

It is indeed a tragedy that people so readily repeat the errors of the past and remain gullible to the false promise of something of value at no cost. Nothing of value comes without a cost. The socialist promise is a mirage and, like many mirages, the reality is one of endless desert with little to quench the thirst and no clear avenue of escape.

THE BOLIVARIAN REPUBLIC OF VENEZUELA

Venezuela has a rocky history replete with decades of political repression and unstable governance, but it had a market economy from the 1910s to the 1950s, and by the mid-1950s, it achieved "a fourth place ranking" in worldwide per capita GDP.[640] Everything changed in 1958, however, when the socialists came to power. Jose Nino records the march to Venezuelan socialism:

> When Venezuela returned to democracy in 1958, it looked like it was poised to begin an era of unprecedented prosperity and political stability. However, Venezeula's democratic experiment was doomed from the start . . . [I]ts very own founder, Romulo Betancourt . . . was an ex-communist who renounced his Marxist ways in favor of a more gradualist approach of establishing socialism. . . [He] believed in a very activist role for the State in economic matters.

* * * *

> Betancourt's administration, while not as interventionist as succeeding . . . governments, capped off several worrisome policies, which included: (1) devaluation of the Venezuelan currency, the Bolivar; (2) failed land reform that encouraged squatting and undermined the property rights of landowners;

[and] (3) the establishment of a Constitutional order based on positive rights and an active role for the Venezuelan state in economic affairs.

Betancourt's government followed-up with considerable tax hikes that saw income tax rates triple to 36%. In typical fashion, spending increases would be accompanied with these tax increases, as the Venezuelan government started to generate fiscal deficits because of its out of control social programs. These growing deficits would become a fixture . . . during the pre-Chavez era.[641]

Hugo Chavez was a socialist, as is his handpicked successor Nicolas Maduro. Chavez inherited from his predecessor Carlos Andres Perez a nationalized oil industry. Perez nationalized that industry in 1975. Over the course of a few decades, Chavez and Maduro succeeded in pillaging oil revenues and redistributing them to select classes within Venezuela, but state management of the oil industry proved inept, incapable of maintaining profitability in an ever-changing global marketplace. As Ivona Iacob explains, Chavez instituted land reforms that confiscated the property of the wealthiest citizens in the country and redistributed it to the poorest.[642] In addition to nationalizing the oil industry, Chavez nationalized the banking, steel, agriculture, gold mining, telecommunications, electricity, tourism and travel, and transportation industries.[643] By 2011, Venezuela had a 27% annual inflation rate. When Chavez died in 2013, inflation stood at 50%. One year later, under Maduro, it grew to 63.4%.[644]

On February 15, 2019, an opinion piece appeared in *USA Today* written by Daniel Di Martino. In 2019, Martino, a Venezuelan expatriate, was a student at Indiana University-Purdue University, Indianapolis. He came to the United States in 2016 at the age of seventeen. In his article, Di Martino explained that when he was fifteen in Caracas in 2014, he remembers standing in line for an hour waiting for groceries and then realizing when he reached the cash register that he forgot to bring with him his government ID. "Without the ID, the government rationing system would not let the supermarket sell my family the full quota of food we needed," he recalled.[645] "It was four days until the government allowed me to buy more."[646] He remembers that following nationalization of the private industries, production levels dropped precipitously, which led to shortages of all kinds, causing long lines to form for the purchase of even basic necessities like "toothpaste or flour."[647] He recalls power outages and water shortages (with running water available for only "about one day per month"[648]) because both had come under government control and resources were no longer available to maintain the electrical grid. "By 2016, my home lost power roughly once a week,"[649] he recalled. The massive government welfare programs and increases in mandatory minimum wages could not be sustained due to the loss of profitable free markets and, so, government payments for those services led "to rampant inflation" with "prices doubl[ing] every few weeks, and the standard of living contin[uing] to plummet."[650] Martino summarizes:

> I watched what was once one of the richest countries in Latin America gradually fall apart under the weight of big government. . . . When Chavez took office in 1999, my parents were earning several thousand dollars a month between the two of them. By 2016, due to inflation, they earned less than $2 a day. If my parents hadn't fled the country for Spain in 2017, they'd now be earning less than $1 a day, the international definition of extreme poverty. Even now, the inflation rate in Venezuela is expected to reach 10 million percent this year. Venezuela has become a country where a woeful number of children suffer from malnutrition, and where working two full-time jobs will pay for only 6 pounds of chicken a month.[651]

Amnesty International has tracked the bleak course of political repression used by Nicolas Maduro to silence dissent from his regime's socialist policies. On February 20, 2019, the organization posted the following account:

> Venezuelan security forces under the command of Nicolás Maduro executed and used excessive force against people, and arbitrarily detained hundreds of others, including teenagers, in an escalation of their policy of repression as a means of controlling the people of Venezuela and particularly to punish residents of impoverished neighborhoods that decided to protest . . .

> The authorities . . . use fear and punishment to impose a repulsive strategy of social control against those who demand change. His government is attacking the most impoverished people that it claims to defend, but instead it murders, detains and threatens . . .

Venezuela has suffered from major human rights violations for years, with shortages of food, medicines, hyperinflation, violence and political repression forcing more than three million people to flee the country since 2015.[652]

Repeatedly, whether the regime leaders call themselves socialists or communists, invariably the shortages of essentials lead people enduring the oppressive weight of government-planned economies to express dissatisfaction. Because dissent threatens government control regimes intent on maintaining socialism and communism, they must depend upon repression, including threats, beatings, arrests, and executions.

THE REPUBLIC OF CUBA

Armando Valladares' account of life in Castro's gulag, *Against All Hope*, should remind us of the excesses that come when protection of individual rights is removed from governance and replaced with protection of "collective rights." Once the legitimacy of government is no longer defined by its proof of commitment to the defense of individual rights, once so untethered, it transgresses into the domain of brute power wielded by those who control the instruments of governance. The glorious promises of the Cuban revolution were dashed from the very moment Fidel Castro assumed dictatorship. Cuban communism, like that of the Bolsheviks described in

Donna Kasseinova's remembrance, was quick to find "enemies" in those with resources and in those who dared voice dissenting viewpoints. Imagine if the censorship now common on America's universities, where speech in favor of the Constitution and free enterprise is denounced by students and faculty, were embodied in law. That is the natural, indeed the inevitable evolution of power, when the rights centric basis of American law is rooted out by the socialists.

Valladares did not believe in communism, but he was a dutiful employee of the Postal Savings Bank. He had "frequently spoken out against communism as a political system because it went against [his] religious beliefs" and his ideals.[653] Without prior notice, one early morning in 1960 Valladares was arrested by Castro's Political Police and taken to Cuba's infamous Isla de Pinos Prison. He spent the next twenty years incarcerated there. Convicted before a revolutionary tribunal with the conviction determined on false charges before he was even tried, Valladares would go on to be tortured, subjected to forced labor, solitary confinement, disease without treatment, and foul food, all because he expressed a dissenting viewpoint, thus making him an enemy of the state. Valladares' treatment came to public attention and became an embarrassment for the Castro regime. In 1982, at the behest of international human rights organizations, Valladares was released. The details of the gross mistreatment he experienced at the hands of agents for an all-powerful socialist state is contained in his chilling autobiographical account, *Against All Hope*.[654]

The pattern of socialist deprivation of individual liberty revealed in the Valladares account in Cuba is mirrored by the experience of Ji Li Jiang in China during the Cultural Revolution.[655]

THE PEOPLES REPUBLIC OF CHINA

It has become a common occurrence for Black Lives Matter and Antifa members to assemble in front of suburban homes in affluent neighborhoods and scream profanities at the occupants and demand that they come out and pledge their support for the Black Lives Matter movement. It has also become common for Black Lives Matter and Antifa members to enter restaurants and outdoor dining areas, confront customers, and demand that they pledge their support for the Black Lives Matter movement, doing so with the threat of violence if the diners' refuse to oblige. There are two essential messages that the rioters are conveying. One is the mantra "black lives matter," which no one of reason disputes (albeit all lives matter, not just those associated with one pigment). Underneath that lies the more important message for the Marxist leaders of the organizations: that private property is not legitimately owned but must be redistributed. And so it is that the BLM protestors yell that the property owned by the people in the suburbs is not really theirs, that it is rightfully the rioters, or that those who chose to pay for a private meal at a restaurant are not entitled to their privacy and not entitled to their meal but that the rioters may take what the private citizens have: It is not rightfully theirs! From the violent demand that no one has a right to private property, it is not a far leap in logic to the conclusion that the mob may take it from the private property owners, may destroy it, or may put it to their own uses.

Those who choose not to respond to the threats with full compliance are excoriated by the mob, ridiculed, spat upon, beaten, robbed or vandalized. In time, if the violence continues to be liberally tolerated by local authorities, the violence will proliferate and escalate. Sooner or later a person who sat down for a family meal at a restaurant or who came home from a day of work to relax in the comfort of a house in the suburbs will face a mortal threat and, if history is our guide, will be physically abused or killed.

Those abuses bring back powerful negative memories for people like Ji Li Jiang. They are the techniques of Maoists in the Cultural Revolution, where the inevitable did happen. Consider the parallels.

In 1966, Ji Li Jiang was twelve and Mao Zedong's Cultural Revolution had just begun.[656]

Ji Li Jiang describes "Class Status" day at her communist school in China when students had to announce whether they were from the working or ruling classes. Those who owned property or whose relatives owned property or had positions where they supervised others were to be denounced and persecuted by the working class.

Yu Jian stood up without hesitation. "My class status is office worker. But before Liberation my father used to be an apprentice. He had to work at the shop counter when he was in his teens, and he suffered all kinds of exploitation by the owner. My father is a member of the Communist Party now, and my mother will join pretty soon." All hands were raised to elect him a Red Successor.

It was [Ji Li Jiang's] turn now. My mind was blank. I did not know what to say. I stood up slowly, the back of my blouse suddenly soaked with sweat.

"My class status is also office worker. My father is an actor . . . ." I stumbled, trying to remember what Yu Jian had said. "He . . . is not a Party member, and neither is my mother. And . . . I don't know what else" I sat down.

"Jiang Ji-li, what is your father's class status?" a loud voice asked.

I slowly stood back up and looked around. Du Hai was staring at me. He sat sideways, one arm resting on the desk behind him.

"My father's class status . . .?" I did not see what Du Hai meant at first . . .

"I know what her grandfather was." [Du Hai] paused dramatically, sweeping his eyes across the class. "He was a—LANDLORD."

"Landlord!" the whole class erupted.

"What's more, her father is a—RIGHTEST."

"Rightest!" The class was in pandemonium.[657]

Ji Li Jiang then documents how her family, because of its property holdings and the positions of its ancestors, became the focal point of class suspicions rendering him a victim in a Cultural Revolution reign of terror, resulting in her father's arrest and imprisonment and in efforts by party representatives to get her to denounce her father and supply evidence against him, supporting the charge that he had a "landlord and rightist mentality."[658]

We see the same kind of scapegoating activity in the BLM organization and Antifa attacks on property owners and private citizens. They demand proof of what they consider to be class, and they demand identity awareness and allegiance to a Marxist ideological message, denouncing all dissent. They condemn property owners and demand that the property be turned over to them, that it is rightfully theirs. They are in line with the communists who victimized Ji Li Jiang and her family, following closely in the vein of those who exploit identity differences as a basis for provoking (and demanding) punitive action to strip those possessed of property of their holdings and publicly humiliate them. The Jiang recollection of Maoist terror is likewise reminiscent of medieval prejudice of the kind revealed in the Salem witch trials (1692–1693).

Authoritarianism shows its darkest side when police power is wedded to market and social control such that it can demand from citizens that they prove their loyalty to the authoritarian cause by condemning people whose only crime is to have disfavored characteristics. That, indeed, is profound prejudice based on class, as ignorant and as malign as any based on race or gender.

Like Ji Li Jiang's story, Nien Cheng endured the horrors of the Cultural Revolution's identity politics. Educated at the London School of Economics, Cheng's crime was to be an employee of Shell Oil Company, to have been educated in the West, and to have lived in a residence that suggested wealth and status. Arrested in 1966 by the Red Guard on false charges of British espionage (said to flow from her London education and her husband's employment at Shell), she would endure brutal deprivation and isolation in captivity as a prisoner, having committed no crime at all. She suffered from repeated interrogations, demands for confession, torture, isolation, and session after session of "re-education." Her daughter was also arrested and incarcerated. It was Cheng's hope in her daughter's survival that inspired her to struggle for survival, despite the harshest conditions. In fact, her daughter was murdered in the same prison for refusing to become a witness against her mother. The death of her daughter, Meiping, was a fact kept from Nien Cheng until her release in 1973, over a decade after her incarceration.

A woman of incredible courage, Nien Cheng at the 1973 end of her ordeal, when told that she could go free, looked her captors in the face and refused to leave the prison until they confessed that she had been wrongfully incarcerated. She writes:

> I was livid. Anger and disgust choked me. While I despised their blatant hypocrisy and shamelessness, I knew deep in my heart that the real culprit was not this man [her Red Guard warden] but the evil system under which we all had to live. I would have to fight, whatever the price, I told myself. I stared back at him and sat down.

> "Haven't you something to say? Aren't you grateful? Aren't you pleased that you can now leave as a free person?" the man said.

> I tried my best to control the rage that made me tremble and said, "I can't accept your conclusion. I shall remain here in the Number One Detention House until a proper conclusion is reached about my case. A proper conclusion must include a declaration that I am innocent of any crime or political mistake, an apology for wrongful arrest, and full rehabilitation. Furthermore, the apology must be published in the newspapers in both Shanghai and Beijing, because I have friends and relatives in both cities. As for the conclusion you just read, it's a sham and a fraud.[659]

Donna Kasseinova, Daniel Di Martino, Armando Valladares, Ji Li Jiang, and Nien Cheng's accounts share a profound truth about socialism and communism and its contrast with the government prescribed by our Constitution with its limits on power. When government replaces the private sector, it inevitably demands compliance to implement the precise commands of the administrative state. In that circumstance, instances of dissent otherwise tolerated as the mark of a robust market of ideas and information threaten fulfillment of the government's uniform commands (becoming obstructions of "justice"). By contrast, when government and the private sector are substantially distinct and the private sector represents the largest faction with the government representing a much smaller faction (one limited in its powers, having no control over the market, and having a rule of law that compels it to protect the rights of individuals), dissent must be tolerated and is commonplace. The people, not the state, are sovereign.

In *The Black Book of Communism*, Stephanie Courtois, Nicolas Werth, Jean-Louis Panné, Andrzej Paczkowski, Karel Bartosek, and Jean-Louis Margolin document the enormous cost in human lives, persecution, loss of individual freedom, loss of employment, and loss of opportunity resulting from communist and socialist regimes worldwide. There has been no force in human history more devastating to human life on the planet than communism and socialism, producing more death and more misery than any other phenomenon, including wars and natural disasters. The Bolshevik Red Terror in Russia killed an estimated two million people between 1917 and 1922. Joseph Stalin's Reign of Terror killed approximately 23.2 million between 1930 and 1938 in the former Soviet Union. Mao Zedong's Great Leap Forward (1959 to 1961) and Cultural Revolution (1966 to 1976) killed a combined 60 million in China. Pol Pot's Khmer Rouge killed approximately 2 million Cambodians between 1975 and 1979. North Korea's communist dictatorship has taken the lives of about 3.2 million.

Professor Rudolph J. Rummel estimates the death toll due to communism to be about 148 million people between 1900 and 1999.[660] The Victims of Communism Foundation conservatively estimates that 100 million have been killed by communist regimes worldwide. *The Black Book of Communism* estimates that figure to be eight-five million to 100 million, explaining, "the Communist record offers the most colossal case of political carnage in history."[661] If the United States leans ever more heavily into socialism, it will add to the tally due to the forced economic changes, which will create mass unemployment, poverty, loss of opportunity, depression, and even death, yielding a rise in misery.

Without freedom, humans fare very poorly indeed. The history of the world has confirmed that fact since the birth of civilization.

The form of government is all-important. Liberty cannot co-exist with socialism. It inures in the republican form of government created by our Constitution. The shift to state ownership, regulation, and control of the market entails not just an assumption of pre-existing operation of enterprise but an infusion of political power to dictate the course of enterprise because the state acts through codified expressions of political will. It is inevitable, then, that when the monopoly of police power under political control, i.e., the state, controls the market, it politicizes the market, making instances of dissent from the politically chosen course an act against the state, inviting those instances to be categorized as crimes. That is the inevitable evolution of a socialist take-over of the United States. As the state gains control over the market, its legal demands carry the force of law, and dissent from those demands is inevitably prosecuted as crime. The universe of private sector freedom shrinks from great to negligible; the American experiment in liberty comes to an end.

The ultimate irony of socialism is its inevitable failure. Promised a workers' paradise and relief from the need to pay for education, healthcare, and survival, the socialist state pillages all sources of wealth, destroys the economic engine of capitalism, and brings down all sources of power competitive with the state. In the end, there is universal mediocrity, mass poverty, depression, and hopelessness, which can itself be the source of a new revolution, one that overthrows the tyranny of socialism and reinstates popular sovereignty and free enterprise. Because the experiment in socialism is always catastrophic, enslaving the people in poverty and misery, it cannot be tolerated indefinitely. The regime in power remains paranoid that the false promises made will be understood to be so by a majority of the people who, at last, will appreciate the lie of socialism. When they inevitably do, the people tend to rise from their poverty, their starvation, and their depression to revolt.

The Democratic Party now wed to socialism plants the seeds of its own destruction. Even if for a season that party succeeds in establishing a socialist state in America on the backs of the most productive elements in society, as it exhausts those elements and goes increasingly into debt, reigniting inflation and destroying value wherever its regulatory tentacles reach, it will be stirring powerful sentiments of opposition. Those will, sooner or later, ignite, culminating in a movement to overthrow the socialist regime and, if we are fortunate, re-establish a government instituted to protect the rights of the governed, both economic and political, such that freedom of choice and free enterprise will be restored. With persistence and good fortune, the Constitution will return.

CHAPTER 15

THE WAY BACK TO LIBERTY AND PROSPERITY

—————

Authoritarians have gained ever-greater control over the instruments of governance in the United States since the end of the Civil War. Bit by bit, from the first major independent regulatory agency, the Interstate Commerce Commission, to the establishment today of a massive administrative state that makes the overwhelming majority of all federal law, the authoritarians have succeeded in removing almost all constitutional barriers to the exercise of tyrannical power. As we witness Marxists rioting in the streets, threatening private property owners, threatening the overthrow of local governments, and promising to topple even the federal government, and as we also witness an entire political party, the Democratic Party, fall under the control of the authoritarians, we should realize that we are on the precipice of change so profound and fundamental as to replace our very form of government, a republic, with a new form, socialism. Those Americans who love liberty now confront a Marxist throng united in their hatred of individual rights, the Constitution, American history, and America itself, and united in their quest to take over all governments, federal, state, and local.

With so many authoritarians active in the streets and in positions of power, how do those of us who cherish liberty and support the Constitution defend life, liberty and property from confiscation and destruction? How do we block the advance of collectivism? How do we ensure fulfillment of the Constitution's Guarantee Clause, whereby in Article IV, Section 4, the United States is to "guarantee in every State in this Union a Republican Form of Government"? The days of taking liberty for granted are over. The modern-day Bolsheviks are literally at the gates. There is no alternative but to become directly involved in local, state, and national politics by uniting with like-minded people who love liberty; arming the freedom-loving citizenry so that all may defend property and liberty from assault; communicating with local, state, and national political leaders so they understand clearly that they are expected to defend life, liberty, and property in all of their official actions; voting in favor of those who will so defend and publicly opposing those who will not; suing to block measures that violate or threaten rights whether from local, state, or federal governments; and educating our youth through sources (such as this book) so they may come to appreciate just how precious their freedoms are and how quickly those freedoms can be taken away and they enslaved by socialist or communist masters, dashing all hopes for self-fulfillment and prosperity.

Organized action is critical. Those of like mind who oppose authoritarianism must not hide from the Marxists who clamor for take-over or from the political creators of an authoritarian state, they must also take to the streets, must defend property against assault, must support the police vocally and insistently, even providing direct financial contributions when municipalities cut off funding, and must use civil litigation against the rioters, tracking them down and making them account for the cost of their acts of destruction. In short, through the use of private detectives, private teams of armed defenders, and private litigation, Americans who love liberty must hold those legally responsible who engage in violence, arson, and looting under the civil law, even if the authorities will not prosecute them under the criminal law.

We must challenge those who seek to destroy liberty in the courts and in Congress; unite in opposition to candidates who favor measures that sacrifice rights; and use every means available to educate youth, voice opposition, and call out all instances of corruption, abuse of power, and crony capitalism.

We will lose our liberties, and may not regain them, unless we oppose those who are untying the United States from its constitutional moorings and transforming the nation into an unlimited socialist government. Here are my recommendations:

1. ***Prepare in advance to defend property against rioters and to obtain and track those responsible for violence, arson, and looting.*** The violence, arson, and looting taking place across the country is meeting with little effective resistance from local and state governments and even from the property owners themselves. Consequently, billions of dollars of property have been lost and, likely, billions more will be lost unless private parties act in instances where the local authorities will not. Everyone who owns commercial or non-commercial property should, at a minimum, obtain and learn how to use nonlethal and lethal weapons for self-defense. Efforts should be made to plan means to deter or rebuff potential assaults. Plans should be made for rapid deployment of armed and trained employees or professional armed guards to use nonlethal weapons in defense of property, and, if necessary, lethal weapons in defense of life. The law affecting use of weapons in each jurisdiction should be carefully studied and followed. In addition, surveillance should be installed to permit monitoring any who trespass and commit acts of violence, arson, and looting. Creative means may be found to encumber those who enter property illegally to afford time for arrest.

2. ***Prepare in advance to sue those who commit acts of violence, arson, and looting.*** Everyone who owns commercial or non-commercial property or who otherwise stands at risk of attack should become familiar with tort law in each jurisdiction. Civil suits should be filed against

those responsible for acts of criminal trespass, violence, arson, and looting. Employing surveillance and tracking, every effort should be made to identify those responsible and then litigate against them. During discovery, every effort should be made to determine if those who have committed the civil wrongs are agents of organizations that have trained, financed or provided weapons to them in support of their acts of violence, arson, and looting, in which case those entities should also be sued, including for civil Racketeer Influenced and Corrupt Organization violations. It is critical that all who engage in civil and criminal wrongs be held to account, and if prosecutors will not pursue criminal charges against the wrongdoers than private parties must pursue civil charges against them, and ideally both criminal and civil charges will be brought.

3. ***Sue organizations that fund and arm rioters and that finance the bail of those who have declared their intent to repeat criminal offenses for civil RICO.*** There is strong evidence that several organizations and groups of individuals have financed and supplied weapons in support of criminal trespass, violence, arson, and looting across the country. There is also strong evidence that several organizations and groups of individuals have paid bail for those incarcerated who have vowed that upon their release they would commit more crimes (and have then made good on their promises). When such organizations finance criminal actions or provide support for them (training rioters, paying for their transportation costs to the locations for a riot, paying for room and lodging of rioters, supplying rioters with weapons, or bailing out rioters who have pledged to commit additional criminal acts upon their release), they oftentimes establish the elements necessary for victims to sue for federal civil Racketeer Influenced and

Corrupt Organizations Act violations. When the evidence meets the elements of the offense, such suits should be filed against these organizations to help recoup the billions lost in property damage.

4. *Sue local and state governments that violate individual rights.* When the predictable consequence of stand down orders in the face of rioting is the loss of property and life, those in government should be held responsible. While precedent concerning sovereign immunity imposes an impediment to successful suit, there are frequently exceptions dependent on the law of each jurisdiction. Government officials who prevent police from defending life and property in the midst of a riot should be made to account for those decisions. If there are exceptions to sovereign immunity within the jurisdictions affected, such as if the government official has acted beyond the scope of his or her official duties or in violation of federal, state, or local law through acts of complicity and support for the rioters, civil suits ought to be filed to make the officials account and pay for their derelictions.

5. *Sue federal government agencies that violate individual rights.* Many of those adversely affected by unconstitutional actions of federal agencies have for too long accepted those impositions rather than litigate against them. We are thus inundated with a complex matrix of overlapping and sometimes contradictory federal regulatory constraints. Many in government favor a substantial and dramatic increase in federal regulatory constraints over all business in the United States. We cannot afford to continue in a complacent and conciliatory manner if we are to avoid a near total loss of individual liberty and property rights. Consequently, when rights are imperiled by government,

those affected need to proceed individually, as businesses, or in industry-wide groups, to challenge the government's actions in court and demand protection for rights. The federal judiciary is populated with many fine jurists who believe in the rule of law and have been appointed largely over the last four years. The Supreme Court likewise now has a majority of jurists who understand the threat posed to liberty and property by the administrative state. Activist judges who view their role as that of a legislature of one are increasingly in the minority in the districts and circuits. Doctrines of judicial deference to administrative agency actions are under assault, with several of the justices of the Supreme Court expressing their disfavor for those doctrines. The time is right to increase litigation against unconstitutional actions by federal agencies. Those harmed by actions of the government should now consider legal steps to vindicate their rights.

6. *Actively and vocally support candidates for Congress and the Presidency who oppose, and support all measures that oppose, vesting power in the administrative state.* When candidates for federal elective office endorse an expansion in regulation, those who cherish liberty should sound the alarm. If we are to reverse the authoritarian takeover of the government, we must begin by giving support to candidates for Congress and the Presidency who oppose, and all congressional measures that oppose, expanding the jurisdiction and power of the administrative state.

7. *Advocate legislation that causes every regulation to be revoked unless passed into law by Congress.* Years ago, Congressman Ron Paul's Chief of Staff, Norm Singleton, and I drafted a bill for Congressman Paul that would cause regulations to be null and void unless codified by

congressional passage within a limited period of time. Were that law to have passed, it would have restored the separation of powers and the substantive meaning of the Constitution's vesting clauses. It would have prevented Congress from avoiding direct responsibility to the electorate for all United States laws, as was constitutionally intended. It would thus ensure that the government was restored to a government based on the consent of the governed.

8. *Advocate legislation that eliminates federal agencies, with the end in view of ending the administrative state entirely.* From its inception to the present, the administrative state has endeavored to overcome the Constitution's barriers to federal power. The administrative state has largely succeeded in attaining that objective. So long as combined legislative, executive, and judicial powers are vested in single entities outside of the Constitution's three branches, the people's liberties will never be safe. It is therefore a constitutional necessity, one consistent with restraining power that invades rights to life, liberty, and property, that we put an end to the administrative state. Legislation is needed to forbid any entity outside of the constitutional branches of government from making law, prosecuting law violations, and adjudicating cases.

9. *Publicly oppose all candidates for elective office on the local, state, and national level who advocate measures that sacrifice rights to life, liberty, and property.* The greatest blessings of liberty come from uniform protection of rights to life, liberty, and property under a consistent body of laws. Candidates who pledge to impose confiscatory taxes, redistribute wealth, and determine which industries may lawfully operate in the United States

are authoritarian in character and enemies of the people's liberties and of a republican form of government. They should be vigorously opposed and defeated on the local, state, and national levels.

10. *Support the Rule of Law and Increased Funding for, and Expansion of, Law Enforcement.* The rioting in urban areas from New York to Seattle is accompanied by official acquiescence in crime, coming in the form of either defunding of the police or reductions in force.[662] In addition, police are increasingly handicapped in their ability to protect themselves and innocent civilians by a host of rules that deny them the discretion to use reactive force in all but the most extreme circumstances.[663] Candidates for local and state office should not be supported unless they commit to the full endorsement of, funding for, and expansion of law enforcement to meet and overcome all threats posed by criminal trespassers, rioters, looters, and arsonists. There needs to be a constant, visible police presence in large numbers throughout the urban areas that are experiencing rioting. Police need to be present in both plainclothes and uniformed divisions, and they need to be given the discretion to interdict acts preparatory to crime (such as the delivery and stockpiling of weapons stashes in the streets; the distribution of weapons; and trespass on private property). The cities need to enforce licensing laws for protests, such that those who intend to protest should first obtain a permit to do so in specifically designated areas subject to reasonable time, place, and manner regulations (such as insistence that protestors not leave public streets made available for the protest and not carry weapons into the protest areas). Protestors should be cabined within the designated public areas, which should be chosen to enable police to assume high vantage points (such as the roofs of

buildings) to enable surveillance and rapid interdiction to stop crime. Law enforcement should be given discretion in the field to arrest every individual in the first instance of criminal activity (e.g., in the first instance of criminal trespass or the throwing of an incendiary device or projectile at police or at property).

Laws should be changed to stiffen the penalties associated with insurrection and prosecutions should be thorough and aimed at achieving lengthy sentences to serve as a deterrent. There should be aggravated penalties and time associated with any act of violence that injures a person or destroys property. Laws should be changed to compel that those who cause damage to property or injury be required to pay restitution in the form of economic damages to the property owners and victims or, if victims are deceased, to their families.

New laws should be passed on the local, state, and national levels to protect law enforcement and the national guard from verbal and physical abuse when that abuse interferes with law enforcement efforts, such as when individuals stand within inches of officers in riot formation and scream at them, spit at them, aim or hurl weapons at them, or direct lasers at their eyes. Police should be given the discretion to make prompt arrests when any such assaults occur and the penalties associated with the actions should provide for at least felony convictions and jail time. The public should support the police and provide them with shelter and protection as needed during times of riot. Localities should amass a sufficient force to double the manpower needed to repulse and combat anticipated violence. Police should never be outnumbered by rioters and should never be denied the full panoply of nonlethal and lethal weapons they may need to repulse any attack on life and property.

11. *Support measures to restore cash bail and make it a felony to contribute money to pay bail for another.* Several jurisdictions have eliminated cash bail, enabling even those accused of violent crimes to go back on the street within hours of arrest and commit new crimes. New York is one of those jurisdictions.[664] Organizations have been formed nationwide, including, e.g., the Minnesota Freedom Fund, and The Bail Project, which pay the bail of rioters. Several hardened criminals have been released back on the streets following arrest because of those payments, and, predictably, some have committed new and heinous crimes following their release. For example, Jaleel Stallings was arrested and charged with attempted murder of a policeman, allegedly having shot a policeman in his squad car with an AK-47-style Draco pistol. Stallings' $75,000 bail was paid by the Minnesota Freedom Fund.[665] Television Station KMSP, St. Paul, Minnesota, reported that the Minnesota Freedom Fund bailed out several people charged with violent crimes, including a woman accused of killing a friend (paying $100,000 for her release) and a twice convicted rapist who was charged with kidnapping, assault, and sexual assault in two separate cases (paying $350,000 for his release).[666] Samuel Lee Scott of St. Louis was released after The Bail Project paid his bail and, thereafter, allegedly murdered his wife. Christopher Stewart of Chicago who was charged with firing a gun at a children's party was released after The Bail Project paid his bail and, thereafter, allegedly committed an act of arson, setting his ex-girlfriend's apartment on fire. The Bail Project paid for at least 12,096 people to be released at a cost of over $26 million.[667] To ensure that those accused of violent crimes and rioting remain in the criminal justice system pending their preliminary hearings and are not released when payments are made by others, laws restoring cash bail and making it a felony to contribute money to pay bail for another need to be passed in every state.

12. ***Support measures to end early release of those arrested for any crime pending a trial on the merits.*** Society bears an unreasonable risk when those arrested for a crime are allowed back on the streets before a trial on the merits.[668] To prevent that risk, laws need to be passed in every state revoking laws that permit early release of those arrested and requiring that those arrested be detained pending a bail hearing and a speedy trial on the merits.

13. ***Support making it a crime punishable by life imprisonment to knowingly provide another with an article for use as an offensive weapon in rioting.*** Rioters in multiple jurisdictions have been supplied with improvised weapons in advance of protest events to aid and support violence, criminal trespass, assaults on police, looting, and arson.[669] Among the items supplied include large quantities of bricks, baseball bats, boards with nails driven through them, bottles filled with ice, commercial fireworks, improvised explosive devices, and Molotov cocktails, among others. To help prevent this arming of rioters in advance of protests, laws need to be passed in every state increasing the penalty to life imprisonment for each instance in which a person or group is proven to have knowingly supplied another with an article for use as an offensive weapon in rioting.

14. ***Support increasing the penalty to life imprisonment without a possibility of parole for arson and to double that penalty for those who commit arson and any act of assault, murder, mayhem, destruction of property, or looting.*** Rioters in multiple jurisdictions have committed extremely destructive acts of arson, including burning buildings with people inside, including children.[670] To help prevent this criminal activity, heightened penalties are

needed. Laws should be passed in each state imposing a penalty of life imprisonment without a possibility of parole for any engaged in arson and double life sentences without a possibility of parole for those who commit arson and any act of assault, murder, mayhem, destruction of property, or looting in addition to the specific acts of arson.

15. *Support the Second Amendment right to keep and bear arms and anti-mob legislation.* All Americans not disqualified by mental illness or prior conviction should be armed and become proficient in the use of non-lethal and lethal weapons for self-defense. The spreading of violence combined with official disallowance of police to prevent destruction and loss of life places every American on notice that he or she may be required to defend life and property against assault from mobs and armed individuals. Consequently, to protect life and property, each American needs to become proficient in the use of non-lethal and lethal weapons for self-defense and knowledgeable of the laws concerning the use of force in self-defense in each jurisdiction. In addition, each American should press for passage of anti-mob legislation that expands the right to use lethal force from defense of life to defense of private property when trespassers refuse to vacate private property on request, create a violent or disorderly assembly on private property, vandalize, or engage in arson.

16. *Educate youth of the true history of the United States (such as that contained in this book), so they are not deceived by an educational establishment committed to a collectivist agenda.* This book contains a concise history of authoritarian threats to Americans' liberties and the foundational principles of the Declaration of Independence and the Constitution intended to eliminate

those threats. It is the side of the story that children in public schools do not receive today but desperately need to know. It is the lesson they must be taught, so that they can be inspired to appreciate the freedoms they have and the threats to those freedoms, and be vigilant in defense of those freedoms and in opposition to the authoritarians who are working to take the freedoms away.

17. *Voice opposition to, and call out, all instances of government corruption, abuse of power, and crony capitalism.* As this book reveals, with the elimination of the Constitution's barriers on government power and with the growth of the administrative state, justice itself has been denied in case after case and corruption has become ubiquitous in government. Those abuses should be called out by the victims, and broadcast by those who cherish liberty, so the wrongs can be investigated, those responsible prosecuted, and justice restored. The administrative state is, as the evidence marshaled here supports, endemically corrupt and a party to protectionism, crony capitalism. By publicizing the abuses and demanding an end to them and by prosecuting those who have broken the law, the rule of law and government accountability can be restored.

18. *Vote in favor of candidates committed to, and measures supportive of, restoration of the limited federal republic prescribed by the Constitution.* We need constitutionalists on the federal court but also in Congress and the White House. We need all who swear an oath to uphold the Constitution to mean it, and to show they mean it by favoring measures designed to restore the limits on government power prescribed in the Constitution. Every citizen can do his or her part by actively supporting candidates for elective office who commit to, and support,

all measures aimed at restoring the limited federal republic defined in the Constitution.

19. ***Support state nullification of federal laws that exceed constitutional limits.*** When the federal government enacts sweeping legislation that eliminates free markets, compels citizens to enter interstate commerce through the purchase of specific kinds of goods or services, or imposes mandates that otherwise transform the states into governments not of a republican form or into mere functionaries of the federal government, the states should avoid compliance, protect their citizens, and sue to enjoin the federal action. The Guarantee Clause must have meaning and no state should be compelled to alter its republican form to accommodate a socialist agenda.

20. ***Oppose public school intolerance of views supportive of the Constitution and the Bill of Rights and public school propaganda that asserts the false dogma that the United States is systemically racist.*** The public schools have become breeding grounds for hatred against the United States, the Constitution, the founding fathers, and limited government. They often instill Marxist principles supportive of a socialist state. Parents of school age children must act to oppose that agenda, demand accurate historical education of the underpinnings of the Constitution and the Bill of Rights, and demand that teachers avoid insinuating their own political views into the classroom to encourage student support for radical political causes, and sometimes violence.

If the United States is transformed by governing elites into a socialist state, the nation will experience the devastation and misery that has marked other socialist and communist nations worldwide. Unlike the rest of the world, we have been blessed with the promise of the Declaration and with a Constitution that protects the rights of the governed. That Constitution is anathema to the administrative state and to socialism. The Constitution is revered by most Americans. All Americans alive today have experienced the blessings of freedom in the market, of capitalism, and of self-determination. When they groan under confiscatory taxation, unemployment arising from market destructive regulation, and loss of opportunity from opportunity foreclosing regulations, they are likely not to groan indefinitely without taking action, but it is critical that they understand why it is that they suffer. The greatest hope is that from any such period of darkness, they may recall the blessings of liberty and the governmental form that brought them prosperity and will then unite to overcome wayward experiments in socialism to restore the government to its republican form.

There can be no secure protection for the rights to life, liberty, and property without a rule of law that is consistently applied without regard to race, creed, color, or religion and against all equally who violate those rights. Every measure to reduce rights protective policing, increase early release of the accused, and avoid imposition of strict penalties against those who violate rights to life, liberty, and property encourages more felonious behavior, indeed encourages the disintegration of the rule of law and society itself. Consequently, every effort should be undertaken to support passage of new state and local laws that heighten the penalties for acts of violence from rioters. Moreover, police need to be equipped with every means necessary to combat rioting, including the most effective and efficient non-lethal and lethal weapons.

The way back to liberty depends on elimination of the administrative state, restoration of all limits on power and in defense of individual rights as prescribed by the Constitution, and restoration of the rule of law. Americans who have watched in horror the movement to destroy the nation must stop watching and start acting to prevent that destruction.

CHAPTER 16
CONCLUSION

———————

Those who favor authoritarian power in government, regardless of their stripe (whether Progressives, Socialists, or Communists) have a long history in the United States, dating back to the Hegelians who justified slavery in the antebellum South. They now stand before us as the Black Lives Matter organization, as Antifa, and as the faction controlling the Democratic Party. Just like their intellectual forebears, they mean to transform the government of the United States from one under the Constitution to one against it; from one that protects individual liberty to one that dictates which endeavors each of us may pursue; from one that does not impose confiscatory taxes and defends rights to private property to one that imposes those taxes and violates those rights; from one that allows workers and entrepreneurs to keep the fruits of their labors to one that confiscates those fruits and redistributes them to politically preferred constituencies; and from one that vests sovereignty in the individual to one that vests sovereignty in the state.

We are witnessing the destruction of the last remaining protections of individual liberty. Assaults that were incremental have now become constant and comprehensive. We may still reverse the course, and restore a Constitution of liberty, but it will take the dedicated and persistent efforts of all true friends of liberty in accordance with the agenda provided in Chapter

15. As we make those efforts, we need to be mindful of a prophetic truth Ronald Reagan gave us on October 27, 1964 at the Republican National Convention:

> Freedom is never more than one generation away from extinction. We didn't pass it to our children in the bloodstream. It must be fought for, protected, and handed on for them to do the same, or one day we will spend our sunset years telling our children and our children's children what it was once like in the United States where men were free.[671]

We owe it to our children to teach them the blessings of liberty and the misery that comes when liberty is taken away. We owe it to them to teach them that we may not take liberty for granted because those who lust for power and seek to use it to acquire control over other people's lives, liberties, and properties are forever present in government. We need to explain to them the remarkable, indeed extraordinary and miraculous, founding history of the nation, revealing to them the greatness of the founding generation, a generation that did not use the power of governance to deprive the people of their rights and gave up power repeatedly despite numerous opportunities to accumulate it and abuse it.

THE AMERICAN FOUNDERS' LEGACY OF GOVERNMENT WITHIN CONSTITUTIONAL LIMITS

The Constitutional Convention from May 25 to September 17, 1787 produced a historic achievement in the evolution of humankind. At no time before did representatives of the people adopt a written constitution aimed fundamentally at protecting the rights of the governed, doing so by, in Thomas Jefferson's words, binding men "down from mischief by the chains of the Constitution." At all times prior and since, revolutions have been driven by authoritarians who, with demagoguery and insincerity, have promised an end to all human suffering and material want through a legally enforced equality achieved by state control of enterprise and redistribution of income (e.g., the French Revolution; the Bolshevik Revolution; the Maoist

Revolution; and the Revolucion Cubana), only to betray those promises, as the authoritarians invariably have used their monopoly of state power to pillage all sources of private wealth, deny all basic liberties, ban all forms of dissent, and enslave the people to fulfill their selfish ambitions.

By contrast, the Constitution of 1787 uniquely represents the product of a revolution where the promise that government would protect the people's political and economic liberties was actually kept, a unique occurrence in the history of the world. Indeed, the Constitution of the United States was (and remains) the only government charter predicated on the notion that government is powerless to deprive people's rights because those rights are neither the government's to give nor the government's to take away; rather, they are pre-political and "unalienable," given to each not by the state but by God. The idea of pre-political, God-given rights which render the people sovereign and make just government possible only with the people's consent is the genius of that political philosopher the founders most often relied upon to create the Constitution, John Locke. Under Locke's construct, it is the solemn and unalterable duty of government to protect the rights given man by God. Indeed, not to do so is tyranny and justifies revolution.

As Alexander Hamilton explained of the Constitution: "I never expect to see a perfect work from imperfect man,"[672] but he regarded the Constitution of the United States as perfect a charter in defense of individual liberties as could be imagined. He wrote that although the Constitution "may not be perfect in every part, [it] is, upon the whole, a good one; is the best that the present views and circumstances of the country will permit; and is such a one as promises every species of security which a reasonable people can desire."[673] And while the art of the possible did not permit immediate resolution of the slavery question, the Declaration and the Bill of Rights compelled that resolution to be had, and it was, in a bloody conflict that nearly destroyed the Union, the Civil War.

This innovation in government, a limited federal republic, is a startling redefinition of the relationship between man and the state, antithetical to the Divine Right of Kings defended by Sir Robert Filmer in his *Patriarcha*, the principal work against which Locke opined in his second treatise on government. The innovation of limited republican government came as a shock to the eighteenth-century world and has remained a unique proof of the triumph of liberty to people everywhere ever since. The extreme humility of those who were elected to power in the fledgling republic, to disclaim that power after limited terms to protect the people's liberties, was indeed so peculiar that it seemed impossible to believe to a keen observer of the American Revolution, King George III of England.

As Jeremy Black explains, rather than delegate away the issue of the rebellious colonies to his ministers, George III "kept a close eye on the details of activities linked to the [Revolutionary] war"[674] which remained "central to [his] thoughts."[675] Indeed, in no small measure, King George staked the future of his government under Lord Frederick North, Prime Minister, on the success of the crown's efforts to reprove the King's "rebellious children."[676] Once colonial representatives became convinced that separation from Great Britain was a necessity, they shifted their blame for the acts against them from Parliament and the King's ministers to the King himself (as revealed in the Declaration of Independence), he having ignored their repeated entreaties to remove the yoke of tyranny from around their necks.

Thomas Paine's *Common Sense* was the most widely distributed publication in the colonies in the late 1770s. John Adams wrote of it: "Without the pen of the author of *Common Sense*, the sword of Washington would have been raised in vain." *Common Sense* received wide distribution outside the colonies, throughout Europe and particularly in Paris and London. Historians regard it as the most influential pamphlet in turning the colonial mind against the crown and in favor of revolution.[677] Indeed, the effect of the American Revolution on the world placed Thomas Jefferson in the unique role of counselor to budding revolutionaries who meant to replicate the struggle for freedom in their own countries, including in Russia, Poland, Greece, and South America. In a June 1, 1795 letter to Tench Coxe, Thomas Jefferson wrote: "[T]his ball of liberty, I believe most piously, is now so well in motion that it will roll around the globe, at least the enlightened part of it, for light & liberty go together. It is our glory that we first put it into motion."[678] Tragically, no country of the world could replicate the American experiment in limited government as each (even intent at the start on a rights revolution) veered predictably to authoritarianism. The unity of the American mind on the principles of revolution never let up, as the influential works of Thomas Paine make clear.

In *Common Sense*, Paine not only condemned monarchy, associating it with tyranny but also the person of George III, a serious offense of seditious libel against the crown. In attempts to avoid prosecution, critics of the crown in England and the colonies ordinarily cast aspersion upon the administration through indirect prose, doing so vaguely (never naming the King). Paine did not disguise his contempt. Rather, he waxed bold referring to George III by name as "the greatest enemy this continent hath,"[679] as that "hardened, sullen-tempered Pharaoh of England,"[680] and as a "wretch,"[681] among other choice epithets. He explained that the King "hath wickedly broken through every moral and human obligation, trampled nature and conscience beneath his feet; and by a steady and constitutional spirit of insolence and cruelty, procured for himself a universal hatred."[682]

Paine's message and the immortal Declaration of Independence met with endorsements from American Whigs in words and deeds. On July 9, 1776, after the New York colonial assembly endorsed the Declaration before a body comprised of members of the public and troops gathered in the common, "the inhabitants of New York City pulled down a gilded equestrian statue of . . . King [George III] erected on Bowling Green in 1770 (its metal was to be used for cartridges) . . ."[683] The statue stood immediately outside the front door of General Washington's headquarters "on lower Broadway, right beside the Battery."[684] Soldiers who were read the Declaration became fleet of foot, barreling down Broadway from the common. They decapitated the statue, parading George III's gilded "head around town to the lilting beat of fifes and drums," melting the entire "four thousand pounds of gilded lead in the statue [into] 42,088 musket bullets" destined for the King's regulars, the red coats.[685]

He who drafted *The American Crisis* on the head of a drum at Valley Forge, and stayed with the troops through that terrible campaign, Paine was so committed to individual rights against authoritarian governments that he daringly returned to England thereafter and worked on his seminal *The Rights of Man* favoring republican revolution and condemning key figures in the British state, right under his Majesty's nose. Anxious to seize that man who since 1776 so vexed him and had maintained such effrontery to the crown, George III demanded that Paine be arrested and hanged. Paine was convicted of seditious libel in 1792 in absentia. Before he could be arrested, apparently on word of the attempt, Paine fled to Paris (as the radical Whig John Wilkes had done decades before and was likewise convicted for seditious libel in absentia).

In Paris, Paine was greatly celebrated and elected to the French Assembly. He became a partisan in the French revolution. Robespierre's Jacobins turned against Paine, falsely labeling him a royalist. They convicted him for treason and incarcerated him in Luxembourg Prison (formerly a palace). They sentenced him to die by guillotine. Paine remained jailed in strangely luxurious accommodations, a palace room. He was allowed to roam about the palace grounds at will during the day but was obliged to return to his room at night. He stayed in comfortable confinement from December 28, 1793 until November 4, 1794, awaiting execution. He received a last-minute reprieve in July 1794 because he was severely ill, which his captors thought sufficient to warrant a delay in the public guillotine spectacle, and then he received a second and final reprieve in November of that year when the future President James Monroe negotiated his diplomatic release and return to the United States.

Many contemporaries were intrigued by the American cause, by heroic figures like the signers of the Declaration of Independence, by General George Washington, and by the pamphleteer and political agitator Thomas Paine. The American Revolution became a *cause celebre* among old European elites who doubted the sincerity of the revolutionary leaders' motivations and believed invariably that George Washington would become intoxicated with power, betray his promise to protect the people's liberties, and assume an authoritarian role, that of absolute monarch or military dictator (like Oliver Cromwell or Napoleon Bonaparte). George III was one of those who suspected as much.

In 1783, the King had an interchange with the American artist Benjamin West then living in London, who was among the King's favorites (appointed historical painter to the court and Surveyor of the King's Pictures). The Revolutionary War had just ended. The King asked West what would become of Washington now, apparently presuming the victor of Yorktown would choose to become a King or a military dictator. "They say he will return to his farm," said West. Flabbergasted, doubting that Washington would miss his chance to become an absolute ruler, George III responded: "If he does that, he will be the greatest man in the world."

The King's statement disclosed not only his suspicion that the rumor about George Washington's plans had to be false but also his high regard for the profound humility it would reveal if it happened to be true. Did Washington sincerely believe Paine's appeal in *Common Sense*: "For in absolute governments the King is law, so in free countries the law ought to be King; and there ought to be no other."[686] Washington did.

On December 23, 1783, at the Maryland State House in Annapolis, the Commander-in-Chief of the Continental Army, then the most popular man in America, if not in the world, appeared not for the purpose of proclaiming himself America's Caesar but to resign his commission and return to a life of repose on his farm at Mount Vernon. "Having now finished the work assigned to me," he said, "I retire from the great theater of action; and bidding an affectionate farewell to this august body under whose orders I have so long acted, I here offer my commission, and take leave of all the employments of public life." He would not be America's dictator. He remained loyal to the cause of liberty, removing the United States from the ordinary plight of the other nations of the world, establishing it uniquely to be a nation that would keep the people sovereign and the state their servant.

Word that indeed Washington had relinquished public life, fame, and the opportunity to seize absolute power left George III astonished and puzzled. His infatuation with Washington grew even more. When he ultimately suffered from delusions during the regency crisis of 1788 and 1789 (either from severe porphyria or arsenic poisoning from its presence in his whig), George III revealed in his addled state the extent of his obsession. Ron Chernow writes:

> [I]n late February [1789] . . . Gouverneur Morris reported
> from Paris an unlikely development in the King's madness.
> "By the bye," he wrote to Washington, "in the melancholy

situation to which the poor King of England has been reduced, there were, I am told, in relation to you, some whimsical circumstances." In a deranged fit, wrote Morris, the King had "conceived himself to be no less a personage than George Washington at the head of the American Army. This shows that you have done something or other which sticks most terribly in his stomach."[687]

General Washington faced two undeniable opportunities in 1783 to lead a military coup to become America's King or dictator, one at Newburgh, New York in March of 1783, and the other at Philadelphia, Pennsylvania, in June of 1783. The most popular man in America, he could seize power, proclaim himself King, and crush all dissent with the loyalty of a very large faction of the Continental Army that fought under him, nearly all of whom were upset because the Continental Congress owed them pensions which had been left unpaid for years. The officers at Newburgh were prepared to urge Washington to seize power or, if not him, General Horatio Gates, but Washington would not hear of it, steadfastly refusing to add his weight to the insurrection, committed unalterably to the principle of American liberty, to the experiment in limited government then unfolding, with no treasonous bone in his body and no desire for personal aggrandizement at the public's expense.

At Newburgh, Washington learned of an attempted mutiny by high ranking officers to force Congress into paying its due to the army, and he quickly acted to suppress the plot by calling a meeting in a building appropriately called the Temple of Virtue. Ron Chernow explains Washington's actions:

> He pleaded with them to oppose any man "who wickedly attempts to open the floodgates of civil discord and deluge our rising empire in blood." Give Congress a chance to address your grievances, he implored the officers, saying he would do everything in his power to help them. Then, in ringing tones, he said that if they trusted Congress to take

action, "you will, by the dignity of your conduct, afford occasion for posterity to say, when speaking of the glorious example you have exhibited to mankind, 'Had this day been wanting, the world had never seen the last stage of perfection to which human nature is capable of attaining.'"[688]

Ever mindful of the precedential effect of his actions, Washington meant for the world to see "the last stage of perfection to which human nature is capable of attaining," a government for the first time on earth dedicated to the protection of the unalienable rights of the people. His mission would not be diverted for selfish causes even if the need was great and, in that, he indeed served posterity selflessly, courageously, and magnificently.

In Philadelphia, the scene would repeat itself on June 20, 1783, but this time to the point of near-complete effectuation. Some 400 former Continental Army soldiers brandishing muskets descended on the Philadelphia Statehouse in which the Continental Congress had convened. The mutineers demanded Congress vote to provide them the back pay they were owed. They threatened to hold Congress hostage until the bill to finance them was passed. The members of Congress urgently requested that the state government of Philadelphia send a force to expel the invaders, but the state would not. Congress then disbanded and moved to Princeton, New Jersey, and thereafter to Annapolis, Maryland, and then to New York City before finally resting in the District of Columbia. The former Continental Army soldiers gave up the enterprise on June 25, 1783. Some of the mutineers were prosecuted and convicted, but they were pardoned by a vote of the Continental Congress. Had Washington been intent on leading a revolution to install himself as an absolute monarch or dictator, the Philadelphia mutiny provided that alternative, but he remained adamantly opposed to any effort to upset the experiment in constitutional government.

That steadfast and repeated refusal to become an authoritarian ruler of America shocked elites the world round not only at these junctures but also at Washington's refusal to serve more than two terms as President. Jeremy Black records:

> George Washington's willingness to give up power and not to seek a presidency for life was important to the creation of the particular American combination of elected legitimacy and responsible stability. There was to be no military dictatorship, and thus no equivalent to the Cromwellian Protectorate or to Bonapartism, in the USA. . . . Given [American revolutionary] assumptions, it was unlikely that Washington would put himself at the head of the officers at Newburgh who, in the winter of 1782–3, considered intimidating Congress into granting concessions over pensions, nor at the head of the troops in June 1783 who briefly held Congress hostage.[689]

George Washington was not alone in his selfless commitment to ensuring the success of America's experiment in a limited government in defense of the people's liberties. The actions of the founding fathers in the American Revolution until the adoption of the Constitution in 1788 and ratification of the Bill of Rights in 1791 reveal in their correspondence, their public deliberations, and their craftsmanship endless agonizing over how best to ensure the protection of individual liberty and to guard against tyranny.

The Constitution itself is a brilliant manifestation of sincere sentiments to create a government that would not invade the people's liberties. In their correspondence, Thomas Jefferson and James Madison worried that "parchment barriers" might not be enough against the inevitable self-serving designs of governors and wondered if the limitations on power and the system of checks and balances built into the Constitution would, over time, continue to be respected enough to counteract evil measures by those who aimed to maximize their political and personal fortunes. They left us with a near-perfect document in defense of liberty, one that held out the promise of guarding against tyranny, if only those who governed would respect the primacy of individual liberty, and if only the public would remain forever vigilant in defense of their liberties. It was a tall order, and they knew it.

The founding fathers well understood that with power beyond constitutional limits comes corruption, as those obsessed with the luxury of using other people's money (tax dollars) and a monopoly on police power invariably advance their own self-interests at public expense. This corruption in fact mirrors the essential agenda of the authoritarians who, as we have seen, overcame the Constitution's rule of law to create an extra-constitutional administrative state to pursue their own self-interests through the unelected and unaccountable rulers of that state.

THE MODERN POLITICAL REALITY OF UNLIMITED GOVERNMENT AND UNLIMITED CORRUPTION

We need not look back far in our nation's history to see direct evidence of abuses tied to unchecked power assumed by those in the highest offices of the federal government. During the Obama Administration, then-Vice President Joe Biden's son, Hunter Biden; brother James Biden; and sister-in-law Sara Biden profited at the expense of the nation, reaping windfalls based on a massive influence-peddling scheme tied to countries that are adversaries of the United States. The evidence confirms that then-Vice President Joe Biden and President Barack Obama, along with Secretary of State John Kerry, were warned of the apparent conflicts of interest by staff who received reports but did nothing to stop them, thus becoming complicit in them.[690] Likewise, former Secretary of State Hillary Rodham Clinton, candidate for President in 2016, conspired with President Barack Obama, Vice President Joe Biden, Director of National Intelligence James Clapper, FBI Director James Comey, and CIA Director John Brennan to propound a false Russian collusion narrative against first candidate and then President Donald J. Trump in an effort to divert attention away from Clinton's own mishandling of State Department emails and collusion with Ukranian and Russian operatives through former and discredited MI-6 agent Christopher Steele.[691] Because both events are profound examples of more widespread corruption within our bloated federal government, both are worthy of careful consideration.

As an initial matter, the stark contrast with the example of George Washington could not be greater. The widespread corruption of the executive branch, revealing extensive self-dealing, dishonors his legacy, breaks trust with the American people, and is compounded by the fact that not only the principals but also numerous sub-actors within the government, through their failure to reveal the illegalities or resign from office after nothing was done to stop them, contributed to the taint of the executive branch and cabinet-level departments.

On September 23, 2020, the US Senate Committee on Finance, chaired by Senator Charles Grassley, released a report entitled "Hunter Biden, Burisma, and Corruption: The Impact on U.S. Government Policy and Related Concerns." The report describes a series of transactions in which the Vice President's son became the recipient of large sums of money from entities and individuals in countries adverse to the United States.

Hunter Biden became a member of the Board of Directors of a Ukrainian energy company called Burisma and received millions of dollars from a corrupt Ukrainian oligarch, Mykola Zlochevsky. Through various corporate entities, Hunter Biden engaged in transactions that netted millions for the Biden family (not only for Hunter himself but also for Joe Biden's brother James and his sister-in-law Sara) along with former Secretary of State John Kerry's stepson, Chris Heinz. Those deals involve, among others, China, Russia, and Kazakhstan.[692]

Because Vice President Biden was tasked by President Obama with overseeing U.S. foreign policy toward Ukraine, the tens of thousands of dollars in payments from the Ukrainian oligarch to his son raise major conflicts of interest concerns voiced directly to the administration by staff but left unheeded. The financial ties undermined U.S. State Department efforts to dissuade the Ukrainian government from corrupt practices involving the Burisma energy company, culminating in the well-televised action of Biden wherein he threatened to withdraw $1 billion in United States loan guarantees if the Ukrainian President did not immediately fire that country's Prosecutor General who planned a corruption investigation of Burisma in which his son then served as a board member. Among the report's key findings are the following: (1) "In early 2015 the former Acting Deputy Chief of Mission at the U.S. Embassy in Kyiv, Ukraine, George Kent, raised concerns to officials in Vice President Joe Biden's office about the perception of a conflict of interest with respect to Hunter Biden's role on Burisma's board. Kent's concerns went unaddressed, and in September 2016, he emphasized in an email to his colleagues [that] 'the presence of

Hunter Biden on the Burisma board was very awkward for all U.S. officials pushing an anticorruption agenda in Ukraine'"; (2) "In October 2015, senior State Department official Amos Hochstein raised concerns with Vice President Biden, as well as with Hunter Biden, that Hunter Biden's position on Burisma's board enabled Russian disinformation efforts and risked undermining U.S. policy in Ukraine"; (3) "In addition to over $4 million paid by Burisma for Hunter Biden's and [Devon] Archer's [the Yale roommate of Secretary of State John Kerry's stepson, Chris Heinz] board memberships, Hunter Biden, his family, and Archer received millions of dollars from foreign nationals with questionable backgrounds"; (4) "Hunter Biden received a $3.5 million wire transfer from Elena Baturina, the wife of the former mayor of Moscow"; (5) "Hunter Biden opened a bank account with Gongwen Dong to fund a $100,000 global spending spree with James Biden [the brother of Joe Biden] and Sara Biden"; and (6) "Hunter Biden had business associations with Ye Jianming, Gongwen Dong, and other Chinese nationals linked to the Communist government and the People's Liberation Army[;] [t]hose associations resulted in millions of dollars in cash flow."

The Senate Finance Committee uncovered a series of transactions, which reveal that Hunter Biden profited from his association with his father, then-Vice President Joe Biden. Further, Biden and Kerry were aware of the financial associations, despite initial denials, and did nothing to stop them, enabling Hunter Biden, Chris Heinz, and Biden college friend Devon Archer to make millions of dollars from adversaries of the United States.

Concerning Secretary of State John Kerry, the Committee specifically found his denials of knowledge that his stepson Chris Heinz, Hunter Biden, and Devon Archer were involved with Burisma Holdings and the corrupt Ukrainian oligarch Zlochevsky were patently false. The Committee concluded: "Former Secretary Kerry's December 2019 denial of having any knowledge about Hunter Biden or Burisma is inconsistent with the evidence uncovered by the Committees. Kerry was briefed about Hunter Biden, Burisma, and Heinz the day after Burisma announced Hunter Biden joined its board. Additionally, Secretary Kerry's senior advisor sent him press clips and articles relating to Hunter Biden's board membership. This appears to be yet another example of high-ranking Obama administration officials blatantly ignoring Hunter Biden's association with Burisma."

The Committee found that Hunter Biden, Chris Heinz, and Devon Archer profited directly from a sale of an American aviation company possessed of technology with military applications to a Chinese-government owned company.

> [T]he Henniges transaction . . . was an Obama-era Committee on Foreign Investment in the United States (CFIUS) approved transaction which gave control over Henniges, an American maker of anti-vibration technologies with military applications, to a Chinese government-owned aviation company and a China-based investment firm with established ties to the communist Chinese government. One of the companies involved in the Henniges transaction was a billion-dollar private investment fund called Bohai Harvest RST (BHR). BHR was reportedly formed in November 2013 by a merger between Chinese government-linked firm Bohai Capital and a U.S. company named Rosemont Seneca Partners. Rosemont Seneca Partners was reportedly formed in 2009 by Hunter Biden, the son of then-Vice President Joe Biden, by Chris Heinz, the stepson of former Secretary of State John Kerry, and by others.

The Committee found that the State Department under Secretary John Kerry was directly responsible for approving the Henniges' transaction despite the evidence of conflicts of interest and the threat to national security, explaining that "[t]he potential conflict of interest in this case was particularly troubling given Hunter Biden's history of investing in and collaborating with Chinese companies, including at least one that clearly poses significant national security concerns." That history preceded and followed the 2015 Henniges' transaction. The Committee found that despite direct media inquiries about the conflicts of interest involving Hunter Biden profiting from associations with known adversaries of the United States, including the Ukrainian oligarch, the Chinese communist government, Kazakh nationals, and the Russian government, the Obama Administration persistently denied the existence of the conflicts and did nothing to stop the profiteering activities by Hunter Biden, James Biden, Sara Biden, Chris Heinz, and Devon Archer.

In March 2016, when Hunter Biden was on the Burisma Holdings board of directors (receiving approximately $83,000 a month[693] despite no knowledge of the business of Burisma (energy production and exploration)), then-Vice President Joe Biden met with then Ukrainian President Petro Poroshenko. Poroshenko wanted assurance from Biden that U.S. government-approved loan guarantees, amounting to about $1 billion, would be forthcoming. The Vice President demanded Poroshenko fire the Ukrainian Prosecutor General Viktor Shokin as a *quid pro quo* for receipt of the already approved loan guarantees. Shokin was then investigating Burisma Holdings and planned to interrogate the company's board members, including Hunter Biden. Vice President Biden boasted at a televised Council on Foreign Relations conference that he told Poroshenko, "I'm leaving in six hours. If the prosecutor is not fired, you're not getting the money . . . Well, son of a b—, he got fired." Shokin's firing appears to have ended the probe.

The Senate Finance Committee report concluded that Hunter Biden, Chris Heinz, James and Sara Biden, and Devon Archer were involved "in a vast financial network that connected them to foreign nationals and foreign governments across the globe" during Joe Biden's tenure as Vice-President and John Kerry's as Secretary of State. The Committee found "Biden and Archer [were] willing partners [with] Chinese nationals connected to the Communist regime. Their work in China began at least in 2009, with the creation of Rosemont Seneca Partners with Heinz, Secretary of State John Kerry's stepson. Then, several years later, Biden and Archer formed BHR with Bohai Capital and received their business license approval in China shortly after Biden visited China with his father, Vice President Biden." The entities and individuals with whom the transactions took place have criminal histories, involving organized crime, prostitution, embezzlement, and fraud and direct associations with enemies of the United States, including Russia and China, which the Committee found to raise not only "conflicts of interest concerns" but also "criminal financial, counterintelligence and extortion concerns."

In short, the evidence plainly reveals that Joe Biden and John Kerry's relatives were able to cash in on their associations with the then-Vice President and Secretary of State, forming financial relationships with foreign individuals and entities adverse to the United States. That corrupt dealing to turn political connections into lucrative personal financial arrangements at the expense of national interests occurred repeatedly, but informed of it, Joe Biden and John Kerry did nothing to stop it. Peter Schweizer documents a series of Biden family business deals at or immediately after Vice Presidential visits to countries antagonistic to the United States. For example, concerning the December 4, 2013 visit to Beijing of the Vice President on Air Force Two with Hunter Biden in tow, Schweizer explains: "Approximately ten days after the Beijing trip, Hunter Biden's Rosemont Seneca Partners finalized a deal with the Chinese government worth a whopping $1 billion. The deal was later expanded to $1.5 billion. As of this writing, the fund's website says its investments amount to more than $2 billion. It is important to note that this deal was with the Chinese government—not with a Chinese company, which means that the Chinese government and the son of the Vice President were now business partners."[694]

The Bidens were thus selling something highly valuable (worth over a billion dollars) other than personal talent. The personal family connections to the Vice President must have given the funding parties the impression that they could secure an advantage for themselves and their countries by wielding influence over the Vice President or, through him, with the administration. Peter Schweizer explains in *Secret Empires*: "A troubling pattern emerges . . . showing how profitable deals were struck with foreign governments on the heels of crucial diplomatic missions carried out by their powerful fathers [Vice President Joe Biden and Secretary of State John Kerry]. Often those foreign entities gained favorable policy actions from the United States government just as the sons were securing favorable financial deals with those same entities."[695]

Schweizer explains a series of corporate entities owned or controlled by Rosemont Seneca Partners, which funneled funds to Hunter Biden and

Christopher Heinz (John Kerry's stepson). One of those entities, Bohai Harvest RST, became a lucrative conduit for funds from China to Biden and Heinz. The special deals entered into with these entities netted millions for Hunter, James and Sara Biden, Christopher Heinz, and Devon Archer. Schweizer explains: "The Rosemont Seneca deal was lucrative for the Bidens and Kerry's stepson, and appears, on behalf of the Chinese government, strategically timed to go along with China's aggressive territorial claims [in the South China Sea]. But it was not the only deal that occurred at this time."[696] The full extent of funds flowing from adversarial states to the Biden and Kerry families in apparent influence-peddling deals has not been uncovered as of this writing. Nevertheless, the dealings that have been revealed suggest the scheme was vast in scope and very lucrative. At a minimum, it suggests extreme negligence on the part of the then-Vice President and the then Secretary of State, at a maximum it suggests a conscious family effort, at least on the part of the Bidens, to profit from high-level positions at the expense of the nation, which raises the specter of numerous potential criminal law violations.

Moreover, in late October 2020, Tony Bobulinski, the CEO of Sinohawk Holdings (a company he described as "a partnership between the Chinese operating through CEFC/Chairman Ye and the Biden family) said he possessed a trove of documents since given to the Senate Finance Committee and the Senate Committee on Homeland Security and Government Affairs, linking Hunter Biden, then-Vice President Joe Biden, and Joe Biden's brother James to an influence-peddling scheme involving a Chinese communist government energy concern, CEFC, and its Chinese communist Chairman Ye. Bobulinski's name surfaced in emails published by the *New York Post*, which had been obtained from a laptop purportedly belonging to Hunter Biden left in a computer repair shop. Bobulinski verified the authenticity of an email from the laptop dated May 13, 2017, in which "remuneration packages" were referenced. The email states: "Hunter has some office expectations he will elaborate" and referred ro a split in proceeds coming from CEFC to the Biden family with "20" for "H" and "10 held by H for the big guy." Bobulinski confirmed that "H" was Hunter Biden and the "big guy" was Joe Biden. Biden has repeatedly denied having any knowledge of his son's business involvement with foreign partners.[697] He also denied on October 22, 2020, during the final presidential debate that he received any money from the Hunter Biden transactions with China, albeit he has denied neither the authenticity of the emails and documents nor that his family members received millions of dollars from foreign entities associated with business transactions in countries adverse to the United States.[698]

Hunter Biden allegedly received millions of dollars from the scheme. Bobulinski claims to have met then-Vice President Biden on two occasions, one on May 2, 2017, in the late evening at the bar at the Beverly Hills Hilton in Los Angeles. He said the meetings were put together by Hunter and James Biden and that there "was no other reason for me to be in that bar meeting Joe Biden than to discuss what I was doing with his family's name and the Chinese CEFC." He said Hunter Biden introduced the Vice President to Bobulinski, stating: "[T]his is Tony, Dad, the individual I told you about that's helping us with the business that we're working on and the Chinese," suggesting knowledge of the interactions by the then-Vice President, contradicting Joe Biden's denials.[699]

The corruption of the Biden family in influence-peddling is at least equaled, if not surpassed, by former Secretary of State Hillary Rodham Clinton who, through the Clinton 2016 presidential campaign's surrogate Fusion GPS, conspired with Christopher Steele, a former head of the British intelligence service's Russia desk, to create a false Trump-Russia narrative (falsely asserting links between Russia and the Trump campaign to rely on Russian hackers to interfere with the 2016 presidential election). The evidence is marshaled and the crimes explained well in two books by Gregg Jarrett, *The Russia Hoax*[700] and *Witch Hunt*[701]. The false narrative was designed to direct attention away from Clinton's own email server scandal.[702] Infamously, Hillary Clinton while serving as Secretary of State had her official emails redirected to a private at-home, unsecured email server, resulting in breaches of security, the Public Records Act, the Freedom of Information Act, and State Department regulations as foreign nationals, including those working for the Chinese communist government, hacked into her unsecured server and obtained information.[703] Among the emails flowing into her private server were some one hundred containing classified information, including identification of secret sources, means, and locations.[704] Under State Department regulations, the Espionage Act, the Public Records Act, and the Freedom of Information Act, it was illegal for the Secretary of State to redirect official emails from the State Department to a personal server. Although repeatedly briefed about the need to use only official State Department protected servers and devices, Clinton relied almost exclusively on her unsecured at-home private server. The firestorm of controversy associated with those dangerous and derelict actions, combined with the FBI investigation into them, created concern for the Clinton campaign, resulting in the decision that a "diversion" was needed. They would try to shift the focus from her real email scandal to what they would concoct as an even greater scandal: The Russians were trying to steal the election with the complicity of Donald Trump!

Hillary Clinton signed off on the clandestine plan, which was then communicated to the White House, the FBI Director, the CIA Director, and the Director of National Intelligence who became accomplices in use of their offices to interfere with the 2016 election in apparent violation of, among other laws, the federal fraud statute, 18 USC Section 1341; the mail and wire fraud statute, 18 USC Section 1343; the federal criminal RICO statute, 18 USC Sections 1961–1968; and the Hatch Act (inapplicable to the President and Vice President). In a recently released September 7, 2016, three-page memo from then CIA Director John Brennan, he informs FBI Director James Comey and his assistant, FBI agent Peter Strzok, that Hillary Clinton had approved a plan to blame Trump for ties to Russian hackers intent on disrupting the 2016 election as a means to divert attention away from her email scandal. The memo refers to "[a]n exchange [redacted] discussing U.S. presidential candidate Hillary Clinton's approval of a plan concerning U.S. presidential candidate Donald Trump and Russian hackers hampering U.S. elections as a means of distracting the public from her use of private email server." Brennan goes on to state that Clinton approved "a proposal from one of her foreign policy advisers to vilify Donald Trump by stirring up a scandal claiming interference by the Russian security service." Brennan briefed President Obama on this effort to vilify Trump with the false accusations in the White House on July 28, 2016. Aware from the start that no reliable evidence supported the accusations, President Obama, FBI Director Comey, and CIA Director Brennan nevertheless made repeated public statements condemning Trump and the Trump campaign for collusion with Russia to interfere with the 2016 presidential election. Moreover, from another declassified document, it is apparent that U.S. intelligence officials referred to FBI Director Comey for investigation Hillary Clinton's approved plan to vilify Trump with these false charges, seeking the referral in the same month as the Brennan memo was written. In congressional testimony, Comey claimed that the referral "didn't ring a bell."

In his blog on the subject, Jonathan Turley summarizes:

> Throughout the campaign, and for many weeks after, the Clinton campaign denied any involvement in the creation of the dossier that was later used to secure a secret surveillance warrant against Trump associates during the Obama administration. Journalists later discovered that the Clinton campaign hid the payments to Fusion [GPS] as "legal fees" among $5.6 million paid to the law firm. *New York Times* reporter Ken Vogel at the time said that Clinton lawyer Marc Elias had "vigorously" denied involvement in the anti-Trump dossier. When Vogel tried to report the story, he said, Elias "pushed back vigorously, saying 'You or your sources) are wrong.'" Times reporter Maggie Haberman likewise wrote: "Folks involved in funding this lied about it, and with sanctimony, for a year." Even when Clinton campaign chairman John Podesta was questioned by Congress on the matter, he denied any contractual agreement with Fusion GPS. Sitting beside him was Elias, who helped devise [the] contract. Later, confronted with the evidence, Clinton and her campaign finally admitted that the dossier was a campaign-funded document that was pushed by Steele and others to the media. Making things worse is the fact that we now know American intelligence flagged Steele's main source as a Russian agent and warned that the dossier

was suspected of containing Russian disinformation from Russian intelligence sources.[705]

Despite mounting evidence that several key Obama Administration officials, including President Barrack Obama, Vice President Joe Biden, FBI Director James Comey, and CIA Director James Clapper were aware of the vacuousness of the Russian collusion narrative, Comey proceeded to rely on the unreliable Steele dossier to obtain multiple warrants against Trump administration officials from the secret Foreign Intelligence Surveillance Court upon sworn affidavits he signed and recommended, with the acquiescence of his colleague Rod Rosenstein, the Deputy Attorney General. Millions of tax dollars were spent on an investigation by Special Counsel Robert Mueller and by Congress that yielded no information of Russian collusion, yet the entire fiasco from the very start was driven by those who knew the allegations to be unsubstantiated and predicated on a false foundation sponsored by an opposition political campaign. Indeed, this was the most extensive and costly political scandal in American history, one that reveals widespread corruption in federal intelligence agencies and the White House and begs for extensive prosecutions against all who participated in this attempt to steal an election and depose a duly elected President on fraudulent charges.

I share Peter Schweizer's sentiments expressed well in *Secret Empires*: "If we are to remain an effective constitutional republic, we must face and win the war on corruption at home. We must not tolerate public service as a front for family enrichment and elite will to power. It is un-American, and has direct and dire effects on policy-making and good governance."[706]

WHOSE VISION OF AMERICA WILL PREVAIL?

The authoritarians who riot in the streets, predominate in the Democratic Party, and aim to make America a socialist or communist nation are enemies of the Constitution and of all freedom-loving Americans. Their lust for power is palpable, and when in power, their propensity to use it for corrupt ends is well documented based on recent events. They mean to destroy the greatest system of government in defense of individual liberty that the world has ever known. They aim to destroy the nation's engine of human progress, free enterprise. They promise to make the administrative state the eventual controller of us all. They promise a country that they will govern where only they will enjoy freedom. They are pillaging America's wealth, violating the rule of law, engaging in lawless behavior, and robbing America of its prosperity and freedom. They despise our history, rewrite it to advance a political narrative contrary to principles in defense of liberty, and wish to make each American ashamed to be an American.

We are left to ask whose vision for America will win out in the struggle over our country's destiny. Will it be the vision of the authoritarians who, like George III, paternalistically presume their wishes for America should replace by force the free choice of each individual, or will it be the constitutionalists who, like George Washington, presume it the sacred duty of government to guard individual liberty against those, like the authoritarians, who would use state power to take our liberties away?

AFTERWORD

Without Abraham Lincoln's persuasive, unrelenting, and consistent intellectual force for union, articulated brilliantly, calmly and with resolute purpose in his June 16, 1858 "House Divided Speech" at the Republican Convention in Springfield, Illinois; in his "Better Angels of Our Nature" 1861 Inaugural Address; and in his "With Malice Toward None" Second 1865 Inaugural Address, it is doubtful that the United States could have survived as one nation. Is there an Abraham Lincoln today who can help save the union a second time?

In humble, nonjudgmental teachings that transcend bitter rivalries and irreconcilable differences, Lincoln spoke to the divine character of humanity: to mercy, to compassion, to the better angels in foe and friend, to the battle weary, to the wounded, to the widow, to the crestfallen on both sides. He spoke to the American soul. He never renounced nor repudiated the Founding Fathers' principles. He never appeased those who demanded that renunciation as a condition precedent for their cessation of hostilities. To them, Lincoln pointed General Grant's terrible swift sword of war unyieldingly until the battle was won, completely and finally.

In his Second Inaugural Address in 1865, unaware that John Wilkes Booth glared at him from the stands near the Capitol podium, Lincoln said: "Fondly do we hope – fervently do we pray – that this mighty scourge of war may speedily pass away. *Yet, if God wills that it continue until all the wealth piled by the bondsman's two hundred and fifty years of unrequited toil shall be sunk, and until every drop of blood drawn with the lash, shall be paid by another drawn with the sword, as was said three thousand years ago, so still it must be said 'the judgments of the Lord, are true and righteous altogether.'"* The first principles of the Declaration of Independence and the Constitution would win out, by force of arms if needed.

Today, as then, we have once again become a people bitterly divided-- riveting our attention on that which divides us and casting aside as trivial that which historically unites us. On the brink of Civil War then, as one half of the voting population abandoned the promise of the Declaration of Independence and clung to a false and depraved system of governance (the institution of slavery) that they said was "ideal" socialism, they convinced themselves in a grand delusion to condemn individual liberty and a republican form of government and capitalist labor (which they tried to convince themselves was abject inhumanity and inescapable misery).

In the midst of Marxist and anarchistic rioting today, one-half of the voting population also abandons the promise of the Declaration of Independence and clings to that same false and depraved system of government (socialism) that they again say is the "ideal" change needed for America. They convince themselves in another grand delusion to condemn individual liberty, a republican form of government and free enterprise (which they try to convince themselves is abject inhumanity and inescapable misery). The stark, ever mounting ideological divisions transform a nation of civil debate into one where incendiary words are quickly replaced with violence and total intolerance of dissent, resulting in a majority wielding economic and political force to deny economic opportunity and freedom of speech to the minority.

All of this in the 1850's presaged the outbreak of Civil War in the 1860's. All of this in 2021 presages the breakdown of the rule of law and essential protections for individual liberty and private property by executive order: cessation of border protections against unlawful entry; destruction of energy independence, fossil fuels, the Keystone XL Pipeline; and raw exertion of executive will in the fashion of a dictator to compel state and local governments to adopt a socialist agenda.

Then: Northerners who pledged allegiance to the promise of the Declaration of Independence and to pay the ultimate price in defense of the Republic and of the republican form of government guaranteed by the Constitution refused to compromise to accept plantation socialism and fought Southerners who renounced the Declaration and demanded a new confederate nation that federalized the authoritarian system of slavery. **Now:** A Democratic party in control of the White House, the House of Representatives, and the United States Senate rejects the Constitution, free enterprise, and individual rights to implement: market stifling regulations; higher taxes; green initiatives that destroy the fossil fuel industry; mass property redistributions; and Soviet-style planned government economies to advance a far-left, socialist green agenda and make America a centralized, socialist nation. The Republican party fights to break the collusion between Big Tech and the Democratic Party that seeks to suppress conservative voices and silence the robust, wide-open debate protected by the First Amendment. The Republican party fights to prevent the politicization of the Supreme Court to ensure judicial independence. The Republican party fights to restore the separation of powers and the system of checks and balances and resurrect the Constitution from the death grip of the administrative state.

Under the Kansas and Nebraska Act of 1854, Congress by a slim majority ruled that state territories upon entering the union could choose for themselves, based on popular sovereignty, whether they would be free or slave. This then led Southerners to try to convert the Kansas territory into a slave state by emigration from the deep South to Kansas in large numbers, resulting in a mini civil war in Kansas that presaged the great Civil War.

Out of the conflict in Kansas there arose an abolitionist farmer named John Brown who with his sons began a violent rampage to end slavery through the massacre of slave-owners at Pottawatomie Creek and then on to Harpers Ferry, West Virginia. At Harpers Ferry, Brown hoped to seize from the federal arsenal the weapons necessary for a national slave insurrection. What Brown hoped to be a revolution against slavery never materialized and was effectively suppressed by the United States military including several who would later become famous for bravery both North and South in the Civil War.

Again presaging its coming was the famous caning attack on United States Senator Charles Sumner on May 22, 1856. Senator Sumner delivered a speech on the floor of the Senate entitled "A Crime Against Kansas." In that speech, he condemned South Carolina and its Senator Andrew P. Butler for supporting the Kansas-Nebraska Act of 1854. He referred to that bill (which Butler co-sponsored with Senator Stephen A. Douglas of Illinois) as "the rape of a virgin territory compelling it to the hateful embrace of slavery," and to Senator Butler himself and South Carolina itself as pretend "chivalrous Knights" who lacked "honor and courage" and who had "chosen a mistress who though polluted in the light of the world is chaste in Butler's sight. I mean the harlot of slavery." Finding all this insufferable and slanderous under the Southern Code of Honor, South Carolina Congressman Preston Brooks, first cousin once removed of Butler, rose to defend his relative and his state.

On May 22, Sumner wrote at his Senate desk, which desk was bolted to the floor. Coming from the House side, Brooks—accompanied by South Carolina representatives Lawrence Keith and Henry Edmondson—entered the Senate chamber as Sumner sat writing. Brooks wielded a gutta percha cane and bashed Sumner over the head with it in unremitting savagery. Disabled by the attack, Sumner could not extricate himself from his bolted desk. He tried unsuccessfully to maneuver to get around it receiving one violent blow after another. Several other members of the chamber moved to Sumner's aid but were rebuffed by Keith and Edmondson, at least one of whom wielded a pistol. Brooks' beating of Sumner continued. With great effort Sumner freed himself and members succeeded in subduing Keith and Edmondson. The house voted to expel Brooks, but the vote failed. To prove his honor Brooks nevertheless resigned and was unanimously thereafter re-elected by his constituents. Sumner was so severely injured that he could not attend a single session of the Senate for the next three years."

The intellectual force for union then as now rests in the true defense of first principles, as articulated in the words of Abraham Lincoln. It was Lincoln's consistent *unwillingness* to compromise on the principles of the Declaration and the Constitution and equally consistent *willingness* to extend the hand of mercy, the abandonment of bile, and the promise of forgiveness and reconciliation (with malice toward none and charity for all) which brought the torn nation together without dooming it to an unholy, self-destructive, and unprincipled devolution into the wickedness and depravity of slavery and socialism.

Consider Lincoln's calls for reconciliation and healing; "With malice toward none; with charity for all; with firmness in the right, as God gives us to see the right, let us strive on to finish the work we are in; to bind the nation's wounds; to care for him who shall have borne the battle, and for his widow, and his orphan--to do all which may achieve and cherish a just, and a lasting peace, among ourselves, and with all nations." And then in his June 16, 1858 House Divided Speech at the Republican State Convention in Springfield, Illinois, Lincoln sealed his fate with the Founders principles: "A house divided against itself cannot stand [Lincoln quoting Christ from the synoptic gospels of Matthew, Mark, and Luke]. I believe this government cannot endure, permanently half slave and half free. I do not expect the union to be dissolved--I do not expect the house to fall-- but I do expect it will cease to be divided. It will become *all* one thing or *all* the other. Either the opponents of slavery, will arrest the further spread of it, and place it where the public mind shall rest in the belief that it is in the course of ultimate extinction; or its advocates will push it forward, till it shall become alike lawful in all States, old as well as new--North as well as South." In Lincoln's, March 4, 1861 First Inaugural Address, after 7 states had already left the union, Lincoln then spoke to the South. "Though passion may have strained, it must not break our bonds of affection. The mystic chords of memory, stretching forth from every battlefield and patriot grave to every living part and heart and hearthstone all over this broad land, will yet swell the chorus of union, when again touched, as surely they will be, by the better angels of our nature." In his immortal November 19, 1863 Gettysburg Address, Lincoln insisted on principle over appeasement: "It is for us the living, rather, to be dedicated here to the unfinished work which they who fought here have thus far so nobly advanced. It is rather for us to be here dedicated to the great task remaining before us-- that from these honored dead we take increased devotion *to that cause for which they gave the last full measure of devotion--that we here highly resolve that these dead shall not have died in vain--that this nation, under God, shall have a new birth of freedom--and that government of the people, by the people, for the people, shall not perish from the earth.*"

The difference between the intellectual force for union then, and now, is that of first principles, as articulated in the words of Abraham Lincoln.

Joe Biden's plans for America call for rejection of America's basic founding principles: the Declaration's promise, the Constitution's limits on power together with the transformation of the federal and state governments into socialist governments in violation of the Guarantee Clause of the Constitution (Article IV, Section 4). He is the antithesis of Lincoln, Lincoln's nemesis.

Who is our Lincoln today? Who can bind the nation's wounds, restore protection for life, individual liberty, and property, return us to peace and prosperity, and preserve the republican form of government guaranteed us in Article IV, Section 4? Who is possessed of an uncompromising commitment to our founding principles and an unshakable willingness to fight for those principles against all odds? And against all enemies foreign and domestic?

Joe Biden misperceives appeasement for compromise and promises for principles. He abandons fundamental protections for rights to liberty and property to satisfy the immediate demands of authoritarian radicals who insist on using government power to take away liberties and suppress dissent from all with whom they disagree, and to take away the properties of all who have earned them in favor of those who have not, but who have his political favor. He is by his own definition a dictator. He takes no offense at tyranny per se. He thinks the tyrant benevolent, if a dictator like unto himself.

Governor Kristi Noem of the great free state of South Dakota exhibits all of the commitments to first principles that Joe Biden lacks. She harbors none of his misperceptions. She knows from whom our rights come (God) and that they are pre-political, superior to the state and unalienable. She knows to whom she owes a duty of protection (to the people, their lives, their liberties, and their estates) and she knows the ends to which just governments are dedicated (to protect the rights of the governed). She takes offense at tyranny in every instance, and most especially when the tyrant appears as a wolf in sheep's cloth, claiming to be benevolent, because she will not be duped into sacrificing the sovereignty of the people to consolidate the power of the authoritarians. She believes in one nation under God.

Joe Biden exercises his own freedom of religion, but he does not believe the rights of the people are bestowed by God, because he believes the state (indeed, himself with an executive order and pen) may take rights away in its (or his) discretion. For Biden, rights are not unalienable. Governor Kristi Noem honors and implements the Constitution. She will not compromise basic principles, as Lincoln would not. She follows the rule of law, foremost of which is the Constitution.

Lincoln would not compromise on basic principle in the four months preceding his March 1861 inauguration. Lincoln was under tremendous pressure to allow a few states to separate from the union and to allow others to remain with slavery inviolate and capable of infinite expansion. Lincoln did not misperceive that request for appeasement as one for compromise, or a promise for a principle. He told George Sumner, "by no act of complicity of mine shall the Republican Party become a mere sucked egg, all shell with no principle in it." If compromise be the principle meant, and if without compromise war would follow, then Lincoln was for war confident that a firm commitment to principle would ensure victory.

There would be no hypocrisy and no dishonor of the American cause. Lincoln understood, as Biden does not, that the very essence of America is in the promise of the Declaration of Independence, in each American's birthright. Lincoln understood that only Americans themselves could destroy their God-given legacy of unalienable rights and individual sovereignty. It would remain each American's blessing unless through sheer stupidity or suicidal ideation each chose to forfeit it for all time. In his January 27, 1838 Lyceum Address, "The Perpetuation of Our Political Institutions," Lincoln prophetically observed: "If destruction be our lot we must ourselves be its author and finisher. As a nation of [the] free we must live through all time or die by suicide."

Jonathan W. Emord,
Hermosa, South Dakota

ABOUT THE AUTHOR

Jonathan W. Emord has practiced constitutional and administrative law before the federal courts and agencies for over thirty-five years. He formerly served as an attorney in the FM Branch of the Federal Communications Commission during the Reagan administration. He is AV-rated by the Martindale Hubbell organization, the highest in legal ability and ethics. He has defeated the Food and Drug Administration eight times in federal court, more times than any other attorney in American history. He is a guest lecturer at Georgetown University Law School and Georgetown University Medical School. He is the American Justice columnist for *USA Today Magazine* and is frequently consulted by the media and members of Congress on issues of constitutional law and regulation. He is the weekly guest host with Robert Scott Bell of the Sacred Fire of Liberty Hour on the *Robert Scott Bell Show*. He is the author of four other critically acclaimed books: *Freedom, Technology, and the First Amendment*; *The Rise of Tyranny*; *Global Censorship of Health Information*; and *Restore the Republic*.

ENDNOTES

1   Rudolph J. Rummel, *Death by Government* (1997); Rudolph J. Rummel, *Statistics of Democide: Genocide and Mass Murder Since* 1900 (1998).

2   Stephanie Courtois, Nicolas Werth, Jean-Louis Panne, Andrzej Paczkowski, Karel Bartosek, and Jean-Louis Margolin, *The Black Book of Communism* x (1999).

3   Jonah Gottschalk, "Shaun king calls for destroying statues of Jesus, smashing stained glass," *The Federalist* (June 22, 2020) @ thefederalist.com.

4   See Gatestoneinstitute.org.

5   Valerie Richardson, "'We are trained Marxists:' Black Lives Matter Co-Founder Featured in GOP Ad," *Washington Times* (Thursday, June 25, 2020) at washington-times.com.

6   David J. Johnson, Trevor Tress, Nicole Burkel, Carley Taylor, and Joseph Cesarie, "Officer characteristics in fatal officer-involved shootings" 32 *Proceedings of the National Academy of Sciences* 116 (Aug. 6, 2019).

7   Amanda Prestigiacomo, "Trooper refuses to kneel to BLM activists: I only kneel to God," *Dailywire* (June 8, 2020) @ dailywire.com.

8   Timothy Fitzgerald, Kevin Hassett, Cody Kallen, and Casey B. Mulligan, "An Analysis of Vice President Biden's Economic Agenda: The Long Run Impact of Its Regulation, Taxes, and Spending," Hoover Institution Study (2020) @ hoover.org.

9   Timothy Fitzgerald, Kevin Hassett, Cody Kallen, and Casey B. Mulligan, "An Analysis of Vice President Biden's Economic Agenda: The Long Run Impact of Its Regulation, Taxes, and Spending," Hoover Institution Study (2020) @ hoover.org.

10   Thomas Jefferson, Autobiography (1821), in 1 *Writings of Jefferson* 122.

11   Georg Wilhelm Friedrich Hegel, *Elements of the Philosophy of Right*, Sect. 57 (1821).

12   C. Bradley Thompson, *America's Revolutionary Mind* 363 (2019).

13   C. Bradley Thompson, *America's Revolutionary Mind* 362 (2019).

14   Eric H. Walther, *The Fire-Eaters* 277 (1992).

15   C. Bradley Thompson, *America's Revolutionary Mind* 373 (2019).

16   Eric H. Walther, *The Fire-Eaters* 229–230 (1992).

17   C. Bradley Thompson, *America's Revolutionary Mind* 373 (2019).

18   Edmund Ruffin, *The Political Economy of Slavery* 9 (1857).

19   C. Bradley Thompson, *America's Revolutionary Mind* 362 (2019).

20   C. Bradley Thompson, *America's Revolutionary Mind* 363 (2019).

21   C. Bradley Thompson, *America's Revolutionary Mind* 364 (2019).

22   James Warley Miles, *The Relation Between the Races at the South* 6 (1861).

23   James Warley Miles, *The Relation Between the Races at the South* 14 (1861).

24   Edmund Ruffin, *The Political Economy of Slavery* 10 (1857).

25   C. Bradley Thompson, *America's Revolutionary Mind* 364 (2019).

26   C. Bradley Thompson, *America's Revolutionary Mind* 365–366 (2019).

27   Eric H. Walther, *The Fire-Eaters* 32 (1992).

28   Walter E. Williams, "Williams: The Devil and Karl Marx," Dailywire.com (September 19, 2020).

29   Walter E. Williams, "Williams: The Devil and Karl Marx," Dailywire.com (September 19, 2020).

30   C. Bradley Thompson, *America's Revolutionary Mind* 371 (2019).

31   Ronald J. Pestritto, *Woodrow Wilson and the Roots of Modern Liberalism* 15 (2005).

32   Eric H. Walther, *The Fire-Eaters* 247 (1992).

33   Karl Marx, *Critique of the Goltha Program* (1891).

34   U.S. Senator James Henry Hammond, Speech to the U.S. Senate (March 4, 1858).

35   Richard Hofstadter, *The American Political Tradition: And the Men Who Made It* (1948).

36   U.S. Senator John C. Calhoun, Speech to the U.S. Senate (February 6, 1837).

37   Abraham Lincoln, Address before the Wisconsin State Agricultural Society (September 30, 1859).

38   C. Bradley Thompson, *America's Revolutionary Mind* 374 (2019).

39   Steven J. Diner, *A Very Different Age* 5 (1998).

40   See generally, Murray N. Rothbard, *The Progressives* 91–92 (2017).

41   Michael McGerr, *A Fierce Discontent* 151 (2003).

42   Gabriel Kolko, *The Triumph of Conservatism* (1963); Murray N. Rothbard, *The Progressive Era* (2017).

43   Murray N. Rothbard, *The Progressive Era* 92 (2017).

44   Murray N. Rothbard, *The Progressive Era* 77 (2017); see also Richard Hofstadter, *The Age of Reason* 8 (1955).

45   Thomas C. Leonard, *Illiberal Reformers* ix (2016); Philip Hamburger, *Is Administrative Law Unlawful?* 451 (2014) ("Thousands of late-nineteenth century American scholars . . . flocked to Germany and returned with ideas about scientific study, which they then introduced into American life. . . . The German scholarship on administrative power thus became the avenue for a sort of learning incompatible with American law."). See also Hofstadter, *The Age of Reform* at 7.

46   Murray N. Rothbard, *The Progressive Era* 235–236 (2017).

47   Murray N. Rothbard, *The Progressive Era* 241 (2017).

48   Steven J. Diner, *A Very Different Age* 203 (1998).

49   Eric Foner, *Who Owns History?* 38 (2003).

50   Richard Hofstadter, *The Age of Reform* 5 (1955).

51   Thomas C. Leonard, *Illiberal Reformers* 9 (2016).

52   Murray N. Rothbard, *The Progressive Era* 39 (2017).

53   Murray N. Rothbard, *The Progressive Era* 42–43 (2017).

54   Murray N. Rothbard, *The Progressive Era* 93–107 (2017).

55   Gabriel Kolko, *The Triumph of Conservatism* 57–58; 59 (1963).

56   Michael McGerr, *A Fierce Discontent* xiii (2003).

57   Richard Hofstadter, *The Age of Reform* 131 (1955).

58   Richard Hofstadter, *The Age of Reform* 81–83 (1955).

59   Richard Hofstadter, *The Age of Reform* 86 (1955).

60   Richard Hofstadter, *The Age of Reform* 100 (1955).

61   Richard Hofstadter, *The Age of Reform* 119–120 (1955).

62   Steven J. Diner, *A Very Different Age* 231 (1998).

63   Edward J. Larson, *Summer of the Gods* 119 (1997).

64   Herbert Spencer, *Principles of Biology*, Volume 1, 444 (1864).

65   Donald J. Pestritto, *Woodrow Wilson and the Roots of Modern Liberalism* 11 (2005).

66   Thomas C. Leonard, *Illiberal Reformers* x (2016).

67   Michael McGerr, *A Fierce Discontent* 64 (2003).

68   Steven J. Diner, *A Very Different Age* 222–223 (1998).

69   Richard Hofstadter, *The Age of Reform* 240 (1955).

70   Steven J. Diner, *A Very Different Age* 230 (1998).

71   Richard Hofstadter, *The Age of Reform* 82 (1955).

72   Alexander Hamilton, James Madison, John Jay, *The Federalist Papers* ("No. 10: The Same Subject Continued (Madison)") 71-79 (Signet Classics reprint, 2003); John Adams, *A Defence of the Constitutions of the United States of America* 3; 290–291, 310 (1788).

73   Thomas C. Leonard, *Illiberal Reformers* xiii (2016).

74   Thomas C. Leonard, *Illiberal Reformers* xiii (2016).

75   Paul A. Lombardo, *Three Generations No Imbeciles* 159 (2008).

76   Paul A. Lombardo, *Three Generations No Imbeciles* xiv (2008).

77   Albert W. Alschuler, *Law Without Values* 1 (2000).

78   Paul A. Lombardo, *Three Generations No Imbeciles* xiii (2008).

79   Thomas C. Leonard, *Illiberal Reformers* 111 (2016).

80   Thomas C. Leonard, *Illiberal Reformers* 99 (2016).

81   Edwin Black, *War Against the Weak* 99 (2012)·

82   Paul A. Lombardo, *Three Generations No Imbeciles* 26 (2008).

83   Paul A. Lombardo, *Three Generations No Imbeciles* 158 (2008).

84   Paul A. Lombardo, *Three Generations No Imbeciles* 89 (2008).

85   Paul A. Lombardo, *Three Generations No Imbeciles* xii (2008).

86   Albert W. Alschuler, *Law Without Values* 1 (2000).

87   Paul A. Lombardo, *Three Generations No Imbeciles* 163 (2008).

88   Paul A. Lombardo, *Three Generations No Imbeciles* 165 (2008).

89   Paul A. Lombardo, *Three Generations No Imbeciles* 78 (2008).

90   Paul A. Lombardo, *Three Generations No Imbeciles* 121 (2008).

91   Paul A. Lombardo, *Three Generations No Imbeciles* 83–89 (2008).

92   Paul A. Lombardo, *Three Generations No Imbeciles* 115 (2008).

93   Paul A. Lombardo, *Three Generations No Imbeciles* 159 (2008).

94   Paul A. Lombardo, *Three Generations No Imbeciles* 160 (2008).

95   Thomas C. Leonard, *Illiberal Reformers* 112 (2016).

96   Thomas C. Leonard, *Illiberal Reformers* 118–119 (2016).

97   Thomas C. Leonard, *Illiberal Reformers* 117 (2016).

98   Thomas C. Leonard, *Illiberal Reformers* 115 (2016).

99   Thomas C. Leonard, *Illiberal Reformers* 115 (2016).

100   Thomas C. Leonard, *Illiberal Reformers* 110 (2016).

101   Thomas C. Leonard, *Illiberal Reformers* 114 (2016).

102   Thomas C. Leonard, *Illiberal Reformers* 114 (2016).

103   Thomas C. Leonard, *Illiberal Reformers* 114 (2016).

104   Paul A. Lombardo, *Three Generations No Imbeciles* x (2008).

105   See generally Albert W. Alschuler, *Law Without Values* (2000).

106   Albert W. Alschuler, *Law Without Values* 59 (2000).

107   Albert W. Alschuler, *Law Without Values* 63 (2000).

108   Paul A. Lombardo, *Three Generations No Imbeciles* 103 (2008).

109   Paul A. Lombardo, *Three Generations No Imbeciles* 103–107 (2008).

110   Trevor Burrus, "The United States Once Sterilized Tens of Thousands—Here's How the Supreme Court Allowed It," *Medium* (Jan. 27, 2016).

111   Paul A. Lombardo, *Three Generations No Imbeciles* x (2008).

112   Paul A. Lombardo, *Three Generations No Imbeciles* xi (2008).

113   Paul A. Lombardo, *Three Generations No Imbeciles* xi (2008).

114   Paul A. Lombardo, *Three Generations No Imbeciles* 121 (2008).

115   Paul A. Lombardo, *Three Generations No Imbeciles* 5 (2008).

116   Paul A. Lombardo, *Three Generations No Imbeciles* 172 (2008).

117   *Buck v. Bell*, 274 U.S. 200 (1927).

118   *Slaughter-House Cases*, 83 U.S. (16 Wall.) 36 (1873).

119   *Plessy v. Ferguson*, 163 U.S. 537 (1896).

120   *Mugler v. Kansas*, 123 U.S. 623 (1887).

121   *Jacobson v. Massachusetts*, 197 U.S. 11 (1905).

122   *Hannibal & St. J.R. Co. v. Husen*, 95 U.S. 465 (1878).

123   *Crowley v. Christensen*, 137 U.S. 86 (1890).

124   *Patterson v. Colorado*, 205 U.S. 454 (1907).

125   Jonathan W. Emord, *Freedom, Technology, and the First Amendment* (1991) 84–86; 87–90 (1999).

126   *Gitlow v. New York*, 268 U.S. 652 (1925).

127   *Schenck v. United States*, 249 U.S. 47 (1919).

128   *Abrams v. United States*, 250 U.S. 616 (1919).

129   Albert W. Alschuler, *Law Without Values* 65–66 (2000).

130   Albert W. Alschuler, *Law Without Values* 66 (2000).

131   Stephen Jay Gould, "Carrie Buck's Daughter," 2 *Constitutional Commentary* 331, 333 (1985).

132   Georg Wilhelm Friedrich Hegel, *Philosophy of History* 39 (1830); Ronald J. Pes-

tritto, *Woodrow Wilson and the Roots of Modern Liberalism* 16 (2005); Stephen R. C. Hicks, *Explaining Postmodernism* 120 (2004).

133   Georg Wilhelm Friedrich Hegel, *Philosophy of Right* 241 (1821); Stephen R. C. Hicks, *Explaining Postmodernism* 123 (2004).

134   Georg Wilhelm Friedrich Hegel, *Elements of the Philosophy of Right*, Sections 258, 259, 261, 269, and 288 (1821).

135   Ronald J. Pestritto, *Woodrow Wilson and the Roots of Modern Liberalism* 9 (2005).

136   Daniel T. Rodgers, *Atlantic Crossings* 76–77 (1998).

137   Daniel T. Rodgers, *Atlantic Crossings* 98 (1998).

138   Daniel T. Rodgers, *Atlantic Crossings* 85–86 (1998).

139   Daniel T. Rodgers, *Atlantic Crossings* 99 (1998).

140   Daniel T. Rodgers, *Atlantic Crossings* 99 (1998).

141   Philip Hamburger, *Is Administrative Law Unlawful?* 449 (2014)

142   Philip Hamburger, *Is Administrative Law Unlawful?* 443 (2014).

143   Philip Hamburger, *Is Administrative Law Unlawful?* 447 (2014).

144   Philip Hamburger, *Is Administrative Law Unlawful?* 455 (2014).

145   Frank Johnson Goodnow, *The American Conception of Liberty and Government* 10–13, 21 (1916).

146   Westel Willoughby, "Administrative Necessity as a Source of Federal Power," *American Political Science Review* (1910).

147   Daniel T. Rodgers, *Atlantic Crossings* 86 (1998).

148   Philip Hamburger, *Is Administrative Law Unlawful?* 468 (2014).

149   Daniel T. Rodgers, *Atlantic Crossings* 85 (1998).

150   Daniel T. Rodgers, *Atlantic Crossings* 86 (1998).

151   Daniel T. Rodgers, *Atlantic Crossings* 86 (1998).

152   Daniel T. Rodgers, *Atlantic Crossings* 88 (1998).

153   Daniel T. Rodgers, *Atlantic Crossings* 89 (1998).

154   Daniel T. Rodgers, *Atlantic Crossings* 91 (1998).

155   Daniel T. Rodgers, *Atlantic Crossings* 91 (1998).

156   Daniel T. Rodgers, *Atlantic Crossings* 95 (1998).

157   Philip Hamburger, *Is Administrative Law Unlawful?* 470 (2014).

158   Richard A. Epstein, *How Progressives Rewrote the Constitution* 7 (2006).

159   Thomas C. Leonard, *Illiberal Reformers* xi (2016).

160   Philip Hamburger, *Is Administrative Law Unlawful?* 459 (2014).

161   Ronald J. Pestritto, *Woodrow Wilson and the Roots of Modern Liberalism* 90 (2005).

162 Daniel T. Rodgers, *Atlantic Crossings* 76 (1998).

163 Daniel T. Rodgers, *Atlantic Crossings* 97 (1998).

164 Daniel T. Rodgers, *Atlantic Crossings* 107 (1998).

165 Woodrow Wilson, "The Study of Administration," 2 *Political Science Quarterly* 197, 201 (1887)

166 Michael McGerr, *A Fierce Discontent* 214 (2003).

167 Daniel T. Rodgers, *Atlantic Crossings* 251 (1998).

168 Philip Hamburger, *Is Administrative Law Unlawful?* 471 (2014).

169 Thomas C. Leonard, *Illiberal Reformers* 104 (2016).

170 Herbert Croly, *The Promise of American Life* 257 (1909).

171 Herbert Croly, *The Promise of American Life* 187 (1909).

172 Herbert Croly, *The Promise of American Life* 465 (1909).

173 H. Wayne Morgan, *William McKinley and His America* (1998); Scott Miller, *The President and the Assassin* (2013).

174 *Standard Oil Company of New Jersey v. United States*, 221 U.S. 1 (1911).

175 Sidney M. Milkis, *Theodore Roosevelt, the Progressive Party, and the Transformation of American Democracy* 233 (2009).

176 Sidney M. Milkis, *Theodore Roosevelt, the Progressive Party and the Transformation of American Democracy* 233 (2009).

177 Sidney M. Milkis, *Theodore Roosevelt, the Progressive Party, and the Transformation of American Democracy* 41 (2009).

178 Theodore Roosevelt, *An Autobiography* 3 (1913).

179 Sidney M. Milkis, *Theodore Roosevelt, the Progressive Party, and the Transformation of American Democracy* 41 (2009).

180 Sidney M Milkis, *Theodore Roosevelt, the Progressive Party, and the Transformation of American Democracy* 55–56 (2009).

181 270towin.com, 1912 Presidential Election.

182 Ronald J. Pestritto, *Woodrow Wilson and the Roots of Modern Liberalism* 8 (2005).

183 Ronald J. Pestritto, *Woodrow Wilson and the Roots of Modern Liberalism* 8 (2005).

184 Ronald J. Pestritto, *Woodrow Wilson and the Roots of Modern Liberalism* 18 (2005).

185 Woodrow Wilson, *Constitutional Government in the United States* 16 (1908).

186 Woodrow Wilson, *The State; Elements of Historical and Practical Politics* 13–14 (1918).

187 Ronald J. Pestritto, *Woodrow Wilson and the Roots of Modern Liberalism* 74 (2005).

188   Ronald J. Pestritto, *Woodrow Wilson and the Roots of Modern Liberalism* 44–45 (2005).

189   Ronald J. Pestritto, *Woodrow Wilson and the Roots of Modern Liberalism* 43 (2005).

190   Judith Edwards, *Abolitionists and Slave Resistance* (2004).

191   Woodrow Wilson, *The State; Elements of Historical and Practical Politics* 12–13 (1918).

192   Ronald J. Pestritto, *Woodrow Wilson and the Roots of Modern Liberalism* 55 (2005).

193   Woodrow Wilson, *The State; Elements of Historical and Practical Politics* 78 (1918).

194   Woodrow Wilson, *The State; Elements of Historical and Practical Politics* 50 (1918).

195   Ronald J. Pestritto, *Woodrow Wilson and the Roots of Modern Liberalism* 77 (2005).

196   Woodrow Wilson, *The State; Elements of Historical and Practical Politics* 60 (1918).

197   Ronald J. Pestritto, *Woodrow Wilson and the Roots of Modern Liberalism* 49 (2005).

198   Woodrow Wilson, *The State; Elements of Historical and Practical Politics* 60–61 (1918).

199   Woodrow Wilson, *The State; Elements of Historical and Practical Politics* 61 (1918).

200   Ronald J. Pestritto, *Woodrow Wilson and the Roots of Modern Liberalism* 80 (2005).

201   Woodrow Wilson, "Socialism and Democracy," in 5 *The Papers of Woodrow Wilson* (Arthur S. Link, ed., 1901) 561 (August 22, 1887).

202   Ronald J. Pestritto, *Woodrow Wilson and the Roots of Modern Liberalism* 123–124; 127; 136 (2005).

203   Woodrow Wilson, *The State; Elements of Historical and Practical Politics* 351 (1918).

204   Woodrow Wilson, *The State; Elements of Historical and Practical Politics* 61 (1918).

205   Woodrow Wilson, *The State; Elements of Historical and Practical Politics* 62–62 (1918).

206   Woodrow Wilson, *The State; Elements of Historical and Practical Politics* 64 (1918).

207   Ronald J. Pestritto, *Woodrow Wilson and the Roots of Modern Liberalism* 17 (2005).

208   Ronald J. Pestritto, *Woodrow Wilson and the Roots of Modern Liberalism* 34 (2005).

209   Larry Walker and Jeremy F. Plant, "Woodrow Wilson and the Federal System," *Politics and Administration: Woodrow Wilson and American Public Administration* 123–124 (1984).

210   John Morton Blum, *The Progressive Presidents* 73 (1982).

211   Walter Lippmann, "Republican Resurrection," *New Republic* 9 (1916).

212   Daniel T. Rodgers, *Atlantic Crossings* 283–284 (1998).

213   Daniel T. Rodgers, *Atlantic Crossings* 381 (1998).

214   Amity Shlaes, *The Forgotten Man* 51 (2007).

215   Amity Shlaes, *The Forgotten Man* 52 (2007).

216   Amity Shlaes, *The Forgotten Man* 54 (2007).

217   Amity Shlaes, *The Forgotten Man* 47–48 (2007).

218   Amity Shlaes, *The Forgotten Man* 80 (2007).

219   Amity Shlaes, *The Forgotten Man* 80-81 (2007).

220   Amity Shlaes, *The Forgotten Man* 81 (2007).

221   Burton Folsom, Jr., *New Deal or Raw Deal?* 32–33 (2008).

222   Kenneth Whyte, *Hoover: An Extraordinary Life in Extraordinary Times* 271; 274 (2017).

223   Jonathan W. Emord, *Freedom, Technology, and the First Amendment* 145–174 (1991).

224   *United States v. Zenith Radio Corporation*, 12 F.2d 614 (N.D. Ill. 1926).

225   Jonathan W. Emord, *Freedom, Technology, and the First Amendment* 145–174 (1991).

226   Kenneth Whyte, *Hoover: An Extraordinary Life in Extraordinary Times* 205 (2017).

227   Congressional Record—Senate, May 5, 1930.

228   John T. Flynn, *The Roosevelt Myth* 78 (1948).

229   Dinesh D'Souza, *The Big Lie* 27 (2017).

230   Dinesh D'Souza, *The Big Lie* 170 (2017).

231   Dinesh D'Souza, *The Big Lie* 171 (2017).

232   Dinesh D'Souza, *The Big Lie* 179 (2017); John P. Diggins, *Mussolini and Fascism: The View from America* 47–48 (1972); David Boaz, "Hitler, Mussolini, Roosevelt," *Reason* (October 2007).

233   David Boaz, "Hitler, Mussolini, Roosevelt" (a review of Wolfgang Schievelbusch, *Three New Deals: Reflections on Roosevelt's America, Mussolini's Italy, and Hitler's Germany, 1933-1939*), Cato Institute, *Commentary* (Sept. 28, 2007) @ cato.org.

234   Dinesh D'Souza, *The Big Lie* 181 (2017).

235   Dinesh D'Souza, *The Big Lie* 180 (2017).

236   Peter H. Irons, *The New Deal Lawyers* 8–9 (1982).

237   William E. Leuchtenburg, *Franklin D. Roosevelt and the New Deal* 36 (1963).

238   John Boettiger, "Maniac Fires on Roosevelt, Cermak Shot; Would Grave," *Chicago Daily Tribune* (March 6, 1933); Theodore N. Pappas, M.D., "The Assassination of Anton Cermak, Mayor of Chicago: A Review of His Post-injury Medical Care," 6 *Surgery Journal*

e105-e111 (2020).

239   Franklin D. Roosevelt, *Looking Forward* 222 (1933); John Morton Blum, *The Progressive Presidents* 108 (1982).

240   John T. Flynn, *The Roosevelt Myth* 34 (1956).

241   John T. Flynn, *The Roosevelt Myth* 38 (1956).

242   John T. Flynn, *The Roosevelt Myth* 45 (1956).

243   David M. Kennedy, "How FDR Derailed the New Deal," *Atlantic Monthly* 87 (1995).

244   Dinesh D'Souza, *The Big Lie* 185 (2017).

245   Dinesh D'Souza, *The Big Lie* 185 (2017).

246   John T. Flynn, *The Roosevelt Myth* 42 (1956).

247   Dinesh D'Souza, *The Big Lie* 185–186 (2017).

248   John T. Flynn, *The Roosevelt Myth* 45 (1956).

249   John T. Flynn, *The Roosevelt Myth* 47 (1956).

250   Burton Folsom, Jr., *New Deal or Raw Deal?* 53 (2008).

251   Burton Folsom, Jr., *New Deal or Raw Deal?* 52–53 (2008).

252   John T. Flynn, *The Roosevelt Myth* 47 (1956); Frances Perkins, *The Roosevelt I Knew* 252 (1946).

253   *Panama Refining Company v. Ryan*, 293 U.S. 388 (1935).

254   Marian C. McKenna, *Franklin Roosevelt and the Great Constitutional War* 91 (2002).

255   Marian C. McKenna, *Franklin Roosevelt and the Great Constitutional War* 90 (2002).

256   Marian C. McKenna, *Franklin Roosevelt and the Great Constitutional War* 90–91 (2002).

257   Jim Powell, *FDR's Folly* 163 (2003).

258   Amity Shlaes, *The Forgotten Man* 14 (2007).

259   Amity Shlaes, *The Forgotten Man* 216 (2007).

260   Josh Blackman, "Amity Shlaes Responds on Schechter Poultry," *The Volokh Conspiracy*, July 31, 2019.

261   *Gundy v. United States*, No. 17-6086, 588 U.S. (2019).

262   *A.L.A. Schechter Poultry Corporation v. United States*, 295 U.S. 495 (1935).

263   Marian C. McKenna, *Franklin Roosevelt and the Great Constitutional War* 104 (2002).

264   Amity Shlaes, *The Forgotten Man* 153 (2007).

265   Peter H. Irons, *The New Deal Lawyers* 112 (1982).

266   Peter H. Irons, *The New Deal Lawyers* 113 (1982).

267   Peter H. Irons, *The New Deal Lawyers* 113–114 (1982).

268   Peter H. Irons, *The New Deal Lawyers* 114–115 (1982).

269   Marian C. McKenna, *Franklin Roosevelt and the Great Constitutional War* 124 (2002).

270   Peter H. Irons, *The New Deal Lawyers* 115–116 (1982).

271   Jim Powell, *FDR's Folly* 132 (2003).

272   Jim Powell, *FDR's Folly* 132 (2003).

273   William E. Leuchtenburg, *Franklin D. Roosevelt and the New Deal* 72–73 (1963).

274   Jim Powell, *FDR's Folly* 133 (2003).

275   William E. Leuchtenburg, *Franklin D. Roosevelt and the New Deal* 73 (1963).

276   Jim Powell, *FDR's Folly* 134 (2003).

277   John T. Flynn, *The Roosevelt Myth* 62–63 (1956).

278   Burton Folsom, Jr., *New Deal or Raw Deal?* 126 (2008).

279   John T. Flynn, *The Roosevelt Myth* 49 (1956).

280   John T. Flynn, *The Roosevelt Myth* 49 (1956).

281   John T. Flynn, *The Roosevelt Myth* 49 (1956).

282   *United States v. Butler*, 297 U.S. 1 (1936).

283   *Carter v. Carter Coal Company*, 298 U.S. 238 (1936).

284   Peter H. Irons, *The New Deal Lawyers* 273 (1982).

285   William E. Leuchtenburg, *The Supreme Court Reborn* 117–118 (1995).

286   Peter H. Irons, *The New Deal Lawyers* 272 (1982).

287   William E. Leuchtenburg, *The Supreme Court Reborn* 110, 114 (1995).

288   William E. Leuchtenburg, *The Supreme Court Reborn* 120 (1995).

289   William E. Leuchtenburg, *The Supreme Court Reborn* 121 (1995).

290   Neal Devins, "Government Lawyers and the New Deal," 438 *Faculty Publications* 247 (1996).

291   Neal Devins, "Government Lawyers and the New Deal," 438 *Faculty Publications* 247 (1996).

292   William E. Leuchtenburg, *The Supreme Court Reborn* 139 (1995).

293   Neal Devins, "Government Lawyers and the New Deal," 438 *Faculty Publications* 248 (1996).

294   Neal Devins, "Government Lawyers and the New Deal," 438 *Faculty Publications*

254 (1996).

295   Neal Devins, "Government Lawyers and the New Deal," 438 *Faculty Publications* 247 (1996).

296   Douglas H. Ginsburg, "Delegation Running Riot," a review of *Power Without Responsibility: How Congress Abuses the People through Delegation* by David Schoenbrod, *Regulation* (1995).

297   William E. Leuchtenburg, *The Supreme Court Reborn* 176 (1995).

298   *West Coast Hotel Co. v. Parrish*, 300 U.S. 379 (1937).

299   *Wright v. Vinton Branch*, 300 U.S. 440 (1937).

300   *Virginia Railway Co. v. System Federation No. 40*, 300 U.S. 515 (1937).

301   *Adkins v. Children's Hospital*, 261 U.S. 525 (1923).

302   *Morehead v. New York ex. rel. Tipaldo*, 298 U.S. 587 (1936).

303   *Wright v. Vinton Branch*, 300 U.S. 440 (1937).

304   *Louisville Joint Stock Land Bank v. Radford*, 295 U.S. 555 (1935).

305   *Virginia Railway Co. v. System Federation No. 40*, 300 U.S. 515 (1937).

306   *National Labor Relations Board v. Jones & Laughlin Steel Corp.*, 301 U.S. 1 (1937).

307   *Helvering v. Davis*, 301 U.S. 619 (1937).

308   Neal Devins, "Government Lawyers and the New Deal," 438 *Faculty Publications* 249 (1995).

309   Jim Powell, *FDR's Folly* ix–x (2003).

310   Burton Folsom, Jr., "Myths of the New Deal," Foundation for Economic Education (August 1, 2002) @ fee.org.

311   Amity Shlaes, *The Forgotten Man* (2007).

312   Burton Folsom, Jr., "Myths of the New Deal," Foundation for Economic Education (August 1, 2002) @ fee.org.

313   Price Fishback, "US Monetary and Fiscal Policy in the 1930s," 26 *Oxford Review of Economic Policy* 385–413 (Autumn 2020).

314   Jim Powell, *FDR's Folly* 87 (2003).

315   Jim Powell, *FDR's Folly* ix (2003).

316   Burton Folsom, Jr., *New Deal or Raw Deal?* 2 (2008).

317   Burton Folsom, Jr., *New Deal or Raw Deal?* 3 (2008).

318   Burton Folsom, Jr., *New Deal or Raw Deal?* 30–31 (2008).

319   Kieran Egan, *Getting It Wrong from the Beginning* 25 (2002).

320   John Dewey, "Impressions of Soviet Russia and The Revolutionary World (1929)" reprinted @ airwatch.com (Oct. 27, 2020).

321   John Dewey, "Impressions of Soviet Russia and The Revolutionary World (1929)" reprinted @ airwatch.com (Oct. 27, 2020).

322   John Dewey, "Impressions of Soviet Russia and The Revolutionary World (1929)" reprinted @ airwatch.com (Oct. 27, 2020).

323   John Dewey, "Impressions of Soviet Russia and The Revolutionary World (1929)" reprinted @ airwatch.com (Oct. 27, 2020).

324   John Dewey, "Impressions of Soviet Russia and The Revolutionary World (1929)" reprinted @ airwatch.com (Oct. 27, 2020).

325   John Dewey, "Impressions of Soviet Russia and The Revolutionary World (1929)" reprinted @ airwatch.com (Oct. 27, 2020).

326   John Dewey, "Impressions of Soviet Russia and The Revolutionary World (1929)" reprinted @ airwatch.com (Oct. 27, 2020).

327   Linda K. Kerber, "The Republican Mother: Women and the Enlightenment—An American Perspective," *Toward an Intellectual History of Women* 43 (1997); Sarah Robbins, "'The Future Good and Great of Our Land': Republican Mothers, Female Authors, and Domestic Literacy in Antebellum New England," 75 *New England Quarterly* 562-591 (2002).

328   Murray N. Rothbard, *The Progressive Era* 421 (2017).

329   Edward J. Larson, *Summer for the Gods: The Scopes Trial and America's Continuing Debate Over Science and Religion* 45 (1997).

330   Edward J. Larson, *Summer for the Gods: The Scopes Trial and America's Continuing Debate Over Science and Religion* 45 (1997).

331   George W. Hunter, *A Civic Biology* 194 (1914).

332   Edward J. Larson, *Summer for the Gods: The Scopes Trial and America's Continuing Debate Over Science and Religion* 187 (1997).

333   Edward J. Larson, *Summer for the Gods: The Scopes Trial and America's Continuing Debate Over Science and Religion* 189 (1997).

334   William E. Leuchtenburg, *Franklin D. Roosevelt and the New Deal* 64 (1963).

335   Amity Shlaes, *The Forgotten Man* 133 (2007).

336   Michael E. Parrish, *Felix Frankfurter and His Times* 206-207 (1982).

337   Michael E. Parrish, *Felix Frankfurter and His Times* 207 (1982).

338   Michael E. Parrish, *Felix Frankfurter and His Times* 231 (1982).

339   Michael E. Parrish, *Felix Frankfurter and His Times* 222 (1982).

340   Jim Powell, *FDR's Folly* 228 (2003).

341   Michael E. Parrish, *Felix Frankfurter and His Times* 230 (1982).

342   Michael E. Parrish, *Felix Frankfurter and His Times* 243 (1982).

343   Amity Shlaes, *The Forgotten Man* 246 (2007).

344   Michael E. Parrish, *Felix Frankfurter and His Times* 245–246 (1982).

345   Michael E. Parrish, *Felix Frankfurter and His Times* 246 (1982).

346   Peter H. Irons, *The New Deal Lawyers* 9 (1982).

347   Peter H. Irons, *The New Deal Lawyers* 9 (1982).

348   Michael E. Parrish, *Felix Frankfurter and His Times* 3 (1982).

349   David M. Margolick, "Letters Show Frankfurter A Secret Voice of Brandeis," *The New York Times* (February 14, 1982).

350   James Grossman, "A Note on Felix Frankfurter," *Commentary* (March 1966).

351   Peter H. Irons, *The New Deal Lawyers* 7 (1982).

352   Peter H. Irons, *The New Deal Lawyers* 8 (1982).

353   Peter H. Irons, *The New Deal Lawyers* 9 (1982).

354   Peter H. Irons, *The New Deal Lawyers* 9 (1982).

355   Amity Shlaes, *The Forgotten Man* 63 (2007).

356   Peter H. Irons, *The New Deal Lawyers* 8 (1982).

357   Amity Shlaes, *The Forgotten Man* 64 (2007).

358   The Progressive Party Platform of 1924 (Nov. 4, 1924) @ presidency.ucsb.edu.

359   Amity Shlaes, *The Forgotten Man* 65 (2007).

360   Daniel T. Rodgers, *Atlantic Crossings* 315 (1998).

361   William E. Leuchtenburg, *Franklin D. Roosevelt and the New Deal* 64 (1963).

362   William E. Leuchtenburg, *Franklin D. Roosevelt and the New Deal* 64 (1963).

363   Michael E. Parrish, *Felix Frankfurter and His Times* 221 (1982).

364   Michael E. Parrish, *Felix Frankfurter and His Times* 220 (1982).

365   William E. Leuchtenburg, *Franklin D. Roosevelt and the New Deal* 149 (1963).

366   Peter H. Irons, *The New Deal Lawyers* 9 (1982).

367   Peter H. Irons, *The New Deal Lawyers* 10 (1982).

368   Peter H. Irons, *The New Deal Lawyers* 10 (1982).

369   Peter H. Irons, *The New Deal Lawyers* 11 (1982).

370   Peter H. Irons, *The New Deal Lawyers* 121 (1982).

371   Jeremiah McCall, *Clan Fabius, Defenders of Rome* (2018).

372   Edward L. Pease, *History of the Fabian Society; The Origins of English Socialism* (2008).

373   Max Horn, *The Intercollegiate Socialist Society, 1905-1921* (1979).

374   Michael E. Parrish, *Felix Frankfurter and His Times* 54 (1982).

375   Stuart Chase, *A New Deal* 252 (1932).

376   Kirstin Downey, *The Woman Behind the New Deal* 24 (2009).

377   Kirstin Downey, *The Woman Behind the New Deal* 29 (2009).

378   Michael E. Parrish, *Felix Frankfurter and His Times* 72 (1982).

379   Kirstin Downey, *The Woman Behind the New Deal* 24 (2009).

380   Kirstin Downey, *The Woman Behind the New Deal* 115 (2009).

381   Peter H. Irons, *The New Deal Lawyers* 124 (1982).

382   Peter H. Irons, *The New Deal Lawyers* 124 (1982).

383   Michael E. Parrish, *Felix Frankfurter and His Times* 227 (1982).

384   Peter H. Irons, *The New Deal Lawyers* 124 (1982).

385   Peter H. Irons, *The New Deal Lawyers* 125 (1982).

386   Peter H. Irons, *The New Deal Lawyers* 125, 236–237 (1982).

387   Herbert Romerstein; Eric Breindel, *The Venona Secrets* 113 (2000).

388   Herbert Romerstein; Eric Breindel, *The Venona Secrets* 114 (2000).

389   Whitaker Chambers, *Witness* 334–352 (1952); "Hearings Regarding Communist Espionage in the United States Government" (Aug. 5, 1948).

390   Herbert Romerstein; Eric Breindel, *The Venona Secrets* 115 (2000).

391   Kathryn S. Olmsted, *Red Spy Queen* 30-32 (2002).

392   Herbert Romerstein; Eric Breindel, *The Venona Secrets* 123 (2000).

393   M. Stanton Evans; Herbert Romerstein, *Stalin's Secret Agents* 78 (2012).

394   Kathryn S. Olmsted, *Red Spy Queen* 32 (2002).

395   Lauren Weiner, "Whitaker Chambers' Pumpkin Patch," *Law & Liberty* (October 31, 2016).

396   Allen Weinstein, *Perjury: The Hiss-Chambers Case* (1997).

397   M. Stanton Evans; Herbert Romerstein, *Stalin's Secret Agents* 79 (2012).

398   M. Stanton Evans; Herbert Romerstein, *Stalin's Secret Agents* 81 (2012).

399   M. Stanton Evans; Herbert Romerstein, *Stalin's Secret Agents* 82 (2012).

400   M. Stanton Evans; Herbert Romerstein, *Stalin's Secret Agents* 2-3 (2012).

401   M. Stanton Evans; Herbert Romerstein, *Stalin's Secret Agents* 3 (2012).

402   M. Stanton Evans; Herbert Romerstein, *Stalin's Secret Agents* 83 (2012).

403   Earl Lathan, *The Communist Controversy in Washington* 119 (1966).

404   M. Stanton Evans; Herbert Romerstein, *Stalin's Secret Agents* 100 (2012).

405   M. Stanton Evans; Herbert Romerstein, *Stalin's Secret Agents* 101–102 (2012).

406   M. Stanton Evans; Herbert Romerstein, *Stalin's Secret Agents* 233 (2012).

407   Herbert Romerstein; Eric Breindel, *The Venona Secrets* 449 (2000).

408   Michael E. Parrish, *Felix Frankfurter and His Times* 56 (1982).

409   Michael E. Parrish, *Felix Frankfurter and His Times* 56 (1982).

410   Michael E. Parrish, *Felix Frankfurter and His Times* 57 (1982).

411   Michael E. Parrish, *Felix Frankfurter and His Times* 65 (1982).

412   Michael E. Parrish, *Felix Frankfurter and His Times* 74 (1982).

413   Michael E. Parrish, *Felix Frankfurter and His Times* 68 (1982).

414   Michael E. Parrish, *Felix Frankfurter and His Times* 169 (1982).

415   David M. Margolick, "Letters Show Frankfurter A Secret Voice of Brandeis," *The New York Times* (February 14, 1982).

416   David M. Margolick, "Letters Show Frankfurter A Secret Voice of Brandeis," *The New York Times* (February 14, 1982).

417   David M. Margolick, "Letters Show Frankfurter A Secret Voice of Brandeis," *The New York Times* (February 14, 1982).

418   John T. Flynn, *The Roosevelt Myth* 144 (1956).

419   Alexander Hamilton, James Madison, John Jay, *The Federalist Papers* (No. 22: "The Same Subject Continued (Hamilton)") 148 (Signet Classics reprint, 2003).

420   Alexander Hamilton, James Madison, John Jay, *The Federalist Papers* (No. 37: "Concerning the Difficulties of the Convention in Devising a Proper Form of Government (Madison)") 223 (Signet Classics reprint, 2003).

421   Alexander Hamilton, James Madison, John Jay, *The Federalist Papers* (No. 39: "The Conformity of the Plan to Republican Principles (Madison)") 237 (Signet Classics reprint, 2003).

422   John Locke, *Two Treatises of Government* 362, 373 (Cambridge University Press reprint 1988); Philip Hamburger, *Is Administrative Law Unlawful?* 381–382 (2014).

423   Alexander Hamilton, James Madison, John Jay, *The Federalist Papers* (No. 47: "The Particular Structure of the New Government and the Distribution of Power Among Its Different Parts (Madison)") 298 (Signet Classics reprint, 2003).

424   Alexander Hamilton, James Madison, John Jay, *The Federalist Papers* (No. 47: "The Particular Structure of the New Government and the Distribution of Power Among Its Different Parts (Madison)") 299 (Signet Classics reprint, 2003).

425   Alexander Hamilton, James Madison, John Jay, *The Federalist Papers* (No. 47: "The Particular Structure of the New Government and the Distribution of Power Among Its Different Parts (Madison)") 299 (Signet Classics reprint, 2003).

426   Alexander Hamilton, James Madison, John Jay, *The Federalist Papers* (No. 47: "The Particular Structure of the New Government and the Distribution of Power Among Its Different Parts (Madison)") 299 (Signet Classics reprint, 2003).

427   Alexander Hamilton, James Madison, John Jay, *The Federalist Papers* (No. 51: "The Structure of the Government Must Furnish the Proper Checks and Balances Between the Different Departments (Madison)") 318–319 (Signet Classics reprint, 2003).

428   Alexander Hamilton, James Madison, John Jay, *The Federalist Papers* (No. 51: "The Structure of the Government Must Furnish the Proper Checks and Balances Between the Different Departments (Madison)") 319 (Signet Classics reprint, 2003).

429   Alexander Hamilton, James Madison, John Jay, *The Federalist Papers* (No. 51: "The Structure of the Government Must Furnish the Proper Checks and Balances Between the Different Departments (Madison)") 319 (Signet Classics reprint, 2003).

430   Alexander Hamilton, James Madison, John Jay, *The Federalist Papers* (No. 51: "The Structure of the Government Must Furnish the Proper Checks and Balances Between the Different Departments (Madison)") 319 (Signet Classics reprint, 2003).

431   Alexander Hamilton, James Madison, John Jay, *The Federalist Papers* (No. 51: "The Structure of the Government Must Furnish the Proper Checks and Balances Between the Different Departments (Madison)") 319 (Signet Classics reprint, 2003).

432   Philip Hamburger, *Is Administrative Law Unlawful?* 234–235 (2014).

433   *Faretta v. California*, 422 U.S. 806 (1975).

434   Philip Hamburger, *Is Administrative Law Unlawful?* 173–174 (2014).

435   Philip Hamburger, *Is Administrative Law Unlawful?* 185 (2014).

436   *Wilkes v. Wood,* 2 Wilson 203 (Dec. 6, 1763).

437   *Entick v. Carrington*, 19 Howell's State Trials 1029 (1765).

438   *Paxton's Case*, Court files Suffolk Vol. 572 (March 1765), No. 100.5156.

439   Philip Hamburger, *Is Administrative Law Unlawful?* 263 (2014).

440   *Daubert v. Merrell Dow Pharmaceuticals, Inc.,* 509 U.S. 579 (1993).

441   Philip Hamburger, *Is Administrative Law Unlawful?* 228–230 (2014).

442   *Crowell v. Benson*, 285 U.S. 22 (1932).

443   *Chevron v. Natural Resources Defense Council,* 467 U.S. 837 (1984).

444   *Pereira v. Sessions*, 585 U.S. (2018).

445   *Marbury v. Madison*, 5 U.S. (1 Cranch) 137 (1803).

446   *Loving v. United States*, 388 U.S. 1 (1967).

447   *City of Arlington v. FCC,* 569 U.S. 290 (2013).

448   Adrian Vermeule, *Law's Abnegation* 51–52 (2016).

449   *United States v. Savings Bank*, 104 U.S. 728 (1881).

450   Gabriel Kolko, *The Triumph of Conservatism* 3 (1963).

451   Murray N. Rothbard, *The Progressive Era* 25 (2017).

452   Murray N. Rothbard, *The Progressive Era* 32–33 (2017).

453   Murray N. Rothbard, *The Progressive Era* 49 (2017).

454   Richard Hofstadter, *The Age of Reform* 97 (1955).

455   Murray N. Rothbard, *The Progressive Era* 67 (2017).

456   Murray N. Rothbard, *The Progressive Era* 69 (2017).

457   Murray N. Rothbard, *The Progressive Era* 75 (2017).

458   Murray N. Rothbard, *The Progressive Era* 73 (2017).

459   Murray N. Rothbard, *The Progressive Era* 77 (2017).

460   Murray N. Rothbard, *The Progressive Era* 97 (2017).

461   Gabriel Kolko, *The Triumph of Conservatism* 25 (1963).

462   Murray N. Rothbard, *The Progressive Era* 98–99 (2017).

463   Gabriel Kolko, *The Triumph of Conservatism* 27 (1963).

464   Gabriel Kolko, *The Triumph of Conservatism* 30–57 (1963).

465   Murray N. Rothbard, *The Progressive Era* 100–107 (2017).

466   Gabriel Kolko, *The Triumph of Conservatism* 4 (1963).

467   Gabriel Kolko, *The Triumph of Conservatism* 4 (1963).

468   Gabriel Kolko, *The Triumph of Conservatism* 5 (1963).

469   Jonathan W. Emord, *Freedom, Technology, and the First Amendment* (1991).

470   Adrian Vermeule, *Law's Abnegation* 1 (2016).

471   Adrian Vermeule, *Law's Abnegation* 1 (2016).

472   Adrian Vermeule, *Law's Abnegation* 4 (2016).

473   Adrian Vermeule, *Law's Abnegation* 31 (2016).

474   *Thompson Medical Co., Inc. v. Federal Trade Commission*, 791 F.2d 189, 197 (D.C. Cir. 1986); *Warner-Lambert Co. v. Federal Trade Commission*, 562 F.2d 749, 753–756 (D.C. Cir. 1977), cert. denied, 435 U.S. 950 (1978).

475   *Pearson v. Shalala*, 164 F.3d 650 (D.C. Cir. 1999), *rehearing denied,* 172 F.3d 721 (D.C. Cir. 1999).

476   *Pearson v. Shalala*, 164 F.3d 650 (D.C. Cir. 1999), *rehearing denied,* 172 F.3d 721 (D.C. Cir. 1999).

477   *Pearson v. Shalala*, 164 F.3d 650 (D.C. Cir. 1999).

478   *Pearson v. Shalala*, 172 F.3d 721 (D.C. Cir. 1999) (denying rehearing *en banc*).

479 Alexander Hamilton, James Madison, John Jay, *The Federalist Papers* ("No. 10: The Same Subject Continued (Madison)") 74 (Signet Classics reprint, 2003).

480 Alexander Hamilton, James Madison, John Jay, *The Federalist Papers* ("No. 78: The Judiciary Department (Hamilton)) 465 (Signet Classics reprint, 2003).

481 Adrian Vermeule, *Law's Abnegation* 25–26 (2016).

482 Adrian Vermeule, *Law's Abnegation* 31–32 (2016).

483 *Chevron v. Natural Resources Defense Council,* 467 U.S. 837 (1984).

484 *Chevron v. Natural Resources Defense Council,* 467 U.S. 837, 842–43 (1984).

485 *Chevron v. Natural Resources Defense Council,* 467 U.S. 837, 843 (1984).

486 *Chevron v. Natural Resources Defense Council,* 467 U.S. 837, 844 (1984).

487 *Auer v. Robbins,* 519 U.S. 452 (1997).

488 *Skidmore v. Swift & Co.,* 323 U.S. 134 (1944).

489 *Skidmore v. Swift & Co.,* 323 U.S. 134, 140 (1944).

490 Philip B. Kurland, Ralph Lerner, *The Founders' Constitution* (1987, Vol. 3, No. 4) 62 (excerpting St. George Tucker, "Blackstone's Commentaries" (1803)).

491 Philip Hamburger, *Is Administrative Law Unlawful?* 133–281 (2014).

492 Philip Hamburger, *Is Administrative Law Unlawful?* 281 (2014).

493 Philip Hamburger, *Is Administrative Law Unlawful?* 260-261 (2014).

494 Joshua D. Wright, "The FTC, Unfair Methods of Competition, and Abuse of Prosecutorial Discretion," *Liberty's Nemesis* (Dean Reuter and John Yoo, editors) 355 (2016).

495 Joshua D. Wright, "The FTC, Unfair Methods of Competition, and Abuse of Prosecutorial Discretion," *Liberty's Nemesis* (Dean Reuter and John Yoo, editors) 357 (2016).

496 Joshua D. Wright, "The FTC, Unfair Methods of Competition, and Abuse of Prosecutorial Discretion," *Liberty's Nemesis* (Dean Reuter and John Yoo, editors) 357 (2016).

497 "The FTC at 100: Where Do We Go From Here?" House of Representatives, Subcommittee on Commerce, Manufacturing, and Trade, Committee on Energy and Commerce, at 34 (Dec. 3, 2013).

498 Samuel Butler, *The Elephant in the Moon, and Miscellaneous Thoughts* 22 (Creative Media Partners reprint) (Circa 1640).

499 69 Fed. Reg. 45616 (July 30, 2004).

500 Steve Suo, "Lobbyists and Loopholes," *The Oregonian* (Oct. 4, 2004).

501 See, e.g., 72 FR 24602 (May 3, 2007) (revoking registration despite no evidence of diversion); 71 FR 39367 (July 12, 2006) (denying application without evidence of diversion), 72 FR 42118 (Aug. 1, 2007) (revoking despite ALJ's recommendation for continued

registration);

502   Compare John J. Fotinopoulos; Revocation of Registration, 72 FR 24602 (May 3, 2007) (revoking despite no evidence of diversion, citing poor security and recordkeeping); David M. Starr; Denial of Application, 71 FR 39367 (July 12, 2006) (revoking based on inexperience and risk of diversion, but no evidence of diversion) with Wild West Wholesale; Revocation of Registration, 72 FR 4042 (January 29, 2007) (revoking based on proof of diversion).

503   *Rubin v. Coors Brewing Co.*, 514 U.S. 476 (1995).

504   Drugabuse.gov; cdc.gov.

505   Jerry Mitchell, "How the FDA helped pave the way for an opioid epidemic," *Clarion Ledger* (Jan. 26, 2018) at clarionledger.com.

506   Jerry Mitchell, "How the FDA helped pave the way for an opioid epidemic," *Clarion Ledger* (Jan. 26, 2018) at clarionledger.com.

507   Jerry Mitchell, "How the FDA helped pave the way for an opioid epidemic," *Clarion Ledger* (Jan. 26, 2018) at clarionledger.com.

508   Dick Carozza, "An Interview with Dr. David Graham, Associate Director of the FDA's Office of Drug Safety," *Fraud Magazine* 39 (September/October 2005).

509   PERC, "Why the Sackett Case Is Far from Over," at perc.org.; *Sackett v. EPA*, 566 U.S. 120 (2012).

510   *Sackett v. EPA*, 566 U.S. 120 (2012).

511   Igor Shafarevich, *The Socialist Phenomenon* 6 (2019).

512   F. A. Hayek, *The Road to Serfdom* 83 (1944).

513   Ludwig Von Mises, *Socialism* 239 (Martino Publishing edition, 2012).

514   Iain Murray, *The Socialist Temptation* 3 (2020).

515   Iain Murray, *The Socialist Temptation* 3 (2020).

516   Iain Murray, *The Socialist Temptation* 24 (2020).

517   Iain Murray, *The Socialist Temptation* 3 (2020).

518   Iain Murray, *The Socialist Temptation* 7–8 (2020).

519   Iain Murray, *The Socialist Temptation* 8 (2020).

520   Iain Murray, *The Socialist Temptation* 8 (2020).

521   Iain Murray, *The Socialist Temptation* 8 (2020).

522   Iain Murray, *The Socialist Temptation* 9 (2020).

523   Iain Murray, *The Socialist Temptation* 9 (2020).

524   Iain Murray, *The Socialist Temptation* 10 (2020).

525   Jeremy Rifkin, *The Green New Deal* 3 (2019).

526   Jeremy Rifkin, *The Green New Deal* 20–21 (2019).

527   Jeremy Rifkin, *The Green New Deal* 21–22 (2019).

528   Jeremy Rifkin, *The Green New Deal* 32–33 (2019).

529   Jack Crowe, "AOC's Chief of Staff Admits the Green New Deal Is Not about Climate Change," *National Review* (July 12, 2019).

530   Jack Crowe, "AOC's Chief of Staff Admits the Green New Deal Is Not about Climate Change," *National Review* (July 12, 2019).

531   Andrew Robinson, "'I shall never forget the kindness.' How England helped Albert Einstein escape Nazi Germany," *Time* (Oct. 1, 2019) @ time.com.

532   F. A. Hayek, *The Road to Serfdom* 112–113 (1944).

533   F. A. Hayek, *The Road to Serfdom* 119 (1944).

534   Thomas J. DiLorenzo, *The Problem with Socialism* 95 (2016).

535   Thomas J. DiLorenzo, *The Problem with Socialism* 96 (2016).

536   Thomas J. DiLorenzo, *The Problem with Socialism* 97 (2016).

537   Thomas J. DiLorenzo, *The Problem with Socialism* 57 (2016).

538   Margaret Thatcher, Interview, Thames TV This Week (February 5, 1976).

539   F. A. Hayek, *The Road to Serfdom* 124 (1944) (quoting Hilaire Belloc, *The Servile State* 46 (1912).

540   Thomas J. DiLorenzo, *The Problem with Socialism* 5–8 (2016).

541   F. A. Hayek, *The Road to Serfdom* 136 (1944).

542   F. A. Hayek, *The Road to Serfdom* 79–80 (1944) (quoting Walter Lippmann, "The Government of Posterity," *The Atlantic* 552 (November 1936).

543   Jonathan W. Emord, *The Rise of Tyranny* 53 (2008).

544   Jonathan W. Emord, *The Rise of Tyranny* 53–59 (2008).

545   Bernard Siegan, *Economic Liberties and the Constitution* 322 (1980).

546   Bernard Siegan, *Economic Liberties and the Constitution* 323 (1980).

547   *Pearson v. Shalala,* 172 F.3d 72 (D.C. Cir. 1999).

548   *Nebbia v. New York*, 291 U.S. 502 (1934).

549   Richard A. Epstein, *The Classical Liberal Constitution* 81 (2014).

550   *Nebbia v. New York*, 291 U.S. 502 (1934).

551   Jonathan W. Emord, "Contrived Distinctions: The Doctrine of Commercial Speech in First Amendment Jurisprudence," *Cato Institute Policy Analysis*, No. 161 (September 23, 1991) at cato.org.

552   Philip B. Kurland, Ralph Lerner, *The Founders' Constitution* (Vol. 1, Ch. 6) 54

(excerpting James Burgh, *Political Disquisitions* (1774)).

553   Allan Brownfield, "A Theme for the Bicentennial Fathers' Fear of Power" (Oct. 1, 1974), Foundation for Economic Education at fee.org.

554   Thomas Jefferson, Letter to Edward Carrington, May 27, 1788, in Paul Leicester Ford, *The Works of Thomas Jefferson* 401 (1904).

555   Thomas Jefferson, "Bill for the More Diffusion of Knowledge" (1799) in *The Papers of Thomas Jefferson* (Vol. 2) 256–235 (1784) @ tjrs.monticello.org.

556   George Washington, "Circular to the States" (June 8, 1783) @ mountvernon.org (retrieved October 29, 2020).

557   George Washington, "Farewell Address" (September 19, 1796) at govinfo.gov.

558   Alexander Hamilton, James Madison, John Jay, *The Federalist Papers* ("No. 48: These Departments Should Not Be So Far Separated as to Have No Constitutional Control Over Each Other (Madison)") 305–306 (Signet Classics reprint, 2003).

559   Phillip W. Magness, *The 1619 Project: A Critique* 104 (2020).

560   Phillip W. Magness, *The 1619 Project: A Critique* 15 (2020).

561   Don Jordan, Michael Walsh, *White Cargo* 76 (2008); Michael A. Hoffman, *They Were White and They Were Slaves* 47 (1991).

562   Michael A. Hoffman, *They Were White and They Were Slaves* 17 (1991).

563   Don Jordan, Michael Walsh, *White Cargo* 12 (2008).

564   Don Jordan, Michael Walsh, *White Cargo* 76 (2008).

565   Don Jordan, Michael Walsh, *White Cargo* 76 (2008).

566   Don Jordan, Michael Walsh, *White Cargo* 13 (2008).

567   Don Jordan, Michael Walsh, *White Cargo* 13 (2008).

568   Don Jordan, Michael Walsh, *White Cargo* 94, 108–111 (2008).

569   Don Jordan, Michael Walsh, *White Cargo* 86 (2008).

570   Rhetta Akamatsu, *The Irish Slaves* 57 (2010).

571   Lerone Bennett, Jr., *The Shaping of Black America* (1975).

572   Don Jordan, Michael Walsh, *White Cargo* 254 (2008).

573   Gary J. Sibio, "Irish Slaves in the Americas," *Virily* (2018) @ virily.com.

574   Don Jordan, Michael Walsh, *White Cargo* 169 (2008).

575   Don Jordan, Michael Walsh, *White Cargo* 87 (2008).

576   Don Jordan, Michael Walsh, *White Cargo* 90 (2008).

577   Michael A. Hoffman, *The Untold History of the Enslavement of Whites in Early America* 6 (1991).

578   Don Jordan, Michael Walsh, *White Cargo* 13; 147; 160–161 (2008).

579   Don Jordan, Michael Walsh, *White Cargo* 17 (2008).

580   Don Jordan, Michael Walsh, *White Cargo* 113 (2008).

581   Don Jordan, Michael Walsh, *White Cargo* 262 (2008).

582   Don Jordan, Michael Walsh, *White Cargo* 13; 127–136 (2008).

583   Michael A. Hoffman, *The Untold History of the Enslavement of Whites in Early America* 55 (1991).

584   Michael A. Hoffman, *They Were White and They Were Slaves* 14 (1991).

585   Robert C. Davis, *Christian Slaves, Muslim Masters* xxiv–xxv (2003).

586   Don Jordan, Michael Walsh, *White Cargo* 12 (2008).

587   Don Jordan, Michael Walsh, *White Cargo* 250–251 (2008).

588   Don Jordan, Michael Walsh, *White Cargo* 253 (2008).

589   Don Jordan, Michael Walsh, *White Cargo* 257 (2008).

590   Larry Koger, *Black Slaveowners* 1 (1985).

591   Larry Koger, *Black Slaveowners* 1 (1985).

592   Larry Koger, *Black Slaveowners* 1–2 (1985).

593   Larry Koger, *Black Slaveowners* 7 (1985).

594   Larry Koger, *Black Slaveowners* 18–19 (1985).

595   Don Jordan, Michael Walsh, *White Cargo* 207–210 (2008).

596   Don Jordan, Michael Walsh, *White Cargo* 212 (2008).

597   Don Jordan, Michael Walsh, *White Cargo* 212 (2008).

598   BlackPast, B. (2009, August 10), "(1776) The Deleted Passage of the Declaration of Independence," retrieved from https://www.blackpast.org/african-american-history/declaration-independence-and-debate-over-slavery/ (citing Thomas Jefferson, The Writings of Thomas Jefferson: Being His Autobiography, Correspondence, Reports, Messages, Addresses, and other Writings, Official and Private (1853–1854)).

599   Thomas Jefferson, The Writings of Thomas Jefferson: Being His Autobiography, Correspondence, Reports, Messages, Addresses, and other Writings, Official and Private (1853–1854).

600   Alexander Hamilton, James Madison, and John Jay, *The Federalist Papers* 262–263 (No. 42: "The Powers Conferred by the Constitution Further Considered (Madison)") (Signet Classics reprint, 2003).

601   Alexander Hamilton, James Madison, and John Jay, *The Federalist Papers* 523 (No. 85: "Concluding Remarks (Hamilton)") (Signet Classics reprint, 2003).

602   C. Bradley Thompson, *America's Revolutionary Mind* 127 (2019).

603   Don Jordan, Michael Walsh, *White Cargo* 19 (2008).

604   *City of Richmond v. J.A. Croson Co.,* 488 U.S. 469 (1989); *Metro Broadcasting, Inc. v. Federal Communications Commission*, 497 U.S. 547 (1990).

605   Thomas Jefferson, "III. First Inaugural Address, 4 March 1801," *Founders Online,* National Archives, https://founders.archives.gov/documents/Jefferson/01-33-02-0116-0004. [Original Source: Barbara B. Oberg, *The Papers of Thomas Jefferson,* Vol. 33, 148-152 (Princeton University Press reprint, 2006)].

606   Thomas Jefferson, "Thomas Jefferson to Isaac H. Tiffany," 14 April 1819, *Founders Online*, National Archives, https://founders.archives.gov/documents/Jefferson/03-14-02-0191. [Original Source: J. Jefferson Looney, *The Papers of Thomas Jefferson,* Retirement Series, Vol. 14, 201-202 (Princeton University Press reprint, 2017).

607   James Madison, "Property" (March 29, 1792) in Philip B. Kurland and Ralph Lerner, *The Founders' Constitution* (Vol. 1), Chapter 16, No. 23 at 598 (1987).

608   James Madison, "Property" (March 29, 1792) in Philip B. Kurland and Ralph Lerner, *The Founders' Constitution* (Vol. 1), Chapter 16, No. 23 at 598 (1987).

609   James Madison, "Property" (March 29, 1792) in Philip B. Kurland and Ralph Lerner, *The Founders' Constitution* (Vol. 1), Chapter 16, No. 23 at 599 (1987).

610   *Lochner v. New York*, 198 U.S. 45 (1905).

611   David E. Bernstein, *Rehabilitating Lochner* 3 (2012).

612   David E. Bernstein, *Rehabilitating Lochner* 23–24 (2012).

613   David E. Bernstein, *Rehabilitating Lochner* 29 (2012).

614   *Lochner v. New York*, 198 U.S. 45 (1905).

615   *Holden v. Hardy*, 169 U.S. 366 (1898).

616   David E. Bernstein, *Rehabilitating Lochner* 1 (2012).

617   *Nebbia v. New York*, 291 U.S. 302 (1934).

618   Alexander Hamilton, James Madison, John Jay, *The Federalist Papers* 289 ("No. 45: The Alleged Danger from the Powers of the Union to the State Governments Considered (Madison)") (Signet Classics reprint, 2003).

619   George Washington, Farewell Address (September 19, 1796) at govinfo.gov.

620   George Washington, Farewell Address (September 19, 1796) at govinfo.gov.

621   George Washington, Farewell Address (September 19, 1796) at govinfo.gov.

622   George Washington, Farewell Address (September 19, 1796) at govinfo.gov.

623   George Washington, Farewell Address (September 19, 1796) at govinfo.gov.

624   George Washington, Farewell Address (September 19, 1796) at govinfo.gov.

625   George Washington, Farewell Address (September 19, 1796) at govinfo.gov.

626   Alexander Hamilton, James Madison, John Jay, *The Federalist Papers* 264 ("No. 42: The Powers Conferred by the Constitution Further Considered (Madison)") (Signet Classics reprint, 2003).

627   Alexander Hamilton, James Madison, John Jay, *The Federalist Papers* 198–199 ("No. 33: The Same Subject Continued (Hamilton)") (Signet Classics reprint, 2003).

628   Alexander Hamilton, James Madison, John Jay, *The Federalist Papers* 258–259 ("No. 41: General View of the Powers Conferred by the Constitution (Madison)") (Signet Classics reprint, 2003).

629   Marty Johnson, "Pelosi says she'd be comfortable with Sanders at top of ticket," *The Hill* (Feb. 26, 2020) @ thehill.com.

630   Marty Johnson, "Pelosi says she'd be comfortable with Sanders at top of ticket," *The Hill* (Feb. 26, 2020) @ thehill.com.

631   Reuters Staff, "True Claim: Poll shows 76 percent of Democrats say they would vote for a socialist for President," March 10, 2020, @ reuters.com.

632   Scott Detrow, "Why 2020 Democracts want endorsements from 'The Squad,'" *NPR* @ npr.org.

633   Douglas Holtz-Eakin, Dan Bosch, Ben Gitis, Dan Goldbeck, Philip Rossetti, "The Green New Deal: Scope, Scale, and Implications," American Action Forum (Feb. 25, 2019) at americanactionforum.org; Kevin Dagaratna and Nicolas Loris, "Assessing the Costs and Benefits of the Green New Deal's Energy Policies," The Heritage Foundation @ heritage.org.

634   Paul Driessen, "Policy Brief: Protecting the Environment from the Green New Deal," The Heartland Institute Policy Brief at 2 @ heartland.org.

635   Paul Driessen, "Policy Brief: Protecting the Environment from the Green New Deal," The Heartland Institute Policy Brief at 3 @ heartland.org.

636   Paul Driessen, "Policy Brief: Protecting the Environment from the Green New Deal," The Heartland Institute Policy Brief at 3 @ heartland.org.

637   Paul Driessen, "Policy Brief: Protecting the Environment from the Green New Deal," The Heartland Institute Policy Brief at 3 @ heartland.org.

638   Thomas Jefferson, "Thomas Jefferson to Joseph Milligan, 6 April 1816," *Founders Online*, National Archives, https://founders.archives.gov/documents/Jefferson/03-09-02-0435 [Original source: J. Jefferson Looney, *The Papers of Thomas Jefferson*, Retirement Series, Vol. 9, 638-640 (Princeton University Press reprint, 2012).

639   Margaret Thatcher, Interview, Thames TV This Week (February 5, 1976).

640   Jose Nino, "Venezuela Before Chavez: A Prelude to Socialist Failure" (May 3,

2017), Mises Institute, @ https://mises.org.

641   Jose Nino, "Venezuela Before Chavez: A Prelude to Socialist Failure" (May 3, 2017), Mises Institute, @ https://mises.org.

642   Ivona Iacob, "Venezuela's Failed Socialist Experiment," *Forbes* (July 24, 2016) @ forbes.com.

643   Jon Miltimore, "8 Venezuelan Industries Hugo Chavez Nationalized (Besides Oil)," Foundation for Economic Education (January 10, 2020) @ fee.org.

644   Ivona Iacob, "Venezuela's Failed Socialist Experiment," *Forbes* (July 24, 2016) @ forbes.com.

645   Daniel Di Martion, "Venezuela was my home, and socialist destroyed it. Slowly, it will destroy America too," USA Today (February 15, 2019) @ usatoday.com.

646   Daniel Di Martino, "Venezuela was my home, and socialism destroyed it. Slowly, it will destroy America too," USA Today (February 15, 2019) @ usatoday.com.

647   Daniel Di Martino, "Venezuela was my home, and socialism destroyed it. Slowly, it will destroy America too," USA Today (February 15, 2019) @ usatoday.com.

648   Daniel Di Martino, "Venezuela was my home, and socialism destroyed it. Slowly, it will destroy America too," USA Today (February 15, 2019) @ usatoday.com.

649   Daniel Di Martino, "Venezuela was my home, and socialism destroyed it. Slowly, it will destroy America too," USA Today (February 15, 2019) @ usatoday.com.

650   Daniel Di Martino, "Venezuela was my home, and socialism destroyed it. Slowly, it will destroy America too," USA Today (February 15, 2019) @ usatoday.com.

651   Daniel Di Martino, "Venezuela was my home, and socialism destroyed it. Slowly, it will destroy America too," USA Today (February 15, 2019) @ usatoday.com.

652   Amnesty International, "Venezuela: Hunger, punishment and fear, the formula for repression used by authorities under Nicolas Maduro" (February 20, 2019) @ amnesty.org.

653   Armando Valladares, *Against All Hope* 2 (2001).

654   Armando Valladares, *Against All Hope* (2001).

655   Ji Li Jiang, *Red Scarf Girl* (1997).

656   Ji Li Jiang, *Red Scarf Girl* (1997).

657   Ji Li Jiang, *Red Scarf Girl* 57–58 (1997).

658   Ji Li Jiang, *Red Scarf Girl* 225–226 (1997).

659   Nien Cheng, *Life and Death in Shanghai* 353 (1986).

660   Rudolph J. Rummel, *Death by Government* (1997); Rudolph J. Rummel, *Statistics of Democide: Genocide and Mass Murder Since 1900* (1998).

661   Stephanie Courtois, Nicolas Werth, Jean-Louis Panne, Andrzej Paczkowski, Karel

Bartosek, and Jean-Louis Margolin, *The Black Book of Communism* x (1999).

662   Jemima McEvoy, "At least 13 cities are defunding their police departments" (August 12, 2020), Forbes @ forbes.com.

663   Heather MacDonald, "There is no epidemic of fatal police shootings against unarmed black Americans" (July 3, 2020), *USA Today* @ usatoday.com.

664   Jon Schuppe, "Fair or dangerous? Days after ending cash bail, New York has second thoughts" (Jan. 7, 2020) @ nbcnews.com.

665   Glenn Kessler, "Kamala Harris tweeted support for a bail fund, but the money didn't just assist protesters" (September 3, 2020), *The Washington Post* @ washingtonpost.com.

666   Glenn Kessler, "Kamala Harris tweeted support for a bail fund, but the money didn't just assist protesters" (September 3, 2020), *The Washington Post* @ washingtonpost.com.

667   Andrew Pacquette, "Want to know who is funding the riots? Look at who is funding The Bail Project, which fees countless criminals" (Sept. 27, 2020) @ lawenforcementtoday.com.

668   Zachary Evans, "Police Chief: Arrested Looters in NYC are immediately released because of bail-reform law" (June 2, 2020), *National Review* @ news.yahoo.com.

669   Lana Andelane, "George Floyd: Pallets of bricks found unattended among protests sparks theories of foul play" (June 1, 2020), MSN News @ msn.com; Jordyn Pair, "Minnesota, New York officials say riots were organized, Chicago officials request federal investigation" (June 1, 2020), DISRN @ disrn.com.

670   A. M. Smith, "Police discover charred body inside building set on fire by rioters in Minneapolis" (August 2020), En-Volve @ en-volve.com; John Salvatore, "Violent rioters burned home with kids inside, then blocked fire fighters from getting in," *Flag and Cross* (June 1, 2020) @ flagandcross.com.

671   Ronald Reagan, "Freedom Speech," 1964 Republican National Convention (October 27, 1964) @ Reagan.com.

672   Alexander Hamilton, James Madison, John Jay, *The Federalist Papers* ("No. 85: Concluding Remarks (Hamilton)") 523 (Signet Classics reprint, 2003).

673   Alexander Hamilton, James Madison, John Jay, *The Federalist Papers* ("No. 85: Concluding Remarks (Hamilton)") 523 (Signet Classics reprint, 2003).

674   Jeremy Black, *George III* 227 (2006).

675   Jeremy Black, *George III* 246 (2006).

676   Jeremy Black, *George III* 220 (2006).

677   C. Bradley Thompson, *America's Revolutionary Mind* 249–251 (2019).

678   Thomas Jefferson to Tench Coxe, June 1, 1795 in Paul Leicester Ford, *The Works of Thomas Jefferson*, Vol. VIII, 183 (1904).

679   Thomas Paine, *Common Sense* 39 (1776) (Covington House reprint, 2016).

680   Thomas Paine, *Common Sense* 38 (1776) (Covington House reprint, 2016).

681   Thomas Paine, *Common Sense* 38 (1776) (Covington House reprint, 2016).

682   Thomas Paine, Common Sense 65 (1776) (Covington House reprint, 2016).

683   Jeremy Black, *George III* 224 (2006).

684   Ron Chernow, *Washington* 230 (2010).

685   Ron Chernow, *Washington* 237 (2010).

686   Thomas Paine, *Common Sense* 45 (1776) (Covington House reprint, 2016).

687   Ron Chernow, *Washington* 570 (2010).

688   Ron Chernow, *Washington* 435 (2016).

689   Jeremy Black, *George III* 434 (2006).

690   Peter Schweizer, *Profiles in Corruption* 91 (2020); Mark Hemingway, "Obama administration knew Hunter Biden was shady, witness admits," *New York Post* (November 15, 2019) at nypost.com; Pat Droney, "The swamp Trump warned about: Biden, Kerry aware of Hunter Biden conflicts with Burisma, did nothing," *Law Enforcement Today* (October 23, 2020) at lawenforcementtoday.com; Emily Goodin, "Senior diplomat tells impeachment probe he warned Joe Biden's staff in 2015 that Hunter's appointment to Ukraine gas board would cause problems—but aide said VP didn't have 'bandwidth' as his older son fought cancer" *Daily Mail* (October 18, 2019) @ dailymail.co.uk.

691   Debra Heine, "Brennan personally briefed Obama on Clinton campaign's Russia collusion operation in 2016," *The Michigan Star* (October 7, 2020) @ themichiganstar.com.

692   Peter Schweizer, *Profiles in Corruption* 47–91 (2020).

693   Peter Schweizer, *Profiles in Corruption* 61 (2020).

694   Peter Schweizer, *Profiles in Corruption* 55 (2020).

695   Peter Schweizer, *Secret Empires* 26–27 (2018).

696   Peter Schweizer, *Secret Empires* 35 (2018).

697   Thomas Barrabi, "Who is Tony Bobulinski, Hunter Biden's former business associate?" (October 22, 2020) @ foxnews.com.

698   Susan Jones, "Bobulinski says he met twice with Joe Biden 'to discuss what I was doing with his family's name and the Chinese'" (Oct. 28, 2020) @ cnsnews.com.

699   Susan Jones, "Bobulinski says he met twice with Joe Biden 'to discuss what I was

doing with his family's name and the Chinese'" (Oct. 28, 2020) @ cnsnews.com.

700   Gregg Jarrett, *The Russia Hoax* (2018).

701   Grett Jarrett, *Witch Hunt* (2019).

702   Andrew McCarthy, "Russian intel alleges Hillary Clinton orchestrated collusion hoax to distract from emails" (September 30, 2020) @ foxnews.com; Gregg Jarrett, *The Russia Hoax* 87–117 (2018).

703   Gregg Jarrett, *The Russia Hoax* 1–20 (2018).

704   Gregg Jarrett, *The Russia Hoax* 10–18 (2018).

705   Jonathan Turley, *Res ipsa loquitur—the thing itself speaks*, "Will Adam Schiff's claims now be blocked on Twitter" (October 21, 2020) @ jonathanturley.org.

706   Peter Schweizer, *Secret Empires* 221 (2018).

A free ebook edition is available with the purchase of this book.

To claim your free ebook edition:

1. Visit MorganJamesBOGO.com
2. Sign your name CLEARLY in the space
3. Complete the form and submit a photo of the entire copyright page
4. You or your friend can download the ebook to your preferred device

Print & Digital Together Forever.

Snap a photo

Free ebook

Read anywhere

CPSIA information can be obtained
at www.ICGtesting.com
Printed in the USA
LVHW092059251121
704454LV00007B/1032

9 781631 953927